THE GOLDEN AGE AND DECLINE OF ISLAMIC CIVILISATION

Volume 1

Islamic Civilisation
An Overview

S.E. Al-Djazairi

MSBN Books

S.E. Al-Djazairi: *The Golden Age and Decline of Islamic Civilisation*, Volume 1: Islamic Civilisation, an Overview. Published by MSBN Books; 2020 edition.

ISBN: 9781976785726

Website: msbnbooks.co.uk
Email: info@msbnbooks.co.uk

Design and Artwork: N. Kern

The author, S.E. Al-Djazairi lectured and researched at the University of Constantine in Algeria. He also tutored at the Department of Geography of the University of Manchester, and worked as a research assistant at UMIST (Manchester) in the field of History of Science.
He has published papers on environmental degradation and desertification, politics and change in North Africa, and problems of economic and social development. He also contributed historical entries to various encyclopaedias.

Recently published works by the same author:
Islam in China (3 vols)
Our Civilisation (5 vols)
The West, Islam, Barbarism and Civilisation
The Destruction of the Environment in/of the Muslim World

CONTENTS

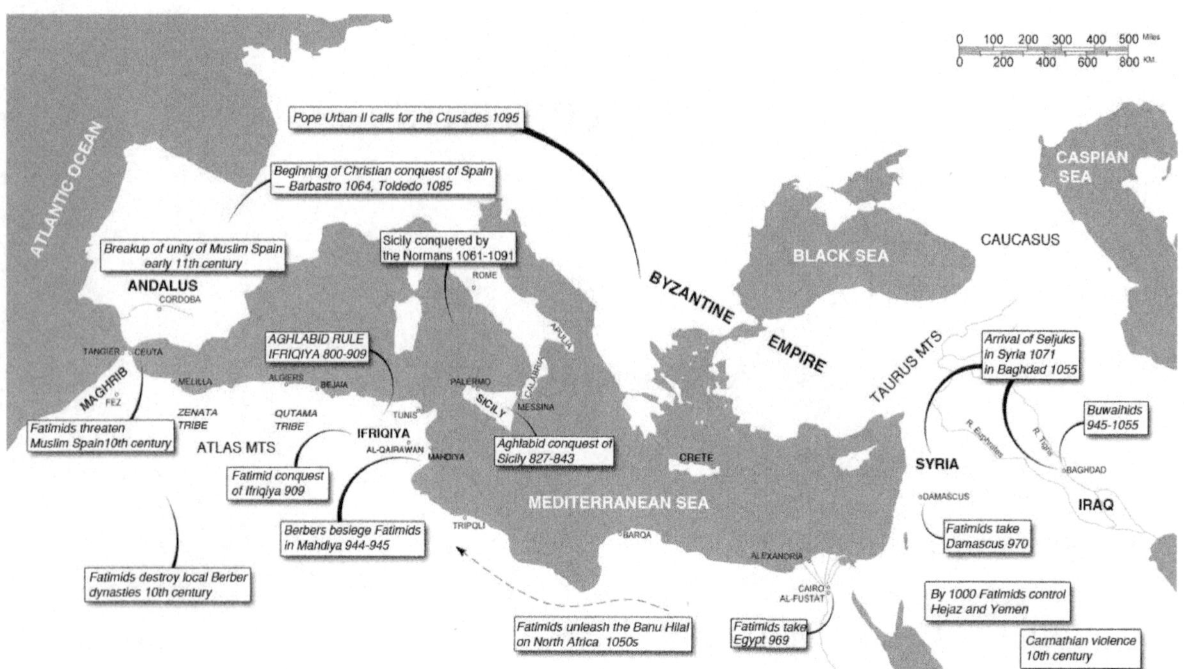

Some major geographic and historic landmarks of the Muslim world in the High Medieval Period.

INTRODUCTION

Muslim civilisation sprang into existence soon after the birth of Islam (7th century C.E). It lasted for a large part of the Middle Ages, and began to collapse in the 13th century following the loss of the great centres of Islamic power and civilisation: Cordova (1236), Valencia (1238), Seville (1248), and Baghdad (1258). All fell in the space of few decades to invading forces. During the same period, in 1260, Damascus and other Syrian towns and cities, core centres of Islamic civilisation, also fell to invading Mongol hordes, completing a chain of disasters. On the particular impact of the Mongols, in Baghdad, in 1258, the palaces, colleges and mosques were plundered and burnt; 'the cultural accumulation of five centuries perished in the flames, and the appalling figure of 800,000 is the lowest estimate given of the number of men, women and children who were slaughtered in the streets and houses.'[1] The Christians gathered in a church under their patriarch were spared.[2] Glubb outlines the event further:

> On 10th February (1258), the Khalif Mustassim gave himself up. Hulagu (the Mongol leader) ordered him to instruct the whole population to gather on the plain outside the walls, where they also were shot, slashed and hacked to death in heaps, regardless of age or sex. Not until 13th February did the Mongols enter the city. For a week, they had been waiting on the walls, not a man daring to leave his unit to plunder. Such iron discipline, unknown in the Middle Ages, goes far to account for their invincibility. The city was then systematically looted, destroyed and burnt. Eight hundred thousand persons are said to have been killed. The Khalif Mustassim was sewn up in a sack and trampled to death under the feet of Mongol horses.

Glubb concludes:

> For five hundred years, Baghdad had been a city of palaces, mosques, libraries and colleges. Its universities and hospitals were the most up to date in the world. Nothing now remained but heaps of rubble and a stench of decaying human flesh.[3]

Syria and Palestine, once thriving regions, famed for their trades, culture and scholarship, suffered a similar fate at the hands of both Mongols and crusaders. Jerusalem's flourishing character prior to the crusades (1095-1291) was noted by the traveller Nasr Eddin Khusraw in 1047. There, he said, goods were cheap and plentiful, beautiful markets and high buildings everywhere, a great number of craftsmen, and each craft with its market.[4] About a hundred thousand people lived

---

[1] J. J. Saunders: *A History of Medieval Islam* (Routledge, London; 1965), p. 181.

[2] Ibid.

[3] J. Glubb: *A Short History of the Arab Peoples (*Hodder and Stoughton, 1969), p. 207.

[4] Nasir Khusraw in A.A. Duri; Jerusalem in the early Islamic period; 7th-11th centuries; in *Jerusalem in History;* edited by K.J. Asali (Scorpion Publishing Ltd, 1989), pp. 105-29; at pp. 118-9.

in the city, which also had a great hospital with rich waqfs (endowments) dedicated to it, from which medicines for its many patients were dispensed and salaries for doctors were paid, and where medicine was taught.[5] In this same 11th century, under the Seljuks, just on the eve of the crusades, famed scholars from both east (Khurasan) and west (Muslim Spain) made the city their destination, many settling there; both the city's scholars and the visitors participating in a rich cultural life.[6] Ibn al-Arabi who gives a vivid picture of such activities was impressed by the majlis (study circles) and scholarly disputations.[7] All this was ended by the crusaders' arrival in July 1099. Storming through the city walls, they slew the whole Muslim population. A contemporary, Abbot Raymond of Agiles of the French town of Du Puy, present during the dramatic moments, wrote:

> When our men took the main defences, we saw then some astonishing things amongst the Saracens. Some were beheaded, and that's the least that could happen to them. Others were pierced through and so threw themselves from the heights of the walls; others after having suffered at length were thrown into the flames. We could see in the roads and in the places of Jerusalem bits and pieces of heads, hands, and feet. Everywhere we could only walk through cadavers. But all that was only little...

The abbot's description moves onto the Mosque of Omar, where:

> There was so much blood... that dead corpses swam in it. We could see hands floating and arms that went to glue themselves to bodies that were not theirs; we could not distinguish which arm belonged to which body. The men who were doing the killing could hardly bear the smoke from the corpses.[8]

The same scale of crusader devastation was inflicted on the remainder of the region as is described in some literature and in part three of this work.[9]

Just as large sways of the Muslim land were put to sword and fire by the Crusaders (in the East) and other Christian armies in the west (Muslim Spain and North Africa), others were suffering similar fate on the Mongol hands; the Baghdad episode one amongst many. The first Mongol invasion of Eastern Islam (1219-1221), under Genghis Khan, to this day remains one of the most brutal episodes ever recorded in history. In three years, more lives were lost than in any similar conflict of such duration notes Saunders.[10] Bukhara, birth-place of Ibn Sina (980-1037) and other illustrious minds of Islam, was razed to the ground in 1220, thousands of women were raped, and 30,000 men (a conservative figure) were massacred.[11] Elsewhere, in Nishapur, Herat, Merw, and other places also famed

---

[5] Ibid.

[6] A.A. Duri: *Jerusalem;* op cit; p. 119.

[7] Ibid; p. 120.

[8] Abbot Raymond of Agiles; in G. Le Bon: *La Civilisation des Arabes* (Syracuse, 1884), p. 249.

[9] G.W. Cox: *The Crusades* (Longmans, London, 1874). S. Runciman: *A History of the Crusades*, 3 vols (Cambridge University Press, 1962). J. J. Saunders, *A History*; op cit.

[10] J.J. Saunders: *The History of the Mongol Conquests* (Routledge & Kegan Paul; London; 1971), pp. 55-6.

[11] W. Durant: *The Age of Faith,* (Simon and Shuster, New York; 1950); p. 339.

for their urbanity, the killing and destruction were many times worse. Ibn al-Athir, who was living through these events, wrote:

> For several years, I put off reporting this event (of the Mongol invasion) I found it terrifying and felt revulsion at recounting it and therefore hesitated again and again. Who would find it easy to describe the ruin of Islam and the Muslims....? O would that my mother had never borne me, that I had died before and that I were forgotten!... It may well be that the world from now until its end... will not experience the like of it again..... Dadjdjal (the Antichrist) will at least spare those who adhere to him, and will only destroy his adversaries. These (the Mongols), however, spared none. They killed women, men and children, ripped open the bodies of the pregnant and slaughtered the unborn. Truly: we belong to God and shall return to Him; only with Him is strength and power.[12]

Decades later, Hulagu, Genghis Khan's grandson, stormed Iraq, Syria and Palestine, and completed the cycle of destruction. Aleppo, a city rich in crafts and scholarship during the rules of Imad Eddin Zangi (r. 1128-1146) and Nur Eddin Zangi (r. 1146-1174),[13] was devastated by the Mongol hordes. In 1260 the city's male population was killed en masse, its citadel, schools, hospitals and bazaars suffered the same fate as Baghdad's, and it is said that one hundred thousand young women and children were taken as slaves.[14] The rest of Syria and Palestine and northern Iraq suffered the same fate. When the Mongol hordes set off towards Egypt, it seemed the end of the last Muslim stronghold had now arrived. At Ain Jalut, in September 1260, the Mamluks registered one of the most decisive victories in the history of Islam, saving both Egypt and the Muslim world from annihilation.[15] The effects of Crusader and Mongol invasions on the Muslim East were dreadful, though. At the time of the crusader invasion, Syria's population stood at 2.7 million inhabitants;[16] two centuries on, despite a revival under the Mamluks, in 1343, it stood at only 1.2 millions.[17]

The decisiveness of the Muslim victory at Ain Jalut can only be appreciated if it is realised that precisely at the time the Mongols were devastating the Muslim East, the Muslim west had just about totally collapsed. In the space of a few years, all the great centres of Islamic power and learning were lost for ever: the Balearic Islands between 1229 and 1235, Cordova, in 1236, Valencia in 1238, Murcia in

---

[12] Ibn al-Athir: *Al-Kamil fi al-Tarikh*; 12 Vols; ed. C.J. Tornberg; (Leiden and Uppsala; 1851-76), xii; pp. 233-4.

[13] A.M. Edde: Alep; in *Grandes Villes Mediterraneenes du Monde Musulman Medieval;* J.C. Garcin editor; (Ecole Francaise de Rome, 2000), pp. 157-75; at p. 157.

[14] J. Glubb: *A Short History*; op cit; p. 207; see also I.M. Lapidus: *Muslim Cities in the Later Middle Ages* (Harvard University Press; Cambridge Mass; 1967), p. 14, for the effects of the Mongol invasion of 1280.

[15] See: A.A. Khowaiter: *Baibars the First*; (The Green Mountain Press; London; 1978). P. Thorau: The Battle of Ayn Jalut: a Re-Examination; in P.W. Edbury: *Crusade and Settlement*; (Cardiff; 1985); pp. 236-41. Ibn al-Dawadari: *Kunz al-Dura;* ed. U. Haarmann; (Freiburg; 1971). Ibn Kathir: *Al-Bidaya wa'l nihaya fi'l tarikh*; Reprint (Beirut; 1977); 14 vols.

[16] J. Cox Russell: Late Ancient and Medieval Population, Transactions of the American Philosophical Society, vol. 48/III, 1958, in Y. Courbage and P. Fargues: *Chretiens et Juifs dans l'Islam Arabe et Turc* (Payot, Paris, 1997); p. 35.

[17] A.N Poliak: The Demographic Evolution of the Middle East: population trends since 1348, Palestine and the Middle East, vol X. no 5, 1938; in Y. Courbage-P. Fargues: *Chretiens*; op cit; p. 35.

1243-4, Jaen in 1246, Seville, in 1248, Tarifa, finally, in 1275-6, completing a chain of disasters which only left Grenada in Muslim hands. Each captured Muslim town and city swiftly turned from beacon of light into yet another haunt of dark medieval Europe.[18] Every defeat meant for surviving Muslims loss of economic, social, and cultural status.[19] Cordova at its fall was full of Christian land-hunters who seized Muslim farms in the hinterland and drove off the inhabitants.[20] On the Island of Minorca, all but one hundred Muslims, were allowed to remain, the rest of the population was rounded up and sold into slavery, 'temporarily glutting' the markets of Ibiza, Valencia and Barcelona.[21] The remaining Muslims had to wear a distinctive garb, and were forced to live in a separate section of each city,[22] or were regularly moved en masse within Spain, such as in 1247, when James I ordered the expulsion from Aragon of 100,000 of them.[23] Those able to maintain their trades were heavily taxed; paying tribute in money, in kind, or in service; their taxes were double those of the Christians.[24] Towards the end of the 13th century, the power and glitter of Muslim Spain were gone, only surviving in the enclave of Grenada for another two centuries, until 1492, before the Muslim presence on the Peninsula was extinguished in 1609-10, and the fate of millions of Muslims and their descendants sank into the meanders of the unknown.[25]

At the dawn of the 14th century, Islam had lost its western lands, Spain and Sicily; North Africa was too weak and divided, facing relentless Christian attacks by sea; whilst the East was somehow convalescing from the Crusader-Mongol episode. Only Egypt, the nascent Ottoman realm, and parts of Muslim India preserved a flicker of learning and power.

Just when some form of recovery began than befell on the land of Islam yet another woe. In the late 14th century, Timur the Lame (Timur Lang) erupted from the east, and with his hordes laid to ruin all that had risen out of the parched land. With his hordes, he slew, raped, and set alight Muslim populations inside their mosques such as in Damascus,[26] and the Jews inside their synagogues such as in Bursa.[27] On departing back to his realm with his loot, in 1402, Timur left a

---

[18] A. F. Calvert: *Moorish Remains in Spain*; (John Lane Company; London; 1906). S.P. Scott: *History of the Moorish Empire in Europe*; 3 Vols (Lippincott Company; Philadelphia and London; 1904). J. Read: *The Moors in Spain and Portugal* (Faber and Faber, London, 1974).

[19] H.C. Lea: *The Moriscos of Spain* (Burt Franklin, New York; 1901), 1968 reprint. T.B. Irving: Dates, Names and Places: The End of Islamic Spain; in *Revue d'Histoire Maghrebine;* No 61-62; 1991; pp. 77-93; at p. 81.

[20] F. F. Armesto: *Before Columbus* (MaCMillan Education; London, 1987), p. 64.

[21] Ibid; p. 36.

[22] W. Durant: *The Age of Faith*, op cit; p. 700.

[23] Ibid.

[24] Sandoval, Lib.xii, & xxviii. In H.C. Lea: *A History of the Inquisition in Spain;* 4 vols (The Mac Millan Company, New York, 1907), vol 3; p. 343.

[25] For the fate of Muslims, one of the best works is R. de Zayas: *Les Morisques et le Racisme d'Etat* (Les Voies du Sud; Paris, 1992).

[26] Johann Schiltberger: *The Bondage and Travels of Johann Schiltberger, a Native of Bavaria, in Europe, Asia, and Africa, 1396-1427*; tr. from the Heildelberg Ms. Edited in 1859 by Friedrich Neumann; London, the Hakluyt Society; 1879; pp. 27-8.

[27] H. A. Gibbons: *The Foundation of the Ottoman Empire* (1300-1403), New York, 1916, p. 257.

shattered Ottoman realm, mountains of skulls from Muslim India to the Syrian coast, having also committed to the desert any remaining towns, cities, and farmlands.[28]

Then, from early in the 15th century, better armed, Christians began to descend on North Africa and occupy one land after the other.[29] Ceuta followed by other Moroccan towns fell to the Portuguese, before the Spaniards completed their reconquista on homeland (capturing Grenada in 1492) and began their conquest of the rest of the Maghrib. Melila, Mers el Kebir, Oran, Bejaia, Tripoli, all falling to them by 1510. It was time for the local Sheikhs to call the Ottomans for rescue, hence the arrival of the Barbarossas and the onset of Ottoman North Africa.[30] Spain and Portugal, the two great Western powers of the modern times (15th-17th centuries) had devised a plan, with Papal blessing and support, for the conquest and division between themselves of North Africa.[31] Had this project succeeded, the fate of the North Africans would have been absolutely similar to that of other people who were also visited by the fervent Portuguese and Spanish crusaders: their total annihilation.[32] Instead, North Africans and Ottomans responded in a centuries long fight back on land and sea, soon to be joined by other Western powers, France most particularly. In this conflict, which this author has examined in some of his other books, Muslims, although surviving as an entity, suffered more losses than their Christian foes, in fact their maritime and coastal trade perishing as a result.[33]

Further east, the local Sheikhs, princes, and Rajas, all weak and divided, some more fickle than others, soon witnessed the arrival of the Portuguese formidable armada, much superiorly equipped than their rag tag gangs.[34] The Portuguese had come on a crusade and to loot riches and spices the East had now become famed for.[35] Soon the Eastern Seas, Ocean, and coastal towns became scenes of destruction and desolation. The Portuguese slew and looted in the Malay

---

[28] E. Gibbon: *The Decline and Fall of the Roman Empire* (W. Smith; London, 1858), Vol VII; 1920; as in pp. 55-6.
[29] W. Heyd: *Geschichte des Levantehandels im Mittelalter*, 1879. Fr ed: W. Heyd: *Histoire du Commerce du Levant au Moyen Age* (Leipzig; 1885-6; reedit; Amsterdam 1967), vol 2, in particular.
[30] E.H. Currey: *Sea Wolves of the Mediterranean*, New York, 1910. C.F. Duro: *Armada Espanola desde la union de los reinos de Castilla y de Aragon; 1476-1664;* 4 vols; (Madrid; 1895); i. R. B. Merriman: *The Rise of the Spanish Empire;* (The Macmillan Company; New York; 1918); vol 2; G. Fisher: *Barbary Legend*; Oxford, 1957.
[31] C.J. Bishko: The Spanish and Portuguese Reconquest 1095-1492; in *A History of the Crusades*; K.M. Setton ed; (The University of Wisconsin Press; 1975); vol 3; pp. 396-456. J. Muldoon: *Popes; Lawyers and Infidels; the Church and Non Christian World; 1250-1550*; (Liverpool; 1979). F. Fernandez Armesto: *Before Columbus* (MaCMillan Education; London, 1987).
[32] For the mass extermination of American natives, who received the same visit at the same time, see: W. Howitt: *Colonisation and Christianity*: Longman; London; 1838. D.E. Stannard: *American Holocaust; The Conquest of the New World;* Oxford University Press; 1992. W. Churchill: *A Little Matter of Genocide*; City Lights Books; San Francisco; 1997.
[33] See this author's Barbary Pirates, especially for sources around the subject.
[34] G. Casale: *The Ottoman Age of Exploration;* Oxford University Press; 2010. S. Ozbaran: A Turkish Report on the Red Sea and the Portuguese in the Indian Ocean (1525). *Arabian Studies* 4 (1978): 81–88.
[35] C. R. Boxer: *The Portuguese Seaborne Empire; 1415-1825*; (Hutchinson; London; 1969); p. 20.

Archipelago.[36] They slew, looted and devastated further west, too. According to Plumb:

> There was nothing haphazard about their path-finding. It was deliberate, well-planned, daringly executed: high technical intelligence was placed at the service of God and profit. And the result was as savage, as piratical an onslaught on the dazzlingly rich empires of the East as the world has ever known. It was not one, however, that seems to have stirred the conscience of any Portuguese commander. For these Orientals were heathens, blacks, Moors, Turks, containing, as one of them wrote, 'the badness of all bad men.[37]

The removal of Islam was another central aim, too. Arabia, including the Holy Sites of Makkah and Madinah were under risk, not just of occupation but of desecration, as well. Albuquerque, had an ambitious plan: to push through the Red Sea to Makkah and, after conquering the Muslim holy city, exchanging it for Jerusalem.[38] Now Selim I (Ottoman Sultan 1512-1520) had to address the situation, and his march south, and the arrival of Ottoman forces at last checked Portuguese rampaging.[39] Safavid collusion with the Portuguese, however, secured the latter's presence in the region and their continued depredations.[40] The Portuguese were soon followed by the Dutch, French and English, who also indulged in looting and rampaging for centuries until there was hardly anything left to loot or rampage through.[41]

The Ottomans managed to help preserve the survival of the Muslim world for a few centuries. Then, when they themselves began their long road onto decline from some time around the late 17th century, there began the final chapter. Soon, one piece of the Ottoman realm after another went its way or was carved up. First the Christian provinces of Europe: Serbia and Greece, then the Muslim provinces.[42] One after the other, Muslim lands began to fall under Western colonial domination.

For decades in places, centuries in others, colonial powers did what they did, and then, one day stepped away some distance, leaving behind a reality of contradictions, exacerbated ethnic divisions, conflicts of culture and identity, ambers of strife, endemic corruption, gin shops, brutal/murderous regimes, the

---

[36] J. Crawfurd: *History of the Indian Archipelago*; Archibald Constable & Company; Edinburgh; 1820.

[37] J.H. Plumb: Introduction in C.R. Boxer: *The Portuguese Seaborne Empire; op cit*; p. xxii-xxiii.

[38] *The Commentaries of the Great Afonso D'Albuquerque,* tr. from the Portuguese edition of 1774 by W. Birch (London: Hakluyt Society); (Burt Franklin Repr; New York, 1970), Vol. III, p. 37. H.V. Livermore, *A New History of Portugal* (Cambridge. 1967), p. 142.

[39] A. Hamdani: Ottoman Response to the Discovery of America and the New Route to India; in *Journal of American Oriental Society*; Vol 101; 1981; pp. 323-330.

[40] H. Morse Stephens: *Albuquerque*; Clarendon Press; Oxford; 1892; p. 77-8. D. Ross: The Portuguese in India, *The Cambridge History of India*, in Six volumes, Cambridge University Press, vol 5, edited by H.H. Dodwell, Cambridge University Press, 1929, pp. 1-27.

[41] W. Howitt: *Colonisation and Christianity*: Longman; London; 1838.

[42] E.L. Clark: *Turkey*; P.F. Collier &Son; New York; 1878. W.E.D. Allen: *The Turks in Europe;* John Murray London, 1919. Sutherland Menzies: *Turkey Old and New*, 2 vols; Allen Lane; London; 1880; vol 2; p. 88 ff.

region in the mess we see today, for, indeed, wherever order and reconstruction seem to begin to prevail, the foreign hands meddle,[43] foment the disorder and violence the land of Islam crumbles underneath, and which the fickle sections amongst Muslims themselves always feed with their efforts, their crimes, their narrowness of minds and souls, their greed, their lives, and at their cost.

*****

Before the 13th century, and straight from the birth of Islam (7th century), the Muslims experienced upheavals of all sorts: political strife, localised wars, epidemics and so on. However, such chaos was contained, and losses were never as grave as in the 13th century. Never before had the foundations of Islamic civilisation, trade, libraries, institutions of learning, or economic infrastructure, suffered destruction on a scale comparable to that of the 13th century and after. The centres of power and civilisation: Baghdad, Cordova, Seville, Murcia, Farghana, Herat, and others, where most scholars came from during the 'golden age' (7th-13th centuries), had all remained in Muslim hands. In the 13th century, however, all these places were lost to Islam, some such as Cordova, Seville, Valencia, and Murcia, forever. Others such as Aleppo, Baghdad, Merw, Khwarizm, Nishapur, and Bukhara were devastated beyond recovery.

Foreign invasions were not alone to blame for Muslim decline, though. Corrupt Muslim rulers and elites also accounted considerably for the decadence of Islamic power. Hence, as Scott points out:

> The character of the Mussulmans of Spain was defiled by all the vices which follow in the train of prodigal luxury and boundless wealth. Among these drunkenness was one of the most common. Personages of the highest rank were not ashamed to appear in public while intoxicated... National degeneracy early indicated the approaching and inevitable dissolution of the empire. The posterity of the (Muslim) conquerors, who in three years had marched from Gibraltar to the centre of France, became in the course of a few generations cowardly, effeminate, corrupt.[44]

And what was proper to Spain was also the case in the Abbasid court; the Caliph supposed to defend the city against the Mongols had a harem of 700 women and slave girls, and a thousand eunuchs to serve them.[45] The Caliph was trampled under Mongol horses, a symbol of decadence of the Caliphate.

In face of all such woes, only the timely intervention of the Mamluks, first, from the mid 13th century, and the Ottoman Turks, between the 14th and 18th centuries,

---

[43] Consult as an instance: J. Salt: *The Unmaking of the Middle East*; University of California Press, 2008.

[44] S.P. Scott: *History*; op cit; Vol II, at pp. 648 and 650.

[45] Baron G. d'Ohsson: *Histoire des Mongols*; La Haye et Amsterdam; 1834;Vol 3; 240.

saved the Muslim realm from total collapse. Then, once Ottoman power declined, especially from the late 18th century onwards, the Muslim world lost its last centre of strength, and fell under colonial tutelage.

*****

Before it collapsed, Muslim civilisation was able to register remarkable achievements. Its legacy is visible in great architectural works, modern sciences and learning. The Arabic numerals, star names, gardens and gardening, hospital care, university learning, libraries, early knowledge of India, China, Scandinavia and far distant lands are some of the legacies of such a civilisation. It was not just Arabs or Muslims who were involved in this great legacy but all ethnic groups and faiths, including Christians and Jews. Islamic civilisation has remained the only truly universal civilisation that has ever existed in the history of humanity. The Islamic policy of inclusion went along with other manifestations of the same nature; medical care, as an example, was afforded to all, and so was education, and even power, at the highest echelons, was open to non-Muslims.

It is these dominant aspects of Muslim civilisation, its rise, accomplishments, and subsequent decline, which are looked at in this work. These are also matters, which Western scholarship has looked at for decades, if not centuries. It is an undeniable fact that without Western scholarly involvement, our knowledge of Muslim civilisation would be extremely poor. The accomplishments of scholars such as Sarton, Wiedemann, Sedillot, Amari, Lombard, Watson, Holmyard, Menocal, Glick, Briffault, Burnett, King, Samso, Hobson, Pinto, Lorch and many others, who have informed us about the culture of Islam, remain, indeed, unique and unsurpassed.[46] It is, in fact, impossible, foolish, even, to ignore Western sources in the study of Muslim subjects.

There are, however, major problems with the overwhelming majority of modern Western scholarship dealing with Islamic subjects. Such scholarship is, for instance, keen to demean Islamic accomplishments when it does not entirely suppress them from knowledge. It is also customary to find the same facts, names, arguments, and worse, the same errors repeated in a wide variety of works. Crucial matters are often set aside, whilst trivialities are dwelt upon. As this work also shows, it is older Western historians who have made the greatest contribution to the understanding of Islamic civilisation.[47] Modern works, with

---

[46] M. Amari: *La Storia dei Musulmani di Sicilia,* 3 vols in 4. Lvi + 2086 p; (Ristampa dell'edizione di Firenze, 1854; 1858; 1868; 1872; Catania; F. Guaitolini.) G. Sarton: *Introduction to the History of Science,* 3 vols, (The Carnegie Institute of Washington; 1927-1948.) L. Sedillot: *Traite des Instruments astronomiques des Arabes*; (Paris, 1834); and other works by the same author. E. Wiedemann: *Aufsatze zur Arabischen Wissenschafts-Geschichte,* 2 vols, (Verlag, Hildesheim-New York, 1970).

[47] It is not, indeed, in the writing of today that one can find the quality of information as can be found in works such as: W. Heyd: *Histoire du Commerce du Levant* (A.M. Hakkert; Amsterdam; 1967). L. Leclerc: *Histoire de la Medecine Arabe*; 2 Vols (Paris, 1876). A. Mieli: *la Science Arabe et son role dans l'evolution scientifique mondiale* Ed, (Leiden, Brill, 1938). J.

some exceptions, are quite poor in comparison. This latter fact will be object of close scrutiny in this work.

This book will not specifically address the issue of the Islamic impact on the Christian West but will touch upon it in many instances. In doing so, this work will highlight one commonly held absurd claim that the science and learning the Christian West recuperated from Islam (in the 12th century, above all) was Greek, and the reason why it was recovered in Arabic was because 'Greek science had been lost to the Christian West, and was recuperated in Arabic from its Muslim guardians.'[48] Yet, contradicting this same claim, we also read that whenever there was any revival at any other time in the Christian West this was due to the Greek legacy, which had been preserved. Hence, in this latter respect, we learn, for instance, that Salerno in southern Italy became the first and mother to all Western universities thanks to its Greek legacy; that Sicily played a leading role in the rise of modern science and civilisation, again thanks to its Greek heritage, that Amalfi, also in the south of Italy, did the same, that the later Rénaissance (16th century) was due to the flow of Greek learning to the Christian West from deceased Byzantium (following its taking by the Ottomans in 1453), and so on and so forth.'[49] Hence, we have two contradictory arguments co-habiting in the Western narrative of the history of science, that on one hand Greek learning was lost to the Christian West, which explains its recovery from Arabic, and on the other, that such Greek learning, in its pristine form, was responsible for the flowering of science and civilisation, whether before the 12th century, or after, or during the 16th –17th century Renaissance.

This is one of the major deficiencies this work will tackle. It will show that it was Islam, the faith, which was, in fact, at the source of Islamic science and accomplishments, and that Greek science was only a tool, a means, just as others were, such as the Hindu, and above all the Chinese legacy, and that most of the basic manifestations of Islamic civilisation had no Greek antecedents of any sort.

This work will particularly dwell on one central issue that has already received the bulk of attention in this introduction: the matter of decline of Muslim civilisation. It will show that whilst Islamic sciences and other aspects of civilisation find support amongst Western historians (a minority), overwhelmingly, Western scholarship, just as most secular 'Muslim' scholars, blame Islam for the decline of Muslim civilisation, setting aside all factors already

Ribera: *Dissertaciones y opusculos*, 2 vols (Madrid, 1928). R. Briffault: *The Making of Humanity* (George Allen, London, 1928). J.W. Draper: A *History of the Intellectual Development of Europe (*George Bell and Son, London, 1875).

[48] Such as the SOAS historian appearing on the BBC program: An Islamic History of Europe, Broadcast on BBC4, 10 April 8.30 p.m, seen by this author. Or any work, and so common an assertion it was found on the covers or back covers of books, such as in R. Fletcher: *Moorish Spain* (Phoenix; London; 1992), back-cover.

[49] Such as in: P. Duhem: *Le System du Monde* (Paris; 1914). B. Lawn: *The Salernitan Questions* (Oxford At The Clarendon Press, 1963). O. Pedersen: *Early Physics and Astronomy* (Cambridge University Press, 1974). P. Chaunu: *European Expansion in the Later Middle Ages;* tr., by K. Bertram (North Holland Publishing Company; Amsterdam; 1979). D. J. Geanakoplos: *Medieval Western Civilisation, and the Byzantine and Islamic Worlds* (D.C. Heath and Company, Toronto, 1979).

looked at above. This is the principal source of contention this work has with such a scholarship.

Before it deals with this issue, in its third and final part, this work, in its first part, offers an overview of Islamic civilisation. This part looks at trade and industry; the urban character as well as gardens, and touches on general aspects of Islamic scholarship.
The second part will focus on Islamic sciences.
The final part will deal with the impact of Islam, the faith, on Muslim civilisation, putting particular emphasis on the Western narrative regarding this issue. This final part will also explain the true reasons for the decline of Muslim civilisation.

It is important to point out here, that whether with regard to Islamic sciences and civilisation, or their historical (mis)treatment, not everything will be covered in this work. Space, time, and above all this author's limits impose restrictions. This work will provide a number of references for a curious audience to fill the gaps. This study aims at an original approach, which can act as a platform for future follow up and improvement.

*All dates in this work are C.E.

ISLAMIC CIVILISATION (AN OVERVIEW)

Muslim society, in its golden age, from the end of the ancient empires to the emergence of the modern states, was a melting pot in time and space, a great crossroads, a vast synthesis, an amazing meeting place.[50]

These few lines capture Muslim civilisation in its thoroughness and in its role in human civilisation as this work will attempt to do, beginning with this, its first part.

This volume, in four chapters, looks at the Islamic economic system, its urban setting, its gardens and its scholarship over its period of glory, from the 7th to the 13th century (although frequent mentions will be made of later times). The aim is to capture the wider picture of Islamic civilisation in its diversity, and look at it from as many new angles as possible; to shed light, of course, but above all bring in new arguments. There is, thus, no need to dwell too long on what other works have dealt with in great abundance, but they will be referred to whenever it is necessary. This work will focus, instead, on matters little touched upon elsewhere, and yet, whose role was vital to the rise of Islamic civilisation and to the progress of civilisation as a whole. This volume, like others, will deal with a central theme in this work: mainstream Western historical mistreatment of Muslim civilisation. It will raise this issue in relation to some of the aspects looked at in the first two chapters, trade and industry, and urbanism. This issue of historical mistreatment is not discussed in the chapter on Muslim scholarship, for it will be abundantly dealt with in the following, Second Volume, on sciences.

[50] M. Lombard: *The Golden Age of Islam*; tr. J. Spencer (North Holland Publishers; 1975), p. 239.

One

TRADE, FINANCE AND INDUSTRY

> Really all Christendom could be supplied for a year with the merchandise of Damascus... There are such rich and noble and delicate works of every kind that if you had money in the bone of your leg, without fail you would break it to buy of these things.

Simone Sigoli, Florentine Pilgrim; 1384.[51]

The words by Sigoli do indeed define the economic prosperity that was once upon a time identified with the Muslim world. They were also expressed two decades or so before Damascus, just as much of Syria, fell to Timur's hordes, whose devastating onslaught in the later years of the 14th century this time ended permanently the glorious history of one of the nations to which modern civilisation is most indebted. Simone Sigoli's words in praise of Syria's accomplishments were far from isolated, and somehow contradict the generalised assumption that Mamluk rule was an era of economic backwardness.[52] Likewise, the thriving economies of Syria, Egypt, and much of the medieval Muslim world, which Lombard, in particular, has faithfully described,[53] also contradict the generally misconceived idea that the arrival of Islam hampered trade, and that Muslims, as a rule, were incapable of industrial innovation. These misconceptions, in this field, as in others, purported by leading figures of Western scholarship, have served as foundations to their followers, who have easily borrowed them and disregarded, all too easily, too, counter arguments that gave a much more favourable role to Islam. To this day, the most popular view on the Muslim role in trade remains that held by Henry Pirenne, a view (and its intrinsic flaws), which has been demonstrated to be the most idiotic of all, historically utterly flawed, by many scholars, and yet it still holds just because it suits the anti Islamic bias. Incidentally, this Pirenne idiocy is similar to another equally idiotic view of Islam and the Prophet, held by Patricia Crone and her acolytes, proved indeed to be utter nonsense, and admitted to be so by Patricia Crone herself and her closest acolyte, Michael Cook, and yet, the same view is adopted and asserted to this moment, in 2017-2018.[54] So, before we digress, let's deal with Pirenne's theory, which is of interest to us here.

---

[51] Visit to the Holy Places of Egypt, Sinai, Palestine and Syria in 1384 by Frescobaldi. Gucci, and Sigoli; tr. T. Bellorini and E. Hoade; Jerusalem; 1948; pp. 183; 182 in R. E. Mack: *Bazaar to Piazza: Islamic Trade and Italian Arts, 1300-1600*; (University of California Press; Berkeley; 2002); p. I.

[52] Such as held by E. Ashtor: *A Social and Economic History of the Near East in the Middle Ages*; (Collins; London; 1976); pp. 280-331.

[53] M. Lombard: *The Golden Age of Islam*; tr. J. Spencer; North Holland Publishers; 1975.

[54] See P. Crone; M.A. Cook: *Hagarism; the Making of the Muslim World*; Cambridge University Press; 1977. Check the internet the many counter arguments, and also how Patricia Crone herself, in 2008 or so admitted the shortcomings of her

1. The Pirenne Theory

In the early 1930s, Pirenne held in his *Muhammad and Charlemagne* that the advance of Islam led to the collapse of economic activity around the Mediterranean, thus driving Europe into the dark ages.[55] In more detail, he asserted:

> European civilisation formed around the Mediterranean by the successive work of Egypt, Syria, Phoenicia, Greece and Rome. The latter, the last worker of an admirable labour, brought into one single state all the people it inherited. The empire founded by Rome, including all, is thus an Empire that was essentially Mediterranean.[56]

He went on:

> From Byzantium, Asia Minor and Egypt, merchants, Jewish, but mostly Syrian continued their supply of it (the West) with luxury goods, rich cloth, and fine wines. By their intermediary it received the gold that was necessary for its currency and the papyrus that was used by copyists and clerks of chancelleries.[57]

Until:

> The brusque irruption of Mohammedanism in the Mediterranean disrupts everything. Syria after its capture by the Muslims no longer sends either ships or merchants to Marseilles; then Egypt falls under the yoke of Islam (642-44), and papyrus no longer reaches Gaul, and as the Muslim invasion grows stronger, maritime traffic, once thriving, now crumbles.[58]
>
> The arrival of Islam brings to an end the use of gold as a currency; causes an end to the import of oriental textiles, an end to the use of papyrus, and puts a stop to the arrival of spices.[59]

Thus:

> The Islamic invasion of the Mediterranean, to my opinion, is the event to which must be attributed the crack which separates Antiquity of European history from that which we usually call the Middle Ages. In shutting the sea and in cutting the West from the Orient, it put an end to the Mediterranean unity, which had constituted for thousands of years the most striking

---

views, and how regardless, her arguments are being adopted by many, most of all, Tom Holland (google his name for his vomit).

[55] H. Pirenne: *Mohammed and Charlemagne* (F. Alcan; Paris-Bruxelles; 1937).

[56] H. Pirenne: Mahomet et Charlemagne, *Revue Belge de Philosophie et d'Histoire* 1, 1922, 77-86, in *Bedeutung Und Rolle des Islam Beim ubergang Vom Altertum Zum Mittelalter*, Paul Egon Hubinger: ed; (Darmstadt, 1968), pp. 1-9. p. 1.

[57] Ibid; p. 7.

[58] H. Pirenne: Un Contraste Economique; Merovingiens et Carolingiens, Revue Belge; 2, 1923, 223-35; in *Bedeutung Und Rolle des Islam*; pp. 10-22; p. 16.

[59] Ibid.

> character, and the condition itself of traditional development of civilisation in that part of the world.[60]

For Pirenne, the arrival of Islam did not just destroy the Europe of Antiquity and cause the end of the Mediterranean community, which had survived the fall of the Roman Empire, worse:

> The sea, once familiar and familial, around which all came together, now becomes alien and hostile.[61]

And:

> The Barbarian invasions altered nothing, but now, the very countries where civilisation was born, are wrested away, and the cult of the Prophet is substituted to the Christian faith, Muslim law to Roman law, Arabic to Greek and Latin... Of the maritime traffic of before we lose all traces.[62]

Pirenne's theory became and has remained a convenient foundation for his followers to see in the Islamic advance of the 7th-8th centuries an explanation to Europe's centuries or so of darkness (5th-15th), and identifying Islam with decline and failure. This seemingly coherent explanation helped Pirenne's rise to the status of remarkable man of learning.[63] For Wiet et al, for instance, 'Reference must be made here to the views brilliantly put forward by the great Belgian historian Henri Pirenne.'[64] Pirenne had been 'spreading the good word,' Coville says,[65] delivering lectures world wide, explaining how it was Islam, instead of the 'Barbarian' invasions of three centuries before (late fifth CE) that had broken a hitherto cohesive and prosperous Western civilisation.

Pirenne's theory was flimsy, though. It was mainly based on the fact that imports of gold and papyrus had 'disappeared' during the Islamic advance, and so could not stand in front of robust challenges. Such challenges came from a number of directions, such as from those who were in agreement with Pirenne with regard to economic regression but who did not accept that the domination of Islam of the Mediterranean basin was the main cause of the phenomenon.[66]

Perroy outlines the main defects of Pirenne's theory by demonstrating that Islam as a faith had no problem with trade, but quite the contrary. The Prophet was a trader; his followers crossed the world from The Sudan to the Volga, from China to Madagascar to trade; and it was, in fact, Islam that 'awakened Western trade.'[67] Pirenne's claim that there was a rupture of links between the East and West is also

---

[60] Ibid; p. 10.

[61] H. Pirenne: Mahomet et Charlemagne; in *Bedeutung*; op cit; p. 8.

[62] Ibid; p. 9.

[63] Hence, on May 18, 1938, a solenal academic session was held in his honour in Brussels (Belgium), which was attended by the Belgian king, Leopold II.

[64] G. Wiet et al: *History of Mankind;* Vol 3: *The Great Medieval Civilisations*; tr. from the French (George Allen & Unwin Ltd; UNESCO; 1975), p. 5.

[65] A. Coville: Les Commencements du Moyen Age d'apres Henri Pirenne, *Journal des Savants,* 1938, pp. 97-104, at p. 97.

[66] Pierre Lambrechts: Les Theses de Henri Pirenne sur la fin du monde Antique et les debuts du Moyen Age, in *Bedeutung*; op cit; pp. 32-57; p. 34.

[67] E. Perroy: *Le Moyen Age* (Presses Universitaires de France, 1956), pp. 113-4.

wrong. In the late 7th century the Gallic bishop Arculf experienced no particular difficulty in getting passage from Christian territory to Muslim and back again, and at Alexandria he was greatly impressed by the volume and the international flavour of commercial exchanges.[68] The fact that Venetian merchants could steal the relics of Saint Mark from an Alexandrian church in the 820s is also proof that merchants of all sorts were still congregating there a century and a half later.[69] Genicot also notes that the ports of Provence (France) had not ceased their activity between the 8th and 10th centuries,[70] and suggests that the decline of the exchange economy could have other causes than the Muslim irruption, especially the state of anarchy of the Frank monarchy after Dagobert.[71] The decline of trade between East and West of the Mediterranean, Perroy, once more observes, was anterior to Islam, and in the period in question, the 8th century, Byzantium kept up its trade with its possessions in Southern Italy and the Adriatic. If there was little traffic beyond that narrow area, it was due to internal conditions within the West and to the monopolistic policies pursued by Byzantium.[72] Byzantium itself pursued its commercial (and other) contacts with Islam. In the 10th century, the Muslim geographer, Ibn Hawqal, spoke of ships coming from the Byzantine Empire to the harbour at Tripoli, and of the international wares that could be found in ports along that coast.[73] A 959 Geniza document reveals a market of the Rum ("Romans"-Greeks or western Christians, indiscriminately) at al Fustat in Egypt, and twice later in the century we also hear of merchants from the Italian city of Amalfi there.[74]

There was also, as this work will amply show, constant cultural, social and economic intercourse between Christian communities living under Muslim and Christian rule. Muslim Sicily, where a substantial Christian minority lived, was not closed to outsiders as several 10th or even late 9th century Christian saints were either born there, or lived there for a time, and we are told of a south Italian "prince" planning to go and consult the doctors at Palermo.[75] Travel by Christian pilgrims to the Holy Land and Jerusalem was also continuous and quite intense. Earl Godwin's eldest son Swegen, Ealdred, Archbishop of York, went to Jerusalem in 1058 in such state as no other before him, and offered 'at our Lord's tomb a golden chalice of wondrous workmanship and price.'[76] Six years later Siegfried of

---

[68] Adamnan, *De locis sanctis,* ed. Denis Meehan (Dublin 1958); pp. 100-2.

[69] Renée Doehaerd, "Méditerranée et économie occidentale pendant le haut Moyen Age," *Cahiers d'Histoire Mondiale (Journal of World History)* 1 (1954) 3; p. 586; see: B.M. Kreuz: Ships, Shipping and the Implications of Change in the early Mediterranean; in *Viator*; 7 1976; pp.79-109; p. 90; and subsequent pp.

[70] F.L. Ganshof, Note sur les ports de Provence du viii au x siecle, in *Revue Historique*, t. CLXXXIV, 1938, p. 28, in L. Genicot: Aux Origines de la civilisation in *Bedeutung*; op cit; pp. 105-19; p. 106.

[71] L. Genicot: Aux Origines de la civilisation... pp. 105-119.

[72] E. Perroy: *Le Moyen Age*; op cit; 113-4.

[73] Ibn Hawqal, *Configuration de la terre:* The Book of the Routes and the Kingdoms, ed., tr. G. Wiet, 2vols. (Paris 1964) 1. pp. 65-6.

[74] S.D. Goitein: *A Mediterranean Society;* 5 Vols, Berkeley; 1967-90; 1.44. For Amalfitans there in 978, see the *Codex Diplomaticus Cavensis,* 8 vols. (Milan/Naples 1874) 2.114-116 (docs. 300, 301).

[75] Byzantion 29-30; 1959-60; pp. 89-173; in B.M. Kreuz: Ships, op cit; p. 91; and subsequent pp.

[76] Ralph Glaber in T.A. Archer: *The Crusades;* (T. Fisher Unwin; London; 1894); p. 17.

Mayence and three other bishops led a motley crowd of seven thousand pilgrims to the Holy Land.[77]

Another claim by Pirenne is that:

> It is a proven fact that the Musulman traders did not install themselves beyond the frontiers of Islam. If they did trade, they did so among themselves.[78]

This, as Denett notes, is a serious misrepresentation of fact.[79] Muslim merchants had established trading colonies in India, Ceylon, East Indies, and even China by the close of the 8th century.[80] The Muslims also sought to trade in the West from the earliest times. In the French river port of Arles in 812 one could find Muslim coins and such wares as Cordova leather, precious stones, and silk cloth, all brought there by Muslim traders.[81] It was, as Denett explains, the hostility to Islam as a faith which forbade the subsequent development and presence of Muslim traders on European soil.[82]

Pirenne's theory had other serious flaws.[83] He cites the scarcity of gold use as a sign of decline, but the passage from gold to silver between 650 and 700, as Perroy remarks, is neither a sign of the collapse of civilisation as believed by Pirenne, nor is it a definitive exhaustion of the stocks of gold of the Occident.[84] Lopez points out that gold did not become scarcer after the Muslim advance; to the contrary, in the 8th century and after, both Muslim coins and their imitations seem to have been fairly common.[85] The abandonment of the gold standard after Louis the Pious, Lopez explains, rather than being due to 'the Muslim irruption,' was instead caused by the insufficient prestige of the Western monarchs.[86] Beyond any doubt, as Bolin and Heyd insist, silver was exported from the Muslim world.[87] 52,000 complete or fragmentary Islamic coins were found in northern European countries dating from the early 8th to the early 11th century.[88] These coin hoards are widely distributed, stretching from Norway and northern Sweden in the north as far as Silesia and the Ukraine in the south, from Schleswig-Holstein and Mecklenburg in

---

[77] Ibid.

[78] H. Pirenne: *Mohammed and Charlemagne*; op cit; p. 174.

[79] D.C. Dennett: Pirenne and Muhammad; in *Bedeutung*; op cit; pp. 120-59; at p. 125.

[80] See W. Heyd: *Histoire du commerce*; op cit; vol 1; p. 28.

[81] Renée Doehaerd, "Méditerranée et économie occidentale pendant le haut Moyen Age," *Cahiers d'Histoire Mondiale (Journal of World History)* 1 (1954) 3.583.

[82] D.C. Denett: Pirenne and Muhammad, in *Bedeutung;* op cit; pp. 120-59; at p. 125.

[83] For an excellent summary of articles devoted to the thesis and its criticism see *Bedeutung* op cit.

[84] E. Perroy: Encore Mahomet et Charlemagne. Revue Historique 212, 1954, 232-8, in *Bedeutung*; op cit; pp. 266-75; at p. 267.

[85] Cf. Bloch, p.13 ff., with bibl in Robert S. Lopez: Mohammed and Charlemagne: A Revision. Speculum 18, 1943, 14-38, in *Bedeutung*; op cit; pp. 65-104; at p. 92.

[86] Cf. especially G.I. Bratianu, *Etudes Byzantines d'Histoire Economique et Sociale* (Paris, 1938), p. 219 ff.; also Bloch, pp. 25-28; R. S. Lopez: Mohammed; p. 98.

[87] W. Heyd: *Geschichte des Levantehandels im Mittelalter* 1, p. 104 ff., in S. Bolin: Mohammed, Charlemagne and Ruric: *Scandinavian Economic History Review*, Vol, I, 1953, pp. 5-39, in *Bedeutung*; op cit; pp. 223-65.

[88] R. Ettinghausen: The Impact of Muslim Decorative Arts and Painting on the Arts of Europe; in J. Schacht and C.E. Bosworth edition: *The Legacy of Islam*; (Oxford at the Clarendon Press; 1974); pp. 292-316; at p. 293.

the west to the Urals in the east.[89] Some of these hoards are real 'treasures troves such as Aladdin's cave;' one of them consisting of more than 11,000 dirhems, in addition to an indeterminate number of fragments, weighing more than 65 lbs.[90] These hoards demonstrate that there were prolonged trade links of these regions with the Islamic world. Bolin, in fact, demonstrates a parallelism of evolution between Europe and the Muslim world, specifically on the monetary level, which 'would have been incomprehensible if there had not been important East-West relations, especially via the North Sea.'[91]

As for the trade in Oriental purple-dyed and embroidered cloths, this was never interrupted in Western Europe, and the decreased use of Oriental cloths among the laymen (if there was a diminution) was largely due to fashion change. The Church did not change fashions, and, in fact, the largest part of the existing evidence of Oriental cloths in Western Europe relates to the Church.[92]

With regard to papyrus, Dennett counters Pirenne:

> Since the Arab conquest of Egypt did not cut off the supply of papyrus at its source, because this material was still found in Gaul a century later and was regularly employed by the Papacy until the eleventh century, it is difficult to say that its disappearance in Gaul is a conclusive proof that the Arabs had cut the trade routes. In the absence of all direct evidence one way or another, it would appear that as a possible hypothesis one might conclude that because parchment could be locally produced, because it was preferable as a writing material, and because, owing to a depreciated coinage, it may not have been more expensive than papyrus, the people of Gaul preferred to employ it.[93]

Dennett is spot on, indeed, for as we shall see in the following chapter, in the Muslim world paper production started and spread from around the late 8th century.[94]

Rather than causing the decline of Western Europe, the Muslim arrival, in fact, stimulated its slow, but undoubted emergence from the Dark Ages, in both economic and cultural terms. Lombard points out how the Muslim arrival 'occurred at a time of exhaustion in Europe, and re-established and amplified international commerce, and contributed to the recovery that characterized the Carolingian Empire.'[95] It was the Muslim advance, he explains, that led the West to regain contact with Oriental civilisation and, through the Muslims, with the major world

---

[89] European discoveries of Cufic coins to 1900 are listed in A. Markov: Topografiia kladovvostochnykh monet, 1910, in S. Bolin: Mohammed, in p. 258.

[90] Ibid.

[91] Ibid.

[92] Cf. Sabbe, op cit, in R. S. Lopez: Mohammed; p. 99.

[93] D.C. Dennett: Pirenne and Muhammad; op cit; at pp. 135-6; See M. Prou: *Manuel de Paleographie Latine et Francaise* (Paris; 1892), pp. 171-90.

[94] Bloom J. (2001). *Paper Before Print: The History of Paper Making in the Islamic World.* Connecticut: Yale University Press.

[95] M. Lombard: L'Or Musulman au Moyen Age, in *Annales ESC* (1947); pp. 143-60.

movements in trade and culture. Whereas the great 'barbarian' invasions of the fourth and fifth centuries, had caused an economic decline in the West under the Merovingian and Carolingian dynasties, the Islamic advance brought with it 'an astonishing development' in this same area.[96]

Gene Heck, likewise, insists:

> Contrary to Pirenne's view, there is powerful source of evidence indicating that not only did the Arab Muslims not cast medieval Europe into its early medieval economic abyss as some scholarship contends but that some three to four centuries later they provided much of the economic stimulus, as well as a multiplicity of commercial instruments, that helped pull up Europe from the "Dark Ages" stifling grip.[97]

J.M. Hobson notes:

> Because of the importance that Italy is accorded to the European commercial revolution, a few points are noteworthy in order to reveal the role of Islam in all this. In fact, as early as the late 8th century, Italy was linked into various sub-systems of the Afro-Eurasian economy straddling Europe, Africa and Asia. It was Italy's direct entry point into this wider and lucrative economy that secured her destiny.[98]
>
> While the Italians played an important role in spreading commercialisation throughout Christendom, they were not the great commercial pioneers portrayed by Eurocentrism.[99]

These points raised by Hobson are indeed critical as will be seen in the following chapters, on how it was precisely thanks to their trading with the Muslim world that the Italian city states were able to import not just economic wealth into Europe (hence the opposite of what Pirenne claims), they also imported means and techniques that taught Europe how to trade efficiently.

Pirenne's theory, finally, is further undermined by the fact that historians who have looked at the domestic history of Europe have noted the decline taking place in the western portion of the Roman empire even earlier than the 5th century; thus centuries before Islam came onto the scene. Lewis even insists that Muslim control of the Mediterranean did not begin in the 7th or 8th century, as Pirenne stated, but in the late 9th and early 10th centuries;[100] a five century gap between Islam and European decline, which makes Pirenne's theory untenable.

Having laid Pirenne's theory to rest, it is now relevant to look at the multiple aspects of Muslim trade, not so much from a quantitative side, which has been

---

[96] M. Lombard: Quand l'Islam Brillait de Mille feux. The article appeared in *Le Temps stratégique* No 20, Spring 1987.

[97] Gene. W. Heck: *Charlemagne, Muhammad, and the Arab Roots of Capitalism*; (Walter de Gruyter; Berlin; New York; 2006); p. 3.

[98] J.M. Hobson: Islamic Commerce and Finance in the Rise of the West, in R.F. Nayef al Rotham ed: *The Role of the Arabic Islamic world in the Rise of the West*, MacMillan, New york, 2012, pp. 84-115 at p. 91.

[99] J.M. Hobson: *The Islamic Origins of Western Civilisation*, Cambridge University Press, 2004, p. 119.

[100] A.R. Lewis: The Moslem Expansion in the Mediterranean, A.D. 827-960; pp. 23-9 in *The Islamic World and the West*; ed: A. R. Lewis (John Wiley and Sons; London, 1970), p. 23.

examined by countless sources, but rather from the qualitative side, how Islam brought diverse and wide stretches of the globe into a vast trading area; and how Islam provided the very foundations to modern commerce. But first, a word on industrial production is necessary to shed some light on the traded goods, and to provide a clearer picture of the Islamic industrial setting that is missing from knowledge at the moment.

2. Industry

Robert Wright, commenting on Landes, holds that:

> Landes spent part of his magnum opus *The Wealth and Poverty of Nations* trying to figure out why the westernmost of Oriental cultures, the Islamic civilisation of the Middle Ages, had not been destined for industrial greatness. His answer, in part: short time horizons. Whereas Europe's pragmatic medieval Christians coolly pursued 'continuing, sustainable profit,' the rampaging Muslims were propelled by 'fighting zeal' and paused 'only for an occasional digestion of conquest and booty.[101]

This view of Muslims as looting hordes, incapable of industrial or economic organisation is, once more, generalised amongst Western scholarship. It is an image reinforced by historical writing and teaching, which claims that industrialisation is a modern, 18th century, Western phenomenon. The English 'Industrial Revolution' of the 18th century is deemed to be the first model of goods produced for a mass market, power-driven machinery playing a central role in the manufacturing process, together with large-scale capital investment through banks and other financial institutions, and a class of entrepreneurs labouring (for profit) to meet the needs of an increasingly urban population. This generally held view, though, is contradicted by historical reality on many grounds.

Firstly, there is nothing such as a sudden revolution, as in this instance, the English spontaneously discovering, building, and installing machinery, warehouses, financial and legal institutions, regulating enterprise, and from amongst them there took place a sudden upsurge of entrepreneurs, and so on and so forth. There was no industrial revolution; things took centuries to evolve; industrialisation proceeded slowly, at times, true, with some leaps, but also with breaks and adjustments of diverse sorts, together with booms and busts, as are occurring in our day.

Secondly, rather than industrial activity being hampered by Islam, it was quite the opposite. From its inception, Islam promoted industrial organisation, wage labour, and private property. With regard to the latter, for instance, the Qur'an

[101] R. Wright: Nonzero: The Logic of Human destiny, at: http://www.nonzero.org/asia.htm

shows no hostility to private property, since it lays down rules for inheritance.[102] The Prophet's Tradition is full of praise for those who engage in enriching themselves so as to be able to help the deprived.[103] Similarly, wage labour is seen in Islam as something perfectly normal; it being a particular case of hiring; one hiring a man's labour power just as 'one hires a boat or a house.'[104] If a man repairs a wall that is collapsing, he has a right to be paid a wage.[105] The only restrictions in Islam derive from moral, religious, and principles of juridical order.[106]

Thirdly, looking through the history of early Islam reveals the existence of a powerful industrial sector geared for mass production. Medieval Muslim geographers describe chief centres of cotton manufacturing in Basra, Khurasan, Herat, Dimyat, Nishapur and Rayy; linen cloth production in Basra, Khurasan and Tinis, centres for silk production in Khuzistan, Bukhara and Fars; preparation of perfumes in Fars and Iraq; paper production in Syria, Iraq, Spain, and Transoxiana, and varied forms of industrial production elsewhere.[107] Islamic manufacturing also relied on the extensive use of power to activate machinery. Referring to technological diffusion, Glick notes, how it is possible to trace the diffusion of paper and sugar manufacture across the Arabic speaking world by noting the appearance of the names of al-warraq (paper maker) or al-Sukkari (sugar maker) in the 9th century.[108] It is likely, therefore, he adds, that paper and sugar processing arrived at the western terminus of diffusion, Islamic Spain, simultaneously along with the vertical wheel and trip hammer assembly, which could also be used for the fulling (pounding) of woollen cloth and for rice husking.[109] Banks and other financial institutions, state administration and its legal apparatus, also played their part in stimulating industrial production in much the same way as we have today. The use of Letters of Credit, for instance, was widespread, and some cities operated stock exchanges, which earned every day nearly 6,500 Dinars in rights of access.[110]

Fourthly, early in Islam, evidence shows the existence of wage labour. Instances include Tunisian lead miners of the 12th century, pearl fishers in the Gulf, and sugar workers in Egypt, who all received fixed wages for definite tasks.[111] In the Arab Peninsula itself, in addition to merchants, a great variety of professional craftsmen were employed within its leading producing sectors such as precious

---

[102] M. Rodinson; *Islam and Capitalism;* tr., by R. Pearce (Allen Lane; London; 1974), p. 14.

[103] M. Hamidullah in *Cahiers de l'ISEA;* Suppl. no 120; Series V; No 3; Dec. 1961; p. 27.

[104] M. Rodinson: *Islam and Capitalism;* op cit; p. 16.

[105] Ibid; p. 14.

[106] As examples available in translation of how hiring, and especially wage labour, are dealt with in religious law, see, for instance, K. Ibn Ishaq: *Abrege de la loi Musulmane selon le rite de l'Imam Malek*; tr. G.H. Bousquet; Vol III (Le Patrimoinel Algiers; 1961), pp. 128-33.

[107] S.M.Z. Alavi: *Arab Geography in the Ninth and Tenth Centuries* (Aligarth; 1965), pp. 97 ff.

[108] T. Glick: Technological Diffusion; in T. Glick, S.J. Livesey, F. Wallis Ed: *Medieval Science, Technology and Medicine*; An Encyclopaedia; (Routledge; London; 2005); pp. 470-2; at p. 471.

[109] Ibid.

[110] E. Gerspach: *L'Art de la Verrerie* (A Quantin Imprimeur, Editeur; Paris; 1885), p. 97.

[111] M. Rodinson: *Islam and Capitalism*; op cit; pp. 52-3.

metals mining, gold and silver smithing and the production of fine jewellery and ornamented swords, metal working, particularly in the manufacture of weaponry, farm equipment, and sundry instruments and house utensils; carpentry, mason work, and the weaving and dying of fabrics.[112]
Fifthly, the quality of Muslim industrial products remained much superior to that of the West down to the 17th century in general, and even after in relation to some items. Many industrial products, such as paper, cotton and silk, sugar, steel, a great variety of earthenware and glass products, chemicals and acids, and many others, were manufactured for centuries in Islam before they were introduced into the West. A reason for the ready acceptance of some Islamic objects, Ettinghausen insists, was their 'obvious aesthetic quality, their harmony, opulence, and often the great richness of their colours.'[113] A further asset especially in the early period was the higher degree of technical skill evident in the execution, far surpassing anything possible in the West.[114] Muslim steel products remained much superior to their Western counterparts until some point in the 18th century.[115] In ceramics production, even the modest Muslim bacini were superior to central and northern Italian ceramics until the 14th century, and Italian potters could not match the artistic quality of the Syrian and Spanish Muslim wares until the late 15th century.[116] Oriental imports became so popular in the West that exceptional efforts were made to imitate them as closely as possible.[117] Confusion still exists between the 16th century Venetian Orientalizing brassware, for instance, and its Islamic models.[118]
Sixth, one of the principal reasons behind the flourishing industrial activity in Islam, and its superiority over its Western counterpart was the role of scientific activity. It will be noted how chemistry, laboratory work, and newly invented acids and other substances proved essential in paper and textile production, the purification of metals, the glazing of ceramics, and other industrial applications. Muslim engineers devised techniques that were widely relied upon in mining, use of water power to activate machinery, the construction of windmills, and so on.
Seventh, as this work will further on show, it was also from Islam that the Christian West derived many of its industrial skills and techniques.[119] Most, if not nearly all, early Western industries and crafts (ceramics, glass making, silk making, and the like), were either a legacy from Islam, or an imitation of Islamic counterparts, and generally had recourse to Muslim craftsmen in their early

---

[112] G.W. Heck: *Charlemagne*; op cit; p. 47.
[113] R. Ettinghausen: The Impact of Muslim Decorative Arts; op cit; p. 295.
[114] Ibid.
[115] C.S. Smith: *A History of Metallography*; (Chicago; 1965); p. 33 ff.
[116] R.E. Mack: *Bazaar to Piazza*; *Islamic Trade and Italian Arts, 1300-1600*; (University of California Press; Berkeley; 2002); p. 4.
[117] Ibid; p. 7.
[118] Ibid.
[119] For further details on this issue, see this author's: *The Hidden Debt to Islamic Civilisation*, Bayt al-Hikmah, Manchester, 2005.

stages of growth (mainly in the East during the Crusades, and also in re-conquered Spain and Sicily).

The following outlines some industrial activities.

Paper Industry

Early Islamic paper-making involved mass manufacturing, the use of machine power and wind and water to activate such machinery. It also anticipated the introduction of innovative processes in response to local conditions and resources and the use of advanced marketing techniques.

The first paper workshop in Islam was established in Baghdad in the years 793/795.[120] It was, however, much earlier, after the conquest of Samarkand, in 704, that Muslims discovered Chinese produced paper.[121] Chinese paper made from bark and the fibres of rags and hemp may possibly have been imported and sold in Samarkand.[122] It was from the Chinese that the Muslims acquired the art of paper making, with a first mill set up in Samarkand itself. The manufacture of paper was favoured in Samarkand by the abundant crops of flax and hemp, as well as by the numerous irrigation canals, as plenty of pure water was then, as now, a necessary requisite for paper- production.[123]

After the first Muslim paper mill was set up in Baghdad in 793-795, paper manufacturing rapidly spread west to Damascus, Tiberias, Syrian Tripoli; the factories set up in Syria benefiting greatly from the favourable conditions for growing hemp.[124] The traveller Nasr Eddin Khusraw (fl. 1030s) said that Syrian paper was similar to that made in Samarkand, but of better quality.[125] High quality Hamawi (Hama-made) paper was used for important diplomatic and religious documents.[126] In general, Syrian paper was regularly shipped to Egypt as it was to the Red Sea ports, and India.[127] Paper production reached Egypt in the late 8th century, and the first extant Muslim document made of paper dates from the year 180 of Hijra (796 of our era) and comes from that country.[128] Complete paper manuscripts have survived from about 900; for example, one in Damascus from the year 266 after the Hijra, a year that began on August 23, 879,[129] and one

[120] G. Wiet et al: *History;* op cit; p. 331.

[121] S.M. Imamuddin: *Muslim Spain* (Leiden; Brill; 1981), p.110; see also: Carreres: Historia de Jativa; p. 48; L. Viardot: *Historia de los Arabes y de los Moros de Espana*; (Barcelona; 1844); p. 239.

[122] D. Hunter: *Paper Making*; (Pleiades Books; London; 1947); p. 60.

[123] Ibid.

[124] M. Lombard: *The Golden Age of Islam*; tr., J. Spencer (North Holland Publishers; 1975), p. 192.

[125] Nasir I-Khusraw: Tr. Schefer; pp. 41; and 58; n. 1, in M. Lombard: *Les Textiles dans le Monde Musulman du VII au XIIem Siecle* (Mouton Editeur; Paris; 1978), p. 203.

[126] T. Walz: Writing materials, in the *Dictionary of the Middle Ages*; Vol 12; J.R. Strayer Editor in Chief, (Charles Scribner's Sons, N. York, 1970 ff), at pp. 697-9.

[127] Ibid.

[128] M. Lombard: *Les Textiles;* op cit; p. 203.

[129] M. Kurd Ali: *Khitat al-sham* IV (Damascus, 1926), 243.

in the Azhar mosque in Cairo from 923.[130] There is an even older manuscript in Leiden, namely, Abu 'Ubayd's book on unusual terms in the traditions of the Prophet; it was written in the year 252 after the Hijra (CE. 865-866), but two-fifths of the work are missing.[131] In Egypt, paper was largely produced at al-Fustat, Fuwwa, and Fayyum. From Egypt, paper-making travelled further west to North Africa and reached Morocco sometime in the 9th-10th century. Fes, in the 12th century, was said to have 400 paper mills.[132] Like much else, from Morocco paper production crossed the Strait into Muslim Spain; the Andalusians, according to the geographer al-Muqaddasi (b. 946-d. end of 10th century), soon excelling at the craft.[133] The town of Jativa, near Valencia, became famed for its manufacture of thick, glossy paper, the *Shatibi,* following a process borrowed from the East.[134] According to the Sicilian based Muslim geographer al-Idrisi (b.1099-1100- d.1166), the paper of Jativa was of such good quality that the like of it was not to be found anywhere else in the world, and that it was exported to the East and the Maghrib.[135] There were also other places in Andalusia of paper production of the heavy, smooth, glazed sort.[136] The quality of Andalusi paper is extolled to this day, Goitein thus remarking that a letter from Grenada, dated 1130, was written on the best paper, almost entirely white, strong, and pleasantly smooth.[137]

By the year 1000, it could be said that paper was in general use throughout the Islamic world, and this had a considerable impact in stimulating the rise of intellectual activities as well as a number of industries. The new product replaced what hitherto were costly and also very rare materials for writing.[138] In contrast with Europe, where paper was a scarce commodity, in the land of Islam it was commercialised in bulk and large quantities. Like papyrus, sheets of paper were sometimes pasted together and sold in large rolls from which the user cut suitable pieces.[139] But most frequently the buyer received the sheets in the format in which they emerged from the frame, and this could vary widely.[140] The sheet was folded to size, and twenty-five such standard sheets were called in Persian *dast,* "hand," translated into Arabic as *kaff* from which subsequently the French "main de papier" was derived. Five "hands" are called a *rizma,* "bundle," which was borrowed by Italian and Spanish *(resma)* and taken over in different forms by other European languages: rame in France, *Ries* (originally *Rizz)* in German, *ris*

---

[130] J. Pedersen: *The Arabic Book*; tr. G. French; (Princeton University Press; 1928); pp. 64-5.

[131] Ibid; p. 47.

[132] K. von Karabacek: *Das Arabische Papier, eine historich-antiquarische Untersuchung* (Vienna; 1887), p. 40.

[133] Al-Muqaddasi: *Ahsan at-taqasim fi Ma'rifat al-Aqalim*; M.J. de Goeje ed., (Bibliotheca geographorum arabicum, 2nd edition, Leiden, 1906), p. 239.

[134] On the paper making industry in Spain, see E.Levi Provencal: *Histoire de l'Espagne Musulmane*; Vol III (Paris, Maisonneuve, 1953), p. 185; and also C.E. Dubler: *Uber das Wirtschaftsleben (*Romania Helvetica XXII; Geneva; 1943), pp. 81-4.

[135] Al-Idrisi: Kitab; pp 192 and 233; in S.M. Imamuddin: *Muslim;* op cit; p. 111.

[136] E. Levi Provencal: *L'Espagne Musulmane au Xem siecle* (Paris; 1932), p. 185.

[137] S.D. Goitein: *A Mediterranean Society;* 5 vols (Berkeley; 1967-88), vol V; p. 288.

[138] G. Wiet et al: *History;* op cit; pp. 331-2.

[139] J. Pedersen: *The Arabic Book*; op cit; p. 67.

[140] Ibid.

in Danish, and of course *ream* in English.[141] In using the paper for books, the sheets were laid inside one another to form a fascicle *(kurrasa),* which consisted as a rule of eight folded sheets.[142]

The advent of cheap and abundant paper fostered cultural activities and mass production of books.[143] Thus, whilst elsewhere, books were 'published' only through the tedious labour of copyists, in the Muslim world, hundreds, even thousands of copies of reference materials were made available to all those wishing to learn.[144] This, in turn, stimulated the trade in books.[145] Markets of bookmakers and bookshops spread in the vicinity of the mosques.[146] The *Warraq* profession (waraq being the Arabic word for paper) developed widely and rapidly.[147] The *Warraqeen* (plural for Warraq) (paper maker) traded mostly in paper, (and quite often, copied manuscripts which they sold to customers.) The more established Warraqs went to considerable length to acquire new manuscripts.[148] Baghdad, most probably, became the first major city where the Warraqeen bookshops appeared.[149] And, from there, these shops spread to other parts of the Muslim world; Cairo, most particularly, became a major centre of the Warraqeen, where, according to Ibn Zulaq, during the Tulunid and Ikhsid rule of Egypt (868-969), there was a special bazaar for the Warraqeen where 'books were offered for sale, and in its shops debates often took place.'[150]

There were other major outlets for mass production of paper. One such outlet was government; as early as the late 8th century Harun al-Rashid's Vizier, Ja'far, introduced paper to government offices.[151] This innovation did not just provide forms for authenticity of legal or governmental documents (as parchment previously used could be washed, whilst paper could not);[152] most of all it set a pattern with which other societies and countries would catch up centuries later. Good-quality papers were also used as gifts for sultans or as a material for currency; and as early as the 9th century, coloured papers were in use for a diversity of purposes: yellow, for instance, favoured in religious circles as it facilitated the memorisation of the Qur'an.[153] Paper was also used for wrapping

---

[141] Ibid.
[142] Ibid.
[143] G. Wiet et al: *History*; op cit; p. 331.
[144] M. Nakosteen: *History of Islamic Origins of Western Education: 800-1350* (University of Colorado Press; Boulder; Colorado; 1964), p. 37.
[145] J. Pedersen: *The Arabic Book*; op cit.
[146] Such as in Damascus, according to Ibn Battuta; I; pp. 207-8; in Fustat: Casanova: Foustat; XXXVIII-XL; in M. Lombard: *Les Textiles*; op cit; p. 205.
[147] M. Sibai: *Mosque Libraries, A Historical Study* (Mansell Publishing Limited; London and New York; 1987), p. 41.
[148] Z. Sardar- M.W. Davies: *Distorted Imagination* (Grey Seal; London; 1990), p. 99.
[149] M. Sibai: *Mosque libraries*; op cit; p. 41.
[150] Ibn Zulaq, *Akhbar Sibawiy al-Misri*, pp. 33, 44 MS 1461; Tarikh Taimur, Egypt; in A. Shalaby: *History of Muslim Education* (Dar al-Kashaf; Beirut; 1954), p. 27.
[151] M. Lombard: *The Golden Age*; op cit; p. 191.
[152] Ibid.
[153] T. Walz: Writing materials, op cit; pp. 698.

goods; in 1035, Nasr Eddin Khusraw, on a visit to Cairo, expressed his astonishment at seeing: 'sellers of vegetables, spices, hardware, provided with paper in which all they sold was immediately wrapped up.'[154] Literate traders also wrote extensively, and there have been found in Egypt remains of their registers, letters and contracts, the 10th century Geniza documents being nearly all on paper.[155] The same Geniza corpus showed the widespread use of paper in books, legal documents, laundry lists, price inventories, and other items, mostly written on paper.[156] In fact, according to a business manual *Irshad ila Mahasin al-Tijara* (A reference to the Virtues of Commerce), written sometime in the 11th or early 12th century, paper was an important object of commerce.[157] The best kind is described as heavy, well polished, pleasant to the touch, and free from worm holes, which can be prevented by means of a species of Indian mint.[158]

The paper industry stimulated a number of crafts and professions, which included dying, ink making, manuscript craftsmanship, and calligraphy. A number of sciences also progressed in the wake of the paper industry. Chemistry, obviously, has the most intricate links with the paper industry, Levey's articles on the subject in the review *Chymia* highlight this. They deal with glues, erasure fluids, and Islamic chemical technology.[159] Levey also draws attention to the pioneering works of the Tunisian, Ibn Badis (1007-1061), who in his *Umdat al-Kuttab* (Staff of the Scribes) in twelve chapters, writes amongst others on: the excellence of the pen, the preparation of types of inks, the preparation of coloured inks, the colouring of dyes and mixtures, secret writing, the making of paper, and so on.[160] Briefly, here, we note, with Levey, how the technology of the manufacture of ink was of great importance to mediaeval Muslims.[161] Inks were usually divided into black and coloured. The former was made up of soot and tannin inks. The soot inks included those called Chinese, Indian, Kufic, Persian, Iraqi, and Nafuran.[162] The major difference among these inks is the material from which the soot was prepared; the sources were usually various botanicals and lampblack. Gum Arabic was a common additive; glair was also in use. Mildly acidic solutions of dilute vinegar or yoghurt were used to arrest or slow down formation of mould.[163] The gallnut and ferrous sulfate inks described in Muslim manuscripts are still used today.[164] Some specialised inks known to the Muslims included an ink which could be used

---

[154] In D. Hunter: *Papermaking: The History and Technique of an Ancient Craft* (Pleiades Books; London; 1943; 1947), p. 471.
[155] M. Lombard: *Les Textiles*; op cit; p. 204.
[156] O.R. Constable: *Trade and Traders in Muslim Spain* (Cambridge University Press; 1994), p. 195.
[157] Anonymous: *Kitab al-Irshad ila Mahasin al-Tijara*; (Cairo AH 1318).
[158] T.W. Arnold: Arab Travellers and Merchants; AD 1000-1500; in A.P. Newton: *Travel and Travellers of the Middle Ages*; (Kegan Paul; London; 1926); pp. 88-103; at p. 94.
[159] In *Chymia*, Quarterly review devoted to the history of chemistry; edited by H.M. Leicester. University of Pennsylvania Press, Philadelphia; Volume 7; (1961).
[160] M. Levey: The Manufacture of inks, Liqs, Erasure Fluids and Glues-A preliminary survey in Arabic Chemical Technology; in *Chymia*; Vol 7 (1961), pp. 57-72.
[161] M. Levey: Chemical Technology in early Muslim Times; in *Scientia*; 96 (1961); pp. 326-30; at p. 326.
[162] Ibid.
[163] Ibid.
[164] Ibid; p. 327.

immediately after preparation, a dry ink, an ink for travellers, a cheap ink for the common people, an ink which did not require fire for its preparation, and a type of ink for religious books.[165]

As noted above, there is nothing pioneering on the part of the Muslims in the invention of paper itself; a Chinese invention, like much else. The Muslims, however, pioneered in other ways. They adapted paper making to their specific conditions, using local materials. They also fostered its development following methods that the industry has retained. The Chinese relied on fibre from the bark of the paper mulberry tree to prepare their material; but short of the substance, the Muslims innovated, using primarily linen as a substitute.[166] In fact, the principal materials which were used in paper making in the land of Islam were the linen of the Egyptian Delta and the Spanish Levant,[167] hemp from Samarkand, Spain,[168] or Syria, the latter being of white colour and excellent quality, and mainly rags.[169] The use of rags, to considerable extent, was due to the widespread use of textile material for items of clothing. In Spain, generally, paper was manufactured from flax and rags.[170] Whilst Pedersen insists that cotton was never used for paper-making, as was formerly supposed,[171] Immamudin claims that papers from Muslim manuscripts preserved in the libraries of Spain show that paper was manufactured both from cotton and linen;[172] and also from *shahdanj* (canamo).[173]

The earliest Muslim manuscript to describe the manufacture of paper is dated Ca. 1025. It says that paper is prepared from flax. There is a fairly full description showing particularly the care exerted in the operation.[174] According to Ibn Badis, the Tunisian author of the treatise, flax was soaked in quicklime, then rubbed with the hands, and spread out in the sun to dry. It was then returned to fresh quicklime. These operations were repeated many times. If was washed free of the quicklime time after time, then pounded in a mortar, washed, and introduced into molds of the proper measure.[175] Here we follow Pedersen's explanation of the rest of the process. The mold consisted of a frame with a screen stretched across it, as in a sieve. A quantity of pulp was placed on the screen and smoothed out to an even thickness.[176] It was then put on a board, possibly felt-covered, and

---

[165] Ibid.
[166] D. Hunter: *Papermaking:* op cit; p. 139.
[167] M. Lombard: *Les Textiles*; op cit; p. 205.
[168] Ibn Awwam*: Kitab al-Filaha* (Le Livre de l'agriculture), tr., by Clement-Mullet; 2 tomes in 3 vols (Paris 1864-1867); I; p. 115.
[169] Wiesner: *Ueber die altesten bis jetzt aufgedundenen Hadernpapiere* (Vienna; 1911), in M. Lombard: *Les Textiles*; op cit; p. 205.
[170] O.R. Constable: *Trade and Traders*; op cit; p. 195.
[171] The account given here and later is based upon von Karabacek's and Wiesner's studies cited above, especially the anonymous Arabic paper mentioned in *MSPER 4;*J. Pedersen, The Arabic Book; p. 65.
[172] In S.M. Imamuddin: *Muslim*; op cit; p. 111.
[173] Banqueri: Agricultura; ii; p. 118; in S.M. Imamuddin: *Muslim*; op cit; p. 111.
[174] M. Levey: Chemical Technology in early Muslim Times; in *Scientia*; 96 (1961); pp. 326-30; at p. 328.
[175] Ibid.
[176] J. Pedersen: *The Arabic Book*; op cit; p. 65.

transferred to a smooth wall, to which it adhered until eventually it became dry and fell away.[177] The sheets, being ribbed by the interlacing pattern of the mold, were now rubbed with a mixture of starch, which had first been pulverized and softened in cold water and then stirred into boiling water. This rubbing process, which was followed by sprinkling, "filled out" the sheet and whitened it.[178] The sheets of paper could now be piled and the stacks pressed prior to individual polishing of each 66 sheet on a board, using agate or onyx, or sometimes glass, as a polishing stone. Cockleshells were originally employed for this process.[179] The last stage, for strengthening the paper and preventing the ink from running, was a "treatment," *'ilãj,* or sizing, as it is known to us. It consisted of immersing the paper in, or rubbing it with, wheaten starch paste, as has been ascertained from the discoveries of paper made in Egypt.[180] Rice water was also employed for sizing, this being a viscous decoction of rice that was strained through a piece of clean linen; less often, use was made of gum tragacanth produced from astragalus. The latter has not been proved from the samples tested, however. Sizing filled up the pores of the paper and made the fibre adhere to each other.[181] Sometimes only one side was smoothed to be used for writing. A pair of sheets would then be glued together with the rough sides facing each other, giving a thick, strong sheet. Al-Muqaddasi says that this was done in Sana' in the Yemen, and sheets of this kind are found in Egypt.[182] Instructions are also given for antiquating the paper with the aid of saffron or fig juice.[183] The use of such paper with an artificially aged appearance could lend itself to abuse. "Old" manuscripts might be fabricated. "Smoothing" *(saql)* of the paper was done by the writer before use. If it was not first-class paper he would smear it with a white substance, then smooth it.[184]

Hunter enlightens us on the technological process, saying that, to beat the cleansed rags to a pulp a trip hammer was put to use. This improved method of maceration was owed to the Muslims.[185] Lombard also comments on this major point of difference between Muslims and Chinese; the Muslims manufacturing paper in mills, relying on machinery.[186] Derry and Williams remark that the process was increased in efficiency by the addition of spikes to tear to pieces the rags, which were the normal raw material.[187]

The use of natural power to activate machinery in paper-making was a decisive breakthrough. By 950, water power was being used in fibre pounding in

[177] Ibid.
[178] Ibid.
[179] Ibid; pp. 65-6.
[180] Ibid; p. 66.
[181] Ibid.
[182] Al-Muqaddasi: *Ahsan al-taqasim;* op cit; III, 100.
[183] J. Pedersen: *The Arabic Book*; op cit; p. 66.
[184] *Irshad*; op cit; VI, 38f.
[185] D. Hunter: *Papermaking;* op cit; p. 139:
[186] M. Lombard: *Les Textiles*; op cit; p. 206.
[187] T.K Derry and T.I Williams: *A Short History of Technology* (Oxford at Clarendon Press, 1960), p. 233.

Baghdad.[188] Hill describes how hydraulic power activated machinery and the technical processes in use.[189] Specific natural conditions affected particular usages of such power. Where the banks of the watercourse were high, as along the Euphrates, at Hama on the Orontes (Syria), at Amasia on the Yeshil Irmak (further east), or at Toledo in Spain, the current of the river itself was used to turn waterwheels, which produced energy for both paper mills, and for other mills (flour production, for instance).[190] Water powered-mills abounded throughout the Muslim world. In the city of Fes, in Morocco, for instance, 400 mills (powered by both water and wind) were working in the year 1184.[191] Not all, possibly, were geared for paper production; some such mills were used for fulling cloth, sawing timber and processing sugar cane.[192] It must be pointed out here that at an early stage, the Muslims compensated for the shortage of water in some parts by relying on wind power.[193]

One of the advantages of paper, Pedersen points out, consists in the fact that it could be manufactured in many different types, both of format and quality.[194] The usual colour was white, of course, but the paper might be given other colours by being dipped in or rubbed with some tinted substance; thus, blue was produced from indigo or aloe, yellow from saffron and lemon, red from the dissolved wax of a mealy bug, olive green from blue with saffron added, green from saffron with verdigris, violet from blue and red.[195] Great importance was attached to these different types in the chancelleries, where for each purpose there was a special type of paper.[196] Ibn al-Nadim gives the names of six different varieties: *al-firauni,* the Pharaonic, which probably imitated Egyptian papyrus; and the other five named after different governors and high officials in the province where paper was produced. The varieties might also be named according to their origins or their format and quality.[197]

---

[188] F. and J. Gies, *Cathedral, Forge, and Waterwheel* subtitled "Technology and Invention in the Middle Ages". Harper Perennial, 1995; p. 97. Joel Mokyr, *The Lever of Riches* subtitled "Technological Creativity and Economic Progress" (Oxford, 1990), p. 41.

[189] See D.R. Hill: *Islamic Science and Engineering* (Edinburgh University Press, 1993), see chapter devoted to water wheels and mills.

[190] See D.R. Hill: *Islamic Science and Engineering.*

[191] A.Djebbar: *Une Histoire de la science Arabe* (Le Seuil; Paris; 2001), p. 350.

[192] D.R. Hill: *Islamic Science and Engineering*; op cit; p. 112.

[193] Carra De Vaux: *Les Penseurs de l'Islam* (Geuthner, Paris, 1921), vol 2; chapter vi: La Mecanique. R.J. Forbes: *Studies in Ancient Technology*; vol II, second revised edition (Leiden, Brill, 1965). D.R. Hill: *Islamic Science*; op cit; A F. Klemm: *History of Western Technology*; tr., by D. Waley Singer (George Allen and Unwin Ltd, London, 1959). Al-Qazwini, *Works;* edit Wustenfeld (Cottingen, 1849), vol II. E. Wiedemann: *Beitrage zur Geschichte der Natur-wissenschaften. X. Zur Technik bei den Arabern* (Erlangen, 1906).

[194] J. Pedersen: *The Arabic Book*; op cit; p. 66.

[195] Ibid.

[196] Ibid; p. 67.

[197] Ibid.

Finally, a word needs to be said about the transfer of paper making processes to the Christian West.[198] The trade required almost five hundred years to find its way into Europe from Samarkand.[199] Both logic and fact, not to speak of geography, Thompson says, show that paper penetrated Europe through Spain, where the Muslims had been manufacturing it for centuries.[200] Long before Europe knew paper, Spanish Christians were acquainted with it; they made an etymological distinction between parchment *(pergamino de cuero)* and paper *(pergamino de pano).*[201] Further proof is to be found in two old paper documents from the monastery of Silos near Burgos. One of these, dating from the 11th century, is a catalogue of the abbey library, written on 157 pages of very white rag paper.[202] The other manuscript (now in the Bibliotheque Nationale) is a Latin glossary in Visigothic characters, not later than the 12th century containing 123 mixed leaves of parchment and paper.[203] Tariff lists, citing tolls collected on Andalusi and Maghrebi paper in towns along the Ebro River in the late 12th century, demonstrate that paper was moving from Muslim to Christian parts in that period.[204] In the 13th century there was introduced the manufacture of paper by Alfonso X into Castile.[205]

The first paper mill to be established in Italy was that of Fabriano, built in 1276.[206] A mill was established at Bologna, in 1293, and another at Padua in 1340. Italy, thanks to a perfected technique became the centre of paper manufacture in Christendom.[207]

In France the first paper mills were those of Troyes, built in 1348.[208] Hitherto, France had used Spanish paper. Like the book-dealers, the early French paper manufacturers were exempt from taxation.[209]

The first use of paper recorded in England dates from 1309.[210] The earliest paper specimen used by Englishmen is found in the account books of Gascony, the English possession in France in the 14th century; most of this paper came from

---

[198] For much lengthier detail and information on this particular matter, see this author's Hidden Debt (part three under chapter on Industry).

[199] D. Hunter: *Paper Making*; Pleiades Books; London; 1947; p. 60.

[200] J.W. Thompson: Paper, The Book Trade and Book Prices; in J. W. Thompson: *The Medieval Library*; (Hafner Publishing Company; New York; 1957); pp. 630-46; at p. 632.

[201] See the ordinance of 1265 by Alphonso X, the Wise, of Castile, in *Recueil des lois d'Alphonse X le Sage de Castille,* ed. by Berni (Valencia, 1759), XVII; iii.

[202] Breviarum et missale Mozarabicum,' included in the 13th century *Vingt livres des etymologies de Saint Isidore;* see M. Férotin, *Histoire de l'abbaye de Silos* (Paris, 1897), p. 275; W.M. Whitehill and J. Perez de Urbel, "Los Manuscritos del real monasterio de Sancto Domingo de Silos," *Boletin de la real academia de la historia,* XCV (1929), 521-601.

[203] L. Delisle, *Mélanges de paléographie et de bibliographie* (Paris, 1880), p. 108.

[204] R.I. Burns: The Paper Revolution in Europe: Crusader Valencia's Paper Industry; *Pacific Historical Review;* 50; 1981; pp. 1-30, at p. 24.

[205] Carreres: Historia de Jativa; I; 1933; p. 48; L. Viardot: Historia; p. 240; in S.M. Imamuddin: *Some Aspects of the Socio Economic and Cultural History of Muslim Spain* (Leiden; Brill; 1965), p. 108.

[206] C.M. Briquet: *Sur les papiers utilisés en Sicile, a l'occasion de deux manuscrits en papier dit de colon* (Palermo, 1892).

[207] J.W. Thompson: Paper, The Book Trade and Book Prices; p. 633.

[208] L. le Clerc, *Le Papier, recherches et notes pour servir a l'histoire du papier, principalement a Troyes et aux environs depuis le XIV' siècle* (Paris, 1926).

[209] D. Hunter: *Papermaking;* op cit; p. 474.

[210] Ibid.

Bordeaux, whence it made its way to England.[211] The first paper mill in England was established in Herefordshire.[212] It is mentioned in Henry VII's *Household Book* under the years 1498-99, but there is an earlier reference to it in the *prohemium* of Bartholomaeus, *De proprietatibus rerum,* printed by Wynkyn de Worde about 1490.[213]

We have seen, Thompson points out, that it took five centuries for paper to penetrate into Europe, despite the disappearance of papyrus. There were at least three reasons why Christendom was reluctant in its acceptance of paper.[214] One was the fragility of paper as compared to parchment, which made chancelleries doubt the permanency of documents inscribed on it. Another reason, Thompson says, was Christian fanaticism, which distrusted and hated everything that came from 'infidel' sources, and paper was then seen as a Muslim-Jewish product. The third reason was the high price of the product, for it being an imported article was almost as expensive as parchment.[215] Gradually the price of paper fell, perhaps because of the new fashion of wearing linen rather than woollen shirts. Also, by the end of the 15th century, Thompson notes, the prejudice against paper disappeared, and this article-now produced in many cities in great quantities and at relatively low prices became, with the help of the printing-press, the foundation of modern civilisation.[216]

Textiles

The textile industry was widely spread throughout the Muslim world and has been abundantly studied.[217] Medieval Muslim geographers provide excellent information on the numbers of looms, the craftsmen employed in the trade, and the burgeoning suburbs gravitating around textile manufacturing centres. Al-Idrisi (1100-1165) counted as many as three thousand farms raising silk worms in the mountains around Jaen in the middle of the 12th century, and al-Shaqundi called this region 'Jaen of the silk' because so many people, both in the city and countryside, were involved in the silk trade.[218] In Sicily, the cultivation of cotton

[211] J.W. Thompson: Paper, The Book Trade and Book Prices; op cit; p. 635.
[212] Ibid; p. 634.
[213] Quoted by B. Botfield: *Prefaces to the First Editions of the Greek and Roman classics and of the Sacred Scriptures* (London, 1861), p. xlviii. See, further, R. Jenkins, "Early Attempts at Paper-making in England, 1495-1586, *Library Association Record,* II (1900), 479 ff.
[214] J.W. Thompson: Paper, op cit; p. 635.
[215] Ibid.
[216] Ibid.
[217] See for instance: W. Heyd: *Histoire du Commerce*; op cit; vol 2; pp. 693-710. N. P. Britton, *A Study of Some Early Islamic Textiles in the Museum of Fine Arts*, Boston; 1938. K. Erdmann: "Turkish Carpets," in *Seven Hundred Years of Oriental Carpets*, H. Erdmann, ed., May H. Beattie and Hildegard Herzog, tr. (1970), pp. 41-60. S.D. Goitein: *A Mediterranean Society*, in 5 vols; vol I, (Berkeley; 1967-1990). Carl J. Lamm: *Cotton in Medieval Textiles of the Near East*; (1937). M. Lombard: *Les Textiles*; op cit. And the excellent work by R.B.Serjeant: *Islamic Textiles* (Librarie du Liban), 1972.
[218] Al-Idrisi: *Opus Geographicum;* v (Naples-Rome; 1975), p. 568. Al-Shaqundi in Al-Maqqari: *Analectes sur l'histoire et la literature des Arabes d'Espagne;* (ed R. Dozy Leiden; 1855-60), ii. p. 146.

was introduced by the Muslims, either from Syria or from the Maghrib.[219] It reached the neighbouring island of Pantellaria, which exported large quantities of this textile product.[220] In Morocco, the irrigated high plains of Dai and Tadla and the Um Rabi' Valley produced considerable quantities of cotton.[221] This made the country into an extremely important centre for cotton manufacturing, and a large share of the manufactured product was exported south to the African continent.[222]
The number of looms and workers involved in textile manufacturing was considerable. In Tinis, in the Egyptian Delta, 5,000 looms were recorded;[223] in Fustat 900 could be found;[224] 4,000 in Tripoli in Syria;[225] in Spain, in Almeria, there were 800 silk weaving looms.[226] It is quite frequent, in fact, to find whole urban conglomerations involved in textile manufacturing, such as in the Egyptian Delta, where a considerable labour force worked.[227]
The manufactured products were of high quality. Al-Muqaddasi refers to the excellent quality of the woven garments produced on the island of Sicily.[228] Scott insists on the strength and delicacy of texture of the textile products, and the extraordinary permanence of the dyes employed in the fabrics.[229]

Syria was a particularly important production centre. Cotton weaving workshops were found in large numbers. Al-Muqaddasi refers to the many cloth manufacturing workshops of Aleppo.[230] From Manbig and Aleppo, cotton of Wadi Butnan was conveyed to the manufacturing centres of Eastern Mesopotamia, and to western Syria.[231] Large silk weaving establishments existed in Tyre, Antioch, Tripoli, and other cities, four thousand weavers being engaged in this craft in Tripoli alone.[232] It seems, according to Lombard, that the Syrian workshops specialised in the production of cloth made of a mixture of silk and cotton; Syria, after all, was the largest producer of both items in the whole Mediterranean Basin.[233] A list of taxes in the city of Aleppo is given by the historian Ibn Shihna for the years 1212-3, which includes the following: the tax on dyeing factories: 80,000 dirhems; the tax on indigo: 20,000 dirhems; the tax on silk: 80,000

---

[219] M. Lombard: *Les Textiles;* op cit; p. 78.
[220] See. M. Amari: *Bibliotheca arabo-sicula*; p. 228.
[221] E.F. Gauthier: Medinat ou dai; *Hesperis;* VI; 1926; p. 24.
[222] M. Lombard: *Les Textiles*; op cit; p. 75.
[223] Nasir I-Khusraw; tr. Schefer; p. 110; n.1; in M. Lombard: *Les Textiles*; op cit; p. 222.
[224] Abd Allatif al-Baghdadi: *Relations d'Egypte;* by M. S. De Sacy (Imprimerie Generale; Paris; 1810-11), p. 409.
[225] E.G. Rey: *Les Colonies Franques de Syrie aux 12em et 13em siecles* (Paris; 1993), p. 215.
[226] Al-Idrisi: *Description de l'Afrique et de l'Espagne;* ed and Fr tr by R. Dozy and M.J. de Goeje (Leiden; 1866), p. 240.
[227] M. Lombard: *Les Textiles*; op cit; p. 223.
[228] Al-Muqaddasi: *Descriptio imperii Moslemici*; ed. M.J. de Goeje; Bibliotheca Geographorum Arabicorum (Leyden; 1876; 2nd ed; 1906), III; p. 239.
[229] S.P. Scott: *History,* Vol II; p. 589.
[230] Al-Muqaddasi: *Ahsan*; Miquel tr. op cit; p. 219; 205.
[231] M. Lombard: *Les Textiles*; op cit; p. 69.
[232] M. Erbstosser: *The Crusades* (David and Charles; Newton Abbot; 1st pub in Leipzig; 1978); p. 131.
[233] M. Lombard: *Les Textiles*; op cit; p. 69.

dirhems.[234] The daily turnover in the cloth trade in the bazaars of the city reached 20,000 Dinars.[235]

In terms of ownership and management of the industry, Muslim rulers had at their disposal workshops for the manufacture of their preferred cloth, and many workshops, privately owned, worked towards meeting the needs of the population and for export.[236] In Muslim Spain, during the reign of Abd Errahman II (r. 822-52), the textile industry of Cordova produced, under the direction of Harith Ibn Bazi, carpets, tapestries, clothes and robes of honour.[237] Abd Errahman III (r. 912-61) also established extensive manufacture of silk and leather.[238] In Egypt, throughout the early Middle Ages, textile manufacture was partly a state owned industry, but there were also private capitalists employing wage workers for their own benefit, at low wages, and under fairly strict supervision of the state.[239] It was the same in the large urban working communities observed in Almeria by Ibn al-Wardi, and in Meknes, in Morocco.[240]
Growing alongside such communities there were other functions, such as those of financiers, warehouse owners, transporters, and others.[241] Casanova notes how in Cairo, special quarters were reserved to cotton merchants,[242] whilst in Baghdad, there was a special wharf for cotton merchants and a special market for the trading of cotton.[243] In Sicily, in 978, the traveller Ibn Hawqal noted a quarter in Palermo called *al-Hara al-Djadida*, or the New Quarter, in which there were various markets including a *Suk al-Tiraziyin*, or market for the makers of *Tiraz* stuffs, a quarter, which was presumably built soon after the capture of Palermo by the Muslims.[244]

Muslim textile products found a large market stretching over the continents. Lombard offers a good picture of this.[245] The coloured garments produced in Basra, near Fes, in Morocco, possibly derived from both linen and cotton, were very much appreciated further south in the African continent, and merchants from the oasis of Sijilmasa traded such items in exchange for gold.[246] Andalusi fabrics made their way to the Christian world as early as the 9th century, as they then appeared in Latin sources, such as when Louis the Pious presented precious fabrics, including a

---

[234] Les *Perles choisies d'Ibn ach-Chihna;* tr. by J. Sauvaget (Beirut; 1933), pp. 163.
[235] E. Gerspach: *L'Art de la Verrerie*; (A Quantin Imprimeur, Editeur; Paris; 1885), p. 97.
[236] M. Lombard: *Les Textiles*; op cit; p. 222; M. Rodinson: *Islam and Capitalism*; op cit; p. 52.
[237] E. Levi Provencal: *Histoire*; op cit; I; p. 257.
[238] J.W. Draper: *A History of the Intellectual Development of Europe*; Revised edition (George Bell and Sons, London, 1875), Vol II; p. 386.
[239] M. Rodinson: *Islam and Capitalism*; op cit; p. 52.
[240] M. Lombard: *Les Textiles*; op cit; p. 223.
[241] See Labib: *Handelsgeschichte Agyptens im Spatmittelalter* (Wiesbaden; 1965), pp. 182; 339. A.M Watson: A Medieval Green Revolution: New Crops and Farming Techniques in The Early Islamic World, in *The Islamic Middle East 700-1900;* edited by A. Udovitch (Princeton; 1981), pp. 29-58; at p. 48.
[242] P. Casanova: Essai de la Reconstitution de la ville d'Al Foustat ou Misr; *Memoire de l'Institut Francais d'Archaeology Orientale*; xxxv (1919).
[243] G. le Strange: *Baghdad Under the Abbasid Caliphate* (Oxford; 1924), pp. 84; 181; 265.
[244] Ibn Hawqal: *Opus Geographicum;* ed. J.H. Kramers; 2nd ed (Leyden; 1938-9), p. 119
[245] M. Lombard: *The Golden*; op cit; pp. 161 fwd.
[246] Al-Biruni: ed. F. Krenkow; *Revue de l'Academie Arabe de Damas*; XIII (1935), p. 341 and fol.

Spanish coverlet to the Abbey of St Wandrille, ca. 823.[247] His son, Charles the Bald, received a variety of textiles as a gift from Cordova in 865,[248] whilst fourteen pieces of Spanish cloth, woven with rich silver thread were cited amongst the ecclesiastical donations of Pope Gregory IV (827-44), and a number of similar items were presented to different churches during the pontificate of Leo IV (847-55).[249] An ecclesiastical vestment in the treasury of the Cathedral of Fermo illustrates how even textiles whose Islamic imagery and inscription did have religious meaning were prized and adapted to new uses.[250] Supposedly owned by Thomas a Becket, Archbishop of Canterbury (murdered 1170), this chasuble (the outer garment worn by a priest celebrating the Eucharist) was made from worn pieces of a gold embroidered silk produced in Almeria, the principal textile centre of Almoravid Spain, in 1116.[251] From the East, Syrian silk cloth was a popular export product, and was regarded as equalling the Chinese in quality.[252] Syria, in the Middle Ages, was in fact, the largest supplier of cotton to the whole Mediterranean world, and its product was also renowned for its quality.[253]

Carpet manufacturing also played a major part in furthering Islamic crafts and skills, and in sharpening Western tastes. The Oriental carpet, as we know it, is assumed to have been brought to the Near East by the Seljuk Turks, when in the middle of the 11th century they moved west from their Central Asian homes.[254] All the early carpets are Turkish. Egyptian carpets date from the second half of the 15th century, whilst the Persians' date from the 16th century.[255] In 1220 Venice established commercial relations with the Seljuks of Rum ruling Eastern Anatolia, where pile carpets with geometric designs were produced from the early 13th century.[256] According to Marco Polo, the carpets produced around Konya were the best in the world.[257] Eastern carpets gradually became appreciated and sought in the West. It was Eleanor of Castile who brought woven carpets to England in 1255 on her marriage to the future Edward I.[258] Gradually the once muddy and straw covered floors of Europe made way to carpets such as we have today.

Just like paper, the Islamic textile industry had a profound effect in stimulating other industries and the rise of technological expertise, both in the Islamic world

[247] O.R. Constable: *Trade and Traders*; op cit; p. 178.
[248] *Gesta sanctorum patnum Fontanellis cocnobii*; xiii. 4; eds F. Lohier and J. Laporte (Rouen-Paris; 1936), p. 102.
[249] *Liber Pontificalis;* n ed. (L. Duschesne; Paris; 1955), pp. 75; 107; 122; 128.
[250] R. E. Mack: *Bazaar to Piazza*; op cit; p. 27.
[251] Ibid.
[252] M Erbstosser: *The Crusades;* op cit; p. 131.
[253] M. Lombard: *Les Textiles;* op cit; p. 69.
[254] R. Ettinghausen: The Impact of Muslim Decorative Arts and Painting on the Arts of Europe; in J. Schacht and C.E. Bosworth edition: *The Legacy of Islam*; (Oxford at the Clarendon Press; 1974); pp. 292-316; at p. 300.
[255] Ibid; p. 301.
[256] R. E. Mack: *Bazaar to Piazza*; op cit; p. 74.
[257] Ibid.
[258] J. Sweetman: *The Oriental Obsession* (Cambridge University Press, 1987), p. 5.

and subsequently in Western Christendom. The cotton industry, for instance, acted on the farming sector and stimulated the rise of dyestuffs such as indigo and other fibres such as linen, which were often mixed with cotton.[259] The chapter on agriculture in the following part will devote much space to this. Cotton impacted on the manufacture of clothing, of course, and also on household articles made of cotton cloth or cotton wool.[260]

As stated above, Western Christendom inherited Muslim industries wherever the Christian armies had the upper hand on their Muslim foe, whether in Spain, Sicily or in the East during the crusades. The textile factories of Palermo, which had fame under the Muslims, carried on under the Normans, of which remnants survive in the regalia of Roger II, preserved in the Treasury of the Holy Roman Empire in Vienna.[261] It is also from Sicily that the art of cloth dyeing spread to Europe.[262] The island was also a leading centre of the silk industry, and even by the 12th century, under Norman rule, silk production seemed to be restricted to Sicily alone, before it spread from there to other regions in the course of the 13th century.[263]
Technical innovations and early manufacturing technologies were introduced in the West via the usual Spanish and Sicilian routes. Textile machinery was already in existence in Muslim Spain centuries before appearing in the rest of Western Christendom. Zozaya notes that the early phase lasting from 825 to 925 was marked by two interesting technological innovations, one of them being the horizontal loom, which appeared, together with the use, well in advance of Christian Europe, of silk thread,[264] as in the shroud of Ona, Burgos (datable to sometime around 925.)[265] The implications are clear: the horizontal loom was already in use in Al-Andalus at least three centuries before the rest of Europe, giving rise to a weaving industry there.[266]
Muslim textile products introduced new linguistic expressions and new varieties of cloth and ideas into the West. This impact occurred very early in Spain. Documented evidence from 916 at the monastery of San Vincente of Ovideo shows a considerable number of Arabic expressions describing textile products and items of clothing.[267] Subsequently and elsewhere, in the wake of the crusades and contact with the Muslim East, there was further impact. Damask, for instance, comes from Damascus; Fustian from Fustat and Muslin from Mosul, in which the respective

---

[259] A. Watson: A Medieval Green Revolution; op cit; p. 47.

[260] See: A.M. Watson: The Rise and Spread of Old World Cotton; in *Studies in Textile History in Memory of Harold Burnham*; ed. V. Gervers (Toronto; 1977), pp. 355-68.

[261] J. D. Breckenridge: The two Sicilies; in *Islam and the Medieval West*; S. Ferber Ed; op cit; pp. 39-59; p.54.

[262] G Le Bon: *La Civilisation des Arabes* (Syracuse; 1884), p. 233.

[263] M. Erbstosser: *The Crusades*, op cit; p. 186.

[264] J. Zozaya: Material Culture in Medieval Spain; in V.B. Mann; T.F. Glick; J. D. Dodds: *Convivencia; Jews, Muslims, and Christians in Medieval Spain* (G. Braziller and the Jewish Museum; New York; 1992), pp. 157-74; at p. 159.

[265] For the horizontal loom, see: M. Returece: El templen:, primer testimonio del telar horizontal en Europe?' *Bolletin de Arqueologia Medieval*; 1 (1987); pp. 71-7.

[266] J. Zozaya: Material Culture; op cit; p. 159.

[267] S. Aguade Nieto: *De la sociedad arcaica a la sociedad campesina en la Asturias medieval* (Universidad de Alcala de Henares, 1988), p. 156.

types of textiles were believed to be manufactured.[268] Other words include cotton, divan, sofa, and mattress, as well as baldachin.[269]

Mining and Metallurgy

Mining, in its diversity, which in many places antedated Islam, developed remarkably during Islamic rule. In Spain, for instance, mining, which had somehow declined during the Visigothic period (prior to the Muslim arrival in 711), was revived and flourished under the Spanish Umayyads (from 755 till late 10th century).[270] There were mines of gold, silver, lead and iron in every district.
Elsewhere, in North Africa, Egypt, Arabia, as in the rest of the realm, mining activities thrived, too. Gold mines were found in western Arabia, Egypt, Africa and in some eastern Islamic lands. A rich gold mining area was called by al-Biruni (973-1050), the Maghrib Sudan. This is the region south of the Sahara in Senegal and on the Upper Niger in Mali. According to al-Idrisi, Wangara (Wanqara) was the most important gold mining centre on the Upper Niger.[271]
Silver was either mined individually or in association with lead ores; the major silver mines were in the eastern Islamic provinces. Other important silver mines were in Spain, North Africa, Iran and Central Asia.[272]
Lead was obtained mostly from galena (lead sulphide), which was quite abundant. This lead ore is often associated with small amounts of silver. Lead ores, especially galena, were exploited in Spain, Sicily, North Africa, Egypt, Iran, Upper Mesopotamia and Asia Minor.[273] It was used for the lining of aqueducts, for the installation of public and private baths and for the roofing of public buildings.[274]
Iron ores were widely distributed throughout the Muslim world. Iron deposits were relatively abundant in Spain, especially to the west of Cordoba in the Sierra Morena and in the vicinity of Seville, where the ore was strip-mined.[275] From iron, steel was refined and was used to make swords and cutlery at Toledo and other towns.[276] In North Africa, about ten mining areas were exploited in Morocco, Algeria and Tunisia.[277] Egypt exploited those ores that were available, for

---

[268] C. Singer: East and West in retrospect in C.J. Singer et al: *History of Technology*; 5 vols; (Oxford at the Clarendon; 1956), vol 2; pp 753-77; p. 764.
[269] R. Ettinghausen: Muslim decorative arts and painting, their nature and impact on the medieval West; in *Islam and the Medieval West*; ed S. Ferber; A Loan Exhibition at the University Art Gallery; (State University of New York; April 6 - May 4, 1975), pp. 5-26; at p. 15.
[270] D.R. Hill: *Islamic Science and Engineering*; (Edinburgh University Press; 1993); p. 208.
[271] Al-Idrisi: *Description de l'Afrique et de l'Espagne*; ed and tr R. Dozy and M.J. de Goeje; (Leiden; 1866); in A.Y. Al Hassan and D.R. Hill: *Islamic Technology;* (Cambridge University Press; 1986); p. 233.
[272] D.R. Hill: *Islamic Science and Engineering*; p. 206.
[273] Ibid.
[274] Ibid; p. 209.
[275] M. Lombard, L'Islam, p. 178; Miguel Gual Camarena, "El hierro en el medioevo hispano," La mineria hispana e iberoamericana, I: 276 n. 5. T. Glick: *Islamic and Christian Spain*; p. 130.
[276] Ibid.
[277] D.R. Hill: *Islamic Science and Engineering*; op cit; p. 207.

example in Nubia and on the Red Sea Coast. Syria was famous for its iron and steel metallurgy; iron ores were obtained in the south and in the mountain ranges between Damascus and Beirut.[278]
Copper and mercury were as important as iron. The former was made into cast or hammered utensils and was a major product of Andalusi trade, the latter mined at the old Roman site of Almadén, was exported throughout the Islamic world for use in the amalgamation of gold.[279] Al-Idrisi mentions the mine to the north of Cordoba, where more than one thousand men worked in the various stages of mining the ores and extracting the mercury.[280]
The alum of Yemen was famous for its quality but according to al Idrisi the major source was in Chad from where it was exported to Egypt and all the countries of North Africa.
Coal was also known and utilised in some areas such as Farghana, where it was mined and sold. It was used as a fuel for ovens and its ashes were used as a cleansing agent.[281]
Precious stones of various kinds were mined. There are several Arabic lapidary works, of which the most famous is al-Biruni's *Kitab al-Jamahir fi ma'rifat al-jawahir* (*Kitab al-Jawahir* in short).[282] Rubies were mined in Badakhshan, emeralds and lapis lazuli from Egypt and turquoise from Nishapur. Crystal was mined in Arabia and in Badakhshan. Diving for pearls was a flourishing industry and corals were obtained from the coasts of North Africa and Sicily.[283]

Muslims developed new techniques of extraction, and also new methods and processes of exploitation of metals for a greater diversity of purposes, and also for export.[284] Comparatively in Europe, it was not until 1536 that the first book on mining-Agricola's *De re metallica*-made its appearance; before that time only a few books were available on lapidary techniques and these had mainly been translated from Arabic.[285] Singer, in particular, has highlighted the pioneering role of Islam in relation to most early technological breakthroughs.[286]
There was diversity of mining technology in Islam because methods differed from mineral to mineral, from country to country, and from one form of ownership to

---

[278] Al-Muqaddasi: *Ahsan Taqasim fi ma'rifat al-Aqalim*; (Leiden; Brill; 1906); repr. Baghdad Muthanna; p. 184.
See also: E. Wiedemann: *Aufsatze zur arabischen Wissenschaftsgeschichte*; (Hildesheim-New York: Georg Olms, Verlag; 1970); vol 1; p. 740.

[279] On copper, S.D. Goitein: *Letters of Medieval Jewish Traders*, (Princeton, 1973); pp. 25, 52, 99 n. 13, 180 n. 7, 192, 261. On mercury, ibid, p. 215; Lombard, L'Islam, p.109.

[280] D.R. Hill: *Islamic Science and Engineering*; op cit; p. 207.

[281] Ibid.

[282] Al-Biruni's *Kitab al-Jamahir li M'arifat al-Jawahir;* edited by F. Krenkow, (Hyderabad, Deccan, 1936).

[283] D.R. Hill: *Islamic Science and Engineering*; op cit; pp. 207-8.

[284] For Muslim engineering skills in this and other areas, see: E. Wiedemann: *Beitrage zur Geschichte der Natur-wissenschaften. X. Zur Technik bei den Arabern.* (Erlangen, 1906). Ibid: `Zur mechanik und technik bei der Arabern' in *Sitzungsherichte der physikalisch-medizinischen Sorietat in Erlangen* (38), 1906.
For exports, and trade in general, see M. Lombard: *The Golden Age*; op cit.

[285] A.Y. Al-Hassan and D.R. Hill*: Islamic Technology;* op cit; p. 236.

[286] C. Singer, ed. *Studies in the History and Method of Science*, 2 vols; (Oxford;) C.J. Singer et al: *History of Technology*; 5 vols; (Oxford at the Clarendon); see vol 2 (1956); particularly pp. 753-777.

another. In any one country there was, in fact, a range of technologies from the primitive to the highly developed.[287] Thus al-Biruni noted how the search for la'l (a kind of ruby) is of two kinds; one of which is to dig the mine under the mountain.[288] As with modern mining there were two major types of operation- the underground and the opencast. In underground mining, one method was to sink shafts vertically into the soil and then drive horizontal passages when the veins were reached. In Syria the shaft of the mine was called the *bir,* i.e. the well, and the horizontal passage the *darb,* i.e. the road.[289] In the Lebanese mountains, a typical shaft was only six or seven metres deep whereas the tunnels were very long. Al-Idrisi saw the mercury mines to the north of Cordoba and was told that the depth from ground level to the bottom of the mine was 250 fathoms (1 fathom=1.8288m).[290] The technique of drilling vertical shafts and horizontal tunnels was a familiar one in the Islamic world since it was used in the construction of qanats.[291] A vivid description of silver mining activities in Panjhir in Khurasan, where 10,000 men were employed in the mining industry, is given by Ibn Hawqal:

> The people of Panjhir made the mountain and the market-place like a sieve because of the many pits. They only follow veins leading to silver, and if they find a vein they dig continuously until they reach the silver. A man may spend huge sums in digging, and he may find silver to such an extent that he and his descendants become rich, or his work may fail because he is overpowered by water or for other reasons. A man may pick a vein and it is possible that another man picks the same vein in another position. Both start digging. The custom is that the miner who arrives first and intercepts the passage of the other miner wins the vein and its results. Because of this competition they execute a work that devils cannot achieve. When one arrives first, the expenses of the other are wasted. If they arrive together they share the vein and then continue digging as long as the lamps are burning. If the lamps are extinguished and cannot be relit, they stop their progress because anyone who reaches that position would die immediately. [In this business] you will see a man start his day owning one million, and by nightfall he owns nothing. Or he may start poor in the morning and by evening become the owner of unaccountable wealth.[292]

Early technological breakthroughs, in this instance water wheels and other similar devices, were used in mining. Hill explains that windlasses were used for hauling ores and materials out of the shafts. A simple but efficient form of windlass was used in the iron mines in Syria and is still used in the construction

---

[287] A.Y. Al-Hassan and D.R. Hill: *Islamic Technology*; op cit; p. 236.
[288] Al-Biruni's *Kitab al-Jawahir;* in A.Y. Al-Hassan and D.R. Hill: *Islamic Technology;* op cit; p. 236.
[289] D.R. Hill: *Islamic Science and Engineering*; op cit; p. 211.
[290] Ibid.
[291] Ibid.
[292] Ibn Hawkal in A.Y. Al-Hassan and D.R. Hill: *Islamic Technology*; op cit; p. 237.

of qanats in Iran for drawing water and in the building industry. To operate this machine an operator sits on a bench on one side of the shaft or well, pulling the horizontal bars of the windlass towards him with his hands and pushing the opposite ones away with his feet at the same time. The material is loaded into a small bucket about 30-35 cm in diameter, which has two handles. The rope is attached to the bucket by hooks fastened at its end. More sophisticated capstans were also used for haulage, when loads were heavier.[293]

Oil lamps were used for illumination. As with qanats, they were useful for aligning the direction of the digging and they were reliable indicators of the adequacy of fresh air supplies.[294]

The devices invented by the Banu Musa Brothers (fl. middle of 9th century) for use in public works such as their 'gas masks' and clamshell grab could have been of use in mining.[295] In particular, their 'gas mask' would have enabled a miner to enter shafts or adits where the air was polluted, although he would still have had to come out of the polluted area at frequent intervals, whilst the clamshell grab would have been useful for dredging up ores that were under water.[296] In their *Book of Ingenious Devices,* they write:

> We wish to explain- how to make a machine by which a person can bring out jewels from the sea if he lowers it, and by which he can extract things which fall into wells or are submerged in the rivers and seas.[297]

Al-Biruni, for his part, mentions a kind of rudimentary breathing apparatus for use by pearl divers. The diver wore an airtight leather helmet from which a tube led to the surface of the water, where its end floated between inflated bladders.[298] In *Kitab al-Jawahir* al-Biruni provides details of the diving operation, and of particular interest is what he has to say about the new type of diving gear. He writes:

> I was told by a man from Baghdad that divers had invented in these days a method for diving by which the difficulty of holding the breath is eliminated. This enables them to frequent the sea from morning to afternoon as much as they wish, and as much as the employer favours them. It is a leather gear which they fit down on their chests and they tie it at the [edges?] very securely and then they dive. They breathe in it from the air inside it. This necessitates a very heavy weight to keep down the diver with this air. A more suitable arrangement would be to attach to the upper end of this gear opposite the forehead a leather tube similar to a sleeve, sealed at its seams by wax and bitumen, and its length will be equal to the depth of diving. The upper end of the tube will be fitted to a large

---

[293] D.R. Hill: *Islamic Science and Engineering*; op cit; p. 211.
[294] Ibid; p. 213.
[295] Banu Musa: *Kitab al-Hiyal*, (The Book of Ingenious Devices,) tr., and annoted by D. R. Hill, Dordrecht: Reidel, 1979; Arabic text, ed. A.Y. al-Hasan; Aleppo: Institute for the History of Arabic Science, 1981.
[296] D.R. Hill: *Islamic Science and Engineering*; op cit; p. 211.
[297] Banu Musa: *Kitab al-Hiyal* in A.Y. Al-Hassan and D.R. Hill*: Islamic Technology;* p. 245.
[298] D.R. Hill: *Islamic Science and Engineering*; op cit; p. 213.

> dish at a hole in its bottom. To this dish are attached one or more inflated bags to keep it floating. The breath of the diver will flow in and out through the tube as long as he desires to stay in the water, even for days.[299]

In organised work, especially in the mines owned by the state, a means of ventilation of wells and mine shafts was always provided, and this matter attracted the attention of Muslim engineers who designed special ventilating machines. The Banu Musa brothers describe a design for

> A machine for use in wells which kill those who descend in them. If a man uses this machine in any well, it will neither kill nor harm him.[300]

This would have been essential, particularly in very deep mines such as those near Cordoba in Spain. Special ventilation shafts were provided or, when several shafts were needed for drainage, these could serve the dual purpose or drainage and ventilation.[301]

Drainage was, of course, the other major problem in mining operations. In state-owned mines such as the silver mines at Zakandar in North Africa, drainage was carried out properly, as the geographer al-Qazwini (d. 1283) reports:

> Here are the silver mines. Anyone who wishes can undertake processing them. There are underground mines in which many people are always working. When they descend 20 *dhira'* [some 10 metres] water appears. The Sultan installs water wheels and water is raised until mud appears. Water is lifted and discharged into a large tank. Another wheel is installed on this tank. It lifts the water and pours it into another tank. On this tank a third wheel is installed. It lifts the water and discharges it on to the surface of the ground to irrigate farms and gardens. This operation cannot be undertaken except by a very rich person. He sits at the mouth of the mine and employs artisans and workers. When the work is done the fifth of the Sultan is put aside and the rest given to him.[302]

The contractual system seems to have been that the Sultan, who owned the mines, installed the drainage and ventilation systems and then let out the actual excavation of the ores and extraction of the silver to contractors.

More sophisticated water lifting machines, such as that described by Taqi al-Din in the 16th century, may have been used for the same purpose.[303]

In the period of the Umayyad and 'Abbasid Caliphs, the output of the mines in their realm was apparently sufficient to meet the demands for some of the most important metals. In later periods when the Muslim world became fragmented

---

[299] Al-Biruni: *Kitab al-Jawahir* in A.Y. Al-Hassan and D.R. Hill: *Islamic Technology;* op cit; pp. 244-5.

[300] Banu Musa Brothers: *Kitab al-Hiyal*; in A.Y. Al-Hassan and D.R. Hill: *Islamic Technology;* op cit; p. 238.

[301] D.R. Hill: *Islamic Science and Engineering*; op cit; p. 213.

[302] Al-Qazwini: *Athar al-Bilad wa Akhbar al-Ibad*; Arabic Text; (Dar Sadir; Beirut; 1960-1); in A.Y. Hassan and D.R. Hill: *Islamic Technology;* op cit; pp. 239-40.

[303] A.Y. Al-Hassan ed: *Taqi al-Din and Arabic Mechanical Engineering, with the Sublime Method of Spiritual Machines;* in Arabic; Institute for the History of Arabic Science (University of Aleppo; Syria; 1977), pp. 165.

into various kingdoms, one often warring with another, many of the Islamic countries needed one or several of the metals and had to import them from non-Islamic regions.[304] Preventing the supply of metals, which served as raw materials for manufactured goods, and bullion for the mints, was used as a weapon in political struggles. Medieval statesmen were of course aware that cutting off the gold supply to the enemy meant weakening his financial resources, and that curbing his supply of iron harmed the production of arms.[305] Wood supply was another important tool of pressure. Al-Idrisi mentions the fact that work on the 'Silver Mountain' between Herat and Sarakhs had to stop because of technical faults and the lack of wood for smelting the ores.[306] The shortage of timber together with the loss of the principal wood producing region, al-Andalus, in the 13th century, were to have a very disruptive effect on the economic system of Islam. It affected its local industries and agriculture which relied heavily on timber for many of their functions. Above all it caused serious harm to the shipping industry, which literally collapsed from the twin effects of the loss of Spain and the blockade on the imports of timber imposed by the papacy on the Muslim world.[307]

Metallurgy

Speaking about native gold, which is collected from gold mines, al-Biruni says that it is usually not free from impurities and therefore this gold has to be refined by smelting or by other methods.

> Gold may be united with stone as if it is cast with it, so that it needs pounding. Rotary mills *(tawahin)* can pulverize it, but pounding it by *mashajin* (a kind of trip- hammer) is more correct and is a much more refined treatment. It is even said that this pounding makes it redder which, if true, is rather strange and surprising. The *mashajin* are stones fitted to axles which are installed on running water for pounding, as is the case in the pounding of flax for paper in Samarqand.[308]

He gives details of the amalgamation process that was used in the mines on a commercial scale:

> After pounding the gold ore or milling it, it is washed out of its stones, and the gold and mercury are combined and then squeezed in a piece of leather until mercury exudes from the pores of the leather. The rest of the mercury is driven off by fire.[309]

---

[304] D.R. Hill: *Islamic Science and Engineering*; op cit; p. 208.

[305] Ibid; p. 209.

[306] Ibid; p. 210.

[307] O.R. Constable: *Trade and Traders in Muslim Spain;* (Cambridge University Press; 1994); p. 196; I.M. Lapidus: *Muslim Cities in the Later Middle Ages* (Harvard University Press; Cambridge Mass; 1967), p. 42.

[308] Al-Biruni: *Kitab al Jawahir,* op cit; p. 234 ff.

[309] Ibid.

After this alloy was removed, separation of the gold from the silver was carried out chemically by what is known as the salt and sulphur process. Nitric acid was used for the separation of gold from silver, a process described by the early medieval chemist, Jabir Ibn Hiyyan (721-815).[310] This is yet another instance of science working in support of economic activity. Gold was tested by cupellation and by other methods. The cupellation process was used extensively both in the laboratory and on an industrial scale. Here the gold was alloyed with lead in a special crucible and then oxidised by means of a strong current of air blown on to the surface of the molten metal. Any base metals such as copper appeared as a scum while the gold and silver remained as a button of silver-gold alloy.[311] Other methods included the touchstone, measuring the specific gravities, and by noting the speed of solidification of gold after it had been removed from the furnace.[312]

Copper was usually obtained from its sulphide ores. It seldom occurred as oxides or carbonates. These latter ores required only the simple treatment of heating with charcoal, while the sulphides required roasting, smelting with fluxes and partial oxidation. A ground-breaking discovery, however, took place in Muslim Spain. The sulphide ores, on exposure to air in the presence of water, are oxidised to soluble sulphates.[313] Muslims then found that if water containing copper sulphate is allowed to flow over iron, pure copper is deposited and the iron dissolved. As iron was cheap and abundant in Spain, this discovery resulted in an efficient method of recovering copper from sulphide ore, and direct mining of copper ore became less necessary.[314]

Bronze is an alloy of copper and tin. It was much used for plain kitchen wares and utensils. It was also the alloy upon which the coppersmiths based much of their work. Bronze was also used in the manufacture of hydraulic components such as valves and taps.[315]

Brass *(shabah, birinj)* is an alloy of copper and zinc, the zinc adding a factor that makes the metal a stronger, harder and less malleable substance than pure copper alone. Various kinds of brass were obtained by varying the zinc content; copper with 20 per cent zinc gives a brass with a colour close to that of gold.[316] Before zinc was known to be a metal, brass was made by heating copper in a mixture of powdered zinc ore and charcoal; as a result, a proportion of the zinc formed close to the copper was diffused into it chemically by a process known as cementation.[317] Later we read in *'Ayn-i-Akhbari* about three qualities of brass containing increasing amounts of zinc; one was ductile in the cold state, the

---

[310] E.J. Holmyard: Jabir Ibn Hayyan in *Section of the History of Medicine*; 1923; pp. 46-57. E.J. Holmyard: *Makers of Chemistry* (Oxford at the Clarendon Press, 1931).

[311] A.Y. Al-Hassan and D.R. Hill*: Islamic Technology*; op cit; p. 247.

[312] For Muslim engineering skills in this and other areas, see: E. Wiedemann: *Beitrage zur Geschichte;* op cit.

[313] D.R. Hill: *Islamic Science and Engineering;* op cit; p. 216.

[314] Ibid.

[315] Ibid.

[316] A.Y. Al-Hassan and D.R. Hill*: Islamic Technology*; op cit; p. 249.

[317] Ibid.

second ductile when heated, but the third was not ductile at all, though it could be cast.[318]

Three main types of iron and steel were utilised in Islamic metallurgical centres; wrought iron *(narmahin),* cast iron *(düs),* and steel *(fuladh).[319]* Wrought iron is soft. It is malleable but cannot be heat-treated. It has many applications provided strength is not required, and it was used as a raw material for manufacturing steel. [320] Cast iron was a well-known material to Islamic chemists and metalworkers. Historians of technology, Hill says, seem to have been unaware, until recently, of its importance in the medieval Islamic world, both as an intermediate and as a final product.[321] According to al-Biruni it was the 'water of iron', and it was 'the liquid which flowed during the melting and extraction of the metal.' The properties of cast iron can be summarised from al-Biruni's *Kitab al-Jawahir* as follows: it is quick to flow like water when smelting iron ores; it is hard and whitish-silvery in colour and its powder has sometimes a pinkish reflection; it does not resist blows, but shatters into pieces-'breakage and brittleness are typical of it'; and it is mixed with wrought iron in crucibles for making steel.[322] In a commentary by al-Jildaki (fl.c. 1339-42) on Jabir Ibn Hiyyan's *Kitab al-hadid* (Book of Iron) we read the following description of the production of cast iron:

> Chapter: Learn, brother, that it is your comrades who found [literally, from *yaskubun*, 'founding'] iron in foundries [especially] made for that purpose after they have extracted it [i.e. the ore] from its mine as yellow earth intermingled with barely visible veins of iron. They place it in the founding furnaces designed for smelting it. They install powerful bellows on all sides of them after having kneaded (*yaluttun*) a little oil and alkali into the ore. Then the fire is applied to it [i.e. the ore] together with cinders and wood. They blow upon it until it is molten, and its entire substance (*jishmuhu wa jasaduhu*) is rid of that earth. Next, they cause it to drop through holes like [those of] strainers, [made in] the furnaces so that the molten iron is separated, and is made into bars from that earth. Then they transport it to far lands and countries. People use it for making utilitarian things of which they have need.[323]

Cast iron was exported to many countries as a raw material. In the 15th century there were at least two commercial brands, one from Iraq the other from the Iranian province of Fars. In Europe the production of cast iron began in the 14th

---

[318] '*Ayn-i-Akhbari* (Source of Information) in A.Y. Al-Hassan and D.R. Hill*: Islamic Technology;* op cit; p. 249.
[319] Al-Kindi: *Risala ila Ba'd Ikhwani fi 'l Suyuf:* Ms Aya Sofya 4832 fols. 170-2 in particular.
[320] D.R. Hill: *Islamic Science and Engineering;* op cit; p. 217; see also: A.Y. Al-Hassan: Iron and Steel Technology in Medieval Arabic Sources; in *Journal for the History of Arabic Science;* Vol 2; No 1; 1978; pp. 31-43.
[321] D.R. Hill: *Islamic Science and Engineering;* op cit; p. 217.
[322] Al-Biruni: *Kitab al-Jawahir*; op cit; 217.
[323] Al-Jildaki: *Kitab al-Hadid*; Ms No 4121; Chester Beaty Library; in A.Y. Al-Hassan and D.R. Hill*: Islamic Technology;* op cit; p. 252.

century but it was not of sufficiently consistent quality for the casting of gun barrels until a century later.[324]

Essentially manufactured steel is iron having a carbon content between that of wrought iron and cast iron. Writing in the middle of the 9th century, al-Kindi (fl.850) described some of the processes in its production.[325] In some cases, steel was made from wrought iron bars by 'cementation', a process whereby iron bars were packed with charcoal and heated until they had absorbed enough carbon from it. However, steel was usually made in the molten state, and at the centres where this was done, one or more of the following methods were adopted:

1. By carbonisation of wrought iron;
2. By decarbonisation of cast iron;
3. By fusion of a mixture of wrought iron and cast iron, which provided two qualities depending on the degree of fusion obtained.[326]

Al Jildaki informs us how rods of cast iron were used to make steel by decarbonisation, or 'crucible steel' as it is usually called:

> As for the steel workers, they take the iron bars and put them into the founding-ovens (*masabik*) which they have, suited to their objectives, in the steel works. They install firing equipment (*akwar*) in them [i.e.' the ovens] and blow fire upon it [i.e. the iron] for a long while until it becomes like gurgling water. They nourish it with glass, oil and alkali until light appears from it in the fire and it is purified of much of its blackness by intensive founding, night and day. They keep watching while it whirls for indications until they are sure of its suitability, and its lamp emits light. Thereupon they pour it out through channels so that it comes out like running water. They then allow it to solidify in the shape of bars or in holes made of clay fashioned like large crucibles. They take out of them refined steel in the shape of ostrich eggs, and they make swords from it, and helmets, lance heads, and all tools.[327]

As reported by al-Biruni, a similar method was used by a Damascene blacksmith named Mazyad b. Ali:

> The crucibles, before being placed in the furnace, were filled with nails, horseshoes and other wrought iron objects as well as marcasite stone and brittle magnesia. The crucibles were then filled with charcoal, placed in the furnace and subjected to hot air blasts for a period, after which bundles of organic matter were thrown into each crucible. After another hour of hot-air blasting the crucibles were left to cool, and the 'eggs' were then taken from the crucibles.

---

[324] D.R. Hill: *Islamic Science and Engineering;* op cit; p. 217.

[325] Al-Kindi: *Risala ila Ba'd Ikhwani fi'l Suyuf;* Ms Aya Sofya 4832 fols. 170-2 in particular.

[326] A.Y. Al-Hassan and D.R. Hill: *Islamic Technology;* op cit; p. 253; A.Y. Al-Hassan: Iron and Steel; *Journal for the History of Arabic Science;* pp. 31-43.

[327] Al-Jildaki *Kitab al-Hadid*; in A.Y. Al-Hassan and D.R. Hill: *Islamic Technology;* p. 253.

In the same passage al-Biruni also describes a method of producing molten steel in crucibles from a mixture of cast iron and wrought iron.[328] Two qualities could be obtained. One resulted if the components were 'melted equally so that they became united in the mixing operation and no component can be differentiated or seen independently'. A second quality of steel was produced if the degree of melting of wrought iron and cast iron was different for each substance, 'and thus the intermixture between both components is not complete, and their parts are shifted and thus each of their two colours can be seen by the naked eye and is called *firind'*.[329]

The *firind* is the distinctive pattern on the blades of 'Damascus' swords, which were in this context the most notable achievement in various metalworking centres in the Orient.[330] Cyril Stanley Smith notes that:

> In comparison with the relative neglect of structure by the European metallurgist, the enjoyment and utilisation of it in the Orient is impressive. In the Orient, etching to display patterns depending on composition differences was in use contemporaneously with the European pattern-welded blade, and was thereafter continually developed to a high artistic level.[331]

Smith observes that the geographical distribution of the Damascus swords seems to have been practically co-extensive with the Islamic faith, and they continued to be made well into the 19th century.[332]

For about a century and a half attempts were made in Europe to reproduce steel comparable in quality to Damascus steel. A large number of metallurgists carried out extensive research into steel making including eminent scientists such as Faraday.[333] The first successful duplication of blades of a true Oriental type was achieved in 1821 by Bréant,[334] an inspector of assays at the Paris mint, whose achievement was the outcome of a suggestion made by an associate named Mérimée who was examining wootz cakes brought from England under the stimulus of Stodart and Faraday's 1819 paper.[335] Against the general opinion of the time, Mérimée had suggested that Oriental Damask was the result of chemical combination and not a mechanical mixture of metals.[336] Bréant's paper, published in 1823, Smith claims, is one of the minor classics of metallurgy.[337] In it he applies to steel Berzelius' principles of chemical combination, and suggests that carbon

---

[328] D.R. Hill: *Islamic Science and Engineering;* op cit; p. 218.

[329] Al-Biruni: *Kitab al-Jawahir,* op cit; p. 256.

[330] See E. Wiedemann: *Aufsatze zur arabischen Wissenschaftsgeschichte*; (Hildesheim-New York: Georg Olms, Verlag; 1970); vol 1; p. 740.

[331] C.S. Smith: *A History of Metallography*; (Chicago; 1965); p. 14.

[332] Ibid.

[333] Ibid; 25 ff.

[334] J.R. Breant: Description d'un procede a l'aide duquel on obtient une espece d'Acier Fondu; in *Bulletin de La Societe d'Encouragement de l'Industrie Nationale*; 1823; 22; pp. 222-7.

[335] Report by Hericart de Thury; *Bulletin Societe Encouragement…* (1821); 20; pp. 37-47; 351-85.

[336] C.S. Smith: *A History*; op cit; p. 26.

[337] Ibid.

added to iron, at the proper temperature, first forms increasing amounts of steel, as a separate "compound," and that as more carbon is added beyond the ideal composition of steel, iron carbide begins to form. On slow cooling a steel of very high carbon content, the "steel" and the carbide will crystallize separately, the crystals being larger the slower the cooling.[338] In other words, it was shown that the blades were made of very high carbon steel (about 1.5-2.0 per cent) and owed their beauty and their cutting qualities alike to the inherent structure of the cakes of steel from which they were forged. The light portion contained numerous particles of iron carbide (cementite) while the dark areas were steel of normal carbon content. The structure was visible, of course, only after etching, which was done with a solution of some mineral sulphate.[339]

Another technique which flourished in Islamic countries and in India in later centuries was a welding technique for gun barrels and swords. This was quite different from that of cast Damascus steel, though it was also called 'Damascus'. Cyril Smith suggests that the technique seems to have originated in the Near East in the 16th century.[340] The manufacture of barrels of this type began in Europe in the 18th century, the earliest detailed description of this type in Europe being by Wasstrom, in 1773, who appreciated all the essential steps involved in the Oriental procedures.[341] During this and the subsequent century great efforts were made. In 1798, Smith, anticipating modern powder metallurgy, noted how William Nicholson made a Damascus-textured metal by compressing mixed filings of steel and wrought iron in a die, restriking the compact at a welding heat and forging it into a plate.[342] He stated that the texture was not fibrous but wavy.[343] Also in 1798, Hermann, a German who was living in Russia and who had established a steel plant in Siberia, presented a paper before the Academy of Sciences in St. Petersburg.[344] He was assisted by Habesci, an Arab who had seen smiths at work in Damascus. Hermann, however, experimented only with welded patterns. He concluded that in order:

> To make a good patterned Damascus steel there should be not over one-third of steel in the welded strip and that twisting and at least six times folding and welding were necessary to give good "flowers" and mechanical qualities.' He preferred to etch in dilute nitric acid, or with a mixture of vitriol or copper sulphate and chalk.[345]

---

[338] Ibid.
[339] Ibid; pp. 25 ff.
[340] Ibid; p. 30.
[341] P. Wasstrom: Beskrifning pa Damascherade skut-gevar af jarn och stal; in *Kogl Vetenskaps Academiens Handlingar*; (1773); 34; pp. 311-8.
[342] C.S. Smith: *A History*; op cit; p. 33.
[343] W. Nicholson: *Nicholson's Journal,* (1798), 1, 468-71.
[344] B.F.J. Hermann: Experiences sur l'acier damasse; *Nova Acta. Acad. Sci. Imp. Petropolitanae*; (1798; published 1802); 12; pp. 352-63.
[345] C.S. Smith: *A History*; op cit; p. 33.

There can be found many references about the existence of foundries in medieval Islamic cities, and state involvement in their management. Al-Qalqashandi (d.1418) in *Subhi al-A'sha*, when discussing government departments in Damascus during the period of 1171-1250, said:

> Of these are several small military departments... such as the department of foundries for iron, copper, glass and others.[346]

Further on, about the departments of the civil service, he added:

> Of these is the department of foundries and the executive in charge of this department is the counterpart of the officer in charge of the military department of foundries.[347]

Ibn Asakir (d.1177), for his part, in his *History of Damascus*, mentions the sites of the iron foundries of the city.[348]

Finally on this subject, as Al-Hassan and Hill point out, we can learn much about Islamic metallurgical equipment from a study of the chemical equipment. The purifying operation was mainly concerned with smelting ores to obtain metals, and according to al-Razi there was 'equipment for melting metals *(ajsad)* and stones', and also equipment for the further processing of these metals. Iron smelting was given special attention in chemistry and it can be assumed that the equipment was a small pilot-plant of what was to become actual metallurgical equipment. Sometimes details of construction were identical.[349] Iron production from ores was effected using blast furnaces. Cast iron was produced by this method before the 10th century. Al-Jildaki gave a description of the smelting process while historians have reported experiments in Egypt on the casting of large cannon at the turn of the 16th century.[350] Crucible steel was melted in small crucibles. The text by al-Biruni describing the manufacture of this kind of steel by a smith in Damascus shows that several crucibles were put into one furnace, and several bellows were used, each operated by two men.[351]

Glass Industry

Abundant accounts from the medieval period testify to a thriving industry, producing glasses of all shapes and colours, in the cities of Alexandria, Cairo, Tyre, Aleppo, Antioch, Damascus, Tripoli, and elsewhere.[352] Syria, for instance, became famed for the art of enamelled glass that would reach its peak of excellence in the 13th century.[353] The existence of specimens preserved since the Middle Ages in

---

[346] Al-Qalqashandi: *Subhi al-A'sha*; Cairo Ministry of Culture; part 4; p. 188.
[347] Ibid; p. 190.
[348] Ibn Asakir: *Tarikh Madinat Dimashq*; Damascus; (Arab Academy of Science; 1954); vol 2; p. 58.
[349] A.Y. Al-Hassan and D.R. Hill: *Islamic Technology;* p. 259.
[350] Al-Jildaki in A.Y. Al-Hassan and D.R. Hill: *Islamic Technology;* p. 259.
[351] Al-Biruni: *Kitab al-Jawahir* in A.Y. Al-Hassan and D.R. Hill: *Islamic Technology;* p. 260.
[352] E. Gerspach: *L'Art de la Verrerie*; (Paris; 1885); p. 97.
[353] W. Durant: *The Age of Faith*, op cit; p. 276.

European Cathedral treasuries, usually mounted in precious metals, is proof of the contrast then existing between the civilisation of Islam and 'the cultural darkness' that affected most of Europe through this long period.[354] The large number of surviving objects in enamelled and gilded glass also bears witness to the extent to which they were appreciated from the time they were created.[355] There is a special interest given to this type of glass in Europe, in the second half of the 19th century, in particular, witness the considerable literature on the subject.[356]

The glass industry thrived most particularly in Syria, but also in Egypt, Palestine and Muslim Spain. Al-Tha'libi (961-1038), in extolling the qualities of Syria, writes:

> Also the thinness and translucence of Syrian glass are proverbially famous; one says more delicate than Syrian glass, or clearer than Syrian glass.[357]

Tyre, in particular, retained a lasting fame for its glass products. Writing during the crusade period, William, Archbishop of Tyre, commented on the fame of Tyrian glass:

> A very fine quality of glass... is marvellously manufactured from sand which is found in this same plain [the Plain of Akko]. This is carried to far distant places and easily surpasses all products of the kind. It offers a material suitable for making most beautiful vases which are famous for their transparency. In this way also, the fame of the city (of Tyre) is spread abroad among foreign peoples, and the profits of the merchants is increased manifold.[358]

There must have been a significant export of glass from the Tyre area to Europe long before that time in order for it to have achieved its high reputation.[359]
Tyre was not alone, though. Aleppo, Damascus and Hama were likewise important centres, and excavations yielded a wide range of material, mostly from the period between 1100 and 1400.[360] Glass of Aleppo and Damascus, which became in the 13th and 14th centuries the leading centres of glass manufacture, must be classified, according to Dimand, among the finest ever produced.[361] Al Kazwini (about 1203-1283), in describing Aleppo, which in the thirteenth century was an important art metropolis, mentions its glass bazaar and the magnificent ware exported thence to foreign countries.[362] An Iranian geographer, Hafiz-i-

---

[354] W.B. Honey: *Glass;* op cit; p. 35.
[355] S. Carboni: *Glass from Islamic Lands;* (Thames and Hudson; 2001); p. 323.
[356] Ibid.
[357] H.J. Cohen: Early Islamic Scholars as glassmakers; in A. Engle ed: *Readings in Glass History;* 2; (Phoenix Publications; 1973); pp. 30-5; at p. 33.
[358] William of Tyre: *A History of Deeds Done Beyond the Sea*; tr. E. Babcock and A.C. Krey; (Columbia University Press; 1943); v. II, 6.
[359] A. Engle: A Study of the Names of Early Glassmaking Families of Europe as a source of Glass History; *Readings in Glass History* 1, pp. 51-65.
[360] D. Whitehouse: Glass in *Dictionary of the Middle Ages*; op cit; vol 5; pp. 545-8.
[361] M.S. Dimand: *A Handbook of Muhammadan Art*; The Metropolitan Museum of Art; (New York; 1958); p. 236.
[362] Ibid.

Abru, speaks of 'the wonderful glass of Aleppo as decorated with elegance and taste.'[363] Glass made in Damascus was especially famous in the time of the Mamluk sultans (mid-late 13th century onwards).[364] It was in Damascus' rich bazaars that Cairo traders found regular supplies of all luxury glass products.[365] Egypt itself continued to produce vessels of all qualities, particularly at Al-Fustat (old Cairo), where excavations yielded immense quantities of glass ranging in date from the eighth century to the later Middle Ages.[366] The quality of Egyptian glass, W.B. Honey remarks, was such, that even in the more sophisticated parts of Christendom, that is the Eastern Roman Empire (Byzantium), 'the art was little regarded apart from its use in mosaics, and such Byzantine glass, as has survived, owes much to the art of Muslim Egypt, if indeed, it is not in many cases actually of Egyptian origin.'[367] Elsewhere, in Palestine, al-Muqaddasi, the late 10th century Muslim geographer, notes that Jerusalem marketed cheese, cotton clothing, mirrors, jars and lamps.[368] The city rose to greater heights during the 11th century as a destination of extensive Christian pilgrimage, which reached a peak in 1065 when a caravan of 12,000 pilgrims arrived from Southern Germany and Holland.[369] In other words, prior to its capture during the Crusades (i.e., before 1099), the city was not just producing glass, it also served as an important export outlet to Western Christendom, which boosted the industry.[370]

There is very little, if any, literature that describes glass manufacture aimed for the mass market, especially in the construction industry. This is a serious flaw when knowing that the industry certainly absorbs most of the glass product, and employs the larger labour force. We have, however, some idea, however small, on how glass was produced in the Muslim world. The glass industry of Aleppo, which was situated in the *Zajjayiye* quarter, obtained its basic materials from the mineral deposits of Jabal Bishri.[371] Dussaud refers to a tributary of the Orontes River which seems to be in the vicinity of Armanaz. This stream, according to Dussaud,[372] "bears the characteristic name of Wadi Abou Kale", presumably because of the abundance of kali (glasswort) growing there.[373] The Syrian industry extracted soda for glassmaking from the ashes of the kali (the Arabic *qali* or *qila*) which grows in the salt marshes and along the seashore.[374] Perhaps the

---

[363] Ibid.
[364] Ibid.
[365] Simon Simeonis; p. 43 in W. Heyd: *Histoire*; op cit; vol 2; p. 710-1.
[366] D. Whitehouse: Glass; op cit; pp. 546-7.
[367] W.B. Honey: *Glass*; Victoria and Albert Museum (Ministry of Education; London; 1946), p. 35.
[368] Al-Muqaddasi, *Descriptio Imperii Moslemici.* ed. M.J de Goeje, (Leiden, 1906), p. 170 (Arabic).
[369] S. D. Goitein: *Palestinian Jewry in Early Islamic and Crusader Times*; (Jerusalem; 1980); p. 18.
[370] R. Hasson: Islamic Glass from excavations in Jerusalem; in *Journal of Glass Studies,* vol xxv; 1983; pp. 109-19; p. 111.
[371] Kamil al-Gazzi: *Nahr al-Dahab*; vol 1; p. Yaqut al-Hamawi, vol. 1, 63; see also C.J. Lamm: *Mittelalterliche Glaser….* Vol 1; text; vol 2 plates; (1930), 1, 492, Note 49.
[372] R. Dussaud: *Topographie Historique de la Syrie Antique et Medievale*; (Paris, 1927), p. 170, n. 5.
[373] A. Engle: Armanaz in Syria and its role in the Medieval Glass Industry; A. Engle ed: *Readings in Glass History;* 2; pp. 1-11; p. 10.
[374] Ibid.

place names mentioned above were sites of this ancient industry, well situated in both cases for the local markets as well as for export.[375]

Whilst Muslims initially inherited the art of glass making from earlier Eastern civilisations, as with other industries, they accomplished substantial breakthroughs. In Spain, Ibn Firnas (d.887) taught artisans the technique of putting the clay in the oven.[376] According to the 16th century historian al-Maqqari, Ibn Firnas established factories, and was the first to make glass out of clay.[377] He, amongst other, advised the glass makers to keep the crystal in the oven for twenty four hours to make it strong.[378] In Egypt, from the 8th to the 10th century, during Tulunid rule and that of their successors, the glassmakers of Fustat (old Cairo) focussed their skill to obtaining their decorative effects by manipulation of the surface of the hot glass.[379] They achieved this by exploiting a variety of techniques: 'by shaping the hot glass with various tools, by the application of threads, by applied and pincered decoration, by mold blowing and by cutting or engraving with the wheel.'[380] In both Egypt and Syria, lamp shades were made in glass adorned with medallions, inscriptions, or floral designs. Under the Tulunids, Abbasids, Fatimids, Ayyubids, and Mamluks, Muslim glass-makers created a new art of decorated glass hardly surpassed at any earlier or later time for strength, design and richness of colour.[381] In fact so impressed were the crusaders by it they pilfered Syrian coloured glasses believing they were cut from precious stones.[382] Glass workers of the early Islamic period experimented in polychrome decoration of the surface. Opaque coloured vessels were made in Egypt and incrustation with glass on another colour, the so-called technique of 'combed' decoration, found its home in Syria.[383] Some of the most sophisticated Egyptian glass vessels were decorated with lustre, a shiny, sometimes metallic effect, achieved by painting copper or silver oxide on the surface of the object, then firing it at a temperature of about 600°C (1112°F.) in reducing conditions.[384] The distinctive Islamic technique of painting nearly colourless or deeply coloured blown glass with enamel colours and gold, which are then fused with glass by refiring, in fact, probably came into being in Syria toward the end of the 12th and the beginning of the 13th century.[385] Elaborating on the technique of gilding and enamelling, Dimand notes several processes: glassmakers applied first the gilt decoration,

---

[375] Ibid.
[376] E. Levi Provencal: *L'Espagne Musulmane*; op cit; p. 184.
[377] P. De Gayangos: *The History of the Mohammedan Dynasties in Spain* (extracted from *Nifh Al-Tib* by al-Maqqari); 2 vols (The Oriental Translation Fund; London, 1840-3), vol I; pp. 148; 425.
[378] Al-Saqati; p. 67; in S.M. Imamuddin: *Muslim;* op cit; p. 118.
[379] R. Pinder Wilson and G. Scanlon: Glass Finds From Fustat; in *Journal of Glass Studies;* vol XV (1973); pp. 12-30; at p. 17.
[380] Ibid.
[381] W.B. Honey: *Glass;* op cit; p. 35.
[382] M. Lombard: *The Golden Age of Islam*; tr. by J. Spencer; (North Holland Publishers; 1975); pp. 188-9.
[383] D.B. Harden et al: *Masterpieces of Glass*; (Allen Press; Oxford; 1968); p. 101
[384] D. Whitehouse: Glass; op cit; pp. 546-7.
[385] R. Pinder-Wilson: Islamic Glass Twelfth-Fifteenth centuries; in *Glass: Five thousand Years*; ed. H. Tait; (New York; 1991); pp. 131-2.

using a pen for the outlines and a brush for larger surfaces. After the first firing, the design was outlined in red and the enamel in various colours was applied thickly according to the design.[386] The semi opaque enamels consisted of a flux containing much lead and coloured with metallic oxides. Green was obtained from oxide of copper, red from oxide of iron, yellow from antimonic acid, and white, which was entirely opaque, from oxide of tin. The blue enamel, the most prominent element in the decoration of this glass was made from pulverized lapis lazuli mixed with colourless glass.[387]

Various dynasties contributed their specific input to this industry as to others. The Seljuk Turks, despite the rather unkind historiography as to their role,[388] have greatly contributed to this industry as to the arts of the countries where they exerted their influence.[389] Enamel painting on glass, just as the damascening of bronze, for instance, reached very high levels during their rule.[390] The typical lamp form also originated in Syria at the time of their rule.[391] Following the Seljuks, in the 13th century Ayyubid and Mamluk periods, pieces with arabesques and Arabic inscriptions were amongst the most popular wares. Their decoration is frequently arranged in horizontal zones of various widths, separated by narrow bands.[392] Some of the figure subjects include polo players and hunting scenes.[393] The lamps for Cairo mosques, made to order for the Mamluk sultans and their emirs, frequently bore their names and badges.[394] The Metropolitan Museum in New York possesses an important collection of such lamps, thirteen of them, and also ten large vessels-basins, bottles, cups, and a tray-and several small beakers and flasks which in quality, Dimand says, is surpassed by none.[395]

The faith of Islam played a major part in stimulating the growth of the glass industry. As Weiss explains, the Muslims transformed their mosques, houses and cities into centres of rich decoration, but in this atmosphere, a special significance was given to glass (just as ceramics): it was required to replace the gold and silver vessels excluded on the grounds of faith.[396] Islam rejects both luxury and the use of precious metals in decoration, most particularly in religious edifices.[397] Weiss

[386] M.S. Dimand: *A Handbook*; op cit; p. 237.
[387] Ibid.
[388] See, for instance: C. Brockelmann: *History of the Islamic Peoples* (Routledge; London; 1950); p. 240. F.B. Artz: *The Mind of the Middle Ages*; 3rd ed revised (The University of Chicago Press, 1980), pp. 175-6. K.N. Chaudhuri: *Trade and Civilisation in the Indian Ocean* (Cambridge University Press; Cambridge; 1985), p. 36. G. Wiet et al: *History*; op cit; pp. 243; 458; p. 663.
[389] D.B. Harden et al: *Masterpieces of Glass*; op cit; p. 101
[390] G. Weiss: *The Book of Glass;* tr. J. Seligman (Barrie and Jenkins; London; 1971), p. 74.
[391] Ibid.
[392] M.S. Dimand: *A Handbook*; op cit; p. 237.
[393] Ibid.
[394] Ibid.
[395] Ibid.
[396] G. Weiss: *The Book of Glass*; op cit; p. 65.
[397] R. Garaudy: *Comment l'Homme Devint Humain* (Editions J A; 1978), p.199-ff see I.R. and L.L al-Faruqi: *The Cultural Atlas of Islam* (Mc Millan Publishing Company; New York, 1986), for a more extensive study of Islam and its impact on society, civilisation, culture etc.

compares this with the situation in the Christian West, where, in contrast to gold and silver and rock crystal with their precious, symbolic properties, glass was not noble enough for its use to be permitted as divine service.[398] Possibly in an effort to supply the thousands of mosques, and also thanks to the input provided by the thriving scientific activity, in chemistry, most particularly, Muslims turned what had hitherto been a craft into an industry, employing large numbers of workers (often working in association).

Technically, the industry called on a variety of collaborative skills. Carboni notes that the technology employed for moulded glass was not that simple, and just as the finished products were sent to the engraver for cold cutting, a mould had to be conceived, prepared, and often cast in bronze before a glass vessel was created.[399] In both cases the glassmaker sought another craftsman's skill in order to accomplish his task, thus making the chain of production more complex.[400] Before beginning his work, a glassmaker would have to obtain a mould from a mould-maker who was perhaps associated with the glass workshop itself or was an independent craftsman working for other craftsmen as well, a skilled metalworker, who would not have limited himself to making moulds for glass factories only.[401] Within this community of artisans, such as in the workshop quarters of Fustat or Nishapur, a glassmaker could, thus, have commissioned the moulds from the neighbouring metalworker.[402]

Whilst it involved various skills, the industry also generated a diversity of products. Djebbar notes how the glass industry led to advances in glasses (for vision) and optical sciences (telescopes).[403] Whitehouse, likewise, points to the enormous contribution of glass to modern science and civilisation.[404] There is an excellent passage by al-Farabi (870-950), which proves that Muslims used telescopes and other sighting devices for the observation of the planets at quite an early date. His passage on the science of mechanics and other devices includes:

> The optical devices used in the production of instruments that direct the sight in order to discern the reality of the distant objects, and in the production of mirrors upon which one determines the points that reverse the rays by deflecting them or by reflection or refraction. With this, one can also determine the points that reverse the sun's rays into other bodies, thus producing the burning mirrors and the devices connected with them.[405]

---

[398] G. Weiss: *The Book of Glass*; op cit; p. 65.
[399] S. Carboni: *Glass From the Islamic Lands*, op cit, p. 197.
[400] Ibid.
[401] Ibid.
[402] Ibid.
[403] A. Djebbar: *Une Histoire*; op cit; pp. 347-9.
[404] D. Whitehouse: Glass Making in T. Glick, S.J. Livesey. F. Wallis editors: *Medieval Science, Technology and Medicine, an Encyclopaedia*; Routledge; London; pp. 199-201; at p. 200.
[405] Al-Farabi: *Ihsa' al-Ulum*; ed. O. Amin; Al-Maktaaba al-Anglo-Misriya (Cairo; 1968), pp. 108-110; in G. Saliba: The Function of Mechanical Devices in Medieval Islamic Society; in *Science and Technology in Medieval Society*; edited by P.O. Long; The Annals of the New York Academy of Sciences (New York; 1985), pp. 141-51; at pp. 145-6.

Further links between glass making and scientific applications for optical purposes, or observation of the sky, are found in Selin's edition of an encyclopaedia under various entries.[406]
Glass vessels also made possible medical diagnosis by uroscopy (inspection of urine samples,) which began in the Islamic world before spreading to Europe.[407] Glass apparatus was also indispensable for scientific experiment.[408] Pinder Wilson and Scanlon list some of the items made of glass that were found in excavations at Fustat.[409] These include window glass, coin weights, vessel stamps and blown vessels. The latter were intended for a variety of purposes, including jars, flasks, ewers, beakers, goblets for containing liquids, toilet flasks and bottles, lamps, specialised vessels such as alembics, druggist measures, and so on.[410]

Exports of Muslim glass, especially Syrian, was a dominant trait of the medieval economy. Syrian ports were very active centres of export, excavations in the port of Tripoli, for instance, yielding considerable amounts of fragments of glasses.[411] The Syrian gilded and enamelled glasses for which the Near East was renowned were exported as far as China, Russia, Sweden and England.[412] Going through the inventories of the time, Heyd points out, reveals bottles, goblets plates of glass, painted or decorated 'in the Damascus manner.'[413] Amongst the many instances is a famous beaker or cup with ornament that is preserved in the museum of Douai, in France. It was part of a bequest recorded in 1329 that included an endowment for poor clergy, and was probably brought from Palestine by a crusader in 1251.[414] Venice, during the crusades, played a central role in this trade. The Genoese were also active. Byrne mentions many times the Levantine wares which Genoese merchants distributed throughout the West, in Spain, southern France and the fairs of Champagne.[415]

Just as with other products, the importation of Muslim glass eventually led to attempts at its imitation in the workshops of Western Christendom. This transfer can be found well explained in works such as Catherine Hess's edition of the *Arts of Fire*, which looks at the Islamic impact on Italian Renaissance in regards to both glass and ceramics; a very beautiful work, indeed.[416] This transfer, like

---

406 H. Selin Editor: *Encyclopaedia of the History of Science, Technology, and Medicine in Non Western Cultures* (Kluwer Academic Publishers. Dordrecht/Boston/London, 1997).
407 D. Whitehouse: Glass Making; op cit; p. 201.
408 Ibid.
409 R. Pinder Wilson and G. Scanlon: Glass Finds From Fustat; in *Journal of Glass Studies;* vol XV (1973); pp. 12-30; at p. 17.
410 Ibid.
411 E. Gerspach: *L'Art de la Verrerie*; op cit; p. 97.
412 D.B. Harden et al: *Masterpieces of Glass*; op cit; p. 102.
413 J. Labarte: Histoire des Arts Industriels; in W. Heyd: *Histoire*; op cit; vol 2; p. 710.
414 W.B. Honey: *Glass*; op cit; p. 46.
415 E.H. Byrne: Genoese Trade with Syria in the 12th century; *American History Review;* Vol 25; 1920; pp. 191-219, at p. 216).
416 C. Hess Editor: *The Arts of Fire, Islamic Influence on Glass and Ceramics of the Italian Renaissance*, The J. Paul Getty Museum, Los Angeles, 2004.

others, has also been studied by this author but from a totally different perspective (more historical than artistic and aesthetical) in another work, and is briefly summed up here.[417] The process was slow, and followed a number of routes, in which the crusader route and the particular role of Venice were central. During the crusades, the Italian states gave considerable logistical assistance to the crusaders in exchange of privileges in the towns and cities they helped capture.[418] For their part in the capture of Tyre, for instance, the Venetians were rewarded with one-third of the port and its hinterland.[419] This created a "state within a state," inhabitants of the Venetian enclave being subject to Venetian jurisdiction, while the king of Jerusalem ruled the rest of the territory. The Venetian *bailo* or consul Marsilio Zorzi reported to the doge in 1243, "In Tyre we have a third of the city, and we have our own complete court, just as the king has his own."[420] When the trading privileges were confirmed for the last time in 1277, it was recognised that Venice had complete parity with the kingdom.[421] Glassworks at Tyre are included among installations referred to in a contract made with the Venetians in 1175, and again in 1243, the latter contract having been made at Acre.[422] Glass making was introduced from Islamic Syria to Venice following a treaty between the Doge Giacomo Contarini and Bohemond VII, prince of Antioch.[423] The treaty mentions duties on broken glass loaded at Tripoli that served as raw material to Venice.[424] The pieces of broken glass, and misshapen bits were carried to Venice so as to be melted down in what were the early stages of the glass industry in that city.[425] Venice also had access to alkali, an essential ingredient for the production of glass, through its merchant colonies in the crusader states.[426] More importantly, the Venetians acquired many and diverse skills from the Syrians (and from the Egyptians, too) with whom they were in close contact during the crusades.[427] Immigrant craftsmen arriving before the fall of Acre (to the Muslims) in 1291 and early European purchasers of the painted glassware might even have had direct knowledge of the Syrian industry.[428] Heyd highlights the role of the Jews of Tyre, who have from one generation to the other exerted amongst the Venetian colony of that city their trades in glass making, and through them much influence was exerted.[429] Engle adds another element to this transfer of skills from the East, stating that during

---

[417] See S.E. Al-Djazairi: *The Hidden Debt*, Part Three; chapter on Industry.

[418] Z. Oldenbourg: *The Crusades;* op cit; pp. 295-6.

[419] S. Carboni, G. Lacerenza and D. Whitehouse: Glass Making in Medieval Tyre; The Written Evidence; *Journal of Glass Studies;* vol 45; p. 2003; pp. 139-49; p. 148.

[420] Ibid; p. 149.

[421] D. Howard, *Venice and the East,* New Haven and London: (Yale University Press, 2000), pp. 30-1.

[422] R. Rohricht ed: *Regni Hierosolymitani*; 1893-1904, 140, 296.

[423] A. Pacey: *Technology*, op cit, p. 50.

[424] S. Carboni: Enamelled Glass production in Venice; in *Gilded and Enamelled Glass from the Middle East*; ed. R. Ward; (London; 1998); pp. 101-2.

[425] M. Lombard: *The Golden Age of Islam*; op cit; pp. 188-9.

[426] R. E. Mack: *Bazaar to Piazza*; op cit; p. 113.

[427] M. Ilg in W. Heyd: *Histoire*; op cit; p. 710.

[428] S. Carboni: Enamelled Glass; p. 101-4.

[429] W. Heyd: *Histoire*; op cit; p. 710.

the crusades, glassmakers from the Syrian-Palestine coast began to be carried (by the Genoese, in particular) in appreciable numbers to northern Italy and the south of France.[430] They would have been needed to make the windows for the great cathedrals being built as a result of the economic prosperity in the West induced by the Crusades, to produce for the fairs, and to lay the foundation of the glass industries of modern Europe.[431]

The decline of the glass industry in the Muslim world is symptomatic of the decline of Muslim civilisation (as will be amply seen in the final part of this work). Carboni, for instance, refers to the high place of enamelled glass in Syrian manufacturing, its exports to the Christian West, and its popularity in subsequent Western literature, and raises questions about its disappearance in the 15th century.[432] This disappearance coincides with that of Syrian manufacturing, which resulted from the invasion and devastation of the country by Timur the Lame in the last years of the 14th and early in the 15th century. Timur burnt the glass manufacture of Damascus, just as the rest of the city and its crafts and industries.[433] In the wake of this assault, whilst pyramids of skulls were made of the inhabitants, Timur only spared one group: master craftsmen whom he carried back to his capital, Samarkand.[434] Following that, Syrian trades and industries, by far the most advanced of the medieval era, totally disappeared.[435] This, Weiss insists, meant that the great days of Syria (and Egypt) were gone for good.[436] And, so from being the leading producer and exporter of glass, skills, and arts, the situation became reversed in the 15th century. Now Venetian workshops executed orders for enamelled glass mosque lamps for the Near East.[437]

Tin Glaze Pottery

Tin Glaze Pottery, under its many other names as: luster-ware, tin enamelled pottery, ceramics, faience, maiolica, delft, and so on, was at the foundation of many modern industries during the industrial awakening of Western Christendom.[438] This industry amounted in the 18th century to several hundreds

---

430 See: A. Engle: A Study of the Names of Early Glassmaking Families of Europe as a source of Glass History; *Readings in Glass History* 1, pp. 51-65. See also: A. Engle: Benjamin of Tudela and the Glass-Makers: A New Perspective; in *Readings in Glass History*; Vol 4; 1974; pp. 32-41; at p. 37.

431 A. Engle: A Study of the Names; op cit.

432 S. Carboni: *Glass From the Islamic Lands;* op cit; p. 323.

433 R. E. Mack: *Bazaar to Piazza*; op cit; p. 113. E. Gibbon: *The Decline and Fall of the Roman Empire*; op cit; vol VII; 1920; pp. 55-6.

434 E. Gibbon: *The Decline and Fall*; vol VII; 1920; pp. 55-6. D. Whitehouse: Glass; op cit; p. 547.

435 G. Sarton: *The Incubation of Western Culture in the Middle East*, a George C. Keiser Foundation Lecture, March 29, 1950 (Washington DC; 1951), Note 35; p. 35. D. Whitehouse: Glass; op cit; p. 547.

436 G. Weiss: *The Book of Glass;* op cit; p. 67.

437 D.B. Harden et al: *Masterpieces of Glass*; op cit; p. 103.

438 For definitions of terms related to the industry, see: E.A. Barber: *Tin Enamelled Pottery*; (Hodder and Stoughton, 1907). To have a fair view of the industry, and the multiplicity of its products, see: G. Savage and H. Newman: *An Illustrated Dictionary of Ceramics*; (Thames and Hudson; London; 1976).

of manufactories producing faience, stretching from France to Poland, passing by Hungary, Denmark, Sweden, Germany, Norway, and throughout much of Europe.[439] A great number of towns and cities owed their reputation to this industry, places such as Nevers in France, for its faience, delft in Holland (for the same named product), and Wedgwood in the UK.
Centuries earlier in the Muslim world, this industry supplied objects of great value for decorative, or other aesthetical, purposes. The Vatican, for instance, owns an Egyptian splash-ware vessel once used as a reliquary, and a white carved semi porcelain cup preserved for its rarity as the chalice of San Girolamo.[440] Islamic lustre-painted bowls, prized for their colour and brilliant surface, were also embedded in the walls of some Italian churches.[441]
Whilst Caiger Smith's work on the subject constitutes what is possibly the best source of the dynamic role played by this industry in both the Muslim and non-Muslim worlds,[442] the following outline will seek to address some of the central issues relating to it. It will focus on early Muslim skills, which contributed to the development of this industry; its role in the overall economic structure of Islam; how it impacted on the West; and finally how, like other industries, it collapsed in the wake of invasions.

Like much else, the early Chinese contribution in this field surpassed that of any other civilisation. Even by the 11th century, when the Muslims had already led the way in the production of glazed pottery, they still remained behind the Chinese in respect to porcelain. Both Ta'libi and Al-Biruni, writing in the first half of the 11th century, refer with admiration to the translucency of Chinese porcelain, to its thinness, and to its resonance when struck.[443] However, as with paper, the compass, and many other products or ideas borrowed from the Chinese, the Muslims transformed the initial product, multiplied its outlets, before, finally, transmitting to the Christian West yet another industry that was to have a determining role in the development of modern economies.

Islam, Lane notes, created a new world of pottery; it was essentially glazed pottery, remarkable for its wealth and colour.[444] At every stage, Lane says,

> One is aware of the exploring hand on the clay, the active mind devising new means to pass colour and glaze successfully through the ordeal of fire.[445]

---

[439] A. Caiger-Smith: *Tin Glazed Pottery*; (Faber and Faber; London; 1973); p. 181.
[440] M.D. Whitman: Ceramics; *Dictionary of the Middle Ages*; op cit; vol 3; pp. 238-40; at pp. 238-9.
[441] Whitman: Ceramics; pp. 238-9. To have a good idea of the beauty and diversity of Muslim objects see G. Fehervari: *Ceramics of the Islamic World in the Tareq Rajab Museum*; (I.B. Tauris; London; 2000). G. Fehervari: *Islamic Pottery* (based on the Barlow Collection); (Faber and Faber; London; 1973).
[442] For such details see A. Caiger-Smith: *Tin Glazed Pottery*; op cit.
[443] In A. Lane: *Early Islamic Pottery*; (Faber and Faber; London; 1947); p. 32.
[444] Ibid; p. 47.
[445] Ibid.

By the 9th century, Muslims produced ware which took Western Christendom until the 15th century to produce comparable ones, where under the names of maiolica, delft, or faience, it remained the Western finest form of pottery for over two centuries more.[446] Under Seljuk rule, in the 12th century, Persia produced translucent white ware, which anticipated the soft paste porcelain of France; the overglaze colours of the minai (pottery decorated in polychrome enameled colours over a cream glaze) technique preceded the enamel colours that appeared in China during the 15th century, and in Europe during the 18th.[447]

Earthenware to receive lustre-painted patterns was covered, when in the biscuit state, with a milky white glaze and fired; its surface was then ready for the lustre decorations.[448] Lustre painting remained a peculiar glory of Islam, imitated a little in Renaissance Italy, but never attempted in the Far East.[449] It is now generally agreed that lustre glazes originated early in the Islamic period, because in all excavations, which have so far been made, no example predating the Arab conquest has been found.[450] To master the technique of mixing and firing lustre glazes, the potters must have worked meticulously and assiduously toward perfecting their methods in an effort to reproduce in 'humble medium' the gold and silver vessels that the *hadith* condemned.[451] Here, again, there becomes obvious the role of the faith in stimulating the development of a craft.
The process of lustre glazing is difficult and complex-as modern ceramists will agree -but by the 9th century the artisans of the Near East had made great progress with their experiments and were able to produce at will lustre glazes of varied tonality, which reflected gold and other metallic colours, as well as iridescent reds, blues, and greens.[452] While lustre sometimes covered the entire surface of fine lead-glazed earthenware, it was also used for painted designs on vessels that had previously been glazed in opaque white. This latter type was imported to Al Andalus and later produced on Spanish soil (from whence it would have a decisive impact on the Christian West, giving origins to our modern faience, and many other products).[453]

From potters' formulas and from modern experimentation we have a fair idea of the materials, which 9th century Muslims used in compounding their lustre glazes. Either metallic copper and silver mixed with sulphur or the bisulphides of these metals (which could be obtained from minerals in their natural states) were calcined to form copper and silver oxides. The compound was ground and mixed

[446] Ibid. For the gap between the wares of Islam and the Christian West, see B. Rackham: *Medieval English Pottery*; Faber and Faber; (London; 1958).
[447] Ibid.
[448] A. Frothingham: *Lustre Ware of Spain*; Hispanic Society of America; (New York; 1951); p. 2.
[449] Ibid.
[450] Ibid.
[451] Ibid.
[452] Ibid.
[453] Ibid.

with red ochre, which contained ferric oxide, and then fluxed with vinegar and painted on the white-glazed earthenware.[454] The vessels were given another firing to reduce the oxides to the metallic state, this time at a low temperature and in a reduction kiln. When they emerged, they were blackened, but with rubbing the coating was removed, and the decorated parts appeared as metallic silver, copper, or gold.[455] The virtues of early Islamic wares, Lane points out, are those perceived by the eye.[456] Potters were fascinated by the behaviour of light:

> Light mysteriously refracted by their lustre pigment; light playing over a carved or subtly modelled surface; light gleaming through the glazed 'windows' pierced in the wall of a vessel, or through the translucent material itself. Black painted ornament swimming under a transparent turquoise glaze is a variant on the same theme. When made opaque with tin oxide, this turquoise glaze seems to soften and purify the light it absorbs; it has an unearthly beauty.... All the colours hold something strange to European eyes; a warm glow and subdued intensity very different from the old brilliance of coloured enamels on Chinese or European porcelain.[457]

The industry was widely spread throughout the Muslim world, and under various dynasties, in diverse places and times, it often incorporated new features. In Iraq, quantities of polychrome lustreware have been discovered at Samarra, court of the Abbasid caliphs, which was founded in 836 and abandoned less than a half century later, so that an approximate date for this pottery is established.[458] Its polychrome metallic glazes show that the potters were experimenting with a difficult technique, contrasting ruby, vermilion, gold, brown, and green lustres on single objects.[459] They may have found that to combine so many tonalities was extremely difficult and did not always work, since about 860 they reduced the number of lustres to yellow and brown.[460] Pottery found at Samarra may not have been made there, for no kilns or wasters were found within the excavated areas. Perhaps the industry was located in several cities such as Baghdad, Basra, and Kufa, any of which may have been a centre of production before the rise of the 'Abbasid capital.[461] There is, in fact, evidence of Kufa and Basra having been centres of glass and pottery manufacture in the writings of al-Ya'kubi, who noted in 890 that when al-Mu'tasim was building Samarra, he brought to the new capital glass blowers, potters, and mat weavers from Basra, and from Kufa, potters and makers of ointments.[462]

---

[454] M. Gomez Moreno Y Martinez: *Ceramica medieval espanola*; (Barcelona; 1924); pp. 28-9. M. Gonzalez Marti: *Ceramica del levante espanol*; (Barcelona, Madrid, 1944); pp. 318-28;

[455] A. Frothingham: *Lustre Ware of Spain*; op cit; p. 3.

[456] A. Lane: *Early Islamic Pottery*; op cit; p. 48.

[457] Ibid.

[458] Ibid; p. 47.

[459] A. Frothingham: *Lustre Ware of Spain*; op cit; p. 3.

[460] A. Lane: *Early Islamic Pottery*; op cit; pp. 14-5.

[461] Ibid; p.11.

[462] A. Frothingham: *Lustre Ware of Spain*; op cit; p. 3.

There are signs that the technique was carried west to Raqqa (Rakka) in Syria and then to Egypt. In both places the painting was mostly done in green and brown from copper and manganese.[463] Quantities of Raqqa pottery passed through the hands of Syrian dealers, who supplied the market with many fine pieces, seen today in museums and private collections.[464] Although some of the Raqqa ware may belong to the 11th century, the majority dates from the 12th century or the 13th, showing decorative elements, which are characteristic of the era of Seljuk rule in Syria and Mesopotamia.[465] The characteristic of Raqqa's pottery was the colour of the lustre, which was usually dark-brown, which is rare in other ceramic centres.[466] The decoration, painted in lustre over a transparent greenish glaze, frequently enhanced by the addition of cobalt blue, consists of arabesques, kufic or Naskhi inscriptions, and occasionally highly stylised birds. The finest wares date from the 12th century.[467]

In Egypt, the growth of the industry was mainly owed to the Tulunid dynasty, which was established there after the Turk, Ibn Tulun, was appointed by the caliph as governor of Egypt (in 879). This dynasty had a profound impact on the cultural and economic life of Egypt. It also provided the foundation for the lustre pottery of the subsequent Fatimid dynasty.[468]

The production of lusterware continued its progress west, and made its initial appearance on the Spanish Peninsula, very possibly during the reign of 'Abd al-Rahman III (912-961).[469] The Spanish role in the vast expansion of this industry will be considered further on.

To the east of Iraq, one of the most creative periods of all ceramic history, Caiger-Smith insists, began in the North West of Persia under the Seljuk Turks.[470] The Seljuk warrior-aristocracy revitalised the cultures of the local peoples, and under their firm administration trade, architecture, metalwork, and pottery likewise flourished.[471] The Seljuks introduced a new composite material for the body of the wares, and new methods of decoration.[472] The main centres of Seljuk production were Rayy in northern Persia, and Kashan, some 125 miles south of modern Tehran.[473] The Seljuk methods outlived them, and spread not only in Iran, but also in Asia Minor, Syria, and Egypt.[474] In Istanbul's library there is a very interesting treatise on the technique of the Seljuk potters written in 1301 by Abu'l Qasim al-Khashan, who himself belonged to a distinguished family of

---

463 A. Caiger-Smith: *Tin Glazed Pottery*; (Faber and Faber; London; 1973); p. 24.
464 M.S. Dimand: *A Handbook of Muhammadan Art*; op cit; p. 189.
465 Ibid.
466 Ibid.
467 Ibid.
468 A. Caiger-Smith: *Tin Glazed Pottery*; op cit; p. 30.
469 A. Frothingham: *Lustre Ware of Spain*; op cit; p. 2.
470 A. Caiger-Smith: *Tin Glazed Pottery*; op cit; p. 43.
471 M. Harami: *Gurgan Faiences*; (Tehran; 1949); A. Lane: *Early*; op cit; 29 ff..
472 G. Fehervari: *Islamic Pottery* (based on the Barlow Collection); (Faber and Faber; London; 1973); pp. 70-1.
473 A. Lane: *Early Islamic Pottery*; op cit; pp. 29-30.
474 G. Fehervari: *Islamic Pottery*; op cit; p. 71.

potters.[475] A considerable amount of information regarding the manufacturing of lustre-ware, as well as the equipment used is found in this treatise. Except for this treatise, Caiger-Smith points out, there are no direct records of the preparation of materials earlier than the 16th century.[476]
A later flourish in Islamic pottery took place under the Ottoman Turks. The kilns of Iznik (Nicea) (north-west Turkey) as O. Aslanapa has shown, were producing pottery long before the appearance of its famous faience tiles and vessels.[477] They were made of red earthenware and decorated mainly in underglaze blue painting.[478] Towards the end of the 15th century, this earthenware was replaced by beautiful faience tiles and vessels. It was these, which made Iznik famous, and perhaps it is not an overstatement to suggest that the wares of Iznik can be regarded as the apex of Islamic potters.[479] Iznik wares were imported into Italy in considerable quantity.[480] Italian potters subsequently imitated the product. The two Iznik patterns that late 16th and early 17th century Italian potters imitated most closely were new, indicating that Italians particularly admired original elements of Ottoman ceramics.[481]

Whilst the Turkish route exerted considerable influence, it was the Spanish route, which was central to the transformation of Western glazed wares. In the history of European ceramics, Frothingham says, the position held by Hispano-Moresque pottery, particularly the lustreware, is one of supreme importance. Had it not been for the pottery introduced first into Spain by the Muslims, ceramic art-forms and techniques would have developed quite differently all over the Continent.[482] The passage of Muslim Spanish lusterware to the Italians, first, and to the rest of the Christian West, has been seen in greater detail by this author in another work.[483] For much better, but much lengthier study of the issue of transmission and impact, the best source is Caiger-Smith's.[484] On the Spanish industry, itself, Alice Frothingham's work remains unequalled.[485] Briefly here, on the Muslim impact on the West, Muslim glazed pottery passed from Muslim Malaga to Christian ruled Manises, near Valencia, in the 14th century. Archives mention the names of Muslim potters working there: such as Suleyman al-Faqui, Azmat al-Malequi and many others as figuring in the contracts for the making of the ware.[486] They were probably encouraged or even persuaded to

---

475 A. Lane: *Early Islamic Pottery*; op cit; p. 32.
476 A. Caiger-Smith: *Tin Glazed Pottery*; op cit; p. 199.
477 O. Aslanapa: *Turkische Fliesen und Keramik im Anatolien*; (Istanbul; 1965).
478 G. Fehervari: *Ceramics of the Islamic World in the Tareq Rajab Museum*; (I.B. Tauris; London; 2000); p. 308.
479 Ibid.
480 A. Caiger-Smith: *Tin Glazed Pottery*; op cit; p. 88.
481 R. E. Mack: *Bazaar to Piazza*; op cit; p. 108.
482 A. Frothingham: *Lustre Ware of Spain*; op cit; p. 277.
483 See S.E. Al-Djazairi: *Hidden Debt*; chapter on industry, under appropriate heading.
484 A. Caiger-Smith: *Tin Glazed Pottery*; op cit; 1973.
485 A. Frothingham: *Lustre Ware of Spain*; op cit.
486 S. Suhrawardy: *The Art of the Mussulmans in Spain*; (Oxford University Press; 2005); p. 132.

settle there by the de Buyl family, the landlords of Manises.[487] Manises soon replaced Malaga as the most important centre for the production of lustre pottery, and would remain so to the 16th century.[488]

Islamic tin glaze were to influence Italian maiolica.[489] The name maiolica (if not derived from Malaga, Arabic Maliqa)[490] points to the influence of the trade with Valencia in Spain via Majorca.[491] It is obvious that Italy, geographically placed between Islamic influences coming direct from the eastern Mediterranean and those coming from Spain to the west, would be the catalyst.[492] Some of the transfers of Muslim Spanish skills and knowledge, and of lustre objects, also travelled to Italy courtesy of the Papal route. The Borgia family, who occupied the Papal throne, were of Spanish-Valencian origins, and commissioned Muslim works for Sala Borgia in the Vatican.[493] Through these routes, the tin glazed earthenware called *maiolica* developed in Italy.[494] The Italians, then, during the 16th century, in particular, spread the art throughout Europe. Caiger Smith traces this laborious spread, following the works of Italian craftsmen.[495] This transfer legated some of the most thriving industries in the Christian West: faience in France, Delft in Holland, Wedgwood in England, and countless more names and factories all over Europe, and subsequently America, employing tens of thousands, if not hundreds of thousands of personnel, and securing the prosperity of more than one region in Europe. By the end of the 18th century, Caiger Smith, says:

> The preceding chapters have traced the passing of the tin glaze technique from land to land and have indicated how each culture in turn adopted the tradition as it first found it, and then began to use it in new ways. The tradition was sufficiently long lived to undergo changes that appear to be transformations. How little there is in common, for instance, between the early tin glaze of Baghdad and Cairo and Dutch gilt and polychrome enamelled wares of the early 18th century! Yet the connections leading from one to the other were direct, and the technique itself remained basically the same. If a Cairo potter or painter of 1100 had been reincarnated in Delft (in Holland) six hundred years later he would have been surprised by some of the decorative style, he would have been impressed by the kilns and the quantity of production, and he would have found the technique itself quite familiar.[496]

---

[487] G. Marti: *Ceramica del Levante Espanol;* (Barcelona; 1944); vol. i, pp. 213-20.
[488] S. Suhrawardy: *The Art of the Mussulmans in Spain*; op cit; p. 132.
[489] J Sweetman: *The Oriental Obsession*; op cit; p. 5.
[490] R. Schnyder: Islamic Ceramics; op cit; p. 34.
[491] J Sweetman: *The Oriental Obsession*; op cit; p. 39.
[492] Ibid.
[493] J Sweetman: *The Oriental Obsession*; op cit; p. 37; S. Suhrawardy: *The Art;* op cit; p. 132.
[494] J. Sweetman: *The Oriental*; op cit; p. 39.
[495] A. Caiger-Smith: *Tin Glazed Pottery*; op cit; pp. 103 ff, in particular.
[496] Ibid; p. 179

In the meantime, just when it had been helping transform the industrial landscape in Europe, the Muslim world, with the exception of Ottoman Turkey, continued to experience decline. The fate of the industry seen here is pretty similar to that of other aspects of Muslim civilisation. Syria like the rest of the Muslim world, perhaps more than any part of the Muslim world, was the leading country in respect to many industries (and scholarship). One of Syria's thriving industrial centres was Raqqa, where kilns produced a characteristic lustre ware.[497] There kilns remained active until the Mongol invasion in 1259, which caused ruin to the area.[498] Once the Mamluks put an end to the Mongol scourge, they gathered the surviving and scattered potters in Damascus. The trade consequently experienced another flurry, the quality of Damascus wares being such that their reputation spread far and wide. French and Italian inventories of the 14th century suggest that Damascus pots were treasured for their own sake, and even mounted on precious metal.[499] In 1420 a Muslim potter of Manises (near Valencia), living under Christian rule, was contracted to make for a Milanese merchant 720 pots *a la domasquina* (on the Damascus model) to match a sample he had been given, probably a somewhat older Syrian jar.[500] By the time that potter had been asked to reproduce a Damascus model, the days of that, and other, Syrian industries were over. In the year 1401, Timur the Lame fell on Syria, and put the country to waste, amongst others setting the potter's quarter of Damascus to fire.[501] In the wake of his massacre of the population, he carried with him to Samarkand, his capital, the craftsmen he had spared.[502] The blossoming art of Samarkand was at the cost of Syria's collapse.

Meanwhile, al-Andalus, or what was left of it (i.e the Grenada enclave), faced a similar fate to other Muslim regions. The curtailment of Muslim maritime power in the mid-14th century, due to the bold intrusions of Christian pirates, was pre-eminent in causing the ruin of the once illustrious Malagan lustre industry.[503] Eventually dependent on the powerful merchant fleets of Cataluna and Valencia, the Muslim potters of Malaga were forced to risk ferrying their products in small coastwise boats to Christian ports where the pottery was then transferred to ships sailing to the desired destinations.[504] The high shipping costs, the taxes for duty and protection, and the heavy breakage must have added considerably to the cost of the pottery. In order to keep prices low, it was easier for artisans to set up their kilns and workshops in Christian Murcia and Valencia.[505] From this time,

[497] A. Lane: *Early Islamic Pottery*; op cit; pp. 57-60; 77-81.
[498] A. Lane: *Later Islamic Pottery*; op cit; p. 15.
[499] See J. Labarte: *Inventaire du mobilier de Charles V, roi de France*; (Paris; 1879).
[500] A. van de Put: *Hispano-Mauresque Ware of the 15th Century*; (London; 1911); p. 8; 15.
[501] A. Lane: *Later Islamic Pottery*; op cit; p. 16.
[502] E. Gibbon: *The Decline and Fall of the Roman Empire*; vol 5; Methuen and Co; Limited; (London; 1923); Chapter LXV; Part II.
[503] A. Frothingham: *Lustre Ware of Spain*; p. 78; see Archivo General De la Corona de Aragon; Barcelona; *Coleccion de documentos ineditos*; (Barcelona; 1850); v. 6; p. 314 ff.
[504] A. Frothingham: *Lustre Ware of Spain*; op cit; p. 78.
[505] Ibid.

Muslim Malaga lost its position as the prime source of lustre-painted pottery in Spain, a distinction that had now become accredited to Christian Manises in Valencia.[506]

Sugar Industry

Sugar production flourished in many parts of the early Islamic world. Like other industries it relied on the use of natural power to activate machinery, produced for a mass market, whilst the refineries were run by the state with some partnership of private manufacturers.[507]
Heyd provides a good chapter on the industry.[508] He explains how sugar cane was initially cultivated in India, Indo-China and also China proper; but neither did the Chinese, nor the Indians, invent the manufacturing processes. For centuries their role consisted in crushing the cane and extracting the juices, which they then thickened on fire. The method of refining sugar via chemical processes was carried out by Muslims who developed this art before taking it beyond the frontiers.[509]

The introduction of sugar cane into Syria followed the Muslim entry into the country in 634, the first mention of the industry being made by Jacob of Edessa (640-70).[510] The industry developed along the coastal area of the extreme east of the Mediterranean, in the centres of cultivation at Laodicea, Tripoli, Sidon, Tyre, Caesarea, Palestina and Acre, whilst inland, the cane was established around Antioch, Aleppo, and Damascus.[511] Production then spread to Egypt. Muslim geographers such as al-Istakhri (fl. 950) make ample descriptions of the industry in both countries.[512] In Damascus, just as in Cairo, whole streets were set aside for sugar refineries.[513] In Egypt, Al-Bakri (b.ca 1010-d. 1094) mentions sugar mills on the left bank of the River Nile, at Terennout, forty miles north west of Cairo.[514] Here, the industry stimulated the growth of the plantation of sugar cane, and from the close of the 8th century, the most fertile land was planted with sugar cane.[515] According to medieval Muslim travellers, there must have been a continuous strip of cane cultivation and sugar mills.[516]

---

[506] Ibid.
[507] M. Rodinson: *Islam and Capitalism;* op cit; pp. 52-3.
[508] W. Heyd: *Histoire du Commerce;* vol 2; op cit; pp. 680-92.
[509] Ibid; pp. 680-1.
[510] C. Brockelmann: *Geschchite der Christlichen Literaturen des Orients* (Leipzig; 1907), p. 47.
[511] N. Deerr: *The History of Sugar* (Chapman and Hall Ltd; London; 1949), vol 1; p. 74.
[512] C. Brockelmann: *Geschchite*; op cit; p. 47.
[513] A.M. Watson: A Medieval Green Revolution; op cit; note 49; p. 58.
[514] Al-Bakri: Descriptions de l'Afrique Septentrionale; in *Journal Asiatique*; 5th series; XII; p. 415.
[515] M. Lombard: *The Golden*; op cit; p. 167.
[516] N. Deerr: *The History of Sugar*; op cit; pp. 87-8.

Sugar was introduced into North Africa in the wake of the Muslim arrival. Abu Hanifa al-Dinawari (d. 895) says that the sugar of Zingis (Tangiers) was the best known to him, a similar statement subsequently found in Al-Bakri, and Al-Idrisi, who wrote:

> When one leaves Egypt, where still some sugar mills are found at Teremut, much carob bean (which affords good syrup) is seen at Mina, and on reaching the fertile lands of the north coast there are great quantities of sugar cane, which gives an enormous yield in Tripoli and Tunis, and among other places at Al-Kayrawan, where there is also manna and jasmine honey of proverbial goodness. The greatest abundance is, however, in the Maghrib where, near Igli, so much is planted that a man's load costs only a quarter of a dirhem, and 1 qantar (100 kgs) of sugar costs only 2 mithqhals, and the sugar produced here supplies the whole of the Maghrib.[517]

In Sicily, where the industry was introduced soon after the Muslim arrival (827 ff.), the geographer, Ibn Hawqal, writing in 950, says:

> The banks of the streams around Palermo, from their sources to their mouths, are bordered by low-lying lands, upon which the Persian reed is grown. The juice is obtained by pressing mills.[518]

Accounts also speak of large sugar production in 10th century Spain; the chief centres being Elvira, Malaga and Seville, especially along the Mediterranean coast.[519]

The making of sugar is described by contemporary Muslim writers, such as Ibn al-Awwam (fl. end of 12th century) (here referring to Abu'l Khair):

> On the manner of making sugar from these (sugar canes), says Abu al-Khair, that when the cane have reached the end of their proper season in the above mentioned time of the month of January, they are cut in small pieces and these are well trodden on or broken in a vine press, or similar presses; that its juice is placed in a clean boiler on a fire to cook and left till it becomes clear, after that it is made to boil again, until it becomes one fourth of its first volume. It is then put into receptacles, forms, or vases made of clay of a peculiar shape, or conical.[520] It is placed in the shade to harden, and the sugar from it is placed in the shade to aerate, and the residue of the cane after the extraction of the juices is kept for the horses because it is pleasing to them and very fattening.[521]

There is a much more detailed description of the same process by the Egyptian al-Nuwairi (d.1331-2):

---

[517] Al-Idrisi: *Geographie*; tr. Jaubert, (Paris; 1836), I; p. 208.

[518] Schack: *Geschichte der Normannen in Sicilia* (Stuttgart; 1889), I; p. 292.

[519] E. Levi Provencal: *l'Espagne*; op cit; p. 167.

[520] N. Deerr notes that this is the earliest statement which makes definite reference to the sugar cone of sugar loaf; in N. Deerr: *The History;* op cit; note p. 81.

[521] Ibn al-Awwam: *Libro de agricultura*, ed. J. A. Banqueri, (Madrid, 1802), in N. Deer: *The History*; op cit; pp. 80-1.

> The cane is carried on the backs of camels and asses, and unloaded at the 'House of the sugar cane.'... Men sit astride on seats and hold in their hands knives which are larger than those used to cut the cane. In front of them are tables. A man takes a number of stalks and cuts them into small pieces, which he throws into the 'House of pouring.' There, they are placed in baskets, which are called *ijara*, and are all of the same size. They are then carried to the mill stone. The cane is laid under the stone which is turned over the lower stone. The juice is pressed out and flows by openings in the base to the holder, the outlet of which is stopped. The cane is then taken to another place. Here it is placed in baskets of plaited work of *halfs* (rushes), which are slit open below and at the sides. These are laid under the wheel of a beam, and by means of the beam the wheel rolls on them until it has crushed them, and the rest of the juice has been pressed out. The juice that is pressed out by the stone mill and the beam *(tacht)* is brought to the same place. The juice is passed through a sieve, which is placed in a kind of frame. From this it flows to a closed vessel, which is called a *bastula*, in predetermined quantity. When this is filled with strained juice it is brought to the place where it is boiled. It is then strained a second time and led to a large boiler *(chabia)*. Into this is poured with straining all that is in the *bastula*. This holds 50 *matr* of juice. Each *matr* is half an official Latin *qintar*. The Latin *qintar* has 200 dirhem. Therefore the *chabia* holds 3,000 *ratl (ratl* = approximately 1lb). This is the content of the *bastula*.'[522]

The industry involved a vast labour force, and tied up large investments in plant and machinery.[523] As a rule, the manufacture and trade of sugar were largely under state monopoly. Early in the 11th century, the Fatimid ruler, Ali Mansur (r. 966-1020) declared a sugar monopoly, and attempted to raise the price by the destruction of stocks.[524] Mamluk sultans and emirs (1250 onwards) acted as factory owners and wholesale suppliers of the commodity.[525] Sugar works were apparently attached to sugar cane fields, and so must have belonged to landowners, but such landowners were in partnership with manufacturers in the province of Girgeh, supplying land and animals, undertaking the construction and upkeep of buildings, and sharing the profits with those responsible for running factories.[526] Sugar made a decisive contribution to state revenue. Taxes were imposed not only on water rights, which sugar shared with other crops, but also on cane, mills, equipment generally, employees, factories as a whole, and on their owners.[527]

---

[522] In E. Wiedemann: *Beitrage zur Geschichte der Naturwissenschaften*; xli; (1915); p. 89.

[523] On the heavy investment in sugar refineries, see P. Berthier: *Les Anciennes sucreries du Maroc et leurs reseaux hydrauliques* (Rabat; 1966), I; pp. 129 ff; M. Benvenisti: *The Crusaders in the Holy Land* (Jerusalem; 1970), pp. 253-6.

[524] Von Lippmann: *Zeitschrift des Vereins der deutsche Zuckerindustrie*; xlvi; 1921; p. 7.

[525] I.M. Lapidus: *Muslim Cities in the later Middle Ages* (Harvard University Press; Mass; 1967), at p. 127.

[526] M. Rodinson: *Islam and Capitalism*; op cit; p. 53.

[527] N. Deerr: *The History of Sugar*; op cit; p. 93.

There is ample evidence of mass production of sugar during times of festivities in 10th century Egypt, when trees were decorated with tiny sugar figures, also evidence, according to Lombard, of progress in its manufacture.[528] Ibn Battuta (1304-1368-9) who in 1336 travelled up the Nile for 600 miles, says that in Cairo, at the serails, every Friday travellers were served with sweetmeats, and at Maulaway, where there were eleven sugar factories, the poor people came into the boiling house without interference to soak their bread in the hot syrup.[529] The finished products also gave rise to many industries such as the making of sweets, pastries, and confectioneries.[530] Confectioners supplied a thriving trade in sweets made from sugar or honey, and almond and fruit pastes; the stalls were abundant in the markets alongside those of syrup makers.[531] Desserts, Lombard reminds us, are after all of Oriental origin.[532]

Whatever may have been the local consumption, there was a great surplus for export. The Egyptian sea trade was mainly with Venice, and also Genoa, and the land trade was mainly to Syria and Persia. Of trade from Morocco, there is mention in English sources; the Durham account rolls (about 1299) refer to Zucker Marrokis, and again in 1310 is found the entry '31 li. De Coukar de Marrok.'[533] Trade of sugar and other commodities was hampered in times of war. There are records of caravans seized, such as one by Richard Coeur de Lion during the Third Crusade.[534] Another 600 camel loads of sugar were seized in 1280 by the Mongols.[535]

Muslims seem to have retained the monopoly of skills in the manufacturing of sugar for centuries. When they arrived in the East, (1096 onwards) the crusaders found that the Syrians were not just expert at growing sugar, but had also mastered the technique of crushing it under presses, extracting the juices, concentrating the substance on fire, then drying it out slowly into sugar.[536] The Crusaders took over the manufacture, and followed precisely the Muslim system of production, using the same Muslim terminology.[537] At Acre, they used Muslim prisoners in the manufacture of sugar.[538] Because the industry remained alien to Europeans for centuries, the Sicilian ruler, Frederick II (d. 1250) made a request to the Marshall Ricardo Filangieri for workers to be sent from Tyre, in Syria, to

---

[528] M. Lombard: *The Golden,* op cit; p. 167.
[529] Ibn Battuta: *Voyages d'Ibn Battuta*, Arabic text accompanied by French translation by C. Defremery and B.R. Sanguinetti, preface and notes by Vincent Monteil, I-IV (Paris, 1968), reprint of the 1854 ed; Vol 1; p. 60. See also pp. 74; and 101.
[530] A.M. Watson: A Medieval Green Revolution; op cit; p. 47.
[531] G. Wiet et al: *History*; op cit; p. 332.
[532] M. Lombard: *The Golden Age*; op cit; p. 167.
[533] Quoted in New Oxford Dictionary under Sugar.
[534] Gale: *Historia Anglicana Scriptores Quinque* (Oxford; 1887-97), ii; p. 407.
[535] Al-Makrisi: *Histoire des Sultans Mamloukes* (Paris; 1840-46), I; p. 38.
[536] Jacques de Vitry in W. Heyd: *Histoire*; vol 2; op cit; pp. 685-6.
[537] W. Heyd: *Histoire*; op cit; vol 2; pp. 685-6.
[538] Michaud-Reinaud: Bibliotheque des croisades; IV; p. 126; in W. Heyd: *Histoire*; op cit; pp. 685-6.

Palermo following the loss of skilled Muslim personnel.[539] In Spain, after it was taken by the Christians (13th century), Muslim artisans retained their leading status in the production of sugar, a role they kept for centuries, even, it would seem, after the final expulsion of the descendants of Muslims from the country in the early 17th century (1609-1610).[540]

Other Products and their Exports

It is, first, worth saying a few words on an important activity that has so far been unmentioned: the Fishing Industry. Muslim fishermen were drawn extremely far from their shores. Along with elements of navigational, shipbuilding (for example, the sternpost rudder) and other maritime technologies, Glick points out, fishing techniques made their way from the Red Sea and Arabian Gulf to al-Andalus as Arab mariners migrated westward or participated in maritime commerce.[541] In Spain, itself, the industry prospered in the 10th century, in particular.[542] A wide variety of means and techniques were used in fishing.[543] Net fishing was particularly widespread. The drag net, *aljerife* (*jarîf*), is a common south Arabian net with two arms, operated from the shore. Other nets of apparent Arab influence or origin are the tuna trap (*almadraba*, from *madraba*); the conical net (*atarraya*, from *tarrâha*); the purse seine (*jareta*, from *sharît*); and the pocket seine (*jabega*, from *shabbak*).[544] Tuna catches were particularly important, and the geographer, Al-Bakri, offers very interesting accounts of tuna fishing in the coastal regions of the province of Sidona during the passage of the fish between the Atlantic and the Mediterranean in the month of May.[545]
Still, with the food industry, we remarkably learn that by the late Middle Ages, a chicken breeding industry had spread in places, particularly in Egypt in the 15th century. A model of a plant, as reconstructed by Sezgin, shows the plant in Luxor, in which eggs were expenditure-bred, with no less than 100,000 chickens hatched in the cycle of 10 days. (L 1.01)[546]

Another item that has also not been mentioned before: inlaid metal work is given attention here. Muslim craftsmen excelled in the art of laying designs in gold and silver in bronze or brass; a skill performed in several ways known generally as

---

[539] *Historia Diplomatica Friderici Secundi*; ed. (J.L. A. Breholles; Paris; 1852-61), vol 5; pp. 574-5.
[540] S.M. Imamuddin: *Muslim*; op cit; p. 92.
[541] T. Glick: *Islamic and Christian Spain*; op cit; p. 244.
[542] E. Levi Provencal: *Histoire de l'Espagne;* vol 3; op cit; (see chapter on economic activities).
[543] C.E. Dubler: *Uber das Wirtschaftsleben;* op cit; pp. 35-39.
[544] R. B. Serjeant, "Fisher-Folk and Fish Traps in al-Bahrain," *Bulletin of the School of Oriental and Asian Studies*, 31 (1968), 489; Braudel, *The Mediterranean*, II: 763; Juan Vernet: *Historia de la ciencia espanola* (Madrid: Instituto de Espana, 1975), p. 86.
[545] Al-Bakri in E. Levi Provencal: *Histoire,* op cit; pp. 297-8.
[546] F. Sezgin: *The Istanbul Museum for the History of Science and Technology in Islam, an Overview*; Istanbul, 2010; p. 179.

Damascening, a term derived from European association of the work with Damascus, where it was certainly practised, although it did not originate there.[547] Muslim inlaid metal work reached perfection about the middle of the 12th century, and kept its excellence for 200 years. The craft was centred around today's northern Iraqi city of Mosul, which was filled with craftsmen renowned for all sorts of artistic products.[548] The influence of Mosul spread to Syria, Egypt and other places. Following the Mongol invasion of the Caliphate, Mosul was entirely devastated in 1262.[549] Thanks to Mamluk patronage, inlaid metalwork was revived, and flourished again in Damascus and Cairo during the second half of the 13th and most of the 14th century.[550] A great number of medieval Muslim objects from that period have reached us often 'in marvellous preservation.'[551] A basin in the Louvre Museum (Paris) (inv. No. MAO 101) bears inscriptions honouring Hugh IV of Lusignan of Cyprus (r. 1324-1359) in both French and bold *thuluth* Arabic, shields with the arms of Jerusalem and a Maltese Cross, and usual early 14th century Mamluk decorations; the French inscription and insignia filling the outlined shields were probably added by another craftsman.[552] A bowl sold in London (Christie's 1966, lot 134) that is decorated with bands of Arabic poetry and birds also bears the arms of Hugh IV.[553]

The influence of Islamic metalwork on the Christian West was very strong towards the end of the 15th century when, at the very end of the period in which the inlay technique was used in the Near East, a large number of basins, bowls, platters, pitchers, and candlesticks executed by this process appeared in Venice, and possibly in other Italian towns as well, and continued to do so during the first half of the next century.[554] As with other industries (as well as sciences) this craft thrived in Europe precisely in the wake of Muslim decline. The decline of the art of inlaying in the Muslim world, Christie points out, occurred precisely at the end of the 14th century, following Timur Lang's invasion and devastation of Syria, most particularly.[555] But whilst it was declining in the East, the art was receiving increased attention in Europe, where it was destined to enjoy 'a brilliant rebirth.'[556] Eastern products became popular in the extravagant pageantry of the petty Italian princes whose workmen adopted them as models and began to emulate their triumphs.[557] In the mid 16th century, the artist and art historian Giorgio Vasari attributed improvements in Italian metalwork to Islamic

---

[547] A.H. Christie: Islamic Minor Arts and their Influence Upon European Work; in T. Arnold. A Guillaume ed., *The Legacy of Islam,* (Oxford; 1931); pp. 108-50; p. 117.

[548] Ibid; p; 118.

[549] G. D'Ohsson: *Histoire des Mongols*; op cit; pp. 371-4.

[550] R. E. Mack: *Bazaar to Piazza*; *Islamic Trade and Italian Arts, 1300-1600*; (University of California Press; Berkeley; 2002); p. 139.

[551] A.H. Christie: Islamic Minor Arts; op cit; p. 120.

[552] D. Storm Rice: Arabic inscriptions on a brass basin made for Hugh IV of Lusignan; in *Studi orientalistici in onore of Giorgio Levi Della Vida*; (Rome; 1956); 2. 390-402. E. Mack: *Bazaar to Piazza*; p. 213; note 3.

[553] E. Mack: *Bazaar to Piazza*; p. 213; note 3.

[554] R. Ettinghausen: Muslim Decorative arts; op cit; p. 16.

[555] A.H. Christie: Islamic Minor Arts; op cit; p. 120.

[556] Ibid.

[557] Ibid; p. 121.

brassware imported from the eastern Mediterranean.[558] In Venice Muslim metal work inspired native craftsmen so much that a distinct Venetian Oriental school arose in which Muslim designs and techniques were adapted to Italian Renaissance taste.[559] The Italians often copied the technique on objects of the same general shape, but added more Western arabesques and linear patterns.[560]

A number of industrial products will be object of attention in the chapters on sciences, but it is worth pointing here how the scientific advance, in chemistry, for instance, stimulated the rise of many industries. Muslim chemical technology of the mediaeval period was 'multifaceted as would be expected in high water period of a civilization,' Levey remarks.[561] Texts involving chemistry have been found which are devoted to perfumery, minting, bookbinding, military techniques, glass and faience, metallurgy, mineralogy, agriculture, and the preparation of drugs.[562] Chemical research and laboratory works stimulated industrial outlets such as cosmetics, soaps, tinctures and their applications in tanning and textiles, distillation of plants, of flowers, the making of perfumes; therapeutic and pharmacy.[563]

The Muslim chemist, Jabir Ibn Hayyan (722-815), was the first to use a laboratory and to make experiment.[564] This allowed him to make discoveries which were applied to industry. Saltpetre, or nitrate of potash, was known to Jabir, and he is the first writer who gives accounts of this salt.[565] This salt was known long before Europeans were acquainted with it, a knowledge, which Thomson explains, was probably one major cause of the superiority of Muslims over Europeans in chemical knowledge; for it enabled them to acquire *nitric acid,* by means of which they dissolved all the metals known in their time, and thus acquired a knowledge of various important saline compounds, which were of considerable importance.[566] Jabir also mentions antimony by name. When speaking of the reduction of metals after heating them with sulphur, he notes, 'the reduction of tin is converted into clear antimony; but of lead, into a dark-coloured antimony, as we have found by proper experience.'[567] In another passage he remarks how antimony 'is calcined, dissolved, clarified, congealed, and ground to powder, so it is prepared.'[568] Jabir also describes processes for the preparation of steel, the

---

[558] R.E. Mack: *Bazaar to Piazza*; op cit; p. 139.
[559] A.H. Christie: Islamic Minor Arts; op cit; p. 121.
[560] R. Ettinghausen: Muslim Decorative arts; op cit; p. 16.
[561] M. Levey: Chemical Technology in early Muslim Times; in *Scientia*; 96 (1961); pp. 326-30; at p. 326.
[562] Ibid.
[563] J. Mathe: *The Civilisation of Islam*, tr. by David Macrae (Crescent Books, New York); A. Djebbar: *Une Histoire*; op cit; p. 334.
[564] E.J. Holmyard: Jabir Ibn Hayyan; in *Proceedings of the Royal Society of Medicine*; vol 16 (1923), pp. 46-57.
[565] T. Thomson: *The History of Chemistry*; H. Colburn and R. Bentley; London; 1830; p. 124.
[566] Ibid.
[567] *Sum of Perfection* (Translated into Latin as *Summa Perfectionis*), book ii. part iii. chap. 10.
[568] T. Thomson: *The History of Chemistry*; op cit; p. 131.

refinement of metals, and also for dyeing, making varnishes to waterproof cloth, preparing hair-dyes, and various other procedures.[569]
Multhauf gives a good account on chemical industries, including the production of heavy chemicals and synthetic substances.[570] Singer has also looked at the early association of chemistry and industry.[571] A Mediterranean based industry of the Middle Ages was the production of alkali, which was essential for glass production.[572] Natron was an impure soda (sodium carbonate), but the ashes of sea or shore vegetation yielded a purer form of soda, called by the Arabs *kali* (hence alkali), and those of inland plants yielded potash (potassium carbonate), both of which were produced in various places.[573] Another early industry was that of oil, the word naphtha, it must be noted, derives from the Arabic *naft*. Under state monopoly, it served many purposes, domestic and non domestic: lighting, energy, sealing vessels and constructions, as a cure for particular diseases, and other usages.[574] Naphtha was also used for military purposes.

The richness of Muslim manufactured products is highlighted by their place in exports to Western Christendom.[575] Northern literature and documents are full of references to Muslim textiles, leather, paper, and other imports.[576] Muslim leather wares, for instance, were highly prized, Cordova' products famed as far as Wales, and leather's wide use in the manufacture of shoes is linguistically demonstrated in the French word 'cordonnier' (shoe maker) and the English equivalent, cordwainer.[577] Muslim glass, and also ceramics, as noted above, were highly prized, and even lower quality Muslim products were highly esteemed elsewhere and served as decorative objects on the most sacred sites such as in churches. In all, something over 1,700 *bacini,* from ceramics originating in Egypt, North Africa, Sicily, Spain (and also Italy and Byzantium) have been counted in northern Italian buildings.[578] In Pisa, in particular, both ceramic and architectural style help put a date on individual *bacini,* and scholarly research relating to these imported items has yielded valuable information on the movement of ceramics between Italy and other regions of the Mediterranean.[579]

---

[569] E.J. Holmyard: *Makers of Chemistry* (Oxford at the Clarendon Press, 1931); p. 59 ff.
[570] R.P. Multhauf: *The Origins of Chemistry* (Gordon and Breach Science Publishers; London, 1993) pp. 160-3.
[571] C. Singer: *The Earliest Chemical Industry* (The Folio Society; London; 1958).
[572] R.P. Multhauf: *The Origins of Chemistry*; op cit; p. 345.
[573] Ibid.
[574] A. Djebbar: *Une Histoire*; op cit.
[575] See for instance: W. Heyd: *Histoire du commerce;* op cit. M.A. *Cook: Studies on the Economic History of the Middle East* (Oxford; 1970). C. Cahen: Commercial relations between the near east and Western Europe from the VIIth to the XIth Century; in: *Islam and the Medieval West*: K.I. Semaan; ed. (State University of New York, Albany; 1980), pp. 1-25. S. D. Goitein: *A Mediterranean Society*, op cit; I; 1967.
[576] O.R. Constable: *Trade and Traders;* (Cambridge University Press; 1994); p. 47.
[577] Ibid; p. 144.
[578] Ibid; p. 191.
[579] In Pisa, 87 buildings and building complexes are known to have been decorated with *bacini.* See H. Blake, "The Bacini of North Italy," *La Ceramique Medievale en Mediterranee Orientale,* p. 93 (and other articles on *bacini* in the same collection). G. Herd and L. Tongiorgi have produced the most extensive studies of these dishes in *I bacini ceramici medievali delle chiese di Pisa,* (Rome, 1981), as well as in their numerous shorter monographs and articles

Artz lists an array of products, which Europe, Asia and Africa imported in great abundance from the Islamic world. These include carved ivories, enamelled glassware, tooled leatherwork of all sorts, tiles, pottery, paper, carpets, illuminated manuscripts, metalwork including damascened swords and vessels, fine cotton cloth, and rich silk fabrics. Today the Islamic sections of 'our museums,' Artz holds, still 'cherish these matchless objects of expert and exquisite craftsmanship.'[580] Durant also notes that Europe imported all its wares and textiles from the Muslim world, or from China, via the Muslim world, the soaps, like the swords of Syria, in particular, being then of great renown.[581] Amongst other Syrian exports were cotton, spices, salt, cereals, pottery, and glass.[582] Metal utensils were also vastly traded, Wiet et al pointing out to the Muslim superiority over their neighbours in this and other industrial crafts.[583]

There is little interest in dwelling on the quantitative side of these and other Muslim exports. It is preferable to examine the foundations of Muslim trade, its organisation and finance, and again, how it impacted on the Christian West precisely in the same manner as industry did.[584]

3. Islamic Fundamentals of Trade and Finance

It is generally claimed that modern banking and commercial techniques owe to the skills and inventiveness of the medieval Italian republics: Venice, above all, but also Genoa, Pisa, Florence, and Amalfi. The Western (Italian) origins of such inventiveness and techniques is summed up by one of the leading Western 'scholars', Chaunu, who tells us:

> The Bill of Exchange was in use between Athens and Pontus, according to the irrefutable evidence in Isocrates' Trapeziticus, but it was lost and forgotten.... Therefore the effective development of commerce really began around 1000, on the eve of three centuries of demographic expansion, which was to encourage intelligence, wealth and durability. The main trade route was between the western end of the Mediterranean and the eastern end, where the Byzantine Empire was populous and therefore wealthy, and the first to resume the techniques and thinking of antiquity.
>
> Eleventh century Italy established the most rudimentary tools of commercial capitalism. Apart from the age-old systems of a loan against security and an exchange of money, we find evidence of the existence of a

---

[580] F.B. Artz: *The Mind of the Middle Ages*; 3rd ed (The University of Chicago Press, 1980), p. 175.
[581] W. Durant: *The Age of Faith*, op cit; p. 276.
[582] A.M. Edde: Alep; in *Grandes Villes Mediterraneenes du Monde Musulman Medieval;* J.C. Garcin editor (Ecole Francaise de Rome; 2000), pp. 157-75; at p. 171.
[583] G. Wiet et al: *History;* op cit; p. 320.
[584] On the Muslim impact on the West, see this author's *The Hidden Debt to Islamic Civilisation;* op cit.

> commercial company in Venice in a text dated 976, and numerous company contracts have been preserved dating from the eleventh century on. For large scale commercial ventures there was the maritime or high risk loan which put the risk onto the money lender. The first colleganza contract appeared in Venice in 1072-3, and in Genoa in the twelfth century, under the Latin name of societas maris, or maritime company. These developments were responsible for the enormous change in commercial methods in the twelfth and early thirteenth centuries. They made possible logistic support for the crusades, which were a sign of the health of Latin Christendom and of her aspirations.
>
> Early rules of partnership were set up, particularly that of salva eunte navi, which put the risk onto the capitalist money lender. The salva eunte navi regulated the un-formalised kind of insurance which is implicit in partnership and the dividing up of risks.[585]

And:

> During the thirteenth century in Italy and Catalonia, cautious instruments of credit were gradually established around the oldest deposit and credit banks. The most important of such instruments was payment 'in writing,' which means by transfers.[586]

And:

> The bill of exchange was the best instrument of credit. It was developed outside the deposit bank by an elite group, the great merchant bankers or merchant exchange brokers who had secure international connections across the fairs of Europe.[587]

Of course Chaunu makes assertions without giving us a single piece of evidence. He certainly relies on his immense reputation of 'great scholar' to do away with such frivolities. The general editor of the English version of Chaunu's work does, indeed, remind us on the very first page of 'Professeur Chaunu's great academic accomplishments.'[588] This is a ridiculous assertion, which fails to convince this author. Indeed, first and foremost to assert that the crusades were a sign of the health of Latin Christendom and her aspirations, as Chaunu does, is repellent, for how can the mass slaughter and rape of Muslims, eating their flesh, and burning of Jews in their homes and synagogues which resulted from this episode be a sign of health? One assumes this is a sign of barbaric depravity, instead. With regard to the matter under discussion here, on the development of commercial methods and new banking techniques, the first criticism of Chaunu's assertion just as with similar ones is that there is no such a thing as techniques or learning disappearing for centuries suddenly to re-appear, fresh, just as centuries before,

---

585 P. Chaunu: *European Expansion in the Later Middle Ages;* tr., by K. Bertram (North Holland Publishing Company; Amsterdam; 1979), pp. 260-1.

586 Ibid; p. 266.

587 Ibid; p. 267.

588 Ibid; General Editor's note.

as he tells us with regard to the Bill of Exchange. This is an idiotic concept of aspects of sciences and civilisation disappearing, and then ten centuries later being recovered by chance. This, unfortunately, is not unique to Chaunu, but is shared by most Western 'historians,' who each in his or her field, use it to justify the sudden appearances of signs of civilisation and sciences in the 12th century, most particularly. By doing this, they do away with the Muslim source of such changes, asserting, instead, that such aspects of civilisation and sciences, hundreds of them, belonged to Greece and Rome initially, had disappeared for over ten centuries, and then were suddenly recovered in the 12th century by Western genius. This work will show countless instances of this sudden recovery after ten or so centuries of loss.

With regard to the specific matter of the Bill of Exchange, debated here, historical evidence shows that contrary to what Chaunu claims, methods and instruments of credit, and all forms of trade associations were known already to the Muslims centuries before the Christian West, and were not invented in Europe.[589] Briefly, here, the second caliph, Umar Ibn al-Khattab (Caliph 634-644), paid for the grains delivered to the state warehouses by cheque.[590] The contemporary use of such cheques in private business dealings appears to have been quite substantial, as taxes to the government were also commonly paid in that manner.[591] With regard to business associations, Goitein, for instance, equates the Muslim *qirad/mudarabah* with the Western *commenda* because this medieval form of business cooperation in Europe was essentially the same as its Muslim counterpart. [592] Likewise, the medieval Italian term *maone* - describing a particular form of corporate association designed to pool risk- derives from the Arabic term *ma'unah,* which means joint efforts to underwrite commercial transportation expenses.[593] More evidence will be provided further on to prove the Muslim pioneering role, and how Islam impacted on the West with regard to every single business practice.

Chaunu is also mistaken when he tells us that commerce developed 'in the year 1000, and that the main commercial route was between both ends of the Mediterranean.' This statement is yet one more proof of how wild assertions are made without any effort to check their veracity. Commerce did not develop in the year 1000, but many centuries earlier. Commercial routes between both ends of

---

[589] A. Udovitch: At the origins of the Western Commenda, in *Speculum* 37 (1962); pp. 198-207. F. Braudel: *Grammaire des Civilisations* (Flammarion, 1987), p. 96. Gene W. Heck: *Charlemagne, Muhammad, and the Arab Roots of Capitalism*; (Walter de Gruyter; Berlin; New York; 2006); p. 110 ff.

[590] Ibn Abd al-Hakam: *Futuh Misr wa Akhbaruha*; (New Haven; 1922), p. 166; see also A.A. al-Duri 1974, p. 170, citing al-Ya'qubi; V. Fisk: *Bankakten aus dem Faijum*; (Goterberg; 1931), pp. 10 ff. Gene. W. Heck: *Charlemagne*; p. 110.

[591] Ibn Abd al-Hakam: *Futuh*; (1961), p. 244. Gene. W. Heck: *Charlemagne*; p. 110.

[592] S.D. Goitein: *Jews and Arabs: Their Contacts through the Ages*; (New York; 1964), p.310; idem. 1967, p.59; M. A. Cook: Commerce; 1974, p. 128.

[593] R. Dozy: R. Dozy: *Supplements aux Dictionaires Arabes*; (Leiden; 1881), p. 82; A. Lieber: Eastern Business practices and Medieval European Commerce; *Economic History Review*; 2nd series; vol 21; 1968; pp. 230, 241; S. Labib: Capitalism in Medieval Islam; *Journal of Economic History*; vol 29; no1; 1969, p. 94; A. Udovitch: A Tale of two Cities; in *The Medieval City*; ed H. Miskimin; D. Herlihy and A Udovitch; (London and New Haven; 1977), p. 149; Geniza document, Taylor Schechter Collection, University Library, Cambridge, no. "TS 10 J, 16, f.17."

the Mediterranean also date from centuries earlier, and were stimulated by both Byzantine and Muslim shipping and commerce above all.
Chaunu and his many followers also fail to acknowledge that the foundations of modern trade were laid in the Islamic world over the period under examination here (7th-13th centuries). Muslim commercial and financial techniques found their way to the Italian cities because it was precisely Italian cities which traded with Muslims.
The following outline will highlight the pioneering role of Islam in establishing the fundamentals of trade and modern finance, centuries before the Italians. It will also demonstrate that these developments were fundamentally Islamic because they had their source in Islam, the faith. Then, albeit briefly, some forms and ways of impact upon the Christian West are looked at.

a. The Islamic Pioneering Role

Relying on a diversity of sources Cahen outlines some of the intricate links that exist between Islam and trade:

> Let us first rid ourselves of an idea that Pirenne himself seem to have had, namely, that Arabs and Islam are marked by a kind of native impotence in economics and trade.[594] No matter what modern developments have been, the Arabs, as far back as pre-Islamic times, organised trade caravans which were at least inter-regional, reaching as far as Syria.[595] Through the Yemen, they were in contact with the Indian Ocean's traffic. Islam was born in a mercantile milieu. Muhammad was a merchant and was not troubled by it. Several of his companions were merchants, and if evidently certain practices of the surrounding states were unknown to them, the reverse was perhaps also true.[596] In any case there was no question of a basic Muslim incapacity to trade.[597]

Trading first and foremost finds a good place in the Islamic religious text and in the sayings of the Prophet (or Tradition). The Qur'an looks with favour upon commercial activity, restricting itself to condemning fraudulent practices and only calling for the abstention from trading during certain religious festivals.[598] The Qur'an does not merely say that one must not forget one's portion of this world (28: 77), it also says that it is proper to combine the practice of religion and material life,

---

[594] Since it would be impossible to list here a bibliography of this immense subject, Cahen points out, he judiciously recommends M. Rodinson: *Islam and Capitalism* (Paris, 1966).
[595] See A. Udovitch: At the origins of the Western Commenda, in *Speculum* 37 (1962); pp. 198-207.
[596] Synthese in A. R. Lewis: *Naval Power and Trade in the Mediterranean, 500-1100* (Princeton University Press; 1951).
[597] C. Cahen: Commercial relations; op cit; at p. 3.
[598] See W. Heffening: Tidjara; in *Encyclopaedia of Islam;* 1st ed; vol 4 (Leiden; 1934), p. 747. See. M. Rodinson: *Islam and Capitalism*; op cit; p. 14.

carrying on trade even during pilgrimage, and goes as far as to mention commercial profit under the name of 'God's bounty' (62: 9-10).[599] In another verse, it says:

> 'Your Lord is He Who makes the ships to sail smoothly for you through the sea, in order that you may seek of His bounty.' (17/ 66)

Equally, the Prophet, himself a trader, just like most of his companions, said:

> 'The merchant who is sincere and trustworthy will (at the Judgment Day) be amongst the prophets, the just and the martyrs; or 'the trustworthy merchant will sit in the shade of God's throne on the Day of Judgment.'[600]

The Prophet commends the merchants to his successors, for

> 'They are the couriers of the world and the trusty servants of God upon earth.'[601]

Consequently, Arnold points out, trade has never implied any disparagement in Muslim eye.[602] Caliph 'Umar said:

> 'There is no place where I would be more gladly overtaken by death than in the market-place, buying and selling for my family.'[603]

The practice of the faith, as this work will amply show, was directly responsible for the upsurge of many sciences and changes including trade. Pilgrimage to Makkah, for instance, just as it stimulated the rise of Muslim sciences such as geography, seafaring, and astronomy, stimulated the growth of trade. Many of the pilgrims fulfilled their religious obligations and at the same time marketed their local products along the route, returning home with foreign goods on which they hoped to make a handsome profit.[604] Here, also as Lieber notes, was a unique opportunity for merchants from far-distant lands to meet and exchange information.[605] It not infrequently happened that a merchant, tempted by the description of some place hitherto unknown to him, continued on his journey after the pilgrimage was over; sometimes even settling down in the new country.[606] From there he would write to members of his family, or to business friends, requesting them to supply him with merchandise for which he had found a market; or he might ship home such goods as he felt could be sold there at a profit.[607]

Where Islam, as with any other aspect of civilisation, interferes is by bringing in a spiritual and ethical dimension to commercial exchange. It is in this spirit that Al-

---

[599] M. Hamidullah in *Cahiers de l'ISEA*; Supplement No 120; Series V; No 3; (December 1961); pp. 26 and fl.

[600] See Wensick: A Handbook of Early Muhammadan Tradition (Leiden; Brill; 1927), in M. Rodinson: *Islam and Capitalism*; op cit; p. 16.

[601] *Kanz al- Ummal* (Haydarabad, AH. 1312-15), ii, No. 4112.

[602] T.W. Arnold: Arab Travellers and Merchants; AD 1000-1500; in A.P. Newton: *Travel and Travellers of the Middle Ages*; (Kegan Paul; London; 1926); pp. 88-103; at p. 93.

[603] Al-Ghazali: *Ihya al-Ulum* (Cairo, AH. 1289), ii, p. 53.

[604] A. Lieber: Eastern Business Practices and Medieval European Commerce, *Economic History Review;* 2nd ser., vol 21; no 2; 1968; pp. 230-43; at p. 230.

[605] Ibid.

[606] A typical example is provided by the career of Abu Muhammad b. Mu'awiya al Marwani, Mus'ab al Zubayri, *Kitab Nasab Quraysh,* ed. E. Levi-Provencal, (Cairo, 1953); E. Levi-Provencal, 'Le Kitab Nasab Quraysh de Mus'ab al Zubayri', *Arabica,* I, (1954), 92-5.

[607] A. Lieber: Eastern Business; op cit; p. 231.

Ghazali, who flourished towards the end of the 11th century, drew a picture of the ideal merchant:
'He must begin his business with a pure intention, be content with gains that can be got by lawful methods, and spend these gains on his family and pious purposes; justice and benevolence are to be the guiding principles of his commercial activity, and in the market he must promote righteousness and check iniquity. He must not come into the market full of greed, and should leave it when he has gained sufficient profit for his wants. He must not neglect the market of the next world, i.e. the mosque, for the market of this life, and in all his actions he must observe the prescriptions of the religious law, remembering that he has to give account of his doings in the Day of Judgment.'[608]

> Into all the details of this picture [says Arnold] it is impossible to enter here, but it is of significance as having been drawn by one of the greatest theologians that the Muslim world has produced and as implying the expectation that the trader would serve as an exemplar of the devout life, and would be a model of righteousness for others to follow.[609]

The earliest known Muslim work on economic ethics consists very largely of a collection of sayings attributed to the Prophet and the early heroes of Islam entitled *Kitab al-Kasab* 'On Earning,' written by a Syrian called al-Shaybani, who died in 804.[610] Al-Shaybani's aim is to show that earning a livelihood is not merely permitted, but is incumbent on Muslims. Man's primary duty is to serve God. A person can only do so if they were properly fed and clothed. This, in turn, can only be reached through productive earning.[611] Another point made by al-Shaybani is that money earned by commerce and industry is more pleasing to God's eyes than money received from the government for civil or military service.[612] The same point is argued by Al-Jahiz (d.869) in an essay entitled *Fi Madh al-Tujar wa Dhamn Ahl al-Sultan* (In Praise of Merchants and in Condemnation of Officials.)[613] Al-Jahiz insists on the security, dignity and independence of merchants in contrast with the uncertainty, humiliation and sycophancy of those who serve the ruler; Al-Jahiz defending the piety and the learning of merchants against their detractors.[614]

The importance of trading amongst Muslims is quite obvious in the early global nature (as far as the world was known then) of Muslim presence in, and

---

608 Al-Ghazali: *Ihya;* op cit; ii; pp. 73-5.
609 T.W. Arnold: Arab Travellers and Merchants; AD 1000-1500; in A.P. Newton: *Travel and Travellers of the Middle Ages*; (Kegan Paul; London; 1926); pp. 88-103; at p. 94.
610 The original work is lost, but it survives in fragments in the author's pupil: Ibn Sama'ah (d. 847) entitled *Al-Iktisab fi'l Rizk al-Muktasab* (Cairo, 1938).
611 In G. Heck: *Charlemagne*; op cit; p. 297.
612 Ibid.
613 See partial translation by O. Rescher: *Excerpte und Ubersetzungen aus den Schriften... Gahiz*, (Stuttgart; 1931), pp. 186-8.
614 Al-Jahiz: *Majmu'at Rasail al-Jahiz*; (Cairo; 1906); p. 155.

exchanges with, foreign markets. Muslim commerce dominated the Mediterranean till the loss of Sicily (1061-1091) and the Crusades (1095-1291), plying between Syria and Egypt at one end, Tunis, Sicily, Morocco, and Spain at the other, and touching Greece, Italy, and Gaul.[615] It captured control of the Red Sea from Ethiopia, reached over the Caspian into Mongolia, and up the Volga from Astrakhan to Novgorod, Finland, Scandinavia, and Germany, where it left thousands of Muslim coins.[616] Muslim shipping was also prominent throughout the Indian Ocean, and as early as 750, and very certainly earlier, there were many exchanges with China as reported by countless sources, especially Chinese.[617] The Muslim merchants' reach was remarkable when one considers the shipping and navigational conditions of the time.[618] The Spanish Muslim, Abu Bakr Al-Marwani (d. 968), for instance, reached the markets of Iraq and India where he amassed 30,000 dinars through trade before losing everything in a shipwreck on the way home to Al-Andalus.[619] After 1100, Indian cotton goods and Chinese porcelain were reaching very remote Indonesian islands (whose main exports were spices) and distant African ports (whence came ivory and gold.)[620] Then, only the Muslim Arabs and Muslim South Asians who led the commerce with China had such a background, and their efforts enabled them to extend their enterprises into the Malay Archipelago.[621] Eventually, the Muslims stimulated Chinese merchants themselves to develop better ocean-going shipping to trade in the region as well.[622] Such achievements testify to the way 'commercial vigour could fashion and enhance civilisation when trade flourished freely and attracted the active participation of local elites.'[623] Which, Abu Lughod notes, contradicts the views that Eastern cultures provided an 'inhospitable environment for merchant-accumulators and industrial developers.'[624] Which also contradicts the assertions made by Chaunu and others that trade awoke in the year 1000 under the aegis of Western Christian tradesmen.

Faith and practice in Islam being closely related, and trade being even seen as an agent to spreading the faith, it is little surprise that trading activities flourished

---

615 W. Durant: *The Age of Faith*, op cit; p. 208.
616 Ibid.
617 A. Pacey: *Technology in World Civilization, a Thousand Year History* (The MIT Press, Cambridge, 1990), p. 12.
For sources on early exchanges (7th century, even time of the Prophet) between Muslims and Chinese see: M. de Thiersant: *Le Mahometanisme en Chine*; Paris; 1878; vol 1. I. Mason: *The Arabian Prophet; A Life of Mohammed from Arabic and Chinese Sources*; which is the translation of a Chinese work by Liu Chai-Lien; Shanghai, 1921.
F.S. Drake: Mohammedanism in the Tang Dynasty; *Monumenta Serica*, Vol. 8 (1943), pp. 1-40; at pp. 23-8.
M. Bretschneider: *On the Knowledge Possessed by the Ancient Chinese of the Arabs and Arabian Colonies,* London, Trubner &co, 1871.
618 Wang Gungwu: *Transforming the Trading World of Southeast Asia*[i] accessed in 1999 at http://hometown.aol.com/wignesh/5Wanggungwu.htm.
619 O.R. Constable: *Trade and Traders*; op cit; p. 80.
620 A. Pacey: *Technology;* op cit; p. 12.
621 Wang Gungwu: *Transforming the Trading World of South-East Asia*; op cit.
622 F. Hirth and W.W. Rockhill. 1911; Ibn Batuta: *Travels in Asia and Africa, 1325-1354*. (London: Routledge and Kegan Paul (Reprint of first edition published in 1929) in Wang Gungwu: *Transforming the trading*.
623 Van Leur 1955; Hall 1985; Briggs 1951; Dumarcay 1985; Stierlin 1984; in Wang Gwugu: *Transforming*; op cit.
624 J.L. Abu-Lughod: *Before European Hegemony* (Oxford University Press, 1989), p. 364.

wherever Muslims established themselves, and wherever they could reach. In this regard, Garaudy points out how agrarian communities based on the Savannah or forest evolved in the 8th century of the Hijra (around 14th century onwards) into great empires, as a result of large scale trade in the geographical area where Islam was present, from Cadiz to China.[625] Such was the intricate relation between trade and the spread of the faith, in many parts in fact, the words for trader and Muslim were synonymous.[626] The intricate link between trade and the spread of the faith is not just obvious in Africa, where the Kingdom of Mali thrived in wealth and glory, but also elsewhere. We are informed that from the 8th to the end of the 15th century the Arabs travelled to China from the Gulf, crossing the Indian Ocean, and passing through the Malay Peninsula, coming to Canton, where they carried trade. Muslims passed through the Straits of Malacca between Sumatra and peninsular Malaysia, crossed the South China Sea, and established trading posts on the southeast coast of China, as well as en route, for example, in Sumatra and on the Malabar Coast of India.[627] In the middle of the 10th century, following the extensive trade links, an important Muslim colony grew in Canton.[628] This contributed largely to the dissemination of Islam in China, and from thence to other surrounding countries.

Further stimulus to trade by the faith, and also evidence of the intricate link between the two, is the fact that Muslims are bound to a strict code and practice of trade as summoned in the Qur'an. The summon to record commercial deals, loans, and other transactions, is clearly stated in the religious text, which goes:

> 'Be not averse to writing down (the contract) whether it be small or great, with (record) the term thereof. That is more equitable in the sight of Allah and more sure for testimony, and the best way of avoiding doubt between you... and have witnesses when ye sell one to another, and let no harm be done to scribe or witness.' (Qur'an II/ 282 ff.)

It is, thus hardly a trait of Muslims innate abilities to develop great skills in commerce, from the early stages recording companies and associations, loans, accounts, and making contracts; they simply had to abide by the directives of their faith, and after centuries they perfected the practice. The greatest contribution of the Muslim world to medieval economic life, Lieber insists, was the development of commercial methods based on writing and recording.[629] This is not just in obedience of the religious text, this was also made possible, Lieber notes, by the high degree of literacy of the Oriental merchant of that time, which, in its turn, was encouraged by the fact that relatively cheap writing materials had long been

---

[625] R. Garaudy: *Comment l'Homme Devint Humain* (Editions J.A, 1978), p. 271.

[626] J.A. Naude: *Islam in Africa*; The South African Institute of International Affairs; 1978; p. 3.

[627] For early Islamic accounts of China, see *Relations des Voyages faites par les Arabes et les Persans dans l'Inde et a la Chine*, ed., et tr. Langles et Reinaud, Paris, 1845, deux petits volumes, Imprimerie Royale.

[628] J.H. Kramers: Geography and Commerce, in *The Legacy of Islam (*edited by T. Arnold and A. Guillaume,) op cit; pp. 79-97; at p. 95.

[629] A. E. Lieber: Eastern Business Practice; op cit; at p. 231.

available in this part of the world.[630] The comparative literacy of the merchants, together with the development of a law-merchant, meant that large-scale commercial operations could now be conducted from the counting-house, whereas previously the merchant had had to be constantly on the move.[631] This change is clearly obvious from the Arabic papyri and papers and especially from the documents of the Cairo Geniza, which date from the 10th to the 13th centuries.[632] The 10th century *Responsa,* or legal opinions, of Sa'adia Gaon, the head of the Jewish Academy at Sura, in Iraq, show how widespread and generally accepted the habit of book-keeping had then become in that part of the world.[633] The fact that Sa'adia wrote his decisions in Arabic rather than Hebrew reinforces the assumption that his opinions were not based on the customs of the Jewish community alone but reflected the spirit of the commercial world of his time.[634]

Muslims also had another formidable tool, which placed them in the vanguard of other nations in regard to any development of the age: a thriving scientific output, which made it easier for them to accomplish what others could not. In this respect, the main contribution of science then was the positioning of the numerals at the beginning of the 9th century, as explained by al-Khwarizmi (780-850). His book on algebra was completed in order to meet the needs of people in solving questions 'Of inheritance, wills, purchase and sales agreements, in surveying, in the cleaning and digging of rivers and canals, in measuring goods and in technical matters.'[635] In discussing the development of accounting methods, Labib notes that after a sale the merchant would enter the profit or the loss in his ledger in such a way as to present the current situation. 'The double entry method' was an important part of a merchant's skill.[636]

Whilst the Muslims had the technical means to perform calculations, which were fundamental to trading operations, Western Christians did not, and so it is quite imbecilic indeed for anyone to claim that Westerners were ahead of Muslims, or that they used these methods of calculation when the numerals only came to use in Europe for such purposes in the early 13th century. This happened courtesy of Leonardo Fibonacci, who was sent to North Africa by his father (a Pisan consul) for the specific purpose to learn such methods, which, he, just as other contemporaries, deemed superior, in fact, vital, for the development of Italian/European commerce.[637] This is all the more the fact when we know that Fibonacci's work, *Liber Abacci* (dated 1202), the most influential early work of

---

[630] Ibid; pp. 231-2.
[631] Ibid; p. 232.
[632] Ibid.
[633] Ibid.
[634] Ibid.
[635] See F. Rosen, ed., *The Algebra of Mohammed ben Musa (al-Khwarizmi)* (London: Oriental Translation Fund, 1831, Reprint: Hildesheim, Olms, 1986).
[636] S. Labib: Capitalism in Medieval Islam; *Journal of Economic History*; vol 29; No1; (1969); p. 92; J. Goody: *The East in the West*, (Cambridge University Press; 1996); p. 67.
[637] W. Montgomery Watt: *The Influence*; op cit; pp. 63-4.
F. Cajori: *A History of Mathematics*; (Chelsea Publishing Company; New York; 1893).

Western mathematics, adopted al-Khwarizmi's methodology and followed his purpose of serving commercial enterprise.[638]

Long before the West, Udovitch explains, Muslim merchants had at their disposal accepted legal mechanisms for extending credit and for transferring and exchanging currencies over long distances.[639] Among the financial tools at their disposal, Gene Heck cites the 'Bank Draft or Letter of Credit *(Suftajah)*, Bond *(Khatt)*; Credit Transfer *(Hawala)*; Bank Deposit; promissory note as well as varying forms of bank cheques (*Khatt/Tawqi/Saqq*).[640]
The first of these, the *suftajah*, or letter of credit, Udovitch explains, allowed a merchant to advance or transfer a sum of money to a business associate at some distant place with 'the full confidence that the transfer would be expeditiously accomplished.'[641] By the 10th century, already, it was customary to pay debts not in cash only, but to settle them by means of letters of credit.[642] There are countless accounts collected from the papyri by Becker to highlight the widespread use of such forms of payment.[643] The "letter of credit" *(suftajah)* was a financial instrument commonly utilised not only in conventional private trade operations but also for transferring public sector funds.[644] The sources suggest that because of such flexibility, they were extensively employed.[645] They could be issued in Makkah or Madinah, for example, and then cashed in a distant city such as Basrah or Kufah - and because they were certified, and deemed valid only when formally signed and stamped by the issuing party, they were readily negotiable credit instruments that could be transacted in remote locations.[646] In 314 H/926, for instance, the Abbasid provincial government of Egypt reportedly sent emissaries to Baghdad remitting tax revenues in the form of three letters of credit *(safatij)* totalling 147,000, 80,000, and 400,000 *dinars* respectively. [647] Sources likewise indicate that the subsequent Ikhshidid administration of Egypt also forwarded its tax proceeds to Baghdad in this manner.[648] Medieval Muslim merchants appear to have used the *safatij* not only as letters of credit, but also as a highly utilitarian expense credit convenience in much the same way that traveller checks are now used.[649] We hear of a man on a long journey with two servants and a guide, whose only earthly riches consisted

---

[638] G. Sarton: *Introduction*; op cit; Volume III; pp. 652-3. A. Djebbar: *Une Histoire de la Science Arabe*; (Le Seuil; Paris; 2001); p. 146. See also Fibonacci's classification and list of contents.
[639] A.L. Udovitch: Trade, in the *Dictionary of the Middle Ages*; op cit; vol 12; pp. 105-8; at p. 106.
[640] G. W. Heck: *Charlemagne*, op cit; p. 109.
[641] A.L. Udovitch: Trade; op cit; p. 106.
[642] W. Fischel: The Origins of Banking in Medieval Islam: *Journal of the Royal Asiatic Society (JRAS)*; (1933); pp. 339-52; and pp. 569-91, p. 574.
[643] H.C. Becker: *Papyri Schott-Reinhard*,(Heidelberg; 1906), vol 1; p. 11.
[644] G.W. Heck: *Charlemagne*; op cit; p. 111.
[645] Ibid.
[646] Al-Sarakhsi: *Kitab al-Mabsut*; (Cairo; 1906; Beirut; 1986); vol 14; p. 37; G. W. Heck: *Charlemagne*; p. 111.
[647] G.W. Heck: *Charlemagne*; p. 111.
[648] A. Lieber: Eastern Business; op cit; p. 234. G.W. Heck: *Charlemagne*; op cit; p. 112.
[649] Al-Duri: *Tarikh al-Iraq al-Iqtisadi*; (Beirut; 1974); p. 169; in G.W. Heck: *Charlemagne*; p. 111.

of two letters of credit consisting of 5,000 Dinars.[650] Indications are that they were equally useful "public sector" tools of financial diplomacy. Money presents were bought from the Ahwaz province for the Caliph's mother in the form of a bill for the amount of 3,000 Dinars.[651] Some 10th-11th century letters of credit were for the huge sum of 40,000 Dinars in the Saharan oasis of Sijilmasa, and many examples of such letters, found at Cairo Genizah,[652] confirm that these instruments of credit were always scrupulously and strictly honoured;[653] just as stipulated in the religious text.[654]

The cheque, in Arabic *Saqq (Sakk)*, as Udovitch explains, is 'functionally and etymologically the origin of our modern cheques.'[655] The use of Saqq was born out of the need to avoid having to transport coin as legal tender due to the dangers and difficulties this represented; the bankers took to the use of bills of exchange, letters of credit, and promissory notes, often drawn up so as to be, in effect, cheques.[656] Cheque payments were made in the very early stages of the Islamic state. Ibn Abd al-Hakam indicates, for instance, that the second caliph, 'Umar Ibn al-Khattab, paid for the grains delivered to state warehouses by cheque.[657] He also states that this ruler would pay governmental wages by cheque prepared by his treasurer, Zayd b. Thabit, which were written on papyrus and certified on their reverse sides by seal, and that this practice was perpetuated into the Umayyad era (661-750).[658] Indeed, the contemporary use of such cheques in private business dealings appears to have been quite substantial, and taxes to the government were also commonly paid in that manner.[659] For any such personal cheque to be valid, it had to be cosigned by at least two witnesses.[660] By the 8th-9th centuries, it seems, cheques had become a common feature of everyday economic life as the bankers would reportedly cash cheques for a fee that could range to as high as ten percent or more.[661] The widespread use of cheques is noted by Nasir-i Khusraw in Aswan in southern Egypt, who further relates that by the middle of the 10th century, most business transactions in Basrah (Basra) were then being carried out by cheque.[662]

---

650 Tanukhi: *Faraj ba'd ash Shidda*; i. pp. 104-5; in W. Fischel: The Origins; p. 575.

651 Tanukhi*: Faraj;* p. 105; in W. Fischel; The Origins; p. 575.

652 See S.D. Goitein: *A Mediterranean Society*; op cit.

653 A.L. Udovitch: Trade; op cit; p. 106.

654 Qur'an: ii.282; iv.33.

655 A. Udovitch: Trade; op cit; p. 106. See also A. Udovitch: *Bankers Without Banks; The Dawn of Modern Banking* (N. Haven; Yale University Press; 1979).

656 L. Massignon in G. Wiet et al: *History*; op cit. at p. 336.

657 Ibn Abd al-Hakam: Futuh; 1922, p. 166; see also A.A. al-Duri: *Tarikh;* 1974, p. 170, citing al-Ya'qubi; V. Fisk: *Bankakten aus dem Faijum*; (Goterberg; 1931), pp. 10 ff. G.W. Heck: *Charlemagne*; p. 110.

658 Ibn Abd al-Hakam 1922, p. 223; G.W. Heck: *Charlemagne,* p. 110.

659 Ibn Abd al-Hakam 1961, p. 244. G.W. Heck: *Charlemagne*; p. 110.

660 Ibn Kathir: *Al-Bidayah wal Nihayah*; (Cairo; 1932; Riyadh; 1966); vol 8; p. 87. G.W. Heck: *Charlemagne*; p. 110.

661 W. Fischel: *Jews in the Economic and Political Life of Medieval Islam*; (London; 1968); p. 21; A. Lieber: Eastern Business; op cit; p. 233.

662 Nasir Khusraw: *Safer Nameh*; ed. C. Schafer; (Paris; 1881); ed., Al-Kashshab; (Cairo; 1945; 1881); p. 64. G.W. Heck: *Charlemagne*; p. 110.

The use of these financial instruments was supported by a widespread network of "money-changers" *(sarraf/sayarifah)* located in the major urban areas who, over time, came to constitute a banking industry.[663] According to Nasir-i Khusraw, in the year 444 H/1052, there were over 200 banks then engaged in both underwriting commercial activities and trading in precious metals bullion in Isfahan alone.[664] Al-Awn Street, in the center of Baghdad appears to have become the "Wall Street of the Middle Ages," with many banking agencies and money-changers located on its premises.[665] These moneychangers would often finance trade transactions using their personal capital resources, and would concurrently take bank deposits, make short-term loans, and issue letters of credit to underwrite other key commercial activities.[666] The bankers benefited from this service, evidence showing the reception of a commission for cashing a *sakk;*[667] the commission rate seeming to be of one dirhem for every dinar.[668] The effective transactional range of such financial instruments also appears to have been impressive. The 10th century geographer, Ibn Hawqal, claims to have witnessed first-hand merchandise sales in North Africa that were paid for by cheques drawn upon a Sijilmasah banking house.[669] At the city of Basrah, by the mid-11th century, anybody could deposit their assets with a changer or banker who handed over a receipt.[670] Any subsequent purchase was then made by means of a draft on the banker, who honoured it when presented by the vendor. Such drafts on bankers were the merchants' exclusive currency.[671] Such methods simplified the manifold mercantile relations, and were fundamental to the rapid and safe settlement of business transactions.[672] That was, Massignon points out, about five centuries before a banking system of worth appeared in Western Christendom.[673]

The development of formal state banking was early, and institutionally went back to the time of Harun al-Rashid (r. 786-809). To administer the financial functions, and to collect sundry *ad valorem* taxes that were levied on the bankers' assets *(mal al-jahbadhah)* as well as to provide oversight of all private banking activities in general, the Abbasid government created a state central banking agency known as *diwan al-jahbadhah.*[674] Indeed, as a result of the vigorous trade expansion that followed the rise of Islam, banks rapidly proliferated throughout its land in a variety of corporate forms.[675] The main role was played by Jewish bankers who,

---

663 G.W. Heck: *Charlemagne*; op cit; p. 112.
664 Nasir I. Khusraw; (1881); p. 253. G.W. Heck: *Charlemagne*; p. 113.
665 Al-Muqaddasi; 1906; p. 183; G.W. Heck: *Charlemagne*; p. 113.
666 Al-Isfahani: *Kitab al-Aghani;* (Cairo; 1868); 1927-1974; vol 11; p. 193. G.W. Heck: *Charlemagne*; p. 112.
667 W. Fischel: The Origins of Banking in Medieval Islam; op cit; p. 578.
668 Ibid; note 4; p. 578.
669 In G.W. Heck: *Charlemagne*; p. 110.
670 G. Wiet et al: *History*; op cit; at p.336.
671 Ibid.
672 W. Fischel: The Origins of Banking in Medieval Islam; op cit; p. 575.
673 L. Massignon: l'Influence de l'Islam; op cit; p. 4.
674 Al-Jahshiyari: *Kitab al-Wuzara wa'l Kutab;* (Leipzig; 1926); pp. 158; 224; 226; 255; G.W. Heck: *Charlemagne*; p. 113.
675 G.W. Heck: *Charlemagne*; op cit; p. 113.

in the entourage of both caliph and ministers in Baghdad, were entrusted with the keeping of both the jewels of the crown and prisoners of the state.[676] Subsequently, under Caliph Muqtadir (r. 908-932), the State Chancellery granted the title of Court Bankers (*Jahabidhat al-Hadra*) to two or three Jewish bankers in Baghdad.[677] Basrah was also a major financial center, and because many of its bankers were Jewish, its principal banking district was known as the "Jewish *(al-Yahudiyah)* quarter."[678] Describing the contemporary financial communities of Egypt and Syria circa 375H/985, for instance, the geographer al-Muqaddasi asserts that most contemporary bankers then were Jews.[679] Two individuals in particular, Yusuf b. Finhas and Harun b. Umran, whom medieval Arabic sources refer to repeatedly as "the two Jewish bankers" *(al-jahbadhan al-yahudiyan),* now rose to great financial prominence at the court of the Abbasid caliph, al-Muqtadir.[680] In fact the development of international banking,[681] Massignon explains, has origins with that Jewish element serving the Abbasid Caliphate in the 9th century.[682]

Every economic venture requires a certain amount of risk, and the greater the lure for profit, the more the risk undertaken. The concept of risk derives from the Arabic 'Rizk' (bounty), which is even stronger than profit. In no culture would economic venture and bounty seem so closely associated than in the Islamic. In tracing the history of commerce, and wealth creation, Peter Jay seized on this particular element to highlight the decisive role of Islamic civilisation in stimulating the growth of international trade, via the techniques already described, and most of all by associating both concepts of risk taking and bounty.[683] Islam thus replaced the fulfilment of localised needs with profit through large commercial exchanges; and the search for ever higher profit demanding increased risk taking. The fundamental reason why risk of capital is a product of Islam is simple: Islam forbids the hoarding of money for the sake of lending it in return for interest on it. Thus, because interest is banned in Islam, a rich Muslim has either to invest his capital in person, or via another party.[684] This way, capital is always circulating rather than remaining static, thus maximising its uses. Besides, by forbidding interest on loans, Islam makes available, and freely, the required capital for those eager for economic venture, and for risk takers. There is no such heavy burden upon the investor of having to borrow at high interest, which cripples investment.

---

[676] Passion d'al-Hallaj; (Paris, 1922,) p. 266 in Louis Massignon: l'Influence de l'Islam au Moyen Age sur la formation de l'essor des banques Juives; *Bulletin d'Etudes Orientales* (Institut Francais de Damas; 1931), vol 1; pp. 3-12; at p. 3.
[677] H. Sabi, *Kitab al-Wuzara*, ed. Amedroz (Leyden, 1904) in Louis Massignon: l'Influence; p. 5.
[678] Miskwayh; 1920-21; pp. 247-8. G.W. Heck: *Charlemagne*; p. 113.
[679] Al-Muqaddasi; 1906; p. 183; G.W. Heck: *Charlemagne*; p. 113.
[680] Al-Jahshiyari; 1926; pp. 158-9; W. Fischel 1933; p. 349; G.W. Heck: *Charlemagne*; p. 113.
[681] See also: W. Fischel: The Origins of Banking in Medieval Islam; op cit; pp. 569-91.
[682] L. Massignon: l'Influence de l'Islam; op cit; p. 4.
[683] P. Jay: The Road to Riches; *BBC;* August; 2000.
[684] See for instance: A. Udovitch: Credit as a mean of investment in medieval Islamic trade; *Journal of Economic and Social History of the Orient* (JESHO); (1967); pp. 260-4.

Speaking of partnership, there is what is known in medieval Europe as the commenda the earlier Arabic equivalent: *qirad*.[685] This was a form of agreement by which an investor advanced capital or merchandise to an agent-manager who was to trade with it and then return to the investor the principal and a previously agreed share of the profits; keeping the other share to himself.[686] If the venture failed, the financial loss was incurred by the investor alone; the agent losing his time and effort. The commenda, thus, had the advantages of both loan and partnership.[687] As in a partnership, profits and risks were shared, and as in a loan, there was no liability for the investor beyond the sum of money handed over to the agent.[688] The last point, Udovitch points out, being especially important in view of the very strict Islamic prohibition of usury.[689]

Whilst it liberalised commerce, Islam, before any other culture, also applied regulations, and a regulatory body to check on the excesses of businessmen and men of finance. The office of The State Inspector (The Muhtasib) ensured that everything functioned within the appropriate code of conduct. Arnold explains how the duties of the Muhtasib consisted in preventing breaches of the civil and religious law, duties which extended to trade and other commercial functions (they also incidentally included the protection of captives from excessive physical burdens, and punishing careless owners of beasts of burden.)[690] The officials under the Muhtasib visited merchants and druggists so as to prevent the use of false weights and measures, or the sale of damaged food and adulterated medicines, and the overcharging and cheating of purchasers.[691] The treatise by the Egyptian Abd al-Rahman Ibn Nasr (12th century), difficult to date precisely, was composed for the use of the Muhtasib, containing most particularly information on weights and measures.[692] Its purpose was essentially to prevent frauds and regulate commercial transactions.[693] Ibn al-Ukhuwwa (d.1329), in his *Handbook for the Muhtasib,* also describes the various duties of the Muhtasib, in regulating markets, and in watching over the quality of the traded goods and their safety.[694] The Muhtasib's authority was enforced by fines and scourging, and from his decision there was no appeal.[695]

---

685 A.L. Udovitch: Trade, in *Dictionary of the Middle Ages*; op cit; p. 106.
686 Ibid.
687 Ibid.
688 Ibid.
689 Ibid.
690 T.W. Arnold: Muslim Civilisation during the Abbasid Period: in *The Cambridge Medieval History*, vol IV; edited by J. R. Tanner, C. W. Previte; Z.N. Brooke (1923), pp. 274-98, at p. 283.
691 S.P. Scott: *History;* op cit; Vol II, at p. 638.
692 G. Sarton: *Introduction to the History of Science*; 3 vols (The Carnegie Institute of Washington; 1927-48), vol 2; p. 298.
693 Ibid.
694 *Ma'alim al-qurba*, ed., and tr. R. Levy (London, 1938), pp 162-163 (tr. p.40); in G E. Von Grunebaum: *Medieval Islam* (The University of Chicago Press, 1954), at pp. 217-8 and p. 165.
695 S.P. Scott: *History;* op cit; vol 2; p. 638.

Most of these early Islamic accomplishments are to be found carried to the Christian West, via the Italians, in subsequent centuries. This Islamic impact, which would normally require a whole book, is summed up here.[696]

b. The Islamic Impact

In the words of Lieber:

> The merchants of Italy and other European countries obtained their first education in the use of sophisticated business methods from their counterparts on the other side of the Mediterranean, most of whom were Muslim.[697]

Gene Heck observes, how as a result of their commercial contacts with the Italian city states, the Muslims then passed on many of their highly developed innovative business techniques on to Venice, Genoa, Amalfi, Gaeta and Pisa, and Marseilles, the very cities wherein many modern economic historians claim that "Western" capitalism was born.[698] Employing business methods directly borrowed from the Muslims, while concurrently benefiting from the strong economic stimuli that their trade demands produced, the Italian merchants, Heck pursues:

> Contributed immensely to the precipitation of medieval Europe's commercial renaissance commencing in the 11th-12th centuries, a prime factor in that continent's eventual emergence from its unfortunate three centuries long experimentation in the "Dark Age economics."[699]

The Italian cities of Genoa, Pisa and Venice, in particular, maintained intense trade links with Anatolia as well as with the Fertile Crescent, Egypt, and North Africa, and because of that were able to learn from their Muslim counterparts many of the institutional arrangements that facilitated long distance and cross-societal trade.[700] The strong Italian presence in the East, and their support for the crusades, in exchange for commercial privileges in captured cities, has already been described above in relation to industry. The Italians also kept the strongest trading links with Muslim Spain and North Africa.[701] In 1133, for instance, a delegation of Almoravid high dignitaries travelled to Pisa and signed a major agreement with the Republic.[702] Both Pisa and Genoa likewise negotiated with the Almohads for trade

---

[696] For further details, see G.W. Heck: *Charlemagne*; op cit; or A.E. Lieber: Eastern; op cit.

[697] A.E. Lieber: Eastern Business Practices; p. 141.

[698] G.W. Heck: *Charlemagne*; op cit; p. 4.

[699] Ibid; pp. 4-5.

[700] M. Amari: *I Diplomi arabi del reale archivio Fiorentino* (Florence, Lemonnier, 1863). M.L. de Mas Latrie: *Traites de Paix et de Commerce, et Documents Divers, Concernant les Relations des Chretiens avec les Arabes de l'Afrique Septentrionale au Moyen Age* (Burt Franklin, New York; originally Published in Paris, 1866), vol 1; p. xv. J.L. Abu-Lughod: *Before European Hegemony* (Oxford University Press, 1989), p. 67.

[701] O. R. Constable: *Trade and Traders*; op cit; M.L. de Mas Latrie: *Traites de Paix et de Commerce*, op cit.

[702] M.L. de Mas Latrie: *Traites de Paix*; op cit; p. 36.

privileges in their domains.[703] During the second half of the 12th century, the two cities sought to extend their commercial powers through treaties with Muslim rulers in Valencia, Denia and the Balearics.[704] Abd-al Mumin, the first Almohad ruler, had in the year 1153 or 1154 concluded a treaty with the Republic of Genoa to secure peace and good rapports between their subjects.[705] An alliance between the two sides was certainly in place by 1161.[706] Almohad treaties with Genoa appear to have been renewed at roughly fifteen year intervals, and generally included clauses guaranteeing safe conduct for shipping, tariff reductions for Genoese traders, and the right to maintain funduqs in Almohad ports.[707] Similar treaties were drawn up between the Almohads and Pisa in the late 12th century, Pisa, though, remaining less favoured than Genoa.[708] In 1166, Abu Yakub Yusuf, son of Abd-Al Mumin, gave back to the Pisans the franchises and possessions they had before in Africa, and recognised their right of Funduq (Fundaco) (storage house) at Zouila, the main outskirt of Al-Mehdia (Tunisia), mostly inhabited by European merchants.[709]

These contacts and exchanges were to have far reaching impacts on the development of modern trade mechanisms, which, as seen under the preceding heading, were known to Muslims for centuries. One of these changes was in accounting methods and the development of similar methods in the Christian West. It was through the Pisan colony in North Africa (in Bejaia, specifically) that the Christian West acquired the first knowledge of mathematics for commerce, via Leonardo Fibonacci.[710] The techniques of modern bookkeeping developed in 13th-14th century Italy as a replacement for the cumbersome Roman numerals with their Arabic equivalents directly borrowed from the Near East in the writings of Leonardo of Pisa-made systematic 'double entry' accounting a much more approachable administrative undertaking.[711]

Next to the knowledge of the bill of exchange, the conception of the joint stock company, Kramers notes, was acquired by the partnership of Muslim and Christian Italian merchants.[712] The Italian merchants, who were intensely engaged in trade with the Near East in the course of the 10th-13th centuries, were exposed first hand to the workings of these innovative instruments-and in this

---

703 O.R. Constable: *Trade and Traders*; op cit; p. 43.

704 *Liber iurium republicae genuensis*; ed. M.E. Ricotti, *Historia patria monumenta*, vii; pp. 152-3; see also M. Amari *I Diplomi arabi*; op cit; pp. 239-40.

705 M.L. de Mas Latrie: *Traites de Paix;* op cit; p. 47.

706 O.R. Constable: *Trade and Traders*; op cit; p. 43.

707 H.C. Krueger: Genoese Trade with Northwest Africa in the 12th century; *Speculum;* 8; (1933); p. 379.

708 O.R. Constable: *Trade and Traders;* op cit; p. 43.

709 Manrangone, *Chron. Pis*, ed. Bonaini in M.L. de Mas Latrie: *Traites de Paix*, p. 48.

710 See: D.E. Smith: *History of Mathematics* (Dover Publications; Inc; New York; 1923; reedited 1951), p. 216.

711 G.W. Heck: *Charlemagne,* op cit; p. 253.

712 J. H. Kramers: *Islamic Geography and Commerce;* extracted from The Legacy of Islam; edited by Sir Thomas Arnold and A. Guillaume (Oxford; 1931); pp. 79-106; reprinted in *The Islamic World and the West;* Edited by A.R. Lewis; op cit; pp. 66-78, at p. 77. R. and D. El Mallakh: Trade and Commerce, in *The Genius of Arab Civilisation,* J. R. Hayes Editor; Source of Renaissance (Phaidon, London, 1976), pp. 193-205; at p. 203.

exposure, they cannot have failed to be impressed with their flexibilities and commercial efficiency.[713] Italy's *commenda* accord, which, Heck remarks, 'became medieval Europe's principal capital-contracting mechanism for engaging productive trade, the then foremost tangible symbol of evolving medieval western capitalism,' was a direct borrowing from the *qirad-mudarabah* of the Islamic East that preceded it in origin.[714] Pryor notes the striking similarities between the two concepts.[715] For instance, under both *Qirad* and *commenda*, transfer of control over the capital in question was prerequisite. Under both, the ownership of the capital remained with the capital investor, although the labour investor retained absolute control over it. In both the *qirad* and *commenda*, there were two separate types of arrangements with respect to the labour investor's freedom to manage the enterprise. Both concepts were similar with respect to the mechanics of how the division of profits was accomplished.[716]

Already noted is how Islam provides a legal/legislative procedure for commercial transactions.[717] These procedures were widened to include not just Muslim inter-trading but also trading with non-Muslims. Amari has collected 84 original documents and 41 diverse pieces, all of which were related to the Maghrib. Many of these were in duplicate, and original contemporary text, relating to exchanges between Muslims and Christians,[718] the oldest dating from 1150.[719] Wiet et al. note how oral precedents became committed to standardised written forms; notarial practice evolving in Italy in the 11th century and spreading through southern France and Spain from the middle of the 12th century. This has afforded private individuals the opportunity, of which they quickly took advantage, of ensuring legal validity for their smallest transactions.[720] Kramers also observes that the treaties that Western nations concluded with Muslim rulers, and the institution of consular representatives in Eastern ports, were important stages in the development of the rules that nowadays govern international trade.[721]

The Islamic impact on modern trade and finance is also obvious through the linguistic legacy from Arabic in regard to fundamental concepts and institutions. Amongst these borrowings are words such as cheque, arsenal, magasin, traffic, tariff, douane (customs), and aval. The impact is not just linguistic, as has been the unfortunate practice on the part of most historians/specialists in Islamic culture to

---

[713] G.W. Heck: *Charlemagne*, op cit; p. 247.
[714] Ibid; p. 245; p. 247.
[715] J.H. Pryor: The Origin of the Commenda Contract; *Speculum*; 52; 1977; pp. 33-6; idem 1983; pp. 148 ff. in G. W. Heck: Charlemagne; op cit; p. 243.
[716] J.H. Pryor; 1977; pp. 33-6; idem 1983; pp. 148 ff.
[717] A.L. Udovitch: Trade, op cit.
[718] M. Amari: *I Diplomi arabi;* op cit.
[719] M.L. de Mas Latrie: *Traites de Paix;* op cit; p.xv.
[720] G. Wiet et al: *History*; op cit; p. 474.
[721] J.H. Kramers: Geography and Commerce; in *The Legacy of Islam,* op cit; at p. 105.

note. Rather borrowing of such expressions expresses the adoption by the West of fundamental concepts upon which the whole modern system of trade and exchange rests. The word *saqq* leading to cheque has already been examined, and it is worth adding that the German and Dutch words for the same thing (Wechsel, wissel) also derive from Arabic.[722] No need here to dwell too long on words such as traffic, for instance, from the Arabic *tafriiq*, meaning 'distribution,' which is the basis for all exchanges. The focus of the World Trade Organisation is indeed on the free movement of goods as the basis of prosperity for all. 'Magazine', particularly in the sense of a storehouse for goods, comes from the Arabic, the Arabic plural *makhazin* being adopted as a singular by the Italian traders of the late Middle Ages (e.g. Genoa or Venice), either direct from an Arabic-speaking country like Egypt or, more likely, from Turkey or Persia, where Arabic plurals were often used as singulars.[723] Then, from Italian *magazzino*, it passed into Old French as magazin (modern *magasin* = 'shop') and then to English.[724] Nowadays, of course, it is most familiar in the sense of a 'storehouse' and as a miscellaneous weekly or monthly periodical.[725] Magasin carries the notion of storage; for centuries the magasins acting as the bases for all European trade dealings in and out of the Muslim world. De Mas Latrie shows that all medieval Western Mediterranean republics, without exception, owned permanent establishments in Muslim coastal towns, maintaining councils and envoys to safeguard their interests and manage their businesses.[726] Around and from the magasins there evolved maritime activity, money exchange, road transport, and various other activities. Among the forms of trade was also the feigned bargain called '*mohatra*,' which has also passed from Arabic into European language.[727]

There is a rich Muslim literature dealing with commerce, which eventually was at the source of similar Western (Italian, primarily, literature). Rosen in his 19th century translation of al-Khwarizmi's (780-850) *algebra*, makes the point that al-Khwarizmi intended to teach:

> What is easiest and most useful in arithmetic, such as men constantly require in cases of inheritance, legacies, partition, lawsuits, and trade, and in all their dealings with one another...[728]

Leonardo Fibonacci's *Liber Abaci* of 1202, which was largely inspired by al-Khwarizmi, is divided into fifteen chapters, some chapters dealing specifically

---

[722] Ibid.

[723] G. M. Wickens: 'What the West borrowed from the Middle East,' in *Introduction to Islamic Civilisation*, edited by R.M. Savory (Cambridge University Press, Cambridge, 1976), pp. 120-5; at p. 121.

[724] Ibid.

[725] Ibid.

[726] M.L. de Mas Latrie: *Traites de Paix*; op cit; p. 84.

[727] J.H. Kramers, Geography and Commerce; op cit; p. 105.

[728] F. Rosen (ed. and tr.), The Algebra of Mohammed ben Musa (1831, reprinted 1986) in entry on al-Khwarizmi by John J O'Connor and Edmund F Robertson: *Arabic Mathematics*, op cit.

with, as follows: Chapter 8: Prices of goods; 9: Barter; 10: Partnership; 11: Alligation; 12: Solutions to Problems.[729]

Al-Khwarizmi's is hardly the sole treatise dealing with the issue. Sarton mentions four Spanish Muslim works on *mu'amalat* (Commercial Dealings Involving Arithmetic) that include works by Al-Majriti (d. 1007) wherein it is said that he wrote a book on the whole of the science of numbers which is called among us *al-mu'amalat.* Al-Zahrawi (936-1013), al-Majriti's contemporary, wrote *Kitab sharif fi'l mu'amalat al tariq al-burhan* (the Noble Book on Mu'amalat in the Demonstrative Manner). The other two were al-Tunbari (d. 1025) and Ibn al-Samh.[730] Sarton insists that due to the fact that all four works came from Spanish Islam, they might well have been very influential on the development of medieval commerce and the transmission of Muslim commercial methods to the Christian world; a transmission which is very much substantiated by the presence of many Arabic words in the Spanish vocabulary.[731]

There is also a considerable amount of Muslim writing defining economic activity, besides establishing early known economic laws. As Gene Heck points out, Muslim writers such as Muhammad B. Hassan al-Shaybani in *Kitab al Iktisab fi al-Rizk al-Mustalab* and al-Dimashki in *Kitab Al-Ishara Ila Mahasin al-Tijara* began formulating then very novel and profound free market economic concepts and theories that would shape the then known intellectual world- and then, more than half a millennium later, would be 'invented by Adam Smith and others in the Renaissance reformationist Christian West.'[732]

The early (11th century) Al-Dimashki's guide: *Kitab al-Ishara Ila Mahasin al-Tijara* (The Book of Guidance to the Benefits of Commerce)[733] begins with an essay on the true nature of wealth, and then proceeds to discuss the necessity of money; how to test a currency; how to evaluate commodities; their prices; how to discern good from defective merchandise; investment in real estate; handicrafts and manufactures; advice for salespeople; the advantages of business; the different types of merchants and their duties; how to avoid fraud; how to keep records, wealth protection, and so on and so forth.[734]

Al-Dimashki's *Kitab* shows a very close relationship, in technique and approach to Pegalotti's *Practica della Mercatura*, which appeared centuries later (between 1333 and 1340 in Florence).[735] A great deal of the merchandise mentioned is the same, as is a lot of the technical terminology, the advice to businessmen, and many of the forms of business relationships.[736]

Beyond the matter of impact is the interesting point raised here by Lewis:

---

[729] D.E. Smith: *History of Mathematics*; op cit; p. 216.

[730] G. Sarton answering Query 23 on Arabic commercial arithmetic; *ISIS*, vol 20; pp. 260-2; p. 261.

[731] Query 23; p. 261-2.

[732] G.W. Heck: *Charlemagne*, op cit; p. 221.

[733] Al-Dimashki: *Mahasin al-Tijara*; tr. H. Ritter, Ein arabisches handbuch der handelswissenschaft; in *Der Islam*; vol VII; (1917); pp. 1-91.

[734] R.D. Mc Chesney: Al-Dimashki in *The Genius of Arab Civilisation*, (J. R. Hayes Ed); op cit; p. 206.

[735] N. Stilman (discussion) in *Islam and the Medieval West*; In K.I. Semaan; ed. op cit; p. 152.

[736] Ibid.

It would be easy to assemble other traditions, and writings of ascetic tendency, that say just the opposite and condemn commerce and those engaged in it. It is, however, noteworthy that centuries before Christian writers were prepared to defend and define the ethics of commerce against ascetic criticism, Muslim writers were willing to do so, and that even a major theologian like al-Ghazali (d.1111) could include, in his religious writings, a portrait of the ideal merchant and a defence of commerce as a way of preparing oneself for the world to come.[737]

4. Means and Resources

A variety of means and resources that could have been placed under this heading have already been looked at. Here focus is on other forms of payment not examined above, and the role of maritime transport.

a. Currencies and Forms of Payment

The Muslim realm was not always perfectly united geographically and politically, and many local rulers minted their own currencies.[738] Also the early caliphs used Byzantine and Persian money, but in 695, the Umayyad Caliph Abd-al-Malik struck an Arab coinage of gold dinars and silver dirhems.[739] The Umayyad Dynasty disappeared in the East but was transferred to Spain. Spanish currency consisted of the Dinar (of gold), which was equal to two dollars (early twentieth century value); the dirhem (of silver), equal to twelve cents; and various small pieces of copper that fluctuated in value.[740] In terms of its weight in gold, Gerspach informs us, a Dinar weighed between 4 and 4.20 grams, the gram of gold.[741]

The medieval usage of currencies and their valuation were studied by Al-Muqaddasi in his treatise *Ahsan at-Taqasim fi Ma'arifat al-Aqalim* (The Best Divisions in the Knowledge of the Climes).[742] He looked at such currencies in every part of the Muslim world, their design, value, multiples, and sub-multiples, their equivalents in goods and merchandise, and so on. Thus, for the Maghrib, he said:

[737] Al-Ghazali in B. Lewis: Sources for the Economic History of the Middle East in *Studies in the Economic History of the Middle East*; Edited by M.A. Cook (Oxford University Press; 1970), pp. 78-92; op cit; at p. 88.
[738] B. Rosenberger: La Pratique du commerce; in *Etats, Societes*; op cit; pp. 245-274; p. 260.
[739] A. Durant: *The Age of Faith*; op cit; p. 208.
[740] S.P. Scott: *History;* op cit; vol 2; p. 636.
[741] E. Gerspach: *L'Art;* op cit; p. 97.
[742] Al-Muqaddasi: *Ahsan at-taqasim fi Ma'rifat al-Aqalim*; from the partial French translation by A Miquel, (Institut Francais de Damas, Damascus, 1963).

> In all the provinces of this region, the standard is the *dinar*, which is lighter than the *mithqal* by a *habba*, that is to say a grain of barley. The coin bears an inscription in the round. There is also the small *rub'* (quarter of a *dinar*); these two coins pass current by number, [rather than the weight]. The *dirhem* also is short in legal weight. A half *dirhem* is called a *qirat*; there is also the quarter, the eighth part, and the sixteenth part which is called a *kharnuba*... All of these circulate by number [rather than by weight], but their use thus does not bring any reduction in price.[743]

Al Muqaddasi, incidentally, also looks at weighs and measures, and for the same region, he informs us that:

The *sanja* (counterpoise weights) used are made of glass, and are stamped just as described about the *ratls*. The *ratl* of the city of Tunis is twelve *uqiya* (ounce), this latter being twelve *dirhems* (weight).[744]

The smallest weight Muslims used in trade was the grain of barley, four of which were equal to one sweet pea, called Arabic carat; which is still in use as a unit of weight, and of precious metals (e.g. so many carats fine).[745]

Forms of payment varied according to the geographical boundaries, but were mostly affected by the nature of the transaction itself. Briefly, payment for large transactions was often on credit, subsequent to the writing of a contract between the parties involved, the buyer acknowledging his debt; which could be settled in stages. Payments could also be made in kind, by cheque or by letter of credit; gold was only used in very large transactions.[746] Payment for small transactions was carried in cash, generally in silver coins.[747] The letter of exchange, already mentioned, in Arabic the *Hawala*, and in Persian the *Suftadjah*, was very much in use, and it consisted in merchant A giving merchant B a letter requiring from a third C, residing in a distant place to advance B an amount which A would reimburse in the future.[748] Dates for reimbursement were, of course, agreed in advance.

Both within and beyond the Muslim world, fresh monetary currents appeared along the great trade routes, and there was no longer, as there had been before the Muslims, 'a linear displacement of the mass of metal,' but a completely new pattern, 'in fact a genuine circuit,' according to Lombard.[749] There have been considerable finds of Muslim coins and currencies in the furthest regions of Europe in recent history. One consisted of more than 11,000 dirhems, in addition to an indeterminate number of fragments, and weighing more than 65 lbs, whilst hoards

[743] Ibid; p. 215.
[744] Ibid.
[745] J.W. Draper: *History*; op cit; Vol II; p. 44.
[746] B. Rosenberger: La Pratique; op cit; p. 261.
[747] Ibid.
[748] Ibid; pp. 261-2.
[749] M. Lombard: *The Golden*; op cit; p. 117.

containing many hundreds or a few thousands of dirhems were common.[750] The geographic distribution of these finds stretches from Scandinavia to Silesia and the Ukraine in the south; and from Schleswig-Holstein and Mecklenburg in the west to the Urals in the east.[751] Although these finds have received a good deal of attention, focus, generally, has been from a collector's point of view. Though this is an interesting matter, it ought not to surpass in attention the real issue that these hoards reveal, indeed, the intensity of the flow of currencies,[752] and of course the dense flow of trade between the Muslims and Europe. These hoards also point to a highly elaborate monetary system, one of the fundamental institutions in the economic life of medieval Near Eastern society.[753]

Heck notes how:

> The Muslim monetary economy played a particularly powerful role in regenerating a parallel financial system in the Christian West-through stimulating bilateral trade, which resulted in greatly increased currency demand, and equally by exposing increasing numbers of Western European merchants to the transactional merits of a superior coinage.[754]

By the onset of the middle ages, the rulers and traders of Europe had developed an appreciation for the transactional value of the superior quality of Muslim money.[755] The Muslim coinage of Spain, in particular, enjoyed a great reputation for both purity and design.[756] Andalusi currency was certainly transported across the frontier from as early as the 8th century.[757] Northern Christian rulers did not mint their own gold until the 13th century, yet various gold coins were used in the north during the medieval period.[758] Andalusi dirhems (silver) appear in Christian documents, usually under the guise of *solidos mahometi, solidos de argento Kazimi,* or *solidos hazimi.*[759] Chalmeta has cited twenty two references to these Kasimi dirhems dating between 933 and 1078.[760] In Sicily, under Norman rule (1091 ff), the unit of coinage in every transaction was the quarter dinar or *rub',* a coin originally minted by the Aghlabids in the early 9th century, later issued in large quantities by the Fatimids, and used widely in Sicily (as in North Africa) through the 12th century.[761] Even the papacy appears to have benefited from the influx

---

[750] European discoveries of Cufic coins to 1900 are listed in A.Markov: *Topografiia kladovvostochnykh monet*, 1910; in S. Bolin, Mohammed, op cit.
[751] S. Bolin: Mohammed, in *Bedeutung,* op cit, at p. 258.
[752] Ibid.
[753] A. S. Ehrenkreutz: Monetary Aspects of Medieval Near Eastern Economic History; in M.A. Cook ed: *Studies*; op cit*;* pp. 37-50; at p. 37.
[754] G.W. Heck: *Charlemagne;* op cit; pp. 234-5.
[755] Ibid; p. 227.
[756] S.P. Scott: *History;* op cit; vol 2; p. 636.
[757] O. R. Constable: *Trade and Traders*; op cit; p. 47.
[758] P. Grierson: Carolingian Europe and the Arabs; the myth of the Mancus; *Revue Belge de Philosophie et d'Histoire*; 32 (1954); pp. 1059-74; at p. 1065.
[759] O. R. Constable: *Trade and Traders*; op cit; p. 48.
[760] P. Chalmeta: Precisions au sujet du monnayage hispano-arabe; in *Journal of Economic and Social History of the Orient*; 24 (1981), pp. 316-8.
[761] O. R. Constable: Cross Cultural Contacts: sales of land Between Christians and Muslims in 12th Century Palermo; in *Studia Islamica;* vol 85; (1998); pp. 67-84; p. 79.

into Europe of Muslim money, as the *Liber Censuum*- an official list of payments made by outlying ecclesiastic establishments to the Holy See in 1180- contains an asset inventory that includes many Islamic dinars.[762] Such widespread use, Cahen points out, confirms the role of Islamic currency 'infusing new blood into commercial relations.'[763]

Local imitations of Muslim coins were fairly common.[764] A great reputation was enjoyed by Islamic gold dinars minted elsewhere. A chart by Bolin that compares Islamic and European coin weighs under Carolingian rule demonstrates that the intrinsic value of the Islamic currency was then so generally admitted that a number of European rulers deliberately imitated it both in its weight and its design in order 'to promote interregional monetary exchange calculations and to enhance the prestige of their own mint proceeds.'[765] Among them the Holy Emperor Charlemagne last currency issue, struck at the onset of the 9th century, precisely matched the Abbasid silver dirhem in weight and even bore Arabic inscriptions from the Qur'an that glorified Allah.[766] Christian mints were also established in South Italy to turn out quarter dinars known as *tari* or *rumi rub'*.[767] In 1072, the Norman conqueror Robert Guiscard issued his own version of the Sicilian quarter dinar which bore the inscription, in Arabic, "Duke Robert, King of Sicily".[768] Later, King Roger II standardised the coin in a form which became known as the *duqiyya* quarter, and sale contracts indicate that these Norman *duqiyya* quarters were the regular and most popular, though not the only, unit of exchange in 12th century Palermo.[769] Christian France, just as Spain and Italy, also used and imitated the gold coins of the Almoravids (called maravedis).[770]

The use of paper money was to revolutionise monetary transactions. Paper money was first adopted in north China by the end of the 11th century, and in the Chin and Southern Sung territories it was in regular use by the 12th century, although it still coexisted with metal coins.[771] Some paper money was printed in Chinese and Arabic in 1294 at Tabriz via block-printing, a method also of Chinese origin.[772] Evidence of this is provided by a contemporary.[773] As with paper, it was the Muslims, who traded directly with the West, who generalised the use and spread of this Chinese invention.

---

[762] M. de Villard: La Montezione nell'Etat Barbarica; *La Revista Italiana di Numismatica*, vol 38; (1926); pp. 22-38; 73-122.
[763] C. Cahen: Commercial Relations; op cit; p. 1.
[764] Bloch, p.13 ff. with bibl; in R.S. Lopez: Mohammed, op cit; pp. 14-38.
[765] A.M. Watson; Back to Gold and Silver; *Economic History Review;* vol 20; No 1; 1967; pp. 11-3.
[766] G.W. Heck: *Charlemagne*, op cit; p. 228.
[767] Stern hypothesized that the word tari, which soon became commonly used for any quarter dinar, was derived from the Arabic word tari, meaning fresh, as in freshly minted. S.M. Stern: Tari, in *Studi Medievali*; 11; (1970); p. 194.
[768] Ibid; p. 189.
[769] O. R. Constable: *Cross Cultural Contacts*; op cit; p. 79.
[770] M.L. Bates: Mints and Money: *Dictionary of the Middle Ages*; op cit; pp. 421-4; p. 423.
[771] J.L. Abu-Lughod: *Before European Hegemony;* op cit; p. 333.
[772] G. Sarton: *Introduction;* op cit; Vol II, p. 764. D. Hunter: *Papermaking;* op cit; p. 474.
[773] G. Sarton: *Introduction,* Vol II, p. 764.

b. Maritime Transport and Trade

> Islam's ancient glories [according to Braudel] were not just its horsemen but also its sailors, Islam, being the society of motion by excellence, which implies sea travel to far places.[774]

Whilst Braudel holds a great place amongst scholarship in the West, when it comes to the appreciation of his view on Muslim naval expertise, it would seem his impact is of little or no value. The generalised view amongst such scholarship, indeed, is that Muslims have no expertise in shipping, or naval enterprise; much worse even, in their (scholarship) view, Muslims regard the sea as the enemy to be feared. Hartmann, for instance, writes:

> Islam has as a rule been afraid of the sea; from the very beginning it was impressed with a sense of the supremacy of the unbelievers on the ocean, and made practically no efforts to dispute their domination.[775]

The generalised claim, in fact, is that Muslim fear of the sea and their naval inferiority largely accounted for their military inferiority and their failure to exploit international sea trade.[776]

The issue with these and similar claims is that they tend to be aired by some historians and then repeated by others without any regard to actual facts. There is, in reality, nothing inherently wrong with Islam in the appreciation of the sea. Rather the opposite. In the Qur'an Muslims are repeatedly enjoined to seek bounty through sea travel (such as Chapter XVII/Verse 66). The Qur'an also says:
'Behold in the creation of the heavens and the earth, in the sequencing of night and day; in the sailing of ships through the oceans for the profit of mankind.' (II/164)
'He drives the ships which by His leave sail the ocean in your service.'(XVI, 14):

Historical evidence, likewise, shows a highly developed Muslim navy whether in the field of warfare or for peaceful purposes. In the field of maritime warfare, as early as the Caliphate of 'Uthman (caliph 644-651), a powerful Muslim fleet was built in Egypt. It inaugurated its operations by capturing Cyprus in 649.[777] Then years later it repulsed a Byzantine fleet off Egypt, attacked the Island of Rhodes in 654, and the following year destroyed a considerable Byzantine naval force.[778] The navy grew in force, and throughout the Muslim world. Further west, a fleet of three hundred Muslim vessels was charged to bring into order the rebellious coastal populations of Majorca and Minorca in 848-9.[779] Four years earlier, following Viking attacks on Seville, Caliph 'Abd Errahman II decided to have a

---

[774] F. Braudel: *Grammaire des Civilisations* (Flammarion, 1987), p. 88; p. 95.
[775] M. Hartmann: China; *Encyclopaedia of Islam*; 1st series; Vol 1; (Brill; Leiden; 1913); pp. 839-54; at p. 844.
[776] Such as found in C. Hillenbrand: *The Crusades, Islamic Perspectives* (Edinburgh University Press; 1999), pp. 556 ff who argues the inferiority of Muslim shipping in the war of the crusades.
[777] G.W. Heck: *Charlemagne*, op cit; p. 60.
[778] Ibid.
[779] E. Levi Provencal: *Histoire*; op cit; p. 107.

stronger fleet built, and shipyards were erected.[780] Under the rule of Al-Hakam II (r. 961-76), a Muslim fleet was able to catch a Viking formation, not far from Silves and decimated it.[781] A great fleet was used by Ibn Abi Amir (Al-Mansur) (d.1002) for his campaigns off the Catalan and Galician coasts in 985, and then in 997; facts, which Levi Provencal notes, highlight the power and potency of the Muslim navy.[782] Fahmy, for his part, devotes the bulk of his work to tracing Islamic arsenals (arsenal=*dar al-sina'a*) and naval centres.[783] Arsenals go back very early, to the rule of the Umayyad Caliph, Mu'awiya (661-680), under whose orders, a number of warships were built in Alexandria.[784] It is also worth noting that the Syrian fleet based in Tartus had become 'the terror of the Aegean' by the end of the 10th century.[785] These and other instances that would be seen further down, in part II (under Geography), highlight the power of the Muslim navy, and refute the generalised view amongst modern scholarship that Muslims feared the sea.

Aside from its military role, the Muslim navy played a crucial part in maritime trade. Descriptions of contemporaries and chants by ancient poets spoke of great ships, heavily laden, and light feluccas mingled.[786] Throughout the medieval period, Muslim ships and merchants dominated the circuit between the Gulf-Red Sea and the south Indian coasts, where they were joined by Indian ships that shared with the Chinese dominion over the second circuit to the Strait.[787] Muslim traders visited the Red Sea on their route to the Mozambican coast, Ethiopia, and Zanzibar and South Africa, and as early as the 10th century, they had a colony in Madagascar.[788] On the Tigris in Iraq in the 12th century, cane rafts were in great use, and in Egypt, commercial transport was very dense on the Nile and the canals.[789] To the west, African boats used to visit regularly the Spanish ports, delivering and carrying both goods and travellers.[790] Goitein has collected details of about 150 ships operating in the Mediterranean and the Nile, whose owners were mainly based in Tunisia.[791]

The dominant role of Muslim medieval shipping is highlighted by the fact that Arabic documents provide a wealth of maritime vocabulary and technical names for the vessels, such as those that carried merchants between Andalusi ports and

---

780 Ibid.

781 Ibid; p.108.

782 Ibid.

783 A.M. Fahmy: *Muslim Naval Organization*; Second edition; (Cairo; 1966); chapters one and Two.

784 Sebeos quoted by Buttler; p. 113; in A.M. Fahmy: *Muslim*; op cit; p. 28.

785 Brooks: Byz. Zeit. 1913; p. 384 in A.M. Fahmy: *Muslim*; p. 61.

786 In G. Wiet et al: *History*; op cit; at p. 325.

787 Janet L. Abu-Lughod: *Before European Hegemony*, op cit; p. 274.

788 F. Braudel: *Grammaire*; op cit. J. Spencer Trimingham: *The Influence of Islam Upon Africa* (Longman, Librairie du Liban; 1980).

789 In G. Wiet et al: *History;* op cit; p. 325.

790 See E. L. Provencal: *Histoire*; Vol iii; appropriate sections for greater detail.

791 S.D. Goitein: Mediterranean Trade in the Eleventh Century: Some facts and problems; in *Studies in the Economic History of the Middle East*; (ed M.A. Cook) op cit; pp. 51-62; at p. 59.

other areas of the Mediterranean.[792] Andalusi Muslim sources cite a variety of vessels. For example, in a sample contract for the hire of boats, the jurist Jaziri (d. 1189) referred to *shani, kharraq, dughaiyas,* and *zawraq* (respectively translatable as a galley, sailing boat, transport vessel, and skiff).[793] Mediterranean vessels varied in size, and a ship described as 'large' may have carried several hundred passengers.[794] In the middle of the 12th century, Usama B. Munqidh mentioned a ship carrying four hundred pilgrims from the Maghrib to the eastern Mediterranean.[795] Geniza letters from the next century confirm these numbers. One mentions a boat travelling to Seville with nearly three hundred Muslims and thirty six or thirty seven Jews, while another refers to a ship bringing four hundred people from Palermo to Alexandria.[796]

Many shipyards built vessels capable of carrying vast cargo of goods and traders and their beasts, but also capable of crossing long distances.[797] Fahmy uses a wide range of contemporary sources to describe the materials used in ship construction, and also naval organisation.[798] Levi Provencal, too, makes a good description of Muslim shipyards in Spain.[799] Spanish shipyards were called either *Dar al-insha* (engineering house), or *Dar sina't al-marakib* (Ship-yards) (or simply *Dar al-sina'a*).[800] Amongst these were Almeria, Alcacer do Sal, Silves, Seville, Algeciras, Malaga, Alicante, and Denia. At Tortosa, near Catalonia, an inscription shows that a shipyard was set up there under Abd Errahman III in 945.[801] Ibn Jubair (Ibn Jubayr) (d. ca. 1217) and al-Idrisi (b. 1101) also cite active shipyards in Sicily.[802] Shipyards supplying boats for coastal and distant traffic were also found on the North African coast and Egypt.[803] In Morocco, Yaqubi (fl.875) refers to a very large complex at Sos.[804] Egypt, which only harboured two shipyards in Byzantine times, had eight under the Tulunids (9th century) and their successors, the Fatimids.[805] To the East, Al-Baladhuri (d. 892) mentions a shipyard at Aqqa on the Syrian coast, others were to be added in the same region under Salah Eddin al-Ayubbi (Saladin) (d. 1193) for commercial and also military purposes.[806] Tyre had yards producing racing vessels, and was not alone among the towns of the Syrian coast in this activity.[807]

---

792 O.R. Constable: *Trade and Traders*; op cit; pp. 24-5.
793 Ibid; p. 25.
794 Ibid; p. 28.
795 Usama Ibn Munqidh: *Kitab al-Itibar*; ed H. Derenbourg (Paris; 1886-93), I.2; p. 61.
796 S.D. Goitein: *Mediterranean Society*; op cit; I; p. 315.
797 As an introduction to the subject, consult, for instance: G. F. Hourani: *Arab Seafaring in the Indian Ocean in Ancient and Early Medieval Times* (Princeton University Press, 1971).
798 A.M. Fahmy: *Muslim Naval Organization*; op cit; chap IV.
799 E.L. Provencal: *Histoire;* op cit.
800 Ibid*;* pp. 321-2.
801 Ibid; pp. 320 fwd.
802 Ibn Jubayr: *The Travels of Ibn Jubayr*; ed de Goeje (Leyden; 1907); p. 327. Al-Idrisi: Description of Italy, p. 85.
803 E. L. Provencal: *Histoire*; op cit; pp. 321-2.
804 Al-Yaqubi: *Kitab al-Buldan*; tr. G. Wiet (Cairo; 1937), p. 348.
805 M. Lombard: *Les Textiles*; op cit; p. 202.
806 Al-Baladhuri: *Futuh al-Buldhan* (Leyden; Brill; 1866), pp. 117-8.
807 G. Wiet et al: *History*; op cit; p. 328.

Timber supply, as Lombard explains, played the fundamental role in ship construction.[808] This explains the subsequent decline and problems that affected Muslim shipping when the Muslims lost (in the 13th century) Al Andalus, which was their timber-supplying region. The near entirety of the Muslim world is located in arid or lightly forested parts. Even where the climate was suitable for forests, Constable rightly points out, Mediterranean trees were fragile and arid conditions slowed their growth.[809] Only a few regions around the Mediterranean basin were capable of supporting forests of this kind, and the scarcity of timber, Glick notes, gave it a "tyranny over trade routes."[810] Muslim Spain was the primary source of production and supply of timber to the rest of the Muslim world.[811] The Iberian Peninsula is (or was) a richly forested part, with pines growing in the Algarve and Murcia in the south, in the mountains of Cuenca and Albarracín, in the hinterland of Tortosa, and on the island of Ibiza.[812] Oaks were found in vast areas, most particularly at what is now Los Pedroches, a forest of evergreen oaks extending far and wide across mountains and high plateaux to Almaden.[813] Oaks were also found in the Algarve, Extremadura, and New Castile. To the south of the Duero was another great belt of oak, respected by the Muslims as 'a strategic barrier,' and the entire northern Meseta was rich in kermes, evergreen, and holm oaks.[814] Timber from Andalusi forests was widely exported as one of the most important commodities supplied to other areas of the Islamic Mediterranean world.[815] The wood was used as a building material, for fuel and charcoal, for artisanry, but above all for ship-building.[816] In the 1050s, Al-Idrisi wrote of Tortosa:

> There are markets, buildings, ateliers and an industry for building large ships from the timber of the surrounding hills. This pine wood is unlike any other, in terms of its length and toughness. It is taken to make masts and yards for ships... this pine timber has no equal in the known world for excellence of reputation, strength, and length. It is transported to all regions of the world, far and near...[817]

South of Tortosa, the mountains around Cuenca also produced many pine trees, whose wood was cut, then thrown into the water of the Jucar river, which carried it to Denia and Valencia on the sea. Because the Jucar actually flowed to a spot south of Valencia, Al-Idrisi felt the need to explain that, at the river mouth, the

---

808 M. Lombard: Arsenaux et bois de marine dans la Mediterranee Musulmane; in *Le Navire et l'Economie Maritime du Moyen Age au 18em Siecle*; Deuxieme Colloque International d'Histoire Maritime (Paris; 1958), pp. 53-106.

809 O.R. Constable: *Trade and Traders in Muslim Spain;* (Cambridge University Press; 1994); p. 197.

810 T. Glick: *Islamic and Christian Spain in the Early Middle Ages* (Princeton University Press, 1979); p. 107.

811 Ibid: p 134.

812 Ibid, p. 133.

813 Ibid.

814 Ibid.

815 O.R. Constable: *Trade and Traders*; op cit; p. 196.

816 Ibid.

817 Al-Idrisi: *Opus Geographicum (Kitab Nuzhat...)* 9 vols; (Rome-Naples; 1970-84), v, p. 555; and *Opus* vii; (Naples-Rome; 1977); p. 734.

timber was "loaded on boats, and taken to Denia, where it was used in the construction of large ships and small boats."[818] In south-western al-Andalus, Silves was also surrounded by forests, producing "large quantities of wood, which is exported from there in all directions," and 'all the lands around [Alcacer do Sal] are covered in pine trees, from which they construct many ships.'[819]
The Muslim loss of Spain in the 13th century was to play a crucial part in causing the demise of Muslim maritime effort in the East.[820] The export of timber to the Muslim world was banned by the papacy,[821] and ships carrying wood to Egypt, in particular, were to become privileged prey of Christian attacks.[822] This, eventually, as the final part of this work will show, caused the demise of Islamic shipping in the crucial sea and ocean going age (15-18th centuries).

Other than timber, ship construction depends on the use of nails, copper chains, cables, anchors, cushions, pads, sails, and other materials.[823] Contemporary sources cite the quantities of materials used and also of the varieties of iron objects.[824] The medieval Muslim Spanish writer on the state inspector, Al-Saqati (fl. end 12th century or beginning of the 13th), at the end of his manual, details various items (ropes, sails, and the like) that were required in order to equip a ship properly, together with materials (including nails and linen) which were necessary for ship construction.[825] The use of nails instead of ropes to tie parts of the boats, which was a major breakthrough in boat construction, was noted by the geographer Ibn Rustah (fl. 903).[826] A series of innovative breakthroughs that were to lead to long distance sea and ocean travel were, indeed, made by the medieval Muslims. One such innovation, despite its name, was the lateen sail, introduced first in the Indian Ocean and then, via the 'lateen caravel,' into the Mediterranean.[827] The advantage of such sail was to allow ships to beat against the wind, unlike the square rigged galleons of the Mediterranean, which could sail only before the wind.[828] Another early, 8th century, development, was the use of tar instead of oil on the wooden decks to prevent them from leaking.[829] This innovation makes good sense due to the availability of the resource in many parts of the Muslim world. The use of the compass in navigation, of course, was crucial as it guided vessels across 'the trackless waters,' independently of the appearance of the stars (and indicated unerringly the course of the caravan in the Desert).[830] The compass, it ought to be

[818] Ibid, v; p. 560.
[819] Ibid; v; p. 543.
[820] I.M. Lapidus: *Muslim Cities in the Later Middle Ages*; op cit, W. Heyd: *Histoire*; op cit.
[821] W. Heyd: *Histoire;* op cit; p. 27.
[822] I.M. Lapidus: *Muslim Cities*; op cit; p. 42.
[823] M. Fahmy: *Muslim;* op cit; pp. 75-85.
[824] Ibid; pp. 81-3.
[825] Al- Saqati: Kitab al-Faqih; pp. 71-2; in O.R. Constable: *Trade and Traders*; op cit; p. 117.
[826] Ibn Rustah: *Al-A'alaq-un-Nafisa* (Leyden; 1891), pp. 195-6.
[827] On this: see R and D. El Mallakh: Trade; op cit; at p.204; W.M. Watt: *The Influence;* op cit; pp. 19-21.
[828] J. Lirola: Arab Navigation in T. Glick, S.J. Livesey, F. Wallis Editors: *Medieval Science, Technology and Medicine*; An Encyclopaedia; (Routledge; London; 2005); pp. 364-6; at p. 365.
[829] Al-Baladhuri: *Futuh al-Buldan*; op cit; pp. 117-8.
[830] S.P. Scott: *History*, op cit, vol 2; p. 634.

remembered, was a Chinese invention, the Muslim contribution being its use in sea journeys, which opened new options for the movement of goods and traders.[831] Likewise, the sternpost rudder is a Chinese invention adopted and diffused by the Muslims, and not as some modern researchers claim, a Scandinavian invention that eventually reached the Muslims.[832] To mount only one rudder in the sternpost which could be operated only by one person proved vastly more efficient than the two traditional lateral oars it replaced.[833]

Other than all these practical aspects, sea trade also involved theory, concepts and documents of commercial and legal sort. Trade through international boundaries, Udovitch explains, required substantial investments of capital to purchase goods, and also to transport them, and care (amidst risks so difficult to imagine today) for them until they could be sold.[834] Thus, commercial enterprises involved the partnership of many investors, and in the case of maritime transportation, a vessel could often be the property of a group of people either as co-owners, or as an association (*shirka*) brought together for that large commercial venture.[835] It was irrelevant whether the crew were of a different ethnic, or religious group from that of the owners. What was relevant, though, and constituted cause for scrutiny, were matters of responsibility over the cargo, compensation for losses, and similar issues, which became the focus of maritime jurisprudence and law.[836] Islamic law, Udovitch points out, was able to reflect the complexities of such large commercial ventures, and provided traders with a variety of means to deal with them.[837] The intricacies of such Islamic law of the sea are detailed in an 11th century treatise.[838]

On another level, Muslims were ever keen to establish and promote commercial treaties including with their Christian foes. Pardessus notes how Maghrebi treaties were very much favourable to relations with the Christians, allowing allied nations to carry on their vessels foreign traders (often from enemy states) and to associate them, in a certain measure, with the privileges, which they themselves enjoyed.[839]

A tale recounted by Arnold may bring this chapter on Muslim shipping to an end in a manner that is both engaging and revealing:

> Apart from the audacious mendacity and the romantic picturesqueness of stories (such as Sindbad The Sailor) [Arnold says] we cannot but admire

---

[831] See *Relations des Voyages faites par les Arabes et les Persans dans l'Inde et a la Chine*, ed. et tr. Langles et Reinaud (Paris, 1845), deux petits volumes, Imprimerie Royale.
[832] J. Lirola: Arab Navigation; op cit; p. 365.
[833] Ibid.
[834] A.L. Udovitch: Trade, op cit; p. 106.
[835] B. Rosenberger: La Pratique du Commerce; op cit; p. 266.
[836] Ibid.
[837] A.L. Udovitch: Trade; op cit; p. 106.
[838] A. Udovitch: An Eleventh century Islamic treatise on the law of the sea: In *Annales Islamologiques*, (Institut Francais d'Archeologie du Caire); Vol 27; pp 37-54; see also: H. Khalileh: *Islamic Maritime Law* (Leyden; 1998).
[839] M. Pardessus: *Collection des lois maritimes*, 6 vols (Paris; 1828-1847), Vol III, pref., p. LXXXII.

the splendid courage and intrepidity of these Muhammadan seamen who set out on such perilous enterprises. These sea captains in the Middle Ages not only possessed a very considerable knowledge of the art of navigation, but they had a high ideal of the responsibilities attached to their profession. One of the earliest of such collections of mariners' tales that has come down to us from the tenth century gives us some little insight into the character of these sea captains, in the record of a conversation that one of them had with a terrified passenger, who for three nights and days had suffered agonies during a violent tempest. "You must know," he said, "that travellers and merchants have to put up with terrible dangers, compared with which these experiences are pleasant and agreeable; but we who are members of the company of pilots are under oath and covenant not to let a vessel perish so long as there is anything left of it and the decree of fate has not fallen upon it; we who belong to the company of ships' pilots never go on board a vessel without linking our own life and fate to it; so long as it is safe, we live; but if it perishes, we die with it; so have patience and commend yourself to the Lord of the wind and of the sea, Who disposes of men's lives as He will."[840]

5. Exchanges with Asia, Africa and Europe

Hariri quotes the words of a Muslim tradesman:

> I want to take Persian saffron to China, where I heard it fetched a good price; then take Chinese porcelain to Greece, then Greek brocar to India, then Indian steel to Aleppo, Aleppo glass to the Yemen, and Yemeni cloth to Persia.[841]

Other than what they say, these lines also capture fully the optimism and enterprise of Muslim traders. Up to the 13th century, the Muslim land extended from the Gulf of Gascony to beyond the Indus, and Muslims were involved in commercial enterprises reaching into Africa, the Near and Middle East, China, India, and Baltic Europe, thus bringing East and West together as never before.[842] There were Muslim trading posts in Sind and Gujarat, near Bombay, and by the end of the 11th century, Muslim merchants are known to have set up permanent establishments in Hungary, testifying, in the words of Wiet et al. of:

> 'Zeal and ability, which Muslim society could call upon in commercial matters.'[843]

[840] Buzurj b. Shahriyar, *'Ajã'ib al-Hind,* ed. P.A. Van der Lith. (Leiden, 1883), p. 22; in T.W. Arnold: Arab Travellers and Merchants AD 1000-1500; in A.P. Newton: *Travel and Travellers of the Middle Ages*; (Kegan Paul; London; 1926); pp. 88-103; at p. 96.

[841] F. Braudel: *Grammaire,* op cit, p. 103.

[842] In G. Wiet et al: *History*; op cit; p. 161

[843] Ibid; p. 163.

The large Muslim coin finds in and around Scandinavia also attest to vast trading links with Scandinavia across Russian lands as far as Byzantium, or crossing the territory of the Khazars, on towards the Caspian and to Baghdad.[844]

This vast geographical stretch can be subdivided into two rough zones of activity: an Eastern trade, towards India, China and Africa, and a Western, in and around the Mediterranean.

a. The Eastern and African Trade

Travels by Muslim merchants to China had begun in earnest, and we have excellent accounts of them. The first such accounts, dating from the 9th century, were those of Suleyman (851), narrated by Abu Zeid Hassan (in 880),[845] who also added more information procured by other Arabs who had visited China.[846] Abu Zeid speaks of boats sailing for China, departing from Basra and Siraf, whilst Chinese boats (much larger than the Muslims') visited Siraf to be loaded with merchandise brought from Basra. Siraf, on the shores of the Gulf, could accommodate the large vessels and Chinese ships that did not reach as far as Basra. From Siraf, boats sailed to the Arabian coast, Muscat, Oman, and then on to India. En route to China, the merchants carried out more transactions; in the so-called islands of 'Lendjebalous', for instance, where they exchanged iron objects for ambergris. The first major Chinese destination was Khanfu (Canton), where Muslim traders had their own establishments.[847] From Khanfu they went as far as the empire's capital, Khomda; a two month journey. In China, merchants procured a variety of goods, particularly silk and porcelain, to be re-sold to Europe. From China also came iron and steel (and obviously techniques associated with their production).[848] Besides their trade, the merchants provided many descriptions and other anecdotal stories about the country; China, according to Muslim merchants, being both safe and well administered; laws concerning travellers securing both good surveillance and security.[849]

Muslims had many trading posts in Sind, Gujarat and Bombay; and on their way to India, the travellers used the Red Sea ports of Jar and Jidda and, in the Gulf, Ubullah, formerly Apologos.[850] With India, as with Ceylon, exchanges concerned mainly spices, dyeing materials, indigo, timber products, diamonds and other precious stones, and semi finished steel ores aimed for the centres of Damascus and

---

844 J. Fontana: *The Distorted Past* (Blackwell, 1995), p. 37.
845 *Relations des Voyages;* op cit.
846 G. Le Bon: *La Civilisation des Arabes*, op cit; p. 369.
847 In Baron Carra de Vaux: *Les Penseurs de l'Islam* (Geuthner, Paris, 1921), vol 2; pp. 53-9.
848 Janet L. Abu-Lughod: *Before*; op cit; p. 323.
849 Carra De Vaux: *Les Penseurs*; op cit; at p. 58.
850 G. Wiet et al: *History*, op cit, at p. 161.

Toledo.[851] India was also reputed for its finer textile products, mostly manufactured in Bengal and in Cambaye, from local cotton supplies.[852] These fine products found great demand amongst Arabs and Persians, and India supplied them in huge shiploads either via Aden or Hormuz.[853] Raw materials were procured from neighbouring parts; from the Malay Peninsula, for instance, Muslims were importing tin.[854]
Foreign colonies of Middle Eastern merchants established themselves earliest on the north-western coast of India where they blended with the local population.[855] By the early days of Islam, the ports of Cambaye and Saymur had already absorbed resident colonies of Arab merchants, some extremely wealthy, as well as sailors from Siraf, Oman, Basra, and Baghdad, whose presence and permanent incorporation was through intermarriage, as the early 10th century geographer Al-Mas'udi observed when he sojourned there.[856] The Islamising of Gujarati merchants, which had begun in the first centuries of Islam, intensified at the end of the 12th and beginning of the 13th centuries when the Turkish Sultanate of Delhi was established.[857] By the mid-13th century, one of the Muslim settlements, Calicut, became the prime port for Muslim traders in south India.[858] Calicut's attraction and reputation were enhanced by the fact that between 500 and 700 ships crammed its port area, and its city markets overflowed with rare spices, aromatic products, pearls, and precious stones, which struck Portuguese imagination, greed, and envy, on their arrival there in the late 15th century.[859] It seems likely that the navigator who guided Vasco de Gama from Malindi, on the East African coast, to Calicut was a Gujarati.[860] The disastrous impact of such Portuguese irruption on Muslim commerce and shipping in the region will be looked at in the final part of this work.

Africa, contrary to the generalised views, had a flourishing trade prior to the Western intrusion from the 15th century onwards. When the Europeans entered West Africa from the coast, Wolf points out, they set foot in a country already dense with towns and settlements, and caught up in networks of exchanges that 'far transcended the narrow enclaves of the European emporia on the coast.'[861] The textiles of Congo and Guinea, for instance, were as high in quality as those of Europe, and Nigerian decorated hides and leather were appreciated in Europe,

---

851 Compiled from chapter 8 of M. Lombard: *The Golden*; op cit.
852 W. Heyd: *Histoire du commerce*; vol 2; op cit; p. 705.
853 Varthema; pp 151; 157 etc in W. Heyd: vol 2; p. 705.
854 Compiled from chapter 8 of M. Lombard: *The Golden;* op cit.
855 Janet L. Abu-Lughod: *Before*, op cit; p. 267.
856 K.N. Chaudhuri: *Trade and Civilisation in the Indian Ocean* (Cambridge University Press; Cambridge; 1985), p. 98.
857 Janet L. Abu-Lughod: *Before*, op cit; p. 267.
858 Ibid.
859 W. Heyd: *Histoire*; Vol 2; op cit; p. 511.
860 Gopal, 1975: 1; Tibbetts, 1981: p. 10; Abu Lughod notes that the rumour that it was the great Arab mu'allim (master sailor), Ahmad ibn Majid, author of a detailed if discursive 15th century navigational manual (see Tibbetts, 1981), who led the Portuguese to the Indian Ocean is patently impossible, since he was already a very old man in 1490 when his *Kitab al-Fawa'id...* was written; in J.A. Lughod: *Before*; op cit; p. 272.
861 E.R. Wolf: *Europe and the People Without History* (University of California Press; Berkeley; 1982), p. 40.

reaching it via North Africa.[862] Muslim traders had visited the Red Sea on their route to the Mozambican coast, Ethiopia, and Zanzibar and South Africa, and as early as the 10th century, they had a colony in Madagascar. There was, of course, an intense caravan trade linking the North of Africa with the southern parts of the continent. And as Trimingham notes, Islam (the faith) has always followed trade routes.[863] Berber merchants (from north of the continent) had carried Islam across the Sahara into Sahilian states before the Almoravid. All nomad people in the north east who were on the trade routes that link the Red Sea with the Nile became Muslim. Equally, the children of many Muslim merchants who had married local women became Muslim and thus contributed to the expansion of the faith.[864] Also coming from Goa or Egypt, Islam penetrated as far as Chad, and met in Nigeria an old black civilisation, which was remarkable for its art, which it soon adopted.[865] In respect to trade itself, Islam legated to African society the concept of special consideration for merchants and trading; and even more importantly, created a trading class. It imposed contractual laws, hence stimulating institutional as well as legal foundations, not just for trade, but for the whole of society, and, of course, it forbade the practice of usury.[866] It was the Western slave trade (16th century onwards), which would interrupt the progresses of the African continent, which Islam had opened to change.[867]

Until the Western intrusion, some African parts, under the aegis of Islam, and acting as great trading centres, became during the high middle ages great centres of civilisation. Mali was one such place. As the remotest place on the gold road, Mali became famous in the Mediterranean world in the 14th century.[868] Its ruler, known as the Mansa Musa (r. 1312-37), reached legendary proportions. He was one of three Mansas to go on the hajj (proof of both power and stability of the Mali state, as the pilgrimage took over a year.) He travelled with 80 or 100 camels, 'each weighed down with 300 pounds of gold. It was the ritual magnificence and wealth of the court of Mali that impressed beholders. 'Everything about the Mansa exuded majesty.'[869] On his return from his pilgrimage to Makkah in 1324, Mansa Musa brought back with him the Muslim poet and architect, Es Saheli, who built the famous mosques and learning academies of Timbuktu and Gao.[870] Timbuktu, then, was seen as a great centre of learning.[871] The news of the Mansa's splendour reached Europe, and in Majorcan maps from the

---

[862] R. Garaudy: *Comment l'Homme,* op cit; p. 271.
[863] J. Spencer Trimingham: *The Influence of Islam Upon Africa*; op cit; p. 38.
[864] Ibid; p. 42.
[865] E. Perroy: *Le Moyen Age* (Presses Universitaires de France, 1956), p. 525.
[866] J.S. Trimingham: *The Influence;* op cit; at p 38; and p. 51.
[867] E Perroy: *Le Moyen Age*, op cit; p. 525.
[868] Felipe. Fernandez-Armesto: *Before Columbus: Exploration and Colonisation from the Mediterranean to the Atlantic 1229-1492* (Mac Millan, 1987), pp. 146-7.
[869] Ibid.
[870] D. M. Traboulay: *Columbus and Las Casas,* (University Press of America, New York, 1994), p. 70.
[871] G.O. Cox: *African Empires and Civilisations* (New York; 1974), p. 161.

1320s, and in the lavish Catalan Atlas of 1375, the ruler of Mali was portrayed like a Latin monarch, save only for his black face:

> Bearded, crowned and throned, with panoply of orb and sceptre, he is perceived and presented as a sophisticate not a savage: a sovereign equal in standing to any Christian prince.[872]

This dazzling impression ended in the mid 15th century, when direct contact with the outposts of Mali was briefly opened up by Portuguese penetration of the Gambia. Mali went into decline. Familiarity bred contempt and, the heirs of the Mansa came to be seen 'as stage niggers.'[873]

Further east of the continent, the same outcomes resulted from the Portuguese intrusion. When they arrived, their aim was to cut out Swahili middlemen and Muslim shippers. They established themselves at Sofala, the nearest port to Zimbabwe, in 1505, and later at Tete, a river port on the Zambezi.[874] Their presence was to have serious repercussions as to be outlined in the last part of this work.

b. Western Trade (The Mediterranean)

There is a widely held view that Mediterranean trade vanished for centuries, only to reawaken in the 12th century (yet another of those tens of changes that took place in that century) following the arrival of the Normans, particularly after they wrested Sicily from the Muslims (1066-89). According to some views, it was 'the spirit of an imperial race,' 'Northern Blood,' that awakened commercial and maritime activity in the Mediterranean.[875] Pirenne and his followers, as seen above, completely denied any Muslim role in the awakening of trade, but instead blamed the arrival of Islam for the decline of Mediterranean commerce. Contrary to such views, Mediterranean trade never died, and the establishment of Islam did not cause any obstacle to trading relations with the Christian West.[876] Ganshof remarks that the ports of Southern Provence had not stopped their activity from the 8th century to the 10th.[877] The Muslim arrival in the Mediterranean, Cahen holds, in fact, found trade links already dismantled by the barbarian invasions of the late 5th century, and a dying trade.[878] It was, as Lombard observes, the Muslims who revitalised exchange, just when Europe was 'exhausted', and so re-established and amplified international commerce.[879] Sabbe also notes how exchanges were both appreciable

---

872 F.F. Armesto: *Before Columbus;* op cit; pp. 146-7.

873 Ibid.

874 A. Pacey: *Technology in World Civilization* (The MIT Press, Cambridge, Massachusetts, 1990), Preface, p. 71.

875 C.R. Beazley: *The Dawn of Modern Geography*; 2 vols (London; 1897), vol 1; p. 130.

876 R. Lopez quoted in G. Wiet et al: *History;* op cit; p. 161.

877 F.L. Ganshof, Note sur les ports de Provence du viii au x siecle, in *Revue Historique*, t. CLXXXIV, (1938), p. 28. The author suggests that the decline of the exchange economy could have other causes than the Muslim irruption, especially the state of anarchy where was sank the Franc monarchy after Dagobert.

878 C. Cahen: *Commercial Relations;* op cit; p. 3.

879 M. Lombard: l' Or Musulman au Moyen Age, in *Annales ESC* (1947); pp. 143-60.

and continuous after the Muslim arrival.[880] Kramers, too, points out how since the 8th century Muslim travellers and merchants were to be found in Italian towns and Constantinople.[881] In the 720s, for instance, St Willibad had found in Naples a ship in from Egypt.[882] The Christian chronicler Theodolphus (d. 821) reports that in his time, a variety of luxury textiles of Near East origin were being imported at Arles (southern France).[883] He says that Arab merchants were bringing to Arles pearls, crystal, textiles, hides, incense, Indian ivory, art objects from Asia, and balsam from Syria.[884] Eastern purpled and silks were now required vestments both in ecclesiastical ceremonies and as the highest symbols of secular authorities at royal courts throughout much of contemporary Europe.[885] Centuries later, in 1173, Benjamin of Tudela found in Montpellier (southern France) many foreign traders, particularly merchants from the Maghrib and Syria, alongside those from Lombardy, Rome, Genoa, Pisa, Egypt, Gaule, Spain, and England.[886] Muslims traded a considerable amount of goods carrying west products such as iron and steel, porcelain and silk from China, spices from India, pearls from the Gulf, precious stones, perfumes, ivory, gold from all parts, and even food stuffs in large quantities.[887]

The lack of appreciation of such exchanges between Islam and Mediterranean Europe, Kreutz asserts, is an instance of how 'antagonism to Islam affects the correct study of history.'[888] She points out, how the 19th century historian Matteo Camera, stirred by his patriotism and devotion to the Church, rid history of Amalfi's commercial exchanges with Islam,[889] contacts which were 'deemed disgraceful' by Beazley, in whose words, Venice, unlike Amalfi, was not

> 'Stained by disgraceful alliance with the Moslems to the damage of Christian lands.'[890]

Yet, Muslim Spanish products, for instance, especially of the refined sort, found great place even amongst the higher echelons of Christian authority. Thus, the Book of Papa 'Liber Pontificalis' refers to fourteen pieces of Spanish textile with silver work.[891] And in the biographies of Pope Gregory IV (Pope 827-844) and of Leo IV (Pope 847-855) Spanish textiles are listed along with those of

---

880 E. Sabbe: l'Exportation des tissus orientaux en Europe occidentale au haut Moyen Age, in *Revue Belge de Philologie et d'Histoire* XIV (1935); 811-48 and 1261-88.

881 J. H. Kramers: *Islamic Geography and Commerce;* repr in *The Islamic World and the West;* Edited by A.R. Lewis (John Wiley and Sons, London; 1970), pp. 66-78, at p. 76.

882 Willibald Hodoeporicon S. Willibaldi: *Itinera Hierosolymitana et Descriptones Terrae Sanctae*; ed. T. Tobler and A. Molinier; 1879; reprint (Omasbruck 1966), p. 256.

883 Theodolphus *MGH* 1884; vol 1; p. 499

884 Ibid; pp. 497-500.

885 G.W. Heck: *Charlemagne,* op cit; p. 173.

886 Itinerar. Terrae Santae." *Bibl. de l'Ecole de Chartes*, 2nd series, Vol III, p. 203.

887 G. Wiet et al: *History;* op cit, at p. 163.

888 B.M. Kreutz: *Before the Normans* (University of Pennsylvania Press; Philadelphia; 1991), p. 79.

889 Matteo Camera: *Memorie storico-diplomatiche dell'antica citta e ducato di Amalfi;* 2 vols; (1876).

890 C.R. Beazley: *Dawn;* op cit; vol 1; p. 170.

891 In S. Imamuddin: *Muslim;* op cit; p. 112.

Byzantium,[892] whilst an English historian writing on the 12th century marriage of Philip of Flanders with Beatrix of Portugal also makes the eulogy of Spanish Muslim made stuffs.[893]

The port of Alexandria was a principal link in the East-West exchange network, and its activities highlight the fact that trade never ceased in the Mediterranean during the medieval period. The Christian pilgrim Arculf (late 7th century), passing through Alexandria, thirty years after the Muslims took the city, met innumerable races taking on provisions.[894] Just as in Antiquity, medieval Alexandria remained the place from where goods from the Orient reached the West; the main emporium, the '*forum publicum utrique orbi*,' as William of Tyre called it.[895] During the 11th-12th centuries, Egypt's chief indigenous exports were flax and linen, commodities eagerly sought by European and North African merchants who frequented the markets of Cairo and Alexandria.[896] According to al-Idrisi (1100-65), the main articles of trade were musk, pepper, cardamom, cinnamon, galingale (khalanj), myrobalan, camphor, coconut, nutmeg, aloe, ebony, shells, ivory, china, all of which came from Asia, plus incense, myrrh, balsams, and benzoin brought from the Hadramut, Somaliland, or the Sudan; and spices, especially pepper (one of the gates of Alexandria was called the pepper-gate.)[897]

Muslim Spain was also a powerful relay between East and West. Al-Andalus was the major channel through which eastern spices, precious metals, textiles, paper, and other items flowed into Europe, and prior to the European awakening in the central middle ages, Andalusian markets supplied many of 'the good things' in Western Christian life.[898] Andalusians could be seen everywhere in the Arab East and North Africa, as well as in the Mediterranean, in places such as Majorca, Minorca, Sardinia, Sicily, Crete and others, in their capacities as students, teachers, merchants, pilgrims, missionaries, civil servants, skilled workers and artisans.[899] Their commercial activities took them to Greece, Italy, France, and also to Northern Europe, where they traded all sorts of goods.[900] In Muslim countries, evidence of their presence can be seen nowadays in Morocco, Algeria, and Tunisia, not only in the arts and architecture of these countries, but in the names of villages and family names.[901]

---

[892] G. Migeon: Arts Plastiques; ii; p. 320; in S.M. Imamuddin: *Muslim*; op cit; p. 112.
[893] G. Migeon: Arts; p. 320; in S.M. Imamuddin: *Muslim*; op cit; p. 113.
[894] G. Wiet: *History*; op cit; p. 161.
[895] G. Sarton: *Introduction;* Volume III; p. 229.
[896] A.L. Udovitch: Trade: op cit; 107-8.
[897] Kammerer, pp. 10-14, 1929; in G. Sarton: *Introduction*; Volume III. p. 229.
[898] O.R. Constable: *Trade and Traders*; op cit; p. 2
[899] A. Chejne: The role of al-Andalus in the movement of ideas between Islam and the West: in *Islam and the Medieval West*; K.I. Semaan; ed., op cit; pp. 110-33; p. 114.
[900] Ibid.
[901] Ibid.

Most of the Muslim exchanges with the non Muslim Mediterranean world were with the Italians. Throughout the 9th century, Kreutz notes, in cultural splendour and affluence, the Islamic Mediterranean world vied with, and in some respects surpassed Byzantium, and over time the south Italian relationship with the Muslim sphere brought increased prosperity, at least to much of Campania.[902] It seems likely that, in the 10th century, many regional churches were embellished with artefacts brought from the Muslim world even if documented references begin only in the early 11th century and then primarily mention 'Spanish' or 'Moorish' textiles.[903] The Muslim historian, Ibn Hayyan (d. 1076), mentions a treaty for peace and commercial security negotiated between the Umayyads and the Counts of Barcelona in 939, and describes a visit to Cordoba by Amalfitan merchants in 942.[904] Ibn Hayyan went on to say that, after this successful Amalfitan visit, 'their successors,' continued to come to al-Andalus and make great profits.[905] Registers from the second half of the 12th century contain roughly fifty contracts for Genoese voyages to Andalusi ports or for sales of Andalusi goods.[906] In 1160, for instance, a Genoese merchant agreed to transport Andalusi textiles from Genoa to Bejaia in Algeria, while another promised to carry goods from Genoa to Bejaia, Oran, Ceuta or Yspania in 1197.[907]

War, and even the crusades (1095-1291), hardly impeded the large presence of Italian traders in North Africa as is well documented by De Mas Latrie.[908] The Pisans, Florentines, Genoese, Venetians, Sicilians had commercial establishments in the Maghrib. Christian funduqs (storage and trading establishments as well as hostels for traders) were principally located in Tunis, El-Mehdia, Tripoli, Bone, Bejaia, Ceuta, and Oran. The Pisans and Genoese disposed of further establishments in Gabes, Sfax, and Sale.[909] The Funduqs gradually became places where the merchants sold their goods, and every funduq became 'a part of Europe'.[910] In Tunis, Bejaia, El-Mehdia and other places, the Venetians had changing offices, public writers, and shops where they sold goods as in the Place of St Mark.[911] The Pisans were seen in Tunisia as old friends, and had a special Funduq, comprising many houses, where they worked in all security. The regard paid to them is obvious in a letter sent by one emir to the Archbishop of Pisa, chief of the government of the republic.[912] The Florentines, too, used Tunis warehouses and benefited from the guarantees granted to their nation.[913] The Genoese were also well established in Bejaia (modern Algeria), reselling products they had imported such as cotton,

---

[902] B.M. Kreutz: *Before the Normans*; op cit; p. 18.
[903] Ibid; p. 142.
[904] O.R. Constable: *Trade and Traders;* op cit; p. 97.
[905] Ibn Hayyan: *Kitab al-Muqtabis fi Tarikh al-Andalus*; v; ed. by P. Chalmeta et al (Madrid-Rabat; 1979), pp. 478-85.
[906] O.R. Constable: *Trade and Traders;* op cit; pp. 42-3.
[907] Giovanni Scriba: *Il Cartolare di Giovanni Scribba*; eds M. Chiaudano and M. Moresco (Roma; 1935), ii; p. 4; # 812.
[908] M.L. de Mas Latrie: *Traites de Paix*; op cit.
[909] Ibid; pp. 88-92.
[910] B. Rosenberger: La Pratique; op cit; pp. 271-2.
[911] M.L. de Mas Latrie: *Traites de Paix*; op cit; p. 89.
[912] Ibid; p. 37.
[913] Ibid; p. 251.

linen and indigo, whilst Bejaia exported to Genoa products, which it imported from other parts, including alum, wax and gold.[914] Genoa, Pisa, and Venice also had good trading links with Morocco; Genoa, most particularly, disposing of privileged links and establishments in the country.[915] Sicilians and Sardinians, too, without neglecting Morocco, were, like the Genoese and the Pisans, in continuous business rapport and interest with Tunis and Oriental 'Mauritania' (eastern Algeria). Also active under patronage of the pavilions of the great maritime cities, were the smaller ports in Liguria and Dalmatia, and the rich merchants of Tuscany and Lombardy.[916] By the rule of Abu Zakaria (began 1228), the main Christian nations owned permanent establishments in Africa, entertaining councils and envoys to safeguard their interests and manage their businesses.[917]

The relationships with the Italian cities were codified in a number of documents. De Mas Latrie refers to Amari's piecing together 84 original documents, the oldest dating from 1150, including 41 pieces related to the Maghrib, many in duplicate and original contemporary text.[918] This is the best collection concerning the relations between Christians with North West Africa in the Middle Ages.[919] Such treaties between the Muslims and the Italian republics guaranteed the security of the merchants, including the possibility of legal recourse, and stipulated precisely the conditions of trade.[920] These treaties had the merit of improving the status of merchants, who with time obtained the right of interpreters, recognition by consular authorities, and wide autonomy of action.[921]

The same intense commercial activities also prevailed within the Muslim realm in the Mediterranean. There is evidence from Muslim sources, Singer points out, that alum was reaching Bejaia, on the Mediterranean coast, and the North African posts by caravan across the Sahara, which illustrates the intensive intricacy of early trade relationships in the Mediterranean.[922] Glick insists that the purchasing power exercised by al-Andalus in virtue of its high standard of living in comparison with the Islamic East was enormous, and the Andalusi played a significant role in Muslim Mediterranean trade.[923] There was strong economic closeness between Muslim Spain and North Africa: in Morocco, for instance, Andalusi merchants sold their own finished cloth (Valencian brocade, according to al-Shaqundî), as well as copper, a staple export.[924] Under the rule of the Almoravids and Almohads (1088-1248) who united Spain with the Maghrib, the great Moroccan cities, Marrakech and Fes, especially, became extensions of the

[914] C. Singer: *The Earliest Chemical Industries* (The Folio Society; London; 1958), p. 82.
[915] M.L. de Mas Latrie: *Traites de Paix*; op cit; p. 64; p. 37.
[916] Ibid; pp. 84; and pp. 88-92.
[917] Ibid; p. 84.
[918] M. Amari: *I Diplomi arabi del reale archivio Fiorentino* (Florence, Lemonnier, 1863).
[919] M.L. de Mas Latrie: *Traites de Paix;* op cit; p. xv.
[920] B. Rosenberger: La Pratique; op cit; p. 271.
[921] Ibid; pp. 271-2.
[922] C. Singer: *The Earliest Chemical Industries*; op cit; p. 82.
[923] T. Glick: *Islamic and Christian Spain;* op cit; p. 130.
[924] Al-Shaqundi in T. Glick: *Islamic and Christian;* op cit; pp. 130-1.

Andalusi urban economy, merchants moving back and forth freely, carrying Spanish goods on camelback.[925] Until the early 11th century, Andalusi commerce with the East was carried through Tunisian towns, with al-Qayrawan and its port, al-Mehdia, playing the leading role.[926] Andalusi merchants stationed in Tunisia were receiving Egyptian or Syrian goods there and selling them on the spot or, if the home market was judged more favourable, shipping them on to Spain.[927] Levi Provencal[928] and Imamuddin[929] have also provided good data on trade within Andalusia itself, involving goods of both ordinary and luxury sort; heavily loaded convoys criss-crossing the country between major towns and cities and to export harbours.[930]

The Muslim loss of Sicily (beginning in 1061), of Spain (13th century) (except for the Grenada enclave, which would fall in 1492), the crippling of the North African trade and coastal economies by recurrent pirate attacks, and the destruction of the Near and Middle Eastern economies by a succession of invaders, crusaders (11th-13th), Mongols (13th), and subsequently Timur (early 15th), all of which will be examined in detail in the final part of this work, meant that from the 13th century onwards, Egypt became the main Muslim trading centre on the Mediterranean. Egypt remained until the 16th century the transit market for Eastern spices and other Oriental products; silk from Spain and Sicily, textiles from various points around the Mediterranean, olive oil from Tunisia, and metals (iron, copper, lead, tin, and mercury) from Spain and other European countries.[931] Metals and, understandably, wood, were prominent in Egyptian imports.[932] In the 16th century, however, Mamluk Egypt was ruined by Christian Piracy in the Mediterranean, in the Red Sea and Indian Ocean.[933] This matter and its overall impact will be discussed in the last part of this work, which examines the central issue of Muslim decline. Before that, this work looks at the Golden Age of Islamic science and civilisation, beginning with an extensive description of the highly advanced (and sophisticated for those times) urban setting and gardens.

---

[925] T. Glick: *Islamic and Christian Spain*; pp. 131.
[926] Ibid.
[927] Ibid.
[928] Other than works by Levi Provencal already referred to, see by the same author: L. Provencal: *Documents Arabes Inedits sur la vie Sociale et Economique en Occident Musulman au Moyen Age* (Cairo; 1955).
[929] S.M. Imamuddin: Commercial relations of Spain with Ifriqiyah and Egypt in the 10th century; *Islamic Culture*; Vol 38 (1964), pp. 9-14. *The Economic History of Spain Under the Ummayads* (711-1031) (Dacca; 1963).
[930] E. Levi Provencal: *Histoire*; op cit; p. 317.
[931] A.L. Udovitch: Trade; op cit; pp. 107-8.
[932] Ibid.
[933] See for instance: W. Heyd: *Histoire*; op cit; I Lapidus: *Muslim Cities*; op cit. W.J. Fischel: "The Spice Trade in Mamluk Egypt: A Contribution to the Economic History of Medieval Islam," in *Journal of the Economic and Social History of the Orient*, 1 (1958). Al Makrizi: *Histoire des Sultans Mamlouks de l'Egypte*, Etienne M. Quatremere, tr., 2 vols. (1837-1845).

Two

CITIES OF ISLAM

When during the crusades (1095-1291), the Western Christians came into contact with the Muslim East, Erbstosser observes, the size and structure of Muslim cities must have been impressive for such crusaders.[934] At the beginning of the 11th century, Tripoli in today's Lebanon, had 80,000 inhabitants and its fortifications enclosed an area of about 12,000 hectares. Not only did it possess a series of palaces, but to crusaders who came from medieval huts of wood and mud, its five and six storey buildings were also an impressive sight.[935] The city also had centralised water supply systems, which were either in the form of cisterns with pipes leading to the houses of the wealthy citizens at least, or, in individual cases, consisting of an integrated mains supply system for the entire city.[936] The same can be said for other cities, where also street lighting had been common in their centres since the 10th century, vegetable oil being used as fuel in Syria, for example.[937] Public baths, with strict male and female segregation and 'sometimes of considerable artistic merit,' were just as familiar a part of the urban scene as the great hospitals, libraries and schools.[938] The streets of Muslim cities were also paved, and many were actual mosaics of different coloured stones, often shaded with canopies stretching between the roofs of the buildings to give shelter from sun and rain.[939] It was, thus, a new and alien world with advanced economic and cultural standards that confronted the crusaders on their arrival.[940]

The same impression prevailed in the west, in Spain. Castro notes how in 1248 the armies of King Ferdinand III conquered Seville after a struggle that gave 'definitive proof of the military impotence of the already decadent Muslims.'[941] But these victorious armies could not conceal their astonishment at what they saw. The Christians had never possessed anything similar in art, economic splendour, civil organisation, technology, and scientific and literary productivity.[942]

> How great is the beauty and the loftiness and the nobility of the Giralda... And it (Seville) has many other great and noble features besides those of which we have spoken [exclaimed one of the witnesses.][943]

---

[934] M. Erbstosser: *The Crusades* (David and Charles; Newton Abbot; Leipzig; 1978), pp. 130-1.
[935] Ibid.
[936] Ibid.
[937] Ibid.
[938] Ibid.
[939] Z. Oldenbourg: *The Crusades*; tr., from the French by A. Carter (Weinfeld and Nicolson; London; 1965), pp. 476; 498.
[940] M. Erbstosser: *The Crusades;* op cit; pp. 130-1.
[941] A. Castro: *The Spaniards; An Introduction to their History*; (University of California Press; 1971); p. 226.
[942] Ibid.
[943] Cronica General; pp. 268-9 in A. Castro: *The Spaniards;* p. 226.

In the mid 13th century the opulence of the port of Muslim Almeria served as a term of reference for the measurement of economic value, just as the mines of Potosi or the treasures of Venice would do later.[944] Cordoba, before its demise in the 11th century, was the most splendid city in Europe. We read in Reinhart Dozy's *Spanish Islam* of its half-million inhabitants, its three thousand mosques, its hundred and thirteen thousand houses, and its twenty-eight suburbs, whilst Richard Ford speaks of nearly a million inhabitants.[945] Joseph McCabe extols the greatness of the city much further:

> In the tenth century Cordova had a population of a million souls, a lavish supply of pure water, and miles of well-paved and lamp-lit streets. . . . There was not [at that time] anywhere in Europe, outside Arab Spain and Sicily, and there would not be for at least two centuries, a single city with 30,000 people, with even the most rudimentary sewerage, with any paved or lamp-lit streets, with a communal supply of pure water, with an elementary regard for hygiene, with a single public bath (and few, if any, private baths) or school, and with even moderately good precautions against theft and violence.[946]

Cities played a fundamental part in the history of Islam, which is somehow paradoxical when recollecting that those who carried the faith throughout the world, from the Himalayas to the Pyrenees, were mainly Arabs and Bedouins 'who never slept between four walls,' says Marcais.[947] A point also noted by Udovitch, who contrasts the desert and oases 'the setting of its birth,' with the cities and towns 'the setting of Islam's growth and maturity.'[948] From Makkah and Madinah, the centres of power, culture, and wealth moved to such urban sites as Damascus, Baghdad, and Samarkand, and to Cairo, Qayrawan, Fes, and Cordoba.[949] Lombard notes that Sao Paulo in Brazil, said to be the fastest growing city in the world (its population rising from 60,000 in 1888 to 2 million in 1950), hardly, in fact, compares with the growth of Baghdad from 500 inhabitants in 762 to nearly 2 million in 800.[950] This was by no means an isolated case. Some of the greatest cities of the Middle Ages anywhere were all founded in early Islam, cities such as Cairo, Al-Qayrawan and Al-Mehdia in Tunisia; Fes and Marrakech in Morocco; and Al-Kufa and Basra in Iraq.[951] The latter two grew exceptionally rapidly, from just small towns, into great cities, Kufa reaching 100,000 inhabitants, and Basra 200,000 in the space of three decades.[952] Samarra's

---

[944] A. Castro: *The Spaniards;* op cit; p. 227.
[945] W. Blunt: *Splendours of Islam;* Angus and Robertson; (London; 1976); p. 37.
[946] Joseph McCabe: The Splendour of Moorish Spain; in W. Blunt: *Splendours of Islam;* p. 37.
[947] G. Marcais: l'Urbanisme Musulman, in *Melanges d'Histoire et d'Archeologie de l'Occident Musulman*; Vol 1; (Gouvernement General de l'Algerie; Alger; 1957); pp. 219-31; at p. 219.
[948] A.L. Udovitch: Urbanism in *The Dictionary of the Middle Ages*; op cit; Vol 12; pp. 306-10.
[949] Ibid.
[950] M. Lombard: *The Golden;* op cit; p. 118.
[951] Ibid.
[952] Ibid; p. 123.

population according to Herzfeld might have reached 1 million in the 9th century.[953] Fustat's medieval population must have risen to between 450,000 and 600,000.[954] Likewise in Spain, sudden and fast rises turned once sleepy towns into large cities. Al-Maqqari (d.1632) refers to an anonymous medieval author who stated that in Spain there were 80 cities of the first rank, 300 of the second, and so many smaller towns and villages that 'only God could count them.'[955] At their peak, Seville contained 500,000 inhabitants; Almeria an equal number; Granada 425,000; Malaga 300,000; Valencia 250,000; Toledo 200,000.[956] Under the Muslims, Cordoba became one of the most important and most populous cities of the Mediterranean.[957] Its population has been variously estimated at between 100,000 and one million, but the latter figure is more plausible as archaeological works in the city have revealed its huge medieval size, which fits with the one million figure.[958] After the construction of two new cities, Madinat al-Zahra (940-941) and Madinat al-Zahira (978), it became in the 10th century a conurbation of more than 15 kilometres.[959]

Islam, the faith, stands central in this urban process. 'To achieve its full social and religious ideal, Islam cannot do without urban life,' explains Marcais, who also observes how, the mosque, central element of the faith, both in religious and political terms, requires both permanence and urbanity; and so 'The mosque creates the Islamic city.'[960] This was obvious not just in the East, but also in the West; the centrality of the mosque in a vast urban setting was obvious in Seville, Valencia and other Muslim Spanish towns.[961]

The extraordinary urbanisation of Muslim society and its urbanity, too, were in sharp contrast with what was prevalent in the Christian West. In medieval times, whilst the strength of Islam was in its great cities, wealthy courts, and long lines of communication, Southern notes, Western Christendom was primarily agrarian, feudal, and monastic.[962] In Europe, the cities of antiquity had disappeared due to economic crises, (5th century) invasions and brigandage; the town was now merely a cramped *castrum* for defence and refuge; the period was marked by the triumph of the large estate and of rural economy 'Barbarisation and ruralisation having spread over almost the whole of the Western World,' says Lombard.[963]

---

953 E.E. Herzfeld: *Geschichte der Stadt Samarra* (Hamburg; 1948), p. 137.

954 M. Clerget: *Le Caire* (Cairo 1934), pp. 126; 238-9. J. Abu Lughod: *Cairo* (Princeton; 1971), p. 37.

955 Al-Maqqari: *Nafh Al-Tib.* Partial translation by P. De Gayangos: *The History of the Mohammedan Dynasties in Spain* (extracted from *Nifh Al-Tib* by al-Maqqari); 2 vols (The Oriental Translation Fund; London, 1840-3), Vol 1; p. 87.

956 S.P. Scott: *History;* op cit; vol 1; pp. 613-4.

957 M. Acien Almansa and A. Vallejo Triano: Cordoue, In *Grandes Villes Mediterraneenes du Monde Musulman Medieval;* J.C. Garcin editor (Ecole Francaise de Rome; 2000), pp. 117-34; at p. 117.

958 A.M. Watson: A Medieval Green Revolution; New Crops and Farming Techniques in The Early Islamic World, in *The Islamic Middle East 700-1900;* edited by A. Udovitch (Princeton; 1981), pp. 29-58; note 45; p. 57.

959 M. Acien Almansa and A. Vallejo Triano: Cordoue; op cit; p. 117.

960 G. Marcais: l'Urbanisme; op cit; p. 219.

961 T. Glick: *Islamic and Christian*; op cit; p. 114.

962 R.W. Southern: *Western Views of Islam in the Middle Ages* (Harvard University Press, 1978), p. 7.

963 M. Lombard: *The Golden;* op cit; p. 119.

Which contrasts sharply with Muslim Cordova, a city of fountains; baths, schools, and much else, its thoroughfares, for a distance of miles, brilliantly illuminated, substantially paved, kept in excellent repair, regularly patrolled by guardians of the peace.[964] In Paris there were no pavements until the 13th century; in London none until the 14th century.[965] The streets of both capitals were often impassable, and it was only at the close of the reign of Charles II (17th century), that even a defective system of street lighting was adopted in London.[966] The contrast was even greater, when considering that a city such as Baghdad at the end of the 9th century had a population exceeding one million people, whilst even in the 13th century, Lombard insists, we are struck by the difference with Western Christendom; cities in Italy, or Flanders, with population not exceeding thirty or forty thousand people.[967] In 1700, London, the most populous city of the Christian West, was only half as large as Cordova was in 900, when Almeria and Seville had 'each as numerous a population as the capital of the British Empire eight hundred years afterwards.'[968] It was only in the 14th century that Paris, the largest city in the Christian West, reached three hundred thousand inhabitants.[969]

There is another, even more striking contrast, which becomes obvious to whomsoever peruses through the literature devoted to Muslim civilisation. This contrast concerns the accounts of contemporary and older Western sources on one hand which extoll the greatness of Muslim cities (and civilisation), and on the other a new form of scholarship that demeans both the accomplishments and impact of Islamic civilisation, as here with regard to the degree of sophistication of the Islamic urban setting.[970] Addressing this matter of scholarly approach is the first concern of this chapter, which will then move on to describe the Islamic urban setting.

1. The Urban Setting: Between Fallacies and Reality

There are three fundamental derogatory myths in relation to the Muslim city, which are dealt with in turn (a, b, and c).

a. A Matter of Definition:

The first of these is the generalised claim that Muslim cities were not cities in the modern sense. Max Weber, for instance, suggests that there were five distinguishing marks of the medieval city: fortification; markets; a legal and

964 S.P. Scott: *History;* Vol 3; op cit; pp. 520-2.
965 Ibid.
966 Ibid.
967 M. Lombard: l'Evolution Urbaine; pendant le Haut Moyen Age; in *Annales,* vol 2 (1957), pp. 7-28; p. 24.
968 S.P. Scott: *History;* op cit; pp. 520-2.
969 M. Lombard: L'Evolution Urbaine; op cit; p. 24.
970 S.E. Al-Djazairi: *Hidden Debt*; op cit; Part One.

administrative system; distinctive urban forms of association, and partial autonomy.[971] Since the Muslim city lacked some of these marks, Weber maintains, they were not cities, just chaotic concentrations of crowds.[972]
Weber is far from being alone in defining the Muslim city as such, and this derogatory definition of the Islamic city is not unique, for every aspect of Muslim civilisation, sciences, history and faith, has been seen from that same derogatory/hostile angle. Briefly here, Muslim universities are thus said not be universities, 'because they lacked a definite date and legal status in their foundation.'[973] Which is odd considering that neither were subsequent European universities, which were also based in every respect (organisation, administration, campus system, certificates, learning...) on Muslim antecedents.[974] The same is also said about Muslim chemistry, defined as an occult practice called alchemy, which is also odd when Western chemistry inherited everything (classification of metals, the use of experimentation, the vocabulary, the laboratory, and other essentials of chemistry) from its Islamic predecessor.[975] And the same with respect to the observatory in Islam, which is deemed not an observatory, when every single feature found in it (use of large instruments, gathering of scientists, prolonged observation, and so on,) was to be found in its successor the Western observatory.[976] And the same is said with respect to Muslim hospitals, described as mere 'maristans.' Muslim civilisation, itself, is said to be a plagiarised form of Greek civilisation, whilst the faith of Islam is said to be a mere corruption of other faiths.[977] Even the military victories of Muslim armies, including that of Ain Jalut in 1260 which broke the devastating Mongol onslaught on Islam, was painted as a pale success against a handful of Mongols,[978] or was only a skirmish, says Saunders,[979] who oddly also says that it was a turning point in history, and that the Mamluk victory at Ain Jalut saved Islam.[980] Hence, Weber's poor view of Islamic cities is neither new, nor unique. Nor can it stand up to scrutiny, as shown by the following.

---

[971] M. Weber: *The City*; D. Marindale and G. Newirth tr. (Glenco; 1958).

[972] In N. AlSayyad: *Cities and Caliphs* (Greenwood Press; London; 1991), p. 34.

[973] H. Rashdall: The Universities of Europe in *The Middle Ages*, ed. F.M Powicke and A.G. Emden, 3 Vols (Oxford University Press, 1936).

[974] J. Ribera: *Dissertaciones y opusculos*, 2 vols (Madrid, 1928). George Makdisi: *The Rise of Humanism in Classical Islam and the Christian West* (Edinburgh University Press, 1990).

[975] E.J. Holmyard: *Makers of Chemistry* (Oxford at the Clarendon Press, 1931).

[976] L. Sedillot: Memoire sur les instruments astronomique des Arabes, *Memoires de l'Academie Royale des Inscriptions et Belles Lettres de l'Institut de France* 1: 1-229 (Reprinted Frankfurt, 1985). A. Sayili: *The Observatory in Islam* (Turkish Historical Society, Ankara, 1960).

[977] Such as found in all works on Islam, such as: C. Brockelmann: *History of the Islamic Peoples*; tr., from German (Routledge and Kegan Paul; London; 1950 reprint).

[978] G. Guzman: Christian Europe and Mongol Asia: First Medieval Intercultural Contact Between East and West; *Essays in Medieval Studies*, Volume 2; pp. 227- 44; at p. 233.

[979] J.J. Saunders: *The History of the Mongol Conquests* (Routlege & Kegan Paul; London; 1971), p. 117.

[980] J.J. Saunders: *Aspects of the Crusades*; University of Canterbury (Canterbury; 1962), pp.67; and p. 64. See also C. Hillenbrand: *The Crusades, Islamic Perspectives* (Edinburgh University Press; 1999), who claims Islamic military successes, as in p 574 ff. were against a weakened foe; often victories and successes only fruit of Islamic folk epic and imagination.

In contrast to the ancient city or to the Western communes of the later Middle Ages, Islamic cities possessed no special legal or corporate status. The town as such is not recognised in Islamic law notes Udovitch.[981] Nor can we identify any institutions for internal governance, such as guilds or municipal councils, which have been used by social historians to deny the title of city to the Islamic city. But as Goitein points out:

> The medieval Islamic city was a place where one lived, not a corporation to which one belonged.[982]

The 'ulama', or religious scholars, Udovitch notes, 'served as a cohesive force within the urban amalgam,' just as did the muhtasib (the state inspector of corporations, trades, and markets) and a number of formal and informal groupings, including the extended families, the neighbourhoods, local constabulary, and religious orders. The Islamic cities represented effective social realities, and as seats of the government or its representatives they guaranteed security; as local markets or international emporiums they provided economic opportunities; and with

> Their mosques and madrasas, their churches, synagogues, and schools, their bathhouses and other amenities, they contained all that was needed for leading a religious and cultured life.[983]

Oldenbourg also notes how in large cities there were schools for all, free for young children and sometimes even for university students; there were public baths at every street corner, as well as many private pools.[984]

Islamic cities pioneered in aspects of modern life which took the Christian West many centuries to catch up with. One such area was the setting up of an efficient communication system through the post, which, although mainly concerned official exchanges, still, in Mamluk times (mid 13th century onwards), linked up the major towns and cities. After he removed the most serious threat to the Muslim world, i.e that of the Mongols, defeating them at Ain Jalut in September 1260, Baybars I, the Mamluk sultan, revived the *barid,* or postal service, to secure regular and relatively swift communication-four days-between the Mamluk capitals of Cairo and Damascus and the more distant cities of his realm.[985] 'Just as the Pony Express operated in the western United States in the 19th century,' Sims observes, 'the solitary Mamluk *barid* riders usually took ways that were more direct but more arduous and with fewer amenities.'[986] Like the caravans, however, the *barid* needed stations for rest, water and stabling, and at its inception, it made use of existing caravanserais wherever possible such as at Qara Khan, midway between Damascus and Homs, where Baybars carved his emblem, a

---

[981] A.L. Udovitch: Urbanism; op cit; p. 310.
[982] D. Goitein: *A Mediterranean Society* in A.L. Udovitch: Urbanism; pp. 310-1.
[983] A.L. Udovitch: Urbanism; pp. 310-1.
[984] Z. Oldenbourg: *The Crusades*; pp. 497-8.
[985] E. Sims: Trade and Travel: Markets and Caravanserais; in G. Michell ed., *Architecture of the Islamic World*; Thames and Hudson; London; 1978; pp. 97-111; at p. 103.
[986] Ibid.

running panther, on its entrance corridor.[987] Gradually, relay-stations were specially constructed for the *barid*. *Barid* stations, 'the precursors of our post offices, were usually rectangular in plan, although the court could be aligned in either direction, with the stables, living quarters, latrines, cistern and storerooms arranged around it in no easily visible order.'[988] Some had mosques, others an *iwan* with a *mihrab* to serve as a place for prayer. Those dating from the 14th century, in particular, are architecturally ambitious and far more carefully constructed, such as the *khan* called as-Sabil, or Khan Manjak, near Inqirata in Syria, which was built in 1371.[989] The Mamluk *barid* posts, Sims concludes, can be seen as a specialised kind of travel architecture of the 13th to the 15th centuries.[990]

Muslim cities, cosmopolitan by nature, were also great centres of commerce, into which caravans flowed from all corners of the East and the West.[991] The commercial role of such centres has been amply described above to require any more space here.

Muslim cities were also administrative centres employing thousands of clerks, cultural centres where sometimes tens of thousands of manuscripts were preserved in public and private libraries, where schools of literature and philosophy of all persuasions met, where men assembled in public squares to discuss the Qur'an; each of these cities a world in miniature; even the small cities, like Homs and Shaizar, had 'an opulence and comfort which European kings might have envied,' says Oldenbourg.[992]

The conclusion, therefore, is that Islamic cities not only met the requirements of the modern city, they were also centuries ahead of their Western counterparts. In support of this latter point, there is no instance of any city in the West, prior to the 18th century, which provided similar services and amenities as found in urban Islam.

b. The segregationist aspect of Urban Islam

There has never been in Islam any segregation approaching the American southern states, or South African apartheid system, or in most modern Western agglomerations today. Islam is not segregationist either as a faith or society.[993] Van Ess observes that there were no ghettos in the Muslim world all the way down to modern times. Members of the same religious community often lived in the same quarter for reasons of family solidarity; but they were not kept apart from Muslims deliberately and on principle. In particular, they were not unclean; they could be

---

987 Ibid.

988 Ibid.

989 Ibid.

990 Ibid.

991 Z. Oldenbourg: *The Crusades*; op cit; p. 498.

992 Ibid.

993 I.e: G. E. Von Grunebaum: *Medieval Islam*; op cit; p. 177 and p. 210. F. Artz: *The Mind*; op cit; p. 137. Joseph Van Ess: Islamic Perspectives, in H. Kung et al. *Christianity and the World Religions* (Doubleday; London, 1986), p. 80.

invited to dinner.[994] Throughout the Muslim world, whether under the Arabs, or the Turks, all ethnic groups and faiths, had access on equal terms to every single amenity or service, and they formed part of the Islamic whole, and shared in opportunities, and even at the highest echelons of society and power.[995] The Jews in Cairo, for instance, are mentioned as practicing the professions of medical doctors, artisans, accountants, and despite professional specialisation, there is no instance of segregation of populations on ethnic or lines of faith with regard to professions and trades.[996] The same was true in other cities such as Cordova, where under Islam there was no evidence of a segregation of the Jewish population from its Muslim counterpart.[997] There is in fact plenty of evidence showing quite the reverse, a dense intermingling of faiths, which also includes the mozarabs (Spanish Christians living under Muslim rule).[998] In fact, segregation in that city followed precisely its capture by the Christians in 1236. As soon it was taken by the Castilians, one of their first measures was to remove both Muslim and Jewish populations, who were then forced to re-locate into isolated neighbourhoods, cut off from access to every form of land communication.[999]

In the instance when the Islamic state intervened to allocate one particular place in a city to a particular group, this was based on the need to guarantee a right of space to a group of people who had lost their worldly rights and possessions elsewhere. For instance, when Al-Hakam I of Spain (r. 796-820) banished the Cordovans in the early 9th century, they were offered a part of Fes to resettle.[1000] The same happened with the Jews, who when banished by the Church in Spain in 1492 found the same space and rights in the Turkish Ottoman urban realm.[1001] Under Ottoman rule, their social status rose, too.[1002] The startling rise of the new port of Algiers was largely due to the influx of Aragon Jews, even if the port itself was established by Kheir-Eddin Barbarossa (early 16th century).[1003] They achieved extraordinary pre-eminence in Morocco during the 16th century as well.[1004] Subsequently, when the Muslims were banished from Spain in 1609-10, they too were allocated parts of towns and cities, farming lands, trades and businesses from Morocco through Algeria to as far as Turkey and Syria.[1005]

---

994 J Van Ess: Islamic Perspectives: op cit; p. 104.

995 Y. Courbage, P. Fargues: *Chretiens et Juifs dans l'Islam Arabe et Turc* (Payot, Paris, 1997), T.W. Arnold: *The Preaching of Islam* (Archibald Constable, Westminster, 1896); R. Garaudy: *Comment l'Homme devint Humain* (Editions J.A, 1978), p. 197.

996 D. Behrens Abouseif; S. Denoix, J.C. Garcin: Cairo: in *Grandes Villes*; op cit; pp. 177-203; p. 185.

997 M. Acien Almansa and A. Vallejo Triano: Cordoue; op cit; p. 124.

998 Ibid.

999 Ibid; p. 118.

1000 E. Levi Provencal: La Fondation de Fes; in *Islam d'Occident* (Librairie Orientale et Americaine; Paris; 1948), pp. 1-32.

1001 Y. Courbage, P. Fargues: *Chretiens et Juifs;* op cit.

1002 F. Babinger: *Mehmed the Conqueror*; tr., from German by R. Manheim; Bollingen Series XCVI; (Princeton University Press); 1978; p. 106 ff.

1003 G. Fisher: *Barbary Legend* (Oxford at the Clarendon Press; Oxford; 1957), p. 38.

1004 H.de Castries: *Une Description du Maroc sous le regne de Moulay Ahmed al-Mansour;* 1596 (Paris; 1909), pp. 119-20.

1005 K. Brown: An urban View of Moroccan History; Sale 1000-1800; in *Hesperis Tamuda;* 12 (1971), 46-63. R. Letourneau: *Fes avant le protectorat* (Paris; 1949), pp. 79-94. J.D. Latham: Towards a study of Andalusian immigration and its place in Tunisian history; in *Cahiers de Tunisie*; 5 (1957), pp. 203-52. H. Uzuncarsili: *Osmanli tarihi*; 2nd ed (Ankara; 1964), 2; p. 194 in A C. Hess: *The Forgotten Frontier* (The University of Chicago Press, Chicago and London, 1978), chap 6; p. 121.

At all times, indeed, the Islamic city offered an image of a vast gathering of multiple faiths and races. Early Basra, for instance, had a substantial population of Hindus, Yemenis, Persians and Arabs.[1006] Muslim Palermo in Sicily included Greeks, Lombards, Jews, Slavs, Berbers, Persians, Tatars and Black Africans.[1007] The monk Theodosius, brought from Syracuse with Archbishop Sophronius in 883, acknowledged 'the grandeur' of the new capital, describing it as:

> Full of citizens and strangers, so that there seems to be collected there all the Saracen folk from East to West and from North to South... Blended with the Sicilians, the Greeks, the Lombards and the Jews, there are Arabs, Berbers, Persians, Tartars, Negroes, some wrapped in long robes and turbans, some clad in skins and some half naked; faces oval, square, or round, of every complexion and profile, beards and hair of every variety of colour or cut.[1008]

And these were no exceptional cases, as Watson points out.[1009] What was found in Palermo in the 9th century could also be seen in Algiers in the 17th; which Lloyd says, was not just clean and well disciplined, but also every visitor remarking on the law and order that prevailed in a city inhabited by persons of every nationality and religion.[1010] The public baths of the city, Fisher notes, were made available to persons of all races and creeds, and even to slaves.[1011]

Islamic buildings, too, in their design, just like the towns, cities and society, betrayed the same cosmopolitan spirit, as Durant notes:

> From the Alhambra in Spain to the Taj Mahal in India, Islamic art overrode all limits of place and time, and laughed at distinction of race and blood.[1012]

c. Islamic Urban System= Chaos

Urban chaos is claimed to be the child of Islam, the faith. Thus, Planhol says:

> Irregularity and anarchy seem to be the most striking qualities of Islamic cities. The effect of Islam is essentially negative. It substitutes for a solid unified collectivity, a shifting and inorganic assemblage of districts; it walls off and divides up the face of the city. By a truly remarkable paradox this

---

[1006] N.L. Leclerc: *Histoire de la medicine Arabe*. 2 vols (Paris, 1876), vol ii, pp. 279-82.

[1007] Al-Maqqari *Nafh al-Tib*, ed. Muhammad M. Abd al-Hamid. 10 vols (Cairo, 1949), vol ii, pp 14-15; al-Khushani *Historia de los jueces de Cordoba por aljoxani*, ed., and tr. J. Ribera (Madrid, 1914), pp. 38-41, in A.M. Watson: *Agricultural Innovation;* op cit; p. 92.

[1008] In C. Waern: *Medieval Sicily* (Duckworth and Co; London; 1910), p. 19.

[1009] A.M. Watson: *Agricultural;* op cit; p. 92.

[1010] C. Lloyd: *English Corsairs on the Barbary Coast* (Collins; London; 1981), p. 25.

[1011] G. Fisher: *Barbary*; op cit; p. 99.

[1012] W. Durant: *The Age of Faith*; op cit; pp. 270-1.

> religion that inculcates an ideal of city life leads directly to a negation of urban order.[1013]

This is part of a wider line of attack of the same order, which AlSayyad has outlined:

> Housing is mainly made up of inward oriented core residential quarters, each allocated to a particular group of residents and each is served by a single dead end street. As for its spatial structure, the Muslim city has no large open public spaces and the spaces serving its movement and traffic network are narrow, irregular and disorganised paths that do not seem to represent any specific spatial conception.[1014]

The anarchy attributed to the Islamic model is refuted by historical evidence, though. Jairazbhoy, for instance, argues:

> First of all irregularity has always been alien to Islamic art, and indeed in architectural designs there is usually an over zealous desire for symmetry. The irregularities of streets in Muslim towns are the result of subsequent haphazard growth.... It is people who are at fault, not the system.[1015]

Historically speaking, AlSayyad demonstrates, the irregularity of forms in Muslim cities as a response to social and legal codes and as a representation of the Islamic cultural system had no foundation. Muslim towns were originally designed according to very regular geometric patterns, and they only achieved an irregular form in later years probably due to many factors.[1016] When Caliph 'Umar ordered the construction of Kufa ca. 638, he strictly specified the widths of the streets: 20 metres for the main roads, with side streets of 10 to 15 metres, whilst alleys were to be 3.5 metres, which was the minimal width allowed.[1017] This, Kennedy observes, was to be a clearly laid out city, not a tangle of alleyways where people settled and built as they wished.[1018]

The outline by Lassner on the foundation of Samarra (today's Iraq) in the 9th century is an excellent illustration of how fundamentally Islamic urban design stands wholly at the opposite end of what stereotypes claim. Samarra, the second great capital of the Abbasid caliphate, was situated along the Tigris some sixty miles (ninety-seven kilometres) north of Baghdad. The city was subject to meticulous planning; several thoroughfares running almost the entire length and breadth of the city.[1019] The main thoroughfare was the "Great Road" (*Shari' al-a'zam*), called al-Sarjah, extending the entire length of the city. With later extensions it ran some 20 miles (32 kilometres) and was reported to have been 300 feet (91 meters) wide at one point. The part of the road that still exists, although somewhat narrower (240 feet or 73 meters), testifies, indeed, to

[1013] Xavier de Planhol: World of Islam (Ithaca; Cornell University Press; 1959), p. 23, in N.AlSayyad: *Cities*; op cit p. 23.
[1014] N.AlSayyad: *Cities*; p. 6.
[1015] R. Jairazbhoy: *Art and Cities of Islam* (New York Asia Publishing House; 1965), pp. 59-60, in AlSayyad, p. 23.
[1016] AlSayyad: *Cities*; p. 154.
[1017] Al-Tabbari: *Tarikh al-Rusul wal Muluk;* ed., M.J. De Goeje et al; 3 vols; Leiden; 1879-1901; vol 1; p. 2488.
[1018] H. Kennedy: *The Great Arab Conquests*, Da Capo Press, Cambridge, 2007; p. 134.
[1019] J. Lassner: Samarra; *Dictionary of Middle Ages;* op cit; vol 10; pp. 642-3.

dimensions that were staggering.[1020] The new mosque was an enormous structure as it was meant to be attended by the entire population of Samarra.[1021] The distinctive feature of the Samarra mosques was an unusual tower surrounded by a spiral ramp that served as a minaret.[1022] The great government buildings, the Friday mosque and the city markets were all situated along al-Sarjah; and it was throughout the entire history of the city the main line from which most of the city's traffic radiated toward the Tigris and inland.[1023] The market areas were subsequently enlarged and the port facilities expanded as part of an energetic program that included the refurbishing and strengthening of already existing structures.[1024] The new mosque was an enormous structure; and as it was to serve the entire population of Samarra (which resided for the most part along the first two thoroughfares inland), three major traffic areas had to be constructed along the width of the urban area. Each artery was reported to have been about 150 feet (46 meters) wide so as to handle the enormous traffic. Each artery was flanked by rows of shops, representing all sorts of commercial and artisanal establishments; the arteries in turn connected to ample side streets containing the residences of the general populace. The Great thoroughfare was extended from the outer limits of Samarra, and feeder channels that brought drinking water flanked both sides of the road.[1025] The use of Samarra as the main residence of the caliph lasted only about fifty years (836-883), but its artistic and architectural impact was of much longer duration.[1026]

And Samarra was not alone. Sketches of all the cities founded under Islam equally had wide roads and spaces, green areas, a multitude of gardens and orchards, whilst perfect geometry and symmetry were fundamental in their design.

Modern writing that contrasts the chaos of Islamic cities with the urbanity and order of Western cities is, furthermore, entirely at odds with contemporary medieval accounts whether these accounts came from Muslim or Christian sources. Without repeating what has been said already, and in a few lines, Islamic cities, as a rule, were paved with stones, and were cleaned, policed, and illuminated at night, whilst water was brought to the public squares and to many of the houses by conduits.[1027] The houses were large buildings, several storeys high, housing numerous families, with terraces on the roofs, internal galleries and balconies, and fountains in the centre of the courtyards.[1028] Living conditions in 16th century Algiers, according to Western contemporary visitors:

[1020] Ibid.

[1021] P. Soucek; Islamic Art and Architecture; *Dictionary of Middle Ages;* op cit; p. 597.

[1022] Ibid.

[1023] J. Lassner: Samarra; *Dictionary of Middle Ages;* op cit; vol 10; pp. 642-3.

[1024] Ibid.

[1025] Ibid; pp. 643.

[1026] P. Soucek; Islamic Art and Architecture; *Dictionary of Middle Ages;* op cit; p. 597.

[1027] F.B. Artz: *The Mind;* op cit; pp. 148-50.

[1028] Z. Oldenbourg: *The Crusades*; op cit; p. 476.

> Compared favourably with those in northern capitals. The domestic architecture, the flowered patios and gardens of the race which built the Alhambra were among the most attractive in the world. Every respectable house had a galleried courtyard and a flat roof embellished with potted plants. An efficient water supply provided numerous fountains and cleaned the streets to a degree unknown in England (or other European countries).[1029]

And long would be the list of early Islamic cities which could boast huge expanses of gardens.[1030] Every city had its countless gardens, and on the outskirts were great orchards full of orange and lemon trees, apples, pomegranates, and cherries.[1031] So inspiring were the Islamic gardens and structures, Westerners sought to replicate them, and Turkey, as an instance, was at once the source of inspiration and the nursery from which many species of plants and flowers were imported by eager Europeans,[1032] (and which you would be lucky to see in public places today (carnations, in particular).

Never mind flowers and gardens, in contrast, in the Christian West, Paris, Mainz, London and Milan were not even like modern provincial cities compared to a capital.

> They were little better than African villages or townships, where only the churches and the occasionally princely residence bore witness that this was an important centre [says Oldenbourg.][1033]

The streets of both Paris and London 'were receptacles of filth, and often impassable; at all times dominated by outlaws; the source of every disease, the scene of every crime.'[1034] The mortality of the plague was a proof of the unsanitary conditions that everywhere prevailed; the supply of water derived from the polluted river or from wells reeking with contamination.[1035] Medieval Muslim visitors to Christian towns complained-as Christian visitors now to Muslim towns do of the filth and smell of the "infidel cities."[1036] At Cambridge, now so beautiful and clean, sewage and offal ran along open gutters in the streets, and 'gave out an abominable stench, so... that many masters and scholars fell sick thereof.'[1037] In the thirteenth century some cities had aqueducts, sewers, and public latrines; but in most cities rain was relied upon to carry away refuse; the pollution of wells made typhoid cases numerous; and the water used for baking and brewing was usually-north of the Alps-drawn from the same streams that received the sewage of the towns.[1038] Italy was more advanced, largely through

---

[1029] In C. Lloyd: *English Corsairs on the Barbary Coast* (Collins; London; 1981), p. 28.

[1030] A.M. Watson: *Agricultural Innovation in the Early Islamic World* (Cambridge University Press; 1983), p. 117.

[1031] Z. Oldenbourg: *The Crusades*; op cit; p. 476.

[1032] J. Harvey: Turkey as a source of garden plants, *Garden History*; vol 4; 1976.

[1033] Z. Oldenbourg: *The Crusades*; op cit; p. 497.

[1034] S.P. Scott: *History*; op cit; Vol 3; pp. 520-2.

[1035] Ibid.

[1036] Munro and Sellery; p. 266, in W. Durant: *The Age of Faith*; op cit; p. 1003.

[1037] In Coulton: Panorama; 304, in W. Durant: *The Age of Faith*; op cit; p. 1003.

[1038] Jackson: Byzantine and Romanesque Architecture; I; p. 142. Barnes: Economic History; p. 165 in W. Durant: *The Age of Faith*; op cit; p. 1003.

its Roman legacy, and through the enlightened legislation of Frederick II for refuse disposal; but malarial infection from surrounding swamps made Rome 'unhealthy, killed many dignitaries and visitors, and occasionally saved the city from hostile armies that succumbed to fever amid their victories.'[1039]

Finally on this, the idea that Islam is at the source of anarchy and asymmetry is, indeed, fundamentally contradicted by the faith and its practice. Gazing at designs on a Muslim prayer carpet, whether these designs are of Makkah, or a mosque interior, or any other motif, will show absolute, perfect symmetry and precision. Anything on the left side of the carpet is found on the other as if computer designed. No Islamic carpet will show asymmetry. Prayer itself, in a mosque (or anywhere else), is perfect order, in the reading of the verses, in the timing of the prayers, in the direction of the prayers, in the numbers of the (rakaas) (prostrations), in the line of worshippers, in the simultaneity and harmony of their prostration, and similar actions. The Qur'an is recited with absolute, perfect orderliness, in form, in sound, in the repetitions, and is perfect in the length of the verses. Everywhere the Qur'an calls on meticulousness and utter exactitude. Exactitude and utmost precision are constantly sought of the faithful in every deed, in making contracts, in inheritance matters, in the way of fasting, in distributing alms, in the way of performing pilgrimage and other rituals. The gardens of Islam are absolute perfect symmetry and order; and so is the art of Islam, as the consultation of any book on Islamic art will show. Islam, in words, loves the orderly and utterly loathes the disorderly. So why do Muslims act in chaotic ways, and why is their urban or built environment chaos itself?

This issue we cannot address here as it is not the venue; we shall deal with it in volume 3, which looks at some of the main causes of the decline of Islamic civilisation.

2. Urban Imperatives

Contrary to today, early Islamic urban growth proceeded alongside order and aesthetics, and was also inclusive of basic amenities. Udovitch has noted how Islamic cities provided economic opportunities, and with their mosques, madrasas, churches, synagogues, schools, bathhouses, and other amenities, contained all that was needed for leading 'a religious and cultured life.'[1040] Oldenbourg equally remarks how both comfort and fullness marked Muslim urban life, which also included basic amenities as well as social and economic services.[1041] This was the case in the better known cities such as Damascus,

[1039] W. Durant: *The Age of Faith*; op cit; p. 1003.
[1040] A.L. Udovitch; Urbanism; op cit; p. 310.
[1041] Z. Oldenbourg: *The Crusades*; op cit; p. 476.

Baghdad, Cairo, and Cordova as well as other cities.[1042] Damascus, for instance, was well supplied with parks, fountains, and public baths; a great commercial and manufacturing industry; public buildings, and great charitable foundations for the care of the sick, orphans, and the aged.[1043] Each craft had its quarter, and on the outskirts of the city the landed aristocrats and the wealthier merchants had magnificent homes surrounded with gardens.[1044] The contemporary Spanish traveller Ibn Jubayr described the city as 'the paradise of the East,' and was mostly impressed by its hospitals and colleges, which he ranked among the 'great glories of Islam.'[1045] Cordoba (Cordova), under the Romans, was in the words of Lombard 'an insignificant affair.'[1046] Under the Muslims, the first Umayyad governor built walls, restored the old Roman bridge, and built water-mills on a jetty, using the river current.[1047] Further transformations and additions were undertaken subsequently, especially in the 10th century under the reigns of Abd Errahmane III, Al-Hakam II, and under Ibn Abi Amir (Al-Mansur). By the end of the century the city was said to have 900 public baths; nearly 100,000 trade establishments and shops; 50 hospitals, and a university with over 20,000 students.[1048] The streets were cleaned, policed, and illuminated at night; water was brought to the public squares and to many of the houses by conduits.[1049] In 12th century Fes, under the Almohads, writes a chronicler, there were 785 mosques and zawiyas; 240 places of convenience and purification, and 80 public fountains, which were all fed with water from springs and brooks. There were 93 public baths and 472 mills within and alongside the walls, not counting those outside the city. The same chronicler goes on to mention 89,036 dwelling houses, 19,041 warehouses, 467 funduqs for the convenience of merchants, travellers, and the homeless; 9,082 shops, two commercial districts, one in the Andalusian district, near the river Masmuda, and the other in the Kairaounese district; 3,064 workshops, 117 public wash-houses; 86 tanneries; 116 dye works; 12 copper-smitheries; and 400 paper making shops.[1050]

The economic sustenance of the Islamic city was no less crucial. Durant points out that cities and towns: 'Swelled and hummed with transport, barter, and sale; pedlars cried their wares to latticed windows; shops dangled their stock and resounded with haggling; fairs, markets, and bazaars gathered merchandise,

[1042] F.B. Artz: *The Mind*; op cit; pp. 148-50.
[1043] Ibid.
[1044] Ibid.
[1045] Ibn Jubayr: *The Travels of Ibn Jubayr*; translated from the original Arabic with introduction and notes, by R.J. C. Broadhurst (Jonathan Cape, London, 1952), p. 256.
[1046] M. Lombard: *The Golden*; op cit; p. 140.
[1047] Ibid.
[1048] F.B. Artz: *The Mind*; op cit; pp. 148-50. I. R and L.L. al Faruqi: *The Cultural Atlas of Islam* (Mc Millan Publishing Company New York, 1986), p. 319. W. Durant: *The Age of Faith*; op cit; p. 302. R. Hillenbrand: Cordova: *The Dictionary of the Middle Ages*; op cit; vol 3; pp. 598-601.
[1049] F.B. Artz: *The Mind*; op cit; pp. 148-50; Al Faruqi: *The Cultural Atlas,* p. 319; W. Durant: *The Age of Faith*; op cit; p. 302; R. Hillenbrand: Cordova; op cit.
[1050] Rawd al-Qirtas in T.Burckhardt: *Fez City of Islam* (The Islamic Text Society; Cambridge; 1992), p. 73.

merchants, buyers, and poets; caravans bound to China and India, to Persia, Syria, and Egypt; and Baghdad, Basra, Aden, Cairo, and Alexandria sent Arab merchantmen out to sea.'[1051]

The workshops of Cordoba employed 13,000 weavers, as well as its armourers and leather workers, whose products were famous throughout the civilised world.[1052] The city innovated in the manufacturing of crystal; its woollens, silks, brocades and craftsmanship in embossed goat leather were all very much prized in foreign markets; and so were its jewellery and ivory carving.[1053] In Konya, the Turkish Seljuk capital, Greek and Armenian carpet merchants continued to gather for centuries after its greatness was past.[1054] The city had a new market place and shops of all kinds, and included caravanserais, built like basilicas, with high-arched aisles to accommodate the camels.[1055] The vast market gardens stretching below the walls into the Anatolian plain were aimed for the supply of its large population.[1056] In Egypt, as early as 690, Marwan I, the Umayyad caliph, had built covered markets on a site on the Nile that was to become the city of Fustat.[1057] During the next four centuries Fustat grew, establishing itself as a chief emporium, rapidly replacing Alexandria as its primary entrepot and leaving only the silk trade to the once-great maritime city.[1058] Fustat was put to the torch in the mid-12th century as a defensive measure on the part of the Fatimid governor of the newer city of Cairo.[1059] Fortunately, Fustat's cultural brilliance and the wealth of its markets are described by such travellers as Al-Muqaddasi (writing in 985) and Nasir-i Khusraw (in 1047). Al-Muqaddasi writes that goods from al-Andalus, from the Turkish lands and from China were all to be found there, stored or being sold in an immense commercial district of long narrow streets that were permanently covered and artificially lit.[1060] In Samarra, likewise, a market area was built, and smaller markets, called *suwayqat*, dealt in basic commodities, specifically, foodstuffs such as grains and meat and other unspecified necessities.[1061] The area across the river had a 'certain bucolic quality' and encompassed twelve villages along major water channels; with a flourishing agriculture, including excellent cash crops, and the taxes earned on the west bank properties represented some 60 percent of the entire tax base for the city.[1062] Urban-rural complementarities in Muslim Spanish towns developed quickly from the 8th century onwards, the international market encouraging

---

[1051] W. Durant: *The Age of Faith*; op cit; p. 208.
[1052] C. Dawson: *Medieval Essays* (Sheed and Ward: London; 1953), p. 220.
[1053] F.B. Artz: *The Mind*; op cit; pp. 148-50; Al- Faruqi: *The Cultural Atlas*, p. 319; W. Durant: *The Age of Faith*; op cit; p. 302. R. Hillenbrand: Cordova; op cit.
[1054] F.F. Armesto: *Millennium* (A Touchstone Book; New York; 1995), pp. 97-9.
[1055] Ibid.
[1056] Ibid.
[1057] E. Sims: Trade and Travel: Markets and Caravanserais; in G. Michell ed., *Architecture of the Islamic World*; (Thames and Hudson; London; 1978); pp. 97-111; at p. 106.
[1058] Ibid.
[1059] Ibid.
[1060] Ibid.
[1061] J. Lassner: Samarra; *Dictionary of Middle Ages;* op cit; p. 642.
[1062] Ibid; pp. 642-3.

concentration of artisan industries in towns whose monetary economy allowed the urban middle class to buy into the surrounding countryside, thus developing tightly interdependent town-huerta (belts of irrigated parcels) complexes whose agricultural surpluses stimulated both urban economic and demographic growth.[1063] Not only were the huertas surrounding most Andalusi towns closely connected with the economic life of the town, but many amongst the urban elite owned country houses (*munyat*; Castilian, *almtinia*) scattered throughout the huerta.[1064] Extramural suburbs, Glick notes, tended to form along the most heavily travelled commercial roads leading from the town, or around palaces and military establishments; Cordova had more than twenty.[1065] The list of thriving industries in each city, as recorded by contemporary geographers, and as outlined in the previous chapter, is long, and confirms the central place of cities in the social, cultural, and economic life of early Islam.

One of the dominant urban necessities is water supply. How water was perceived and appreciated in medieval Muslim society is well caught in these lines by Lapidus:

> With water, streets could be wet down, the dust settled, the heat eased, and the air freshened. Water brought calm, music, and blossom. Urbanity depended upon it. Without water, the fruit gardens, which in the Arab consciousness are the gardens of paradise, could not survive. In the chronicles, governors who provided water were always well remembered. They were the eternal benefactors of the settlement who assured its viability, prosperity, and civilization. What more could be said for the glory of a reign![1066]

Should one ponder briefly on the chaos and waste prevailing in the water supply of Middle Eastern and North African towns and cities today,[1067] one marvels at the achievements of early Islam. Early Islamic society, much impregnated by the faith, knew and appreciated the place of water in civilisation, its preciousness, the need to salvage it, and preserve it to the very maximum, and that without an abundant supply of water, neither the necessities nor the amenities of civilisation could exist.[1068] The quality of beverages depended on the purity of water; and, likewise, without water, paper, leather, soap and dyed cloth could not be produced, nor in Islam could proper worship be carried on.[1069] So medieval Islamic cities became recipients of extremely advanced systems of water management and supply, and for all purposes. Islam's third Caliph, 'Uthman Ibn

---

[1063] T. Glick: *Islamic and Christian*; op cit; p. 111.

[1064] Ibid; p. 115-6.

[1065] Ibid.

[1066] I.M. Lapidus: *Muslim Cities in the Later Middle Ages, (*Harvard University Press; Cambridge Mass; 1967), pp. 69-70.

[1067] K. Sutton-S.E. Zaimeche (1992) 'Water resource problems in Algeria.' *Mediterranee* 76. Aix en Provence, pp. 35-43.
S.E Zaimeche (1991): 'Feeding the population in semi arid lands: An assessment of the conditions of three North African countries: Morocco, Tunisia and Algeria.' *Maghreb Review*, Vol 16. Nos 3-4; pp. 165-77.

[1068] I.M. Lapidus: *Muslim Cities in the Later Middle Ages,* op cit p. 69.

[1069] Ibid; p. 70.

Affan (Caliph 644-656), by way of example, had a network of wells and canals installed along the Makkah-Al-Basrah pilgrimage-commercial route.[1070] Makkah, itself, possessed three reservoirs, which were filled from the canals dug by the order of Zubaida from Bani Amr.[1071] In Samarra, where water had been brought by pack animals, feeder channels, which flowed all year-round, were now extended from the river.[1072] The Great Thoroughfare extended on the outer limits of the city, and feeder channels that brought drinking water flanked it on either side.[1073] Baghdad, with a population in excess of 800,000 (10th century) was served by a system of canals that gave it access to the sea, stimulating its trade and manufacture.[1074] In 993, the public baths in the city were counted and were found to number 1500.[1075] Many more baths were found in cities and towns, and fountains in public and private estates.[1076]

Throughout the Muslim world, the typical system was the conduct of water by stream, canal, or qanat (underground conduit) into the city, where it was stored in cisterns, then, conduits from these cisterns, often underground, led to the various quarters, and into residences, public buildings and gardens.[1077] Qanats and other systems, and their construction, will receive more attention in the following part, in the chapters devoted to Agriculture and technology and engineering. Here, briefly, the point to make is that *Qanats* vary considerably in size. Those in mountainous areas are usually short, shallow, tunnels only tens of meters long and several deep, which draw surface water from small patches of alluvium.[1078] Others are major engineering feats such as those which supply water to the cities of Kirman, Yazd, and Birjand. At Kirman, *qanats* extend more than 50 kilometres southward to penetrate the water table at the base of the Kuhi Jupar.[1079] Literally thousands of vertical shafts, the deepest 100 to 125 meters, dot the Kirman Plain marking the courses of an unknown number of galleries which carry water to the city.[1080] As a rule, the surplus water flowed out of the city into the irrigation system.[1081]
Syria and Palestine witnessed a great upsurge in the construction of water supplies during Mamluk rule. The Sultan, emirs, and governors took charge of

---

1070 G.W. Heck: *Charlemagne*, op cit; p. 43.
1071 Al-Muqaddasi: *Ahsan al-Taqasim*; (De Goeje ed) op cit; p. 74.
1072 J. Lassner: Samarra; op cit; pp. 642-3.
1073 Ibid; pp. 643.
1074 F.B. Artz: *The Mind;* op cit; 148-50.
1075 A.A. Duri: Baghdad; *Encyclopaedia of Islam*; vol 1; (1960); p. 899.
1076 D.R. Hill: *A History of Engineering in Classical and Medieval Times* (Croom Helm; 1984); p. 31.
1077 Ibid.
1078 P. Ward English: The Origin and Spread of Qanats in the Old World; in M.G. Morony ed: *Production and the Exploitation of Resources*; (Ashgate; 2002); pp. 273-84; at p. 273.
1079 P.H.T. Beckett, "Qanats around Kirman," *Journal of the Royal Central Asian Society* 40 (1953) pp. 47-58; Paul Ward English, *City and Village in Iran* (Madison, 1966), pp. 135-40.
1080 P. Ward English: The Origin and Spread of Qanats; op cit; p. 273.
1081 This was the arrangement in many cities such as Zaranj in Sijistan, and Nisbin in northern Syria. See Ibn Hawqal: *Kitab Surat al-Ard*; ed. J.H. Kramers; 2nd ed., of vol 2 (Brill; Leiden; 1938), p. 414; Ibn Jubayr: *Rihla*; Arabic text ed., W. Wright (Brill; Leiden; 1852), 2nd ed., by M. de Goeje (Brill; Leiden; 1907) p. 239.

providing water to places large or small. Sultan Baybars (d. 1277) and his successors improved the water supply of Hebron, Safad, and the village of Balatunus.[1082] Emirs, and especially those of the Gharb, mountain chiefs of the Lebanon, repaired water canals in Beirut and built aqueducts, and other Syrian towns were similarly assisted.[1083] Water for the holy places of Jerusalem and Hebron was also the responsibility of the Sultan and the emirs he appointed as administrators. For over a decade and a half between 1313 and 1328 a major canal and cistern project was carried out to supply Jerusalem with water.[1084] Further repairs were made at the expense of Sultan Barquq in 1384, and a century later Sultan Qayitbay restored the aqueducts at the request of qadis, sheikhs, and other notables of the city.[1085] General supervision probably lay with the governors of the cities, but the market inspectors and royal commissioners also had some responsibilities.[1086] Of the Syrian cities, Damascus was most favoured with an extensive and complete water system. The rivers Barada, Qanawat, and Banyas supplied the city through two sets of underground canals, one for fresh water, which brought water to mosques, schools, baths, public fountains, and private homes, and the other for drainage.[1087] During the reign of the Mamluk ruler, Tankiz (r.1312-1340), this system was cleaned, repaired, and overhauled to insure the distribution of water in the centre of the city.[1088] Canals were brought into new quarters in 1497, and other repairs and improvements were made at about that time.[1089] Antioch enjoyed a plentiful supply of running water for its gardens and the consumption of its inhabitants; water was carried by miles of underground pipes to the more luxurious dwellings to feed fountains.[1090]
Further east, in Samarkand, water was conducted in a lead lined channel carried on a bridge, which was necessary due to the fact that the land around the city had been excavated to provide clay for the building of the city.[1091] The geographer al-Istakhri (d. middle of 10th century) says that in the city, there was provision of water for the thirsty, and rarely did he see an inn, a street corner, or a square without arrangements for iced water 'in God's name.'[1092] He adds that water circulated in an old moat of the fortress from where it was carried to the market by means of lead pipes.[1093] Another medieval geographer, Al-Ya'qubi (d. 897 or 905), holds that northern towns such as Qumm and Nishapur had underground water systems which supplied water to the houses of the town.[1094]

[1082] I.M. Lapidus: *Muslim Cities in the Later Middle Ages*; op cit; p. 71,
[1083] Ibid.
[1084] Ibid.
[1085] Ibid.
[1086] Ibid; p. 72.
[1087] Ibid; p. 70.
[1088] Ibid.
[1089] Ibid.
[1090] Z. Oldenbourg: *The Crusades*; op cit; p. 476.
[1091] G. Wiet et al: *History*; op cit; p.316; Al-Istakhri: *Kitab Masalik wal-Mamlik*; ed. De Goeje (Leyden; 1927), p. 177.
[1092] Ibid; p. 140.
[1093] Ibid; p. 216.
[1094] Al-Yaqubi: *Kitab al-Buldan*; ed. De Goeje (Leyden; 1891), p. 274.

In the Muslim west, in Marrakech, qanats were built in the 11th century during the reign of the Almoravids.[1095] Today some 85 qanat systems are found on the Haouz plain, 40 of which are functioning and carry water to the city.[1096] In Fes, the geographer Ibn Hawqal, in the 10th century, noted that its markets were washed daily, whilst three centuries later, most homes were crossed by 'streams,' and in each house, regardless of its size, there was a saqqia (running fountain).[1097] Water in the city was also used to wash the streets and to operate between 300 and 400 waterwheels.[1098] The urban facilities of Algiers were of high quality. Its water supply was drawn from cisterns outside the walls, and was later enlarged with the construction of aqueducts under Ottoman supervision by a refugee engineer from Grenada.[1099] At Al-Qayrawan, in Tunisia, centuries earlier, an underground system, 25 kilometres distant from the city, filled a large decantation basin, from where water passed to another larger one, which then took water to the city, both basins dating from the 9th century, Aghlabid era.[1100] In the same country, at al-Mehdia, the geographer al-Bakri describes in great detail the engineering works, which carried waters of the Meyanech to the great mosque, relying on aqueducts and large water raising wheels.[1101] When the Muslims entered Sicily in the 9th century, they established new irrigation techniques, built public baths, and introduced water in many forms to garden and courtyard.[1102] In Spain, the Guadalquivir (The Great River) was spanned by 'a noble bridge' of seventeen arches, which, Lane Poole says, 'testifies to the engineering powers of the Muslims.'[1103] In Seville, the Almohads put an end to the labours of the water carriers by the construction of an Aqueduct. 10th century Andalusia, Scott remarks, was traversed in every direction by magnificent aqueducts, whilst Cordova was 'a city of fountains.'[1104]

By far, some of the greatest engineering works in the field were accomplished by the Ottoman Turks. When they took Constantinople in 1453, the city, just like the empire was agonising. By the time they firmly established themselves, the whole configuration changed. In order to revive Istanbul, sultans and viziers (high officials) of the Ottoman dynasty donated *kulliyes* under the *Vakif (Wakf)* (Religious Endowments) system.[1105] The construction, maintenance, and control of the water supplies and various urban facilities that made up the *kulliye* were

---

1095 A.W. Pond: *The Desert World;* (New York; 1962); pp. 175-6.

1096 G.S. Colin: La Noria maroccaine; *Hesperis;* 14; pp. 38-9.

1097 H. Ferhat: Fes; in *Grandes Villes Mediterraneenes;* op cit; pp. 215-33; p. 225.

1098 Ibid.

1099 W. Spencer: The Urban Achievements in Islam: Some Historical considerations; in *Proceedings of the First International Symposium for the History of Arabic Science* (Aleppo; 1976), pp. 249-60; at p. 259.

1100 G. Marcais: l'Urbanisme; op cit; p. 226.

1101 Al-Bakri in G. Marcais: l'Urbanisme; op cit; p. 226.

1102 J. Lehrman: Gardens; Islam; in T*he Oxford Companion to Gardens*; ed., by G. Jellicoe et al (Oxford University Press; 1986), pp. 277-80 at p. 279.

1103 S. Lane-Poole: *The Moors in Spain* (Fisher Unwin; London; 1888), pp. 135.

1104 S.P. Scott: *History*; vol 3; op cit; p. 520.

1105 Y. Kimiyo: The Water supplies and Public Fountains of Ottoman Istanbul; in O. Atsuyuki ed. *Islamic Area Studies With Geographical Information Systems*; (Routledge; Curzon; London; 2004); pp. 162-83; at p. 163.

carried out through this donation system.[1106] So effective was the system, in the mid-16th century, at the peak of Ottoman prosperity and power, a Spanish doctor who worked for Admiral Sinan Pasha (died 1553) was astonished at the great number of public fountains in the city of Istanbul.[1107] Water from Halkali (northwest of Istanbul) and Kirkcesme (in the *Kagithane* region, north of Istanbul) were carried from the outskirts to Istanbul, inside the city walls. Sixteen water supplies were used to transport the Halkali water to the city, collectively seen as the Halkali Aqueducts.[1108] Mohammed II (the Conqueror) (reigned 1444-46, then 1451-81) was the first to embark on construction of a water supply to transport Halkali water to the city, by initiating the construction of the first (Fatih) Halkali Aqueducts.[1109] The main objective of the Fatih Aqueduct was to supply water to the similarly named *kulliye* built between 1463 and 1470. Fatih *kulliye* was the first large-scale *kulliye* built under the Ottomans, including a mosque in the centre, and in surrounding areas, 16 colleges, a school for the study of the Qur'an, a library, a hospital, accommodation facilities and a soup kitchen for the poor.[1110] The royal chief architect, Sinan, completed the Kirkcesme Water Supply that carried Kirkcesme water to the city during the reign of Suleyman I (Sultan 1520-66) in 1554-63.[1111] The Kirkcesme Water Supply constituted a large network in areas that the earlier Halkali water did not reach. *Tezkireti-Bunyan* that chronicles the life of Sinan records the following statement of Suleyman concerning its construction:

> My intention is that this water should reach every district of the city; let fountains be built where the life of the land is right. Where it is too high, let wells be dug that they be filled by conduits from the city's water supply. Let the elderly, frail widows and little children everywhere fill their pitchers and cups, let them pray for the continuation of my prosperity.

Mimar Sinan and Tezkiret-i Bunyan (Sozen 1989).[1112]

All these gigantic engineering endeavours were the task of a highly organised and regulated state apparatus, under whose payroll there was a considerable labour force, and operating according to established scientific models as can be found in The *Kitab al-Hawi,* an anonymous Iraqi treatise of the early 11th century.[1113] In a section devoted to quantity surveying, instructions are given for calculating the quantities of earth to be excavated from canals of given lengths, widths and depths and for converting these quantities into manpower requirements.[1114] The canal banks were reinforced with bundles of reeds, and the man-hours required

[1106] Ibid.
[1107] F. Carim: *Kanuni Devrinde Istanbul,* (Istanbul: Yeni Savas Matbaasi; 1964).
[1108] Y. Kimiyo: The Water supplies; op cit; p. 163.
[1109] Ibid; p. 164.
[1110] Ibid; p. 165.
[1111] Ibid; p. 164.
[1112] M. Sozen ed. *Mimar Sinan and Tezkiret-I Bunyan*; (Turkiye Istanbul: Emlak Bankasi; 1989).
[1113] C. Cahen, 'Le Service de l'irrigation en Iraq au debut du XI siècle' in *Bulletin d'Etudes Orientales*, vol. 13 (1949-51), pp. 117-43.
[1114] D. Hill: *A History of Engineering*; op cit; p. 42.

for preparing and placing the bundles are clearly stated. For excavation, the number of diggers was first calculated, then the number of carriers was added, a number which depended on the distance the spoil had to be transported. Overheads for additional workers and supervision were then added. There was a set price for each task, so in the end a Bill of Quantities was produced which would provide the estimate for the cost of the works and serve as a guide for the recruitment of labour.[1115] Or, if the project was let out to subcontract, which was often the case, the Bill of Quantities would be the main document for awarding the contract and for the subsequent measurements and payments.[1116] From this document, and elsewhere, Hill insists, we get a picture of a highly organised state enterprise, with an army of bureaucrats, engineers and surveyors, controlling a very large labour force, whose productivity and rates of pay were closely specified.[1117] Although the calculations in the *Kitab al-Hawi* are only 'worked examples', they were probably based upon typical jobs done by the department in the past. The numbers of men resulting from the calculations are between 500 and 1,600, and there must have been a number of projects of this size at any given time. We also have reports such as the one for the district of Marw, which gives the labour force for the irrigation department as 10,000 men.[1118] This sort of organisation was at least six centuries ahead of anything similar in the Christian West, where only until the time of the French king, Louis the XIV (Ruled 1643-1715), were any works of a similar scale undertaken.

As with most other manifestations of early Islamic glory, whilst the faith acted as the motivating force, the practical impetus for such great accomplishments resulted from the then current scientific upsurge which provided solutions to practical problems. The chapter dealing with engineering in the next part will give an extended overview of how Muslims met the challenges and the needs for water supply, whether for irrigation of their fields, or for the demands of the faith, or their urban needs. Here briefly, we note Muslim engineering ingenuity in the construction of the magnificent reservoirs at al-Qayrawan (Tunisia). There, two impressive linked cisterns were constructed for receiving the waters of the Wadi Merj al-Lil when it was in flood.[1119] These cisterns, which still stand, were completed in 862. Although they appear to be circular, both are actually polygonal, the larger having a diameter of just under 130 metres, the smaller one a diameter of 37.4 metres. The smaller receives the waters of the wadi and acts as a settling tank; a circular duct, several metres above its base connects it to the larger cistern, which has a depth of about eight metres. On leaving the larger cistern, the water is decanted a second time into two oblong covered cisterns.[1120]

[1115] Ibid.
[1116] Ibid.
[1117] Ibid.
[1118] Ibn Hawqal: *Kitab Surat al-'Ard,* Arabic text ed. J.H. Kramers, 2nd ed., of vol. 2 of BGA (Brill Leiden, 1938), pp. 635-6.
[1119] K.A.C. Creswell: *A Short Account of Early Islamic Architecture*; Penguin Books; London; 1958; pp. 291-2.
[1120] K.A.C. Creswell: *A Short Account of Early Islamic Architecture*; pp. 291-2.

Muslim engineers also needed to provide techniques that strictly controlled the use of water under conditions of drought and scarcity. Al-Jazari, for instance, devised automata that allowed the sparing use of water.[1121] The principle of the siphon, Scott also notes, was familiar to the Muslims eight hundred years before it was known in France, and was utilized to a remarkable degree in the Muslim Hydraulic system.[1122] An excellent detailed illustration of how the siphon was developed can be found in the *Kitab al-Hayal* by the Banu Musa brothers (fl. early 9th century).[1123]

Baths dominated the Islamic urban and social landscape, and were found alongside numerous pools, as frequent washing is part of religious duty for Muslims.[1124] Hot baths were thus in use in the Muslim world from the 7th century onwards.[1125] The baths of Damascus, meticulously constructed, were numerous; the historian, Ibn al-Asakir pointing out that during his era, the second half of the 12th century, there were forty public baths within Damascus, and another seventeen in its suburbs.[1126] Two centuries before him, the geographer al-Muqaddasi, when in the city, exclaimed: 'There are no baths more beautiful, no fountains more wonderful.'[1127]

In his time, water was piped from the hot springs in Tiberias to Damascus' hot baths.[1128] Many such baths were still working in 1914, 24 hours a day, and they were also hostels for travellers coming from distant lands to spend a night in warmth and comfort.[1129] In Aleppo, in the middle of the 13th century, Ibn Shadad counted 70 baths in the city itself and another 93 in the suburbs, to which could be added thirty or so private baths.[1130] In Algiers, great care was lavished on the hammams (baths), two of which were constructed by high-ranking officials for the public at private expense.[1131] In Muslim Spain, public baths could be found even in the smallest village; in the middle of the 10th century, Cordova alone had 900, whilst, as Scott notes, in the 18th century, in contrast, there were not as many in all of Europe.[1132] The Muslims were in the habit of taking a bath daily, and accordingly, baths were generally reserved for men in the mornings and women in the afternoons.[1133]

The baths were built on the traditional plan: a vestibule for undressing followed by a number of rooms, each of which was hotter than the other serially, and

---

1121 Al-Jazari: *The Book of Knowledge of Ingenious Mechanical Devices*, tr. D.R. Hill (Dordrecht, Boston, 1974).
1122 S.P. Scott: *History*; op cit; vol 2; p. 601.
1123 A. Bir: *The Book of Kitab al-Hiyal of Banu Musa Bin Shakir* (IRCICA; Istanbul; 1990).
1124 Z. Oldenbourg: *The Crusades*; op cit; p. 476.
1125 D.R. Hill: *A History of Engineering*; op cit; p. 44.
1126 Referred to by Thierry Bianquis: Damas in *Grandes Villes Mediterraneenes;* op cit; pp. 37-55; at p. 46.
1127 Al-Muqaddasi: *Ahssan al-taqassim;* op cit; p. 157.
1128 Al-Istakhri: *Kitab al-Masalik wa'l Mamalik;* ed. M.G. al-Hini (Cairo; 1961), pp. 44-5.
1129 T. Bianquis: Damas; op cit; p. 46.
1130 Ibn Shadad: *Al-Alaq al-Khatira*; ed. D. Sourdel (Damascus; 1953), pp. 291-302; in A.M. Edde: Alep; in *Grandes Villes Mediterraneenes;* op cit; pp. 157-75; at p. 166.
1131 W. Spencer: the Urban Achievements; op cit; p. 259.
1132 S.P. Scott: *History;* op cit; vol 3; pp. 520-2.
1133 S.M. Imamuddin: *Muslim;* op cit; p. 208.

finally a cooler one for re-adjustment to the external temperature.[1134] Writing early in the 14th century, the Egyptian Ibn al-Ukhuwwa describes the bath as having three chambers:

> The first chamber is to cool and moisten, the second heats and relaxes, the third heats and dries.[1135]

The baths and the supply tank had to be thoroughly cleaned every day.[1136]

Like most aspects of Islamic civilisation, baths had an intricate link with the faith. Lane Poole notes how:

> The monks and nuns boasted of their filthiness, insomuch that a lady saint recorded with pride the fact that up to the age of sixty she had never washed any part of her body, except the tips of her fingers when she was going to take the mass. While dirt was characteristic of Christian sanctity, the Muslims were careful in the most minute particulars of cleanliness, and dared not approach their God until their bodies were purified.[1137]

The elimination of Islam from Spain thus required the destruction of baths, both public and private.[1138] One of the first acts of Isabella after the conquest of Grenada (1492) was the demolition of baths on account:

> Of the scandal the sight of apartments devoted to ablution and luxury caused every good Christian, as well as for the reason that their use was always considered entirely superfluous in a monastic institution.[1139]

Philip II (1527-1598) ordered the destruction of all public baths on the ground that they were relics of infidelity.[1140] Recurrently measures were passed that all baths, public and private, were to be destroyed, and that 'no one in future was to use them.'[1141] As an earnest enforcement, all baths were forthwith destroyed, beginning with those of the king.[1142] Everyone clean and neat gave the suspicion 'of being a Muslim who regularly performed their ablutions.'[1143] One, Bartolome Sanchez, appeared in the Toledo Auto da fe of 1597 for bathing, and although overcoming torture, he was finally brought to confess and was punished with three years in the galleys, and perpetual prison and confiscation.[1144] Michael Canete, a gardener, for washing himself in the fields while at work, was tried in 1606: there was nothing else against him but he was tortured.[1145] This hostility to bathing was

---

[1134] Ibid; p. 209.

[1135] Ibn Al-Ukhuwwa: *Ma'alim al-Qurba fi Ahkam al-Hisba*; ed., R. Levy; Arabic text with abridged English translation (Gibb Memorial Series) (London; New Series; 1938), pp. 149 ff.

[1136] D.R. Hill: *A History of Engineering;* op cit; p. 44.

[1137] S. Lane Poole: *The Moors*; op cit; pp. 135-6.

[1138] T.B. Irving: Dates, Names and Places: The end of Islamic Spain; in *Revue d'Histoire Maghrebine;* No 61-62 (1991); pp. 77-93; p. 85.

[1139] S.P. Scott: *History;* op cit; Vol II, p. 261.

[1140] S. Lane Poole: *The Moors;* op cit; pp. 135-6.

[1141] Luis del Marmol Carbajal: *Rebelion y Castigo de los Moriscos de Granada* (Bibliotheca de autores espanoles, Tom. XXI); pp. 161-2.

[1142] H. C. Lea: *A History of the Inquisition of Spain*, 4 vols (The Mac Millan Company, New York, 1907), vol 3; p. 336

[1143] T.B. Irving: Dates, names and places; op cit; p. 81.

[1144] H.C. Lea: *The Moriscos of Spain*; (Burt Franklin; New York; 1968) reprint; p. 129.

[1145] Ibid.

not the prerogative of Spain alone, but was an expression of generalised hostility to bathing, seen, in many respects, as a sign of Muslim degeneracy. Anti Islamic polemicists claimed that Islam was effected by a deliberate policy of promiscuity.[1146] Bathing, thus, remained highly unpopular in the West until fairly recent times. It has been observed that Shakespeare made few references to bathing or washing; and that the 16th and 17th centuries, Conner observes, were an insanitary period in European history.[1147] In these circumstances European travellers to the Muslim East were often prepared to admit that Middle-Eastern peoples were more cleanly than their own.[1148] Fynes Moryson found that the Turks, above all, kept their bodies and clothing clean as a matter of religion; perhaps in frequency of bathing they might be rivalled by the Germans, but:

> Surely the Germanes use it not for cleanlinesse, but to dry up the Grosse humours which they get by intemperate drinking.[1149]

However, David Urquhart later argued that the hot bath 'produces, with cleanliness, habits of self-respect, which are incompatible with intoxication.'[1150] Later in the 17th century Grelot was impressed by the number of public lavatories in Istanbul, with fountains in them, and kept very clean, in contrast to Europe, where such facilities were rare and even church walls were besmirched.[1151]

Contrary to the view found in most writing on Islamic medieval cities, Marcais insists, it is entirely erroneous to believe that the Muslims released their used waters, sewage, or refuse to the street.[1152] Sanitary regulations were, in fact, maintained to a high degree, and a thorough system of drainage prevailed. Seven centuries after the cities of Spain had been drained by a system of great sewers, their streets kept free from rubbish, and subjected to daily cleansing, Scott observes:

> Paris was still worthy of its ancient appellation of Lutetia, "The Muddy;" the way of the pedestrian was blocked by heaps of steaming offal and garbage; and droves of swine, the only scavengers, roamed unmolested through court-yard and thoroughfare.[1153]

Sewage systems under the city of Muslim Valencia were large enough to admit a cart with ease, and the smallest could be traversed by a loaded beast of burden.[1154] Cordoba was well equipped with a good sewage system, which made

---

[1146] E. Said: *Orientalism*; (London; 1980); p. 188; and R.W. Southern: *Western Views of Islam in the Middle Ages;* (Harvard; 1962); pp. 30-1.
[1147] P. Conner: On the Bath: Western Experience of the Hamam; in *Renaissance and Modern Studies*; vol 31; (1987); pp. 34-42; at p. 35.
[1148] Ibid.
[1149] F. Moryson: *Itinerary*; London; 1617; pt 1; Bk.3; ch. 4; p. 265; and pt. III. Bk. 1 ch 3; p. 44.
[1150] D. Urquhart: *The Pillars of Hercules*; (London; 1850); ii; 80.
[1151] W.J. Grelot: *A Late Voyage to Constantinople*; Tr. J. Phillips; (London; 1683); pp. 193-4; in P. Conner: On the Bath; p. 36.
[1152] G. Marcais: l'Urbanisme; op cit; p. 226.
[1153] S.P. Scott: *History;* op cit; vol 3; pp. 520-2.
[1154] Ibid; vol 1; p. 613.

it possible to evacuate waste.[1155] In the cities of the East, Oldenbourg notes, the conditions of hygiene and comfort were closer to those of the 19th century than to anything in the Middle Ages.[1156] And so it was in North Africa, even in flat cities such as Al-Qayrawan, where such a system would have been hard to establish.[1157] So effective was the system that when the French entered the city of Fes (early in the 20th century), they found it adequate enough to leave it untouched.[1158] This applies to other parts; excavation showing this to be the case in Fustat (Cairo), where each house, probably, had its own cesspool, in some cases linked by piping to a general drainage network.[1159] The task of making certain that the whole sewage system worked fell to the urban sewage cleaner, operating as part of the city corporation, under the jurisdiction of the Muhtasib.[1160]

Central in the provision and upkeep of all such works and structures were purely Islamic, religious, endowments, *waqfs*. The provision of drinking water, which as noted, was considered a meritorious action, resulted in many individuals building qanats and constituting them into *waqfs*, whether in a town, or a particular quarter of a city.[1161] Canals and a fountain were built for the sanctuary of Hebron between 1453 and 1461. Though the Mamluk emirs paid for most of the water projects, *waqfs* were often left for the maintenance of the canals.[1162] In Tunis, water supply was taken in charge by both central administration and religious endowments.[1163] Often, the founder of a *waqf* laid down the rules, as in one instance, that the water, when it reached the town, should be let into the houses and cisterns, and that as soon as one place had taken water, the remainder should be let into the next place, and that at times when water was scarce, no one should use more than was necessary.[1164] The founder also stipulated that rice (which demands huge amounts water) should not be cultivated with the water of the *waqf*, which has to flow into the town. Many wells, as well as fountains, in both bazaars and streets of towns were also constituted into *waqfs*.[1165]

Drinking water in the towns came under the Muhtasib's general supervision, and if water conduits were in a state of disrepair, it was his duty to have them repaired, and under certain situations could order the townspeople to do so, and if the source of drinking water was polluted, he could order them to resolve the problem.[1166] Likewise, after *qanats* came into widespread use in the Muslim World, a body of

---

1155 M. Acien Almansa and A. Vallejo Triano: Cordoue; op cit; p. 126.
1156 Z. Oldenbourg: *The Crusades*; op cit; p. 498.
1157 G. Marcais: l'Urbanisme; op cit; p. 227.
1158 Ibid.
1159 G. Wiet et al: *History*; op cit; p. 318.
1160 G. Marcais: l'Urbanisme; op cit; p. 226.
1161 A.K.S. Lambton: Ma'; in *Encyclopaedia of Islam*; op cit; vol 5; new series; at p. 876.
1162 I.M. Lapidus: *Muslim Cities in the Later Middle Ages*; p. 72.
1163 S. Denoix: Bilans in *Grandes Villes*; op cit; p. 294.
1164 A.K.S. Lambton: Ma'; op cit; p. 876.
1165 Abd al-Husyan Sipinta: *Tarikhiya-yi awkaf-I Isfahan*; 1967; p. 360, in A.K.S. Lambton: Ma'; op cit; p. 876.
1166 R. Levey: *The Social Structure of Islam* (Cambridge; 1957), p. 337.

customs and law *(shari'a)* developed to regulate the water-supply system.[1167] The earliest known codification of this law is the *Kitabi Qani* or Book of *Qanats* which was in existence in the 11th century.[1168] Its original purpose was to protect *qanat* owners in a risky but essential investment in permanent agricultural settlement, the law of *harim* ("borders"), for example, gave the owner protection over territory surrounding his qanat and prohibited the sinking of new mother wells within one kilometre of existing *qanats.*[1169]

Health and social organisations, equally, in their foundation, management and upkeep, were the outcome of strictly Islamic forms of organisation, especially religious endowments, complemented by measures from the central authority. The latter was heavily involved in the construction and setting up of hospitals and hostels, for instance.[1170] One of the earliest hospitals was established in old Cairo, at al-Fustat, in 872 by Ibn Tulun, a former slave of Turkish origin, who rose in the military ranks to become governor of the city. In both construction and management, the hospital absorbed vast resources, which came chiefly from the bazaar and from other *waqfs.*[1171] The patients were given a special garment and beds, and were served meals and medications, whilst physicians attended to the patients every day. Every Friday Ibn-Tulun visited the hospital, inspected the supplies, conferred with the physicians and visited the patients.[1172] A number of Muslim hospitals, such as the Adudi in Baghdad, the Qala'un in Cairo and the Mansur in Marrakech, were outstanding in their size, their furnishings and equipment, and the quality of their staff.[1173] Even allowing for the Oriental tendency to exaggerate, Whipple points out, their wealth and revenues made possible the magnificence of these establishments.[1174] The director had charge of the administration, supervision of the supplies and medicaments and the furnishing of the hospital; in some instances he had charge of the *waqfs* of the hospital, but the actual professional work was left to the physicians, in the hands of the physician-in-chief or dean, assisted by the heads of the different specialties.[1175] As for the hostels, some of their aims were to provide shelter to the poor, the elderly, or those without family or relatives to care for them.[1176]

[1167] P. Ward English: The Origin and Spread of Qanats in the Old World; in M.G. Morony ed. *Production and the Exploitation of Resources*; Ashgate; 2002; pp. 273-84; at p. 282.

[1168] A special assembly was convened in Khwarizm in the 9th century by 'Abdullah ibn Tahir to write this book of laws on *qanats,* because in the other books on law (fiqh) and in the Traditions of the Prophet *qanats* are not mentioned. A.K.S. Lambton, *Landlord and Peasant in Persia* (London, 1953), p. 217.

[1169] P. Ward English: The Origin and Spread of Qanats; p. 282.

[1170] A.M. Edde: Alep; in *Grandes Villes Mediterraneenes;* op cit; pp. 157-75; at p. 169.

[1171] A. Whipple: *The Role of the Nestorians and Muslims in the History of Medicine;* facsimile of the original book, produced in 1977 by microfilm-xerography by University Microfilms International (Ann Arbor, Michigan, U.S.A; 1977), p. 93; and A. Issa Bey: *Histoire des hopitaux en Islam*; Beirut; Dar ar ra'id al'arabi; 1981; pp. 112-5.

[1172] A. Issa Bey: *Histoire;* op cit; pp. 112-5.

[1173] A. Whipple: *The Role*; op cit; p. 80.

[1174] Ibid.

[1175] Ibid; p. 81.

[1176] A.M. Edde: Alep; op cit; p. 169.

There were also hostels for the care of poor women, widows, divorced, and unmarried girls, who could not be taken in charge by their relatives.[1177]

Endowments, again, financed such institutions. In Aleppo, it is known that a share of profits from lands and orchards, mills and shops, and baths were constituted into *waqfs*, and were devoted to the financing of hospitals (and also of mosques and madrasas).[1178] Nur Eddin Zangi (r. 1146-1174) instituted a waqf for a hospital for destitute men in Aleppo, which was extended in 1257 to also include a ward for women.[1179] This hospital, which was further transformed in the Mamluk period, was mainly to serve the poorer sections of the population.[1180] This was not the sole example, for under the Mamluks, many *waqfs* funded hospitals and also convents for the poor.[1181] The hospital of the Mamluk sultan, Qala'un, for example, was supported by the income from all of his commercial properties, including each of his warehouses (locally known as *funduq).*[1182]

Other than hospitals, endowments also funded diverse social amenities, those aimed at the destitute in particular. The second of the two *khans* built by Sultan Qayitbay in 1480-1, after the sultan had made the pilgrimage to Makkah, was endowed for the benefit of the poorer inhabitants of Madinah.[1183] The revenues of the Tiryaki Carsi (originally a drug dispensary) in Istanbul, across the avenue from its parent mosque, the Suleymaniye, and the Misr Carsi (the Egyptian or Spice Bazaar), part of the foundation of the Yeni Valide on the Golden Horn, were both permanently attached to the *kulliyes* of which each formed part.[1184] All these services relied largely on group solidarity.[1185] This was possible because the Muslim does not just have the personal duty imposed by the faith to help those in distress, through the zaqat (alms), one of the five pillars of Islam, but also in all Islamic cities there was found a network aimed for the care of the sick, the poor, women, or those whose relatives failed to care for.[1186]

Order and security in the Islamic city, finally, were early imperatives, too. All cities had a police force, in Baghdad, the *Sahib al-Shurta* (the Police Chief) being the most powerful figure in the urban administration.[1187] In Aleppo, various institutions of Seljuk origin policed the city.[1188] The same in the Islamic west, such as in Tunis, where the city centre was policed, and so were the suburbs and the surrounding gardens, as well as the markets.[1189] In the same country, in Al-

[1177] Ibid.
[1178] S. Denoix: Bilans, in *Grandes Villes Mediterraneenes;* op cit; p. 294.
[1179] Ibid.
[1180] A.M. Edde: Alep; op cit; p. 169.
[1181] S. Denoix: Bilans; op cit; p. 294.
[1182] E. Sims: Trade and Travel: Markets and Caravanserais; in G. Michell ed., *Architecture;* op cit; pp. 97-111; at p. 110.
[1183] Ibid.
[1184] Ibid.
[1185] D. Behrens Abouseif; S. Denoix, J.C. Garcin: Cairo: in *Grandes Villes;* op cit; p. 194.
[1186] Ibid.
[1187] S. Denoix: Bilans; op cit; p. 287.
[1188] Ibid.
[1189] Ibid.

Qayrawan, the police deployed agents watching public order. It was under the command of a chief who was second in power to the local governor.[1190] The *Wali al-Madina*, or the city's local governor, a man of the law, had the duty to ensure order in the city. There was also a wide distribution of police stations within the city.[1191] In Spanish cities, Scott and Glick note, order was kept by a strong and well-organised police, patrolling the thoroughfares day and night.[1192] Cordoba was policed by at least three distinct forces, each of them with its specific functions.[1193]

3. Construction Skills, and Aesthetics

> It is only necessary to go through the literary and artistic works of the Arabs, [says Le Bon] to notice that they always sought to embellish nature. The characteristic of Arabic art is imagination, the brilliant, splendour, exuberance in decoration, fantasy in the details. A race of poets- and poets doubled with artists. Having become rich enough to achieve all their dreams, they bred those fantastic palaces which seem to be sculptures of marbles engraved with gold and precious metals. No other people has possessed such marvels, and none will ever posses them. They correspond to an age of youth and illusion gone for ever. It is not this epoch of cold and utilitarian banality, which humanity has now entered where they could be sought.[1194]

Similar impression of Muslim artistic accomplishments is conveyed by Talbot Rice:

> The Period of Samarra's supremacy (836-83), so far as art was concerned, was one of the most brilliant in Islamic history; at no time before had so much been built in so short a space of time or had such elaborate decorations been devoted to so large a number of houses as well as mosques and palaces. As one wanders over this immense field of ruins one can but marvel at the age which was responsible for such lavishness.[1195]

Madinat al-Zahra (in Cordova) in Scott's words:

> From a royal villa, Medina al-Zahra insensibly expanded into a miniature city. Around the palace clustered the luxurious dwellings of the courtiers, the merchants, and the officers of the army. The avenues were lined with trees, whose foliage formed a continuous arch. Not a house could be seen that was not embosomed in gardens abounding with gushing water and rare exotics. Even the sides of the Sierra had been stripped of the sombre growth of the evergreens which had originally covered them, and, planted

---

[1190] M. Sakly: Kairouan in *Grandes Villes Mediterraneenes*; op cit; pp. 57-85; p. 73.
[1191] Ibid.
[1192] T. Glick: *Islamic*; op cit; p. 115. S.P. Scott: *History*; op cit.
[1193] M. Acien Almansa and A. Vallejo Triano: Cordoue; op cit; pp. 117-34; at p. 128.
[1194] G Le Bon: *La Civilisation;* op cit; p. 402.
[1195] D. Talbot Rice: *Islamic Art* (Thames and Hudson; London; 1979 ed), p. 97.

> with fig and almond trees, appeared in all the beauty of luxuriant foliage and fragrant blossoms. Not far away, extensive plantations of the sweetest of flowers gave to the locality the name of Gebal al-Wardat, the Mountain of the Rose.[1196]

There is a specialised Western literature in praise of Islam's construction skills and beauty seen in buildings such as the Great Mosque of Damascus, The Dome of the Rock in Jerusalem, the Alhambra in Grenada, and the Blue Mosque of Istanbul. Lambert, Calvert, Harvey, Talbot Rice, Creswell, Marcais, Ettinghausen, and others, have brought to general appreciation such Islamic greatness.[1197] Creswell, for instance, makes an excellent case for the walls and Baghdad gate of Raqqa, the fortified palace of Ukhaidir, 120 miles south of Baghdad, or the buildings of Samarra.[1198] Calvert makes one of the best studies of the Muslim remains in the Spanish cities of Cordoba, Seville and Toledo.[1199]
These accounts of Islamic brilliance seem to conflict with more recent claims that tend to belittle this legacy, that of some dynasties, in particular. Ashtor, for instance, is extremely disparaging towards the Seljuk Turks and Mamluks. About the former, and in regard to their lack of construction skills, he says:

> The attentive reader of the Arabic chronicles of the Seljukid age becomes aware of these facts at time and again he comes across reports of bridges falling down and dams bursting. For often the chronicler reveals that it was not simply the consequence of negligence but of bad construction and ineffective repairs.[1200]

Just as other historians of Islamic civilisation,[1201] he in fact blames the entire decline of Muslim civilisation on the Seljuks.
Looking at historical evidence, however, contradicts his, and others' views. First and foremost, it was the Seljuks who united and saved the Muslim world from total disintegration in the 11th century.[1202] It was also the Seljuks who stood in defence of the Muslim world when the crusaders arrived in 1096, and the great early leaders who led the Muslim armies such as Mawdud, Imad Eddin Zangi, and Nur Eddin Zangi were either of Seljuk stock or associated with them.[1203] In regard to cultural and other accomplishments, the medieval revival of arts and crafts that took place in Iran, Mesopotamia, Syria, and Asia Minor did so under Seljuk

---

1196 S.P. Scott: *History;* op cit; vol 1; p. 630.
1197 See for instance: K.A.C. Creswell: *Early Muslim Architecture*, 2 Vols (1932-40). A.F. Calvert: *Moorish Remains in Spain*; 3 vols; (John Lane Company; London; 1906). E. Male: *Art et artistes du Moyen Age* (Paris 1927), pp. 30-88. G. Marcais: *Manuel d'Art Musulman* (Paris; 1926). G. Marcais: *l'Architecture Musulmane d'Occident*, (Paris 1954). H. Terrasse: *L'Art hispano mauresque des origins au 13em siecle* (Paris; 1933).
1198 K.A.C. Creswell: *A Short Account on early Islamic Architecture* (Scholar Press; 1989).
1199 A. F. Calvert: *Moorish Remains in Spain*; op cit; 1906.
1200 E. Ashtor: *A Social and Economic History of the Near East in the Middle Ages* (Collins; London; 1976), p. 244.
1201 G. Wiet et al: *History*; op cit; pp. 7; 156-7; 243; F.B. Artz: *The Mind;* op cit; p. 175-6; D. Campbell: *Arabian Medicine*; op cit; (see also final part, the section on Orthodoxy).
1202 E. Gibbon: *The Decline and Fall*; op cit; p. 232 ff.
1203 W.B. Stevenson: *The Crusaders in the East*; Cambridge University Press; 1907.

rule.[1204] Seljuk architectural skills were evident during the crusades, especially in their prompt and accomplished ways in repairing any damaged structures, whether in time of peace or war. At Nicaea, for instance, during the first crusade, an attempt by the crusaders to cause the city walls to collapse by mining was repaired overnight.[1205] Seljuk engineering skills were in fact so advanced that the crusaders learnt from them the art of fixing bridges and structures falling into disrepair, or following earthquakes.[1206] The Seljuk capital Konya, towards the end of the 12th century, was impressive, a sizeable and splendid city 'of the size of Cologne', according to contemporary Western visitors.[1207] It was laid in the form of a rectangle with rounded corners, and was enclosed by 108 great stone towers; the Pentagonal citadel built surrounding the hill.[1208] A palace kiosk rivalled the honeycomb vaulted interior of the Capella Palatina at Palermo; the inside of the cupola of the Buyuk Kataray Medrese, decorated in the mid 13th century still glimmers in blue and gold on triangular pendentives.[1209] The caravanserais, built like basilicas, had high-arched aisles.[1210] The mosque of Ani in Armenia; the magnificent portal of the mosque of Diwrigi in Konya; the immense mosque of Ala-Uddin; the cavernous porch and embroidery like facade of the Sirtjeli Madrasa; the Great Mosque of Mosul; the tower of Tughril Beg at Rayy; the tomb of Sinjar at Merw; the dazzling mihrab of the Alaviyan Mosque at Hamadan; the ribbed vault and unique squinches of the Friday Mosque at Qasvin, and there, too, the great arches and mihrab of the Haydaria Mosque: these are but a few of the structures that remain to prove the skill of Seljuk architects and the taste of Seljuk kings, Durant notes.[1211] But more beautiful than any of these, Durant continues, is the masterpiece of the Seljuk age, the Masjid-i-Jami, or Friday Mosque, of Isfahan. Like Chartres or Notre Dame, it bears the labour and stamp of many centuries; begun in 1088, it was several times restored or enlarged, and reached its present form only in 1612, but the larger of the great brick domes carries the inscription of Nizam al Mulk (Seljuk minister d. 1092) and the date 1088.[1212] The porch and the sanctuary portals, one eighty feet high, are adorned with mosaic tiles hardly rivalled in all the history of that art; the inner halls are roofed with ribbed vaults, complex squinches and pointed arches springing from massive piers. The mihrab (1310) has a stucco relief of vine and lotus foliage, and Kufic lettering, unsurpassed in Islam.[1213] Concluding his account, Durant insists:

> Such monuments laugh out of court the notion that the Turks were barbarians. Just as the Seljuk rulers and viziers were among the most

---

[1204] M.S. Dimand: *A Handbook of Muhammadan Art*; (The Metropolitan Museum of Art; New York; 1958); p. 262.

[1205] M. Erbstosser: *The Crusades;* op cit; p. 123

[1206] J. Harvey: The Development of Architecture, in *The Flowering of the Middle Ages*; ed J. Evans (Thames and Hudson; 1985), pp. 85-106.

[1207] F.F. Armesto: *Millennium* (A Touchstone Book; New York; 1995), pp. 97-9.

[1208] Ibid.

[1209] Ibid.

[1210] Ibid.

[1211] W. Durant: *The Age of Faith*; op cit; pp. 316-7.

[1212] Ibid.

[1213] Ibid.

> capable statesmen in history, so the Seljuk architects were among the most competent and courageous builders of an Age of Faith distinguished by massive and audacious designs. The Persian flair for ornament was checked by the heroic mood of the Seljuk style; and the union of the two moods brought an architectural outburst in Asia Minor, Iraq, and Iran, strangely contemporary with the Gothic flowering in France.[1214]

Also in praise of Seljuk achievements is Talbot Rice, who says:

> Though every part of the Islamic world was responsible for the production of works of art of every type, there seem, as we look back today, to be certain especially outstanding arts that we can associate with particular areas or ages; glass with Syria, pottery and miniatures with Persia, or metalwork with modern Mesopotamia, for example, and if we were to follow up this line of thought it would be certainly architecture and architectural decoration that we would associate with the Seljuk of Rum. All over Asia Minor there survive to this day a mass of mosques and madrasas in a very distinctive style and boasting decorations either in carved stone or tile work which are among the finest in all Islam.[1215]

Talbot Rice notes how the Seljuks were the first to develop fine buildings planned as caravanserais, some of which were of considerable size, some almost palaces, and their architecture of the finest sort.[1216]

Other Islamic ethnic groups, Mamluks and Berbers, above all, are also derided for lacking in skills and care for aesthetics.[1217] This, once more, is contradicted by evidence. The Mamluk legacy, for instance, continued to influence Islamic art up to the 20th century.[1218] In their time (mid 13th century onward), they erected hundreds of religious and secular edifices in Cairo, their capital, as well as in the provinces, employing traditional plans, such as hypostyle mosques, four-'wan madrasas, and square mausoleums.[1219] Between 1250 and 1517 they completed some 2,279 projects throughout the territory under their rule according to the catalogue prepared by Michael Meinecke.[1220] His list includes a total of 930 documented projects in Cairo, 253 for Damascus, 232 for Aleppo and 147 for Jerusalem.[1221] Substantial remains survive of 500, almost half of which are in Cairo.[1222] 'The Mamluks' choice of structures,' Ross Burns remarks, 'freed the urban landscape from reliance on stand-alone symmetry, introducing more dynamic relationships between buildings, their individual elements and their

---

1214 Ibid; p. 317.
1215 D. Talbot Rice: *Islamic Art*; op cit; p. 165.
1216 Ibid; pp. 165-6.
1217 Such as: C. Brockelmann: *History of the Islamic Peoples* (Routledge; London; 1950). E. Ashtor: *A Social and Economic History;* op cit.
1218 E. Atil: Mamluk art: *Dictionary of Middle Ages*; op cit; vol 8; p. 69.
1219 Ibid; pp. 69-70.
1220 R. Burns: *Damascus, A History;* Routledge; London; 2005; p. 208.
1221 M. Meinecke: Mamluk Architecture, in *Damaszener Mitteilung*; 1985 a; 165; M. Meinecke: Die mamelukische Architektur….. Gluckstadt; J.J. Agustin; 1992.
1222 R. Burns: *Damascus, A History*; op cit; p. 208.

surrounds.'[1223] Their buildings were lavishly decorated with carved stone, stucco, and marble mosaics and panels, the most outstanding features of Mamluk architecture being soaring tiered minarets, massive carved domes and entrance portals, and marble mihrabs.[1224] The elaborate floral and geometric patterns of the carved stone-work gave these structures their distinctly Mamluk character.[1225]

Berber accomplishments, which will form a major part of discussion in the final part of this work, although generally passed in silence in historical narrative were equally obvious. They can be seen in the 12th century, both in Spain and North Africa, under the Almohad dynasty.[1226] The Giralda Tower of Seville, which took over twenty years to complete (1172-1195) was the work of the Almohads.[1227] It first served as a minaret and observatory, being 300 feet tall, with a base of 43 square feet. It originally had four copper spheres on top which could be seen from miles away, but which were brought down by an earthquake.[1228] It is today a cathedral tower from which one can contemplate a panoramic view of Seville and the Guadalquevir River.[1229] The Great Mosque of Tlemcen (western Algeria) (1082 restored in 1136) is typical of this phase; comparatively small, yet its ornament is lavish, whilst the horseshoe arch has been evolved to an exaggerated degree and the multi-lobed arches and the pierced stonework of the dome are amazingly intricate; which creates a 'picturesque and delightful' effect.[1230]

As a rule, for centuries Muslims erected the most sublime constructions found anywhere, and their techniques and methods retained the admiration of their Western knowledgeable audiences and imitators. It is very opportune here to remind how from the 18th century onwards, the Alhambra has been a source of inspiration for countless European and American poets, writers, painters, and composers, including in the 20th century, the Andalusian composer Manuel de Falla and the poet Frederico Garcia Lorca.[1231] It is now the most celebrated tourist attraction in Spain.[1232] It was not alone. From the Muslim remains of Spain, Calvert, referring to the Gate of the Sun, in Toledo, writes:

'This magnificent gate of rough stone, with its towers of brown granite, has been rightly described as one of the world's masterpieces. Yet here again the pen is powerless to do justice to its beauty; and to describe its proportions and decoration is to complicate, rather than explain, the impression that is conveyed by the camera. The square towers, with their semi-circular fronts, and the great

---

[1223] Ibid.
[1224] E. Atil: Mamluk art: *Dictionary of Middle Ages*; op cit; Vol 8; pp. 69-70.
[1225] Ibid.
[1226] D. Talbot Rice: *Islamic Art*; op cit; p. 149.
[1227] A. Chejne: *Muslim Spain, Its History and Culture* (The University of Minnesota Press; Minneapolis; 1974), p. 367.
[1228] Ibid.
[1229] Ibid; p. 368.
[1230] D. Talbot Price: *Islamic Art;* op cit; p. 149.
[1231] M. Danby: *Moorish Style*; Phaidon Press; London; 1995; p. 41.
[1232] Ibid.

central arch resting on two Moorish columns, and the zones of ornamental arches above the horse-shaped openings, comprise a Moorish gem against a Spanish sky, a miracle of loveliness upon a rough and naked rampart. But how, cries Hannah Lynch, to write of this Puerta del Sol, that "thing of beauty even among -crowded enchantments! It is to pick one's way through superlatives and points of exclamation and call in vain on the goddess of sobriety to subdue our tendency to excess and incoherence. Put this matchless gate in the middle of the desert of Sahara; it would then be worth making the frightful journey alone to look at it. However far you may have journeyed, you would still be for ever thankful to have seen such a masterpiece-incontestably a work of supreme art, perhaps the rarest thing of the world." Whether the writer intends her high eulogy to be applied generally to any "work of supreme art," or to the Puerta del Sol in particular, most people who have come under the witching influence of the art of the Moors, will not deny that it is well deserved.'[1233]

A spectacular decorative form invented by Islamic architects in the 11th and 12th centuries, Stokstad observes, was the muqarnas, or 'stalactite', vault or ceiling (as seen in the ceiling of nave of Capella Palatina in Palermo (1140), an ingenious system of corbels and squinches.[1234] Muqarnas could be used structurally in ceilings and vaults and decoratively in marble, plaster, and tile, and wherever architectural decoration was called for.[1235] The vault, Stokstad explains, may be built of masonry or wood and is often purely decorative.

> Concentric rows of concave cells are corbelled out one above another in an interlocking triple squinch so that the vertical axes of the cells alternate and the upper seem to grow out of the lower. The weight of a muqarnas vault over a square bay does not rest on the corners of the square but on two points along each wall-that is, on the eight points of an octagon inscribed within a square plan. The completed honeycomb-like structure is typically Islamic in its intricate geometric design and its disguise of underlying logic by a dizzying multiplication of forms.[1236]

Such was the enduring impact of this Muslim style in 1919 Hans Poelzig was commissioned to remodel the Grosse Schauspielhaus in Berlin for Max Reinhardt, the famous theatrical producer.[1237] Poelzig used an abundance of stalactite shapes such as muqarnas, which, with skilfully articulated coloured lighting, created a cave like space that was compared at the time to 'an Oriental dream.'[1238] This design was to influence the approach to cinema design in Britain in the 1930s.[1239]

[1233] A.F. Calvert: *Moorish Remains in Spain*; op cit; vol 3: Toledo; p. 433.
[1234] M. Stokstad: *Medieval Art*; (Westview Press; Cambridge; 2004); p. 146.
[1235] Ibid.
[1236] Ibid.
[1237] M. Danby: *Moorish Style*; op cit; p. 217.
[1238] Ibid.
[1239] Ibid.

The inner architectural innovativeness in order to serve practical necessities a well as the beauty of Muslim buildings has also exhausted the lyrical skills of older generations of Western scholars and admirers, and also a few modern ones. Oriental master builders, for instance, in seeking to reinforce their structures, introduced rows of columns into the masonry to have binding effect; and from the 12th century onwards, the walls of ramparts and citadels often were strengthened by buttresses.[1240] Private residences showed similar innovative spirit. Particular arrangements, for instance, were made to deal with the rigours of climate as during the hot season, the rich residents of Baghdad lived in cellars, whilst others made use of *punkahs*, which were large fans suspended from the ceiling; whilst the terraces of Cairo, in particular, generated summer ventilation by means of air-traps opening to the north.[1241]

Light, as Jones insists, has in Islamic architecture a decorative function.[1242] 'It extends the patterns, forms and designs, into the dimension of time. As the day progresses, so the forms change according to the angles of light and shade, as in a kaleidoscope. Light and shade create strong contrasts of planes and give texture to sculpted stone and stuccoed or brick surfaces. As light filters through wooden apertures, stucco and marble screens and patterned coloured glass windows, it projects further patterns on the surfaces behind and beneath, an ephemeral and ever-changing overlay of colours and shadows. The effect is intensified by the artificial lighting system used. Hanging glass lamps, decorated with painted calligraphy and geometric and floral patterns and often held in perforated and patterned metal containers, were intended to cast not a clear beam but a patterned projection on to already patterned surfaces, creating extra layers of design. The patterns on the lamp would be of the same type as those on the walls and ceiling and therefore would produce a harmonious environment both dynamic and restful.'[1243]

The stunning effect of the interior lighting of the Mosque of Cordoba is perfectly captured by Scott.[1244] This interior, by reason of its vast extent and its comparatively low ceiling, was more or less obscure, even at noon-day, and lamps were kept constantly burning by its aisles; two hundred and eighty chandeliers of brass and silver suspended from its arches, the oil used in them being perfumed with costly essences; the largest of these containing 1454 lamps, and measuring 38 feet in circumference; and its reflector containing 36,000 pieces of silver fastened with rivets of gold. Beauty was enhanced by the gems, and by the combined effect of the mirrors, the light was increased, thus, to nine times its original intensity. During the entire month of Ramadhan the mosque was

---

1240 G. Wiet et al: *History;* op cit; p. 317.

1241 Ibid; p. 318.

1242 D. Jones: The Elements of Decoration: Surface, pattern, and Light; in G. Michell ed.; *Architecture*; op cit; pp. 161-75; at p. 173.

1243 Ibid.

1244 S.P. Scott: *History*; op cit; vol 1; p. 663.

illuminated with twenty thousand lights. An enormous taper, weighing sixty pounds, was placed in the Maksurah. Its dimensions were calculated with such accuracy that the wax was completely consumed during the last hour of the last day of the festival.[1245] The intensity of light due to the great number of lamps used is no exaggeration, or unique. Artz speaks of the Mosque of Damascus being lit by thousands of hanging lamps of metal and of enamelled glass.[1246]

Just as light, water, too, has an important decorative place in Islamic architecture, Jones points out. Domestic fountains in reception rooms were very common, certainly in Sicily, Egypt, Syria and Turkey. Generally it was the *shadurwan,* a slab of decorated marble, monochrome or inlaid, tilted at such an angle as to allow a gentle flow of water over its surfaces, which provided the opportunity for a clever interplay of patterns between the running water and the textured surface underneath it and their reflections on ceilings and walls.[1247] A striking example of interplay of light and shade filtered through marble screens and projected on a stream of water is found in the interior of the Rang Mahall, a pavilion in the palace complex of Shah Jihan in the Red Fort in Delhi. There, water is channeled in an open canal that runs through the whole length of the building, in and out of rooms, under screens and platforms, cutting through the floor which it decorates and of which it forms a part.[1248]

4. Impact from Within, and Impact on the West

The point of departure of Islamic construction and design, obviously, is the mosque, and in a chronological order the first such mosque: the Prophet's (PBUH) Mosque. Artz in his thorough and lengthy description of this edifice and those that followed captures the central element of faith as the fundamental determinant of both design and decoration.[1249] The Prophet's mosque was a small dwelling, built in 622 at Madinah under his direction, but was to evolve, and serve as the model for most of the later mosques. The whole structure was a square enclosure, entirely surrounded by walls of brick and stone. One side of the enclosure was roofed with palm branches covered with mud and supported by palm trunks.

Chronologically, it would seem quite remarkable, but the earliest mosque of Islam after that of the Prophet was built in China. This came in the years of diplomatic exchanges between the Prophet and foreign rulers that took place between 628 and 630.[1250] According to Drake:

[1245] Ibid.

[1246] F. Artz: *The Mind;* op cit; p. 148.

[1247] D. Jones: The Element of Decoration; op cit; p. 174.

[1248] Ibid.

[1249] F.B. Artz: *The Mind*; op cit; pp. 172-4.

[1250] M. de Thiersant: *Le Mahometanisme en Chine*; Paris; 1878; vol 1.

> Attention has already been called to an ancient mosque at Hang-chou, for which a T'ang (a dynasty which ruled in China at the time of the Prophet) date is claimed. J.F. Moule's note in *Friends of Moslems* (after Fitch's Hangchow Itineraries) reads: "The oldest of the three mosques is said to have been built originally about 630 CE., in the T'ang dynasty. The present building dates from the 17th century. It has two ancient tablets in Arabic. The Ahung in charge claims that this mosque was built by the uncle of Mohammed himself, Ka Hsing by name..."
> A special interest attaches to this Hang-chou inscription, in that Hang-chou (Khansa) may be taken to be included with its ancient port Kan-p'u, in the great T'ang dynasty depot and Muslim centre of the Arab records – Khanfu.[1251]

The next mosque, built in today's Iraq in 639, was erected on exactly the same plan as the Prophet's Mosque, but the roof was supported by marble columns.

Within eighty or ninety years of the Madinah mosque, all the features of the congregational mosque had evolved. Inside the basic square plan was now added a large open forecourt with a fountain for ablutions in the centre and a shaded colonnade around the sides. Within, everything was arranged for the central act of worship: prayer. Prayer in Islam is more rewarded if performed in a group, and the first row is the most rewarded. Thus, as everyone wished to be near the front, the prayer area of the mosque was thus shaped in a rectangular form; the prayer hall of the Great Mosque at Damascus being 131 meters wide and only 38 meters deep. The annual pilgrimage to Makkah, which brought Muslims from all parts of the realm into contact, contributed greatly to the standardisation of the form of the mosque and also other types of building. However, the structural materials used in both mosques (as in palaces,) (brick, stone, marble, or clay), depended on what was popular in any particular region. Styles also varied, whether with respect to minarets, which followed, with some modifications, the traditional shape of the towers of the countries where they were built. The minaret was the tower from where the call to prayer was made.

The mosques, although generally not too ostentatious externally, were lavishly decorated within with glazed tiles, low flat carvings known as arabesques, rich marble, carpets, and stained-glass windows. However, human and animal forms were strictly forbidden by the Qur'an. Islam also opposes luxury.

> 'He who drinks from gold and silver vessels drinks the fire of Hell,' says a Hadith (Prophetic Saying/Muslim tradition.)

F.S. Drake: Mohammedanism in the Tang Dynasty; *Monumenta Serica*, Vol. 8 (1943), pp. 1-40; at pp. 23-8.
M. Bretschneider: *On the Knowledge Possessed by the Ancient Chinese of the Arabs and Arabian Colonies,* London, Trubner &co, 1871.
[1251] F.S. Drake: Mohammedanism in the Tang Dynasty; op cit, pp. 28-33.

In order to avoid the forbidden, the Muslims, Artz notes, made vessels and tiles of earthenware and covered them with gold lustre; they inlaid steel, brass, copper, and bronze objects with fine bands of gold and silver; and they often carved arabesques on every surface, even in a place like the mihrab. The typical Islamic decoration was based on interlacing lines and geometric designs, and used much colour. Coloured tile and carved and painted arabesque are in fact the common decorative means of Islam. The designs of both tiles and arabesques showed great taste, ingenuity, and inventiveness. Muslims Arabic calligraphy, 'the most beautiful that man has devised, as a common decorative motif,' as Artz holds, uses the text of the Qur'an.[1252] Light inside mosques, in its profusion, also adds to the internal majesty of the building. Carpets, with their perfect unity of design and harmony, the vastness of the interiors, the quietness that could be found within mosques at most times, and the perfumes of incenses also combine to enhance the beauty within. The ceilings are generally high, with the huge domineering interior of the dome at the centre of the building, creating at times an awe inspiring feeling within the onlooker.

Durant explains the architectural revolution, which transformed the old courtyard of the mosque into the madrasa or collegiate mosque throughout Eastern Islam. As mosques increased in number, it was no longer necessary to design them with a large central court to hold a large congregation; and the rising demand for schools required new educational facilities.[1253] From the mosque proper, generally crowned with a dominating dome-four wings or transepts spread, each with its own minarets, a richly decorated portal, and a spacious lecture hall.[1254] This revolution in design was continued by the Mamluks (mid 13th century onwards) in mosques and tombs firmly built in stone, with massive doors of damascened bronze, lit by windows of stained glass, and brilliant with mosaics, carvings in coloured stucco, and such enduring tiles 'as only Islam knew how to make.'[1255]

The mosque of Cordova is certainly one of the most written about edifices for its aesthetics as much as its impact on subsequent buildings.[1256] In its earliest form it was a courtyard mosque of rectangular plan, with a sanctuary of eleven aisles similar to that of the original al-Aqsa mosque at Jerusalem and with horseshoe arches like those topping the arcades of the Umayyad Mosque in Damascus.[1257] Al-Maqqari supplies a large number of quotations from his predecessors who admired the mosque as the best and greatest ever built.[1258] The mosque construction was

---

[1252] Ibid.
[1253] W. Durant: *The Age of Faith*; op cit; pp. 317.
[1254] Ibid.
[1255] Ibid.
[1256] See, for instance, E. Lambert: Histoire de la Grande Mosquee de Cordoue, *Annales de l'Institut d'Etudes Orientales;* 2; (1963); A.A. Salem: Cronologia de la mezquita mayor de Cordoba; *Al-Andalus;* 19 (1954), etc.
[1257] D. Talbot Rice: *Islamic Art;* op cit; p. 77.
[1258] Al-Maqqari: *Nafh Al-Tibb*; op cit; vol 2; pp. 60 ff.

begun by Abd Errahman I in 786, and was enlarged in 833 by Abd Errahman II.[1259] Abd Errahman III and his immediate successors introduced major alterations such as in 950, when he ordered the construction of a minaret 89 yards high.[1260] Al-Hakam II, who succeeded him in 961, built a dome for the mihrab, placed the minbar near it, and brought water to the mosque in canals made of stone.[1261] Al-Mansur (late 10th century) added further enlargements. The mosque is both a very remarkable structure and represents something quite new, notes Talbot Rice, for the dome is supported on a series of intersecting ribs.[1262] The hexafoil arches in two tiers also represent a new and original departure in Islamic architecture.[1263] In its final shape, the mosque contained the finest artistic expressions of the Andalusians, some say it had 360 arches, each receiving the rays of the sun every day of the year; 1,293 marble columns supporting its roofs, and its many ample doors were covered with finely decorated copper.[1264]

The Muslim impact on subsequent Western construction techniques is a vast subject only touched upon succinctly here.[1265] The Cordova mosque, just described, had a great impact on the architecture of the Christian Churches.[1266] One particular area of impact was the horse shoe arch, which Artz notes was first used by Muslims in the construction of the Mosque of Damascus, hence a very early innovation, which they spread widely as they did with pointed arches.[1267] Exteriors of buildings were also done following the Muslim model, such as can be seen near Barcelona on the side of the Catalan church of San Cugat del Valles.[1268] This square tower is crowned with the same top as if 'to evoke a Spanish Muslim minaret' of the prototype built in the 10th century in Cordova under Abd Errahman III.[1269] Lambert insists that during the Romanesque era, architects and decorators from France and Spain certainly borrowed heavily a great number of forms whether directly or indirectly from Oriental forms, which they imitated with great freedom, transposing them, often in a different spirit from that which has inspired them.[1270]

1259 D. Talbot Rice: *Islamic Art*; op cit; p. 77.
1260 Al-Maqqari: *Nafh al-Tibb*; op cit; pp. 84 ff; in A. Chejne: *Muslim Spain,* op cit; p. 365.
1261 Ibid.
1262 D. Talbot Rice: *Islamic Art;* op cit; p. 77.
1263 Ibid; p. 79.
1264 Al-Maqqari: *Nafh al-Tibb*; op cit; pp. 67; 84; 89; in A. Chejne: *Muslim Spain*; op cit; p. 365
1265 For excellent outlines on the matter see: M. S. Briggs: Architecture, in *The Legacy of Islam,* edited by T. Arnold and A. Guillaume (Oxford University Press, first edition, 1931), pp. 155-79; J. Harvey: The Development of Architecture, op cit. A. F. Calvert: *Moorish Remains in Spain*; op cit. A. Fikry: *L'Art Roman du Puy et les Influences Islamiques*; 2nd ed. Soest; (Davaco; 1974). E. Lambert: *L'Art Musulman d'Occident*; (Paris; 1966). H. Terrasse: *L'Art Hispano-Mauresque*; (Paris; G. Van Oest; 1932).
1266 Gomez Moreno: *Iglesias mozarabes* (Madrid; 1919), see also Gomez Moreno: El arte islamico en Espana y en el Magreb; vol 5 of *Historia del Arte* (Madrid, nd).
1267 F. Artz: *The Mind;* op cit; p. 148.
1268 E. Lambert: L'Art Hispano Mauresque et l'Art Romant; *Hesperis*; 17; pp. 29-43; at pp. 38-9.
1269 Ibid.
1270 Ibid; p. 43.

Pilgrimage played a major role in the transfer of Muslim techniques to the Christian West. Much, if not most of the Muslim Spanish influence travelled along the pilgrimage routes, most particularly between Santiago de Compostela, in north-west Spain, and south-west France.[1271] One major route ran from the Le Puy, some 100 km to the south west of Lyons, passing through Conques, Cahors and Moissac in Languedoc, to join with the two more northerly routes to cross the Pyrenees.[1272] The Cathedral at Le Puy (12th century) displays a great wealth of Muslim detail: painted and cusped arches; stone walling with horizontal stripes, corresponding to the alternate voussoirs in contrasting stone over the doorways and blind arcading; masonry panels with pattern work; wooden doors carved in low relief with Kufic inscriptions; and nearly one hundred capitals of Muslim patterns.[1273]

The Crusades were a particular point in history when countless construction skills (and masons) were transferred from the Muslim East to the Christian West. Citing Harvey, the architectural historian, Cochrane explains how it was in Anatolia that skilled Turkish masons used techniques subsequently employed by the Crusaders in their own buildings, sometimes by using local workmen they brought with them back to Europe. Cochrane refers to the use of pointed arches by the Seljuk Turks to repair bridges affected by an earthquake in the year 1114, which soon became familiar in the West.[1274] Briggs outlines further influences on subsequent developments in the West.[1275] He shuns the Church and 'pedantic humanists' of the Renaissance for 'the blindness to such influence,' and emphasises Islamic influences on constructions in Europe from Sicily to mainland Italy, France, and also England, even on the architecture of Christopher Wren.[1276] That influence also extends to military architecture copied from early constructions in Baghdad (8th century,) Salah Eddin's citadel at Cairo, and the citadel of Aleppo (Syria).[1277] Influence, which Briggs also traces to the Crusades.[1278]

Muslim masons were greatly used in Christian parts, especially following Christian military victories and conquest of former Muslim territory. An early instance was the capture of Barbastro in the north-east of Spain in 1064. An army of Normans and Frenchmen, with the blessing of the Pope and under the command of William VIII, Duke of Aquitaine, took many Muslim prisoners, sending several thousands to France, 1500 to Rome and 7000 to Constantinople.[1279] Singers, musicians and

1271 E. Male: *L'art religieux du XIIe siècle en France* (Paris, 1922).
1272 V.I. Atroshenko and J. Collins: *The Origins of the Romanesque*; (Lund Humphries; London; 1985); p. 82.
1273 Ibid; pp. 82-3.
1274 J. Harvey: 'The Origins of Gothic Architecture,' *Antiquaries Journal* 48, 1968, pp. 91-4, in L. Cochrane: *Adelard of Bath* (British Museum Press; 1994), pp. 35-6.
1275 M.S. Briggs: Architecture, pp. 155-79.
1276 Ibid; pp. 167-8.
1277 Ibid.
1278 Ibid; p. 179.
1279 J. Harvey: The Development of Architecture, op cit; p. 86.

other artists were included, but also the Muslim corps of engineers which had defended Barbastro.[1280] These craftsmen possessed technical skills hitherto unknown north of the Alps and Pyrenees.[1281]

In subsequent centuries, following the Christian capture of Spain (1236 ff), Muslim masons as well as Muslim skills were used abundantly in Christian territory. Calvert notes how in its churches and its old houses, Seville is rich in 'Moorish' influences, and exhibits abundant traces of 'Morisco' art, which prevailed against the material dominancy of the Christian conquerors.[1282] Muslims who remained as subjects of Ferdinand became the most lavishly-remunerated artisans of the city.[1283] They pursued the practice of their craft in the dwellings of the rich and in the churches of the "infidel." The church of San Marco has a beautiful 'Moorish' tower built in imitation of the Giralda of Seville, and second only to the minaret tower of the cathedral in point of height; San Gil is a Christianised Mosque; Santa Catalina reveals the survival of 'Moorish' art in its façade, while its principal chapel is Gothic.[1284] Muslim architects from Grenada were also employed by Castilian monarchs in the construction of palaces, and even by church authorities in the ornamentation of cathedrals.[1285] In nearly all the sacred edifices of antiquity the combination of 'Moorish' and Renaissance architecture betrays 'an incongruity of style and sentiment' which is only to be found among the Christian churches of Spain.[1286]

> And if the Catholic kings, who were sworn to the extirpation of the Muslims [Calvert says] allowed the Moors to build their churches in the style of temples devoted to Allah, it is not surprising that many of the finest private residences of the city retain a Moorish design, and possess a distinctly Oriental atmosphere.[1287]

Contacts between Normans and Muslims also explain the ambitious architectural programme which became obvious in northern France and in England shortly before, and in the generation succeeding, the Norman Conquest of 1066.[1288] Following their occupation of Muslim Sicily, beginning in 1061, Norman rulers modelled their palaces on those of their Muslim predecessors.[1289] Norman architects in Sicily and southern Italy gracefully assimilated the Muslim pointed arch (the symbol of the Gothic) in buildings such as the magnificent cloister of Monreale; it was taken up at Monte Cassino and appears in great abundance at Cluny (France).[1290] The Normans took the leading role in the dissemination of the

---

1280 Ibid;
1281 Ibid.
1282 A. F. Calvert: *Moorish Remains in Spain*; op cit; vol 2; Seville; p. 388.
1283 Ibid.
1284 Ibid.
1285 S.P. Scott: *History*; op cit; vol 2; p. 222.
1286 A. F. Calvert: *Moorish Remains in Spain*; op cit; vol 2; Seville; p. 388.
1287 Ibid.
1288 S.P. Scott: *History*; op cit; vol 2; p. 222.
1289 V.I. Atroshenko and J. Collins: *The Origins*; op cit; p. 75.
1290 Ibid.

Gothic style in northern Europe. While many details are still unsure, Harvey notes, we may say that Gothic sprang into being from the impact upon the Normans of Eastern symbols and knowledge.[1291] Its cradle included a large area of north-western, western and Mediterranean Europe, notably England, geographical France, and parts of Italy.[1292]

Finally here, the impact of Islamic architecture on the Christian West was so powerful as to endure for centuries, affecting the centres of Renaissance Christendom, Italy, primarily, an impact studied by Mack and Howard, in particular.[1293] Here, briefly, reference is made to Francesco Borromini, one of the many architects to be influenced by Islamic antecedents. He was inspired by the helicoidal minarets of Samarra and Ibn Tulun (Cairo) for the dome of S. Ivo alla Sapienza in Rome (in the 1660s).[1294] 'The stepped roof of S. Ivo is patterned after that of the Mausoleum of Halicarnassus: the lantern follows the Round Temple of Baalbek: the helical spire recalls the traditional concept of the Tower of Babel, and the bulbous crown is derived from Dutch models which themselves originate from finials of minarets.'[1295] From the sketch of the lantern by Borromini preserved in the Albertina in Vienna, the comparison with the minaret of the Great Mosque of Samarra is particularly obvious.[1296] The Church of S. Gregorio in Messina has been erroneously attributed to Guarini, once again in the 1660s, a few years after Borromini's S. Ivo. The architect of the Sicilian building-with all probability built at least two centuries later-used S. Ivo as inspiration for the spiral roof of the campanile.[1297]
The Muslim influence on Western architecture has endured till even more recent times, and in his rightly titled, *The Oriental Obsession,* Sweetman offers the best account of such an influence.[1298]

[1291] J. Harvey: *The Gothic World: 1100-1600*; (B.T. Batsford; London; 1950); p. 54.
[1292] Ibid.
[1293] D. Howard: *Venice and the East;* (Yale University Press; 2000).
R.E. Mack: *Bazaar to Piazza: Islamic Trade and Italian Arts, 1300-1600*; (University of California Press; Berkeley; 2002).
[1294] M.V. Fontana: The Influence of Islamic Art in Italy; in *Annali;* vol 55; (Napoli; 1995); pp. 296-317; at p. 307.
[1295] W. Born: "Spiral Towers in Europe and Their Oriental Prototypes", *Gazette des Beaux-Arts* 6th S, (1943) 24, pp. 233-48; p. 234.
[1296] M.V. Fontana: The Influence of Islamic Art in Italy; op cit; p. 307; note 26.
[1297] See picture attributed to Guarini, in Born 1943; fig. 8.
[1298] J. Sweetman: *The Oriental Obsession*: (Cambridge University Press, 1987).

Three

THE GARDENS OF ISLAM

Throughout the Muslim world there prevails today an excessive passion for concrete only matched by an equally strong contempt for greenery. Everywhere the observer is struck by the sight of greenery in fast retreat: forests devastated for road construction; quarrying scarring for ever once stunning landscapes; ugly housing projects staining what was once pristine; vandalising of the country proceeding for economic purposes, or for no purpose at all; orchards uprooted for urban expansion; farming lands given priority for concreting for whatever end; gardens and green areas left to abandonment; rivers, streams, and waterways once upon a time with limpid waters today just open sewages, and everywhere you look, anywhere you step, trash so much of it, you think the land of Islam has become a huge garbage dump. Amongst the Muslim communities settled in the West, it is the same sore impression you get; Muslims priority deed on acquiring the property of the Infidels being to concrete their gardens.
Islam, any observer would conclude, the source of this all.
Nothing, though, could be further from the truth, as will be seen in this chapter. Nothing, indeed, could highlight better the contrast between the early Islamic state and its love for gardens and gardening and the decayed Muslim world of today. Even when at war, early Muslims shunned vandalising. Abu Bakr, the first Caliph (632-634), in setting the war machine in motion, gave the strict order that no palm trees were to be destroyed, no cornfields burnt, no orchards cut down.[1299] Unlike the Greeks, who ravaged the fields of the fellow Greeks with whom they were at war, cutting down their olive groves, the Muslims were at pains to avoid destruction and, as soon as possible, restored peaceful government and prosperity to the countries they overran.[1300] At peace, early Muslims distinguished themselves as garden lovers, plant collectors and experimenters in exotic plants, and in impacting on the West in all that had to do with gardens and gardening.[1301]

Today's Muslim passion for concrete and hostility to greenery is a new phenomenon, just like Muslim hostility to books and reading, again in contrast with early Islam. It is also the same contrast which affects any other aspect of civilisation, whether in respect to order and discipline of the past as against the chaos of today, or cleanliness of the past as against the filth which stains the Muslim land today, or the spirit of inventiveness and high intellect of the past which also contrast with the comatose state of brains today, and much else which surely baffles any person with historical literacy, and which surely prompts them

[1299] J. Harvey: *Medieval Gardens* (B.T. Batsford Ltd; London; 1981), p. 37.
[1300] Ibid.
[1301] A. Watson: *Agricultural,* op cit.

to ask but what on earth happened to these people to descend so low? This author can only venture his opinion in volume 3, not here, for we don't wish to spoil the picture of early Muslim gardens.

1. Early Islamic Passion for Gardens and Gardening and its Source

In the words of garden historians, the inhabitants of the early Islamic world were, to a degree that is difficult to comprehend today, 'enchanted by greenery'.[1302] In 'a civilisation, which thought of itself as a garden, gardening was naturally an esteemed art,' notes Armesto.[1303]

> In a mountain of lush greenery [says Marcais] Nature finds its home. Here, no place for vegetal mosaics laid on the ground as in Europe, but pieces of orchards where fruit trees and ornamental plants cohabit in a sort of green disorder where ease and abundance prevail. Trees of almonds, pomegranates, peaches, cherries, oranges, lemons, entangle their branches in the middle where rises the darker obelisk of a cypress tree. Nearly always, there can be heard the sound of wings because here birds find sanctuary. They are never disturbed; they can eat the fruit, or drink the water; they are part of the decor.[1304]

Scott describes how the Muslims:

> Introduced on a diminished scale the hanging gardens of Babylon. In floral ornamentation they had no superiors. They contrived labyrinths, artificial grottoes, concealed fountains. They traced texts and inscriptions by means of gorgeous blossoms on a ground of living emerald. The intricate designs of tapestry were imitated by an infinite variety of flowering plants, whose tints blended in perfect harmony, like the colours of the material they were intended to represent. They acquired such dexterity in the culture of roses that, at all seasons of the year, they bloomed in profusion in every garden.[1305]

From the far eastern parts, on the frontiers with China, to its western shores on the Atlantic, the land of Islam was united in greenery. 'Long indeed would be the list of early Islamic cities which could boast huge expanses of gardens,' Watson holds.[1306] Literary and archaeological sources find origins of gardens as early as

---

[1302] D. Sourdel: Baghdad: Capitale du Nouvel empire Abbaside; *Arabica* ix (1962; pp. 251-65. D. Goitein: A Mediterranean Society; op cit; J. Sourdel Thomine: *La Civilisation de l'Islam* (Paris; 1968), J. Dickie: Nosta Sobre la jardineria arabe en la espana Musulmane; *Miscelanea de estudios arabes y hebraicos* XIV-XV (1965-6); pp. 75-86. G. Marcais: Les Jardins de l'Islam; in *Melanges d'Histoire et d'Archeologie de l'Occident Musulman;* 2 Vols (Alger; 1957), pp. 233-44.

[1303] F.F Armesto: *Millennium;* A Touchstone Publication, (Simon and Shuster New York; 1995), p. 35.

[1304] G. Marcais: Les Jardins; op cit; p. 240.

[1305] S. P. Scott: *History;* op cit; vol 2; p. 605.

[1306] A. Watson: *Agricultural,* op cit, p. 117.

the 730s, and stretching to the whole Islamic world.[1307] Every city had its countless gardens, and on the outskirts were great orchards full of orange and lemon trees, apples, pomegranates, and cherries.[1308] In the 10th century, Bukhara consisted of a walled city measuring a league in every direction, and was surrounded by towns, palaces and gardens, which were in turn encompassed by a wall that must have been 100 miles in circumference.[1309] The land around Bukhara was turned into a vast garden growing not just a rich variety of fruits and vegetables, but many flowers.[1310] In private gardens, around splashing fountains, roses, water lilies, violets, myrtle, iris, sweet marjoram, lemon and orange trees were grown, some in great quantities for commercial ends, particularly for the manufacture of perfumes.[1311] Thirty thousand bottles of the essence of red roses were sent each year to the caliph of Baghdad.[1312] About 150 miles upstream of Bukhara, lay the city of Samarkand, for many miles around the city the fertile lands extended, watered by innumerable canals.[1313] In Turkey, Ettinghausen says:

> Devotion, if not mania for pretty flowers, was prevalent everywhere, and in their multitude; fondness for tulips in 16th century Turkey, in particular, having a profound influence on Europe.[1314]

Further to the west, Al-Fustat, Old Cairo, with its multi-storey dwellings, had thousands of private gardens, some of great splendour.[1315] Cairo also had several garden palaces and many courtyards, and this devotion is in the courtyard tradition in several older private houses that remain to this day.[1316] Basra, in Iraq, is described by early geographers as a veritable Venice, with mile after mile of canals criss-crossing the gardens and orchards.[1317] Nisbin, also in Iraq was said to have 40,000 gardens of fruit trees, and Damascus 110,000.[1318] One Garden in the city of Samarra of the 9th century consisted of 432 acres, 172 of which being gardens with pavilions, halls and basins.[1319] In Baghdad, the gardens of the palaces reached down to the Tigris, and from its farther bank the old town looked down from the west with its domes and its palaces.[1320] When in the early 10th century two Byzantine ambassadors arrived in Baghdad, they could not conceal their fascination at what they saw:

1307 R. Ettinghausen: Introduction; op cit; p. 3.

1308 Z. Oldenbourg: *The Crusades*; op cit; p. 476.

1309 D.R. Hill: *A History of Engineering in Classical and Medieval Times* (Croom Helm; 1984), p. 26.

1310 F.R. Cowell: *The Garden as a Fine Art* (Weidenfeld and Nicolson; London; 1978), p. 72.

1311 Ibid.

1312 Ibid.

1313 D.R. Hill: *A History of Engineering*; op cit; p. 26.

1314 R. Ettinghausen: Introduction; in *The Islamic Garden*, ed., by E.B. MacDougall and R. Ettinghausen (Dumbarton Oaks; Washington; 1976), p. 5.

1315 G. Wiet: *Cairo, City of Art and Commerce* (Norman Oklahoma; 1964), pp. 17; 19; 22.

1316 J. Lehrman: Gardens; Islam; in T*he Oxford Companion to Gardens*; ed. by G. Jellicoe et al (Oxford University Press; 1986), pp. 277-80 at p. 279.

1317 Al-Duri: *Tarikh al-Iraq* (Baghdad; 1948), pp. 26.8.

1318 Yaqut: *Muaajam*; op cit; vol iv; p. 787.

1319 In R. Ettinghausen: Introduction; op cit; p. 3.

1320 M.L. Gothein: *A History of Garden Art* (Hacker Art Books; New York; 1979), pp. 146-8.

> The New Kiosq is a palace in the midst of two gardens. In the centre was an artificial pond of tin (or lead), round which flows a stream in a conduit, also of tin, that is more lustrous than polished silver.... All around this tank extended a garden with lawns with palm trees... four hundred of them... The entire height of those trees, from top to bottom was carved in teakwood, encircled with gilt copper rings. And all these palms bore full grown dates, which in almost all seasons were ever ripe and did not decay. Round the sides of the garden also were melons... and other kind of fruit.[1321]

Equally stunned by eastern greenery were the incoming crusaders (1095-1291). Dreesbach notes that the passages from the French literature of the crusading period, which describe the Orient, show that the things, which 'impressed themselves on the minds of historian, chronicler and poet' were the richness of gardens and orchards and the fertility of the fields.[1322] Thus, William of Tyre's *History* goes:

> The plain of Antioch is full of many rich fields for the raising of wheat and abounding in springs and rivulets.[1323]

And on the neighbourhood of Damascus:

> There are great number of trees bearing fruits of all kinds and growing up to the very walls of the city and where everybody has a garden of his own.[1324]

Crossing into North Africa, where Islamic gardens appeared in the 9th century,[1325] one learns of a multitude of gardens, surrounding and inside cities such as Tunis, Algiers, Tlemcen, and Marrakech, places which today are not conspicuous for their greenery.[1326] Large gardens of the wealthy had flowers selected for their fragrance, as well as fruit and other trees and vegetables, and water for irrigation was often drawn from a well or from a river by water wheel.[1327] These gardens were used for pleasure, and occasionally contained a lake, but there were also smaller enclosed gardens or patios, set out formally, in the Islamic courtyard tradition.[1328] In Tlemcen, Leo the African marvelled at the cherries without rivals anywhere else. He saw water wells and fountains gushing with fresh, cool waters, and all around vines growing grapes of all colours and extremely delicate flavours, and cherries so plentiful, and figs so delicious he had never seen the like anywhere else he had been, as well as peaches, walnuts, almonds, melons, and many other fruit.[1329] Many luxurious country houses surrounded Algiers, and were

---

1321 E. Herzfeld: Mitteilungen uber die Arbeiten der zweiten Kampagne von Samarra,' *Der Islam* 5 (1914); p. 198.

1322 Dreesbach: Der Orient; 1901; pp. 24-36, in J.K. Wright: *The Geographical Lore of the Time of the Crusades* (Dover Publications; New York; 1925), p. 238.

1323 Historia; IV; 10; Paulin; Paris ed. vol I; pp. 134-5 in J. K. Wright: *The Geographical Lore*; p. 239.

1324 Historia; XVII, 3; Paulin Paris ed. vol ii; p. 141 in J. K. Wright: *The Geographical Lore*; p. 239.

1325 J. Lehrman: Gardens; Islam; op cit; p. 279.

1326 Torres Balbas: La Ruinas de Belyunes o Bullones; *Hesperis Tamuda* v (1957) 275-96; 275 ff; G. Marcais: Les Jardins de l'Islam; op cit.

1327 J. Lehrman: Gardens; op cit; p. 279.

1328 Ibid.

1329 Leon the African in G. Marcais: Les Jardins; op cit; p. 241.

renowned for their gardens.[1330] A visitor once counted 20,000 gardens, and all around the city grew all sorts of fruit trees; great varieties of flowers, and all sorts of plants; abundant fountains, and in these gardens, among the lush greenery, families used to come and find enjoyment and solace.[1331] In Tunisia, where once thrived urbanity and greenery there is today parched desert land; the region between Gafsa and Feriana, today a desert, had in Islamic times about 200 villages.[1332] Tunis, according to an early 16th century Turkish observer, had fifty thousand houses, each 'resembling a sultan's palace', and orchards and gardens on the fringes of the city.[1333] In each of these gardens, were villas and kiosks, pools and fountains, and the scent of jasmine overpowered the air. There were water wheels, too, and such an abundance of fruit people hardly paid any attention to them.[1334]

In Spain, writers speak endlessly of the gardens and *lieux de plaisance* of Seville, Cordova and Valencia; the suburb of Valencia having so many orchards and flower gardens that the city looked 'like a maiden in the midst of flowers, the scent of which perfumed the air.'[1335] The city was called by one writer 'the scent bottle of al-Andalus.'[1336] Market gardens, olive groves, and fruit orchards made some areas of Spain-notably around Cordova, Granada, and Valencia- 'garden spots of the world.'[1337] In the 10th century, all the country around Cordoba was one great garden, and according to al-Maqqari, 50,000 villas were set 'like stars in the firmament' in the countryside all around the city.[1338] Inside and around the city there were palaces of recreation in the midst of beautiful ornamental gardens.[1339] Murcia, according to Al-Maqqari was 'filled with scented flowers, singing birds, and water wheels with rumorous sound.'[1340] According to the same author, the banks of the Guadalquevir were decorated with fine buildings and beautiful pleasure gardens.[1341] The Island of Majorca, won by the Muslims in the 8th century, became under their husbandry:

> A paradise of fruits and flowers, dominated by the date palm that later gave its name to the capital.[1342]

The gardens of Almeria extended for a radius of twenty miles north, east, and west from the harbour.[1343] In Grenada, the famed pleasure garden of the Nasrid

---

[1330] J. Lehrman: Gardens; Islam; op cit; p. 279.
[1331] In G. Marcais: Les Jardins; op cit; p. 241.
[1332] A. Solignac; p. 382; in A.M. Watson: A Medieval Green Revolution; op cit; Note 44; p. 56.
[1333] S. Soucek: Tunisia in the Kitab-I Bahriye of Piri Reis, *Archivum Ottomanicum,* Vol 5, pp. 129-296, p. 197.
[1334] Ibid.
[1335] S.M. Imamuddin: *Muslim Spain* (Leiden; E. J. Brill; 1981), p. 85.
[1336] Al-Maqqari: *Nafh al-Tib;* op cit; vol I; p. 67; H. Peres: *La Poesie Andaluse en Arabe Classique au Xiem Siecle* (Paris; 1953), pp. 115ff.
[1337] W. Durant: *The Age of Faith*; op cit; p. 298.
[1338] Al-Maqqari in E. Hyams: *A History of Gardens and Gardening* (J.M. Dent and Sons Ltd; London; 1971); p. 82.
[1339] Al-Maqqari: *Nafh al-Tib*; op cit; pp. 211-2.
[1340] J. Harvey: *Medieval Gardens;* op cit; p. 38.
[1341] Al-Maqqari: *Nafh al-Tib*; vol I; I; pp. 57-8.
[1342] W. Durant: *The Age of Faith*; op cit; p. 298.
[1343] S.P. Scott: *History*; op cit; vol 2; 614.

period was *Jannat al-Arif* (Sp. Generalife) (The Garden Of The Inspector Of The Very High Garden), known for its luxuriant trees and the healthiness of its air.[1344]

Like every science, and like every single aspect of Islamic civilisation, behind the passion and devotion to gardens and gardening, natural beauty and greenery, was the faith, Islam, and its central element, the Qur'an. Thus, we read in the Qur'an:

> 'Surely the God fearing shall be among gardens and fountains.' (Qur'an 51/15).
> 'And those on the right hand; what of those on the right hand?
> Among thornless lote trees
> And clustered plantains,
> And spreading shade,
> And water gushing,
> And fruit in plenty
> Neither out of reach nor yet forbidden,
> And raised couches.' (Qur'an 56/27-34)

And equally:

> 'But for him who feareth the standing before his Lord there are two gardens.
> Which is it, of the favours of your Lord, that ye deny?
> Of spreading branches.
> Which is it, of the favours of your Lord, that ye deny?
> Wherein are two fountains flowing.
> Which is it, of the favours of your Lord, that ye deny?
> Wherein is every kind of fruit in pairs.
> Which is it, of the favours of your Lord, that ye deny?
> Reclining upon couches lined with silk brocade, the fruit of both gardens near to hand.
> Which is it, of the favours of your Lord, that ye deny?
> Therein are those of modest gaze, whom neither man no jinni will have touched before them.
> Which is it, of the favours of your Lord, that ye deny?
> (In beauty) like the jacinth and the coral stone.
> Which is it, of the favours of your Lord, that ye deny?
> Is the reward of goodness aught save goodness?
> Which is it, of the favours of your Lord, that ye deny?
> And beside them are two other gardens.
> Which is it, of the favours of your Lord, that ye deny?
> Dark green with foliage.
> Which is it, of the favours of your Lord, that ye deny?
> Wherein are two abundant springs.

[1344] Al-Maqqari: *Nafh al-Tib*; II; p. 360; n. 12.

Which is it, of the favours of your Lord, that ye deny?
Wherein is fruit, the date palm and pomegranate.'
(Qur'an LV: 46-68).

The expression: 'Gardens underneath which rivers flow' is the most repeated expression in the Qur'an (thirty seven times) for 'the bliss of the faithful.'[1345] Picturesque as the Qura'nic descriptions of the heavenly garden may be,' Shimmel holds, 'we can only imagine what it may be like.' Sura 57/21 specifies its extension:

'And a Garden the breadth whereof is as the breadth of heaven and earth...'

and sura (77/41):

'...Shades and fountains and such fruits as their hearts desire.'

Descriptions of the heavenly garden, which Schimmel explains, are consistent and give an impression of greenery and gushing fountains.[1346]

Faith and greenery also predominate in the words of poets, here the Egyptian Dhu'n-Nun (d.859):

'O God, I never hearken to the voices of the beasts or the rustle of the trees, the splashing of the waters or the song of the birds, the whistling of the winds or the rumble of the thunder, but I sense in them as testimony to Thy Unity, and a proof of Thy incomparableness, that Thou art the All Prevailing, the All Knowing, the All True.'[1347]

Yunus Emre, the medieval mystic of Anatolia, in a little poem, describes Paradise in these simple words:

'Sol cennetin irmaklari
Akar Allah deyu deyu.....
The rivers all in paradise
Flow with the word Allah, Allah,
And every longing nightingale
He sings and sings Allah, Allah;
The branches of the Tuba tree
The tongue reciting the Qur'an,
The roses there in Paradise,
Their fragrance is Allah, Allah...'[1348]

Garden historians were prompt to see such connections between faith and the early Islamic passion for gardening.[1349]

[1345] A.Schimmel: The Celestial garden in Islam; in *The Islamic Garden*, op cit; pp. 13-39; at p. 15.
[1346] Ibid; p. 17.
[1347] Ibid; p. 24.
[1348] *Yunus Emre Diwani;* ed. A. Goplinarli (Istanbul; 1943), Nr. 477.
[1349] G. Marcais: Les Jardins; op cit; J. Dickie: Nosta Sobre la jardineria arabe en la espana Musulmane; *Miscelanea de estudios arabes y hebraicos* XIV-XV (1965-6); pp. 75-86.

> When a whole people can anticipate the paradise of afterlife as a garden, there can be little doubt about their enthusiasm for gardens on aesthetic grounds and still less doubt about their high significance in the every day life of those times [says Cowell].[1350]

Ettinghausen, too, notes that:

> If the garden was such a ubiquitous art form in the Muslim world, being both socially and geographically extensive, there must have been specific reasons for this propensity... and first comes the idea of Paradise as a reward for the Muslim faithful, a garden, descriptions of which have played an important part in the Muslim cosmography and religious belief.[1351]

Early Muslims everywhere, Watson holds, 'made earthly gardens that gave glimpses of the heavenly garden to come.'[1352] Every garden was meant to be a little paradise as Ettinghausen put it 'for the happy owner' carefully protected from the hustle and bustle of the city and its odours.[1353] The spread of Islam saw many gardens established, since not only did they provide climatic relief in those parts of the world, but they granted foretaste of the reward promised to the faithful, as well as a less spiritual but attractive reflection of the traditional royal-pleasure garden.[1354] And the earthly visions of Paradise have inspired the construction of gardens; rivers flowing through paradise helping architects to conceive the canals as they flow through the gardens, each part of the garden being in some way a similitude of Paradise.[1355]

'In laying out and ornamenting gardens,' Immamudin says, 'kings and nobles, rich and poor, theologians and laymen, all participated with equal zeal and enthusiasm and, as a result, each villa, each palace and each town was a delight to the eye.'[1356] Rulers in the days of Islam, when not versed into scholarly passion, were equally passionate about their gardens; they and their surrounding elites laying out their beautiful gardens in palaces for recreation both on river banks and in mountain valleys and on mountain tops, supplying them with water in abundance.[1357] Some such gardens had great splendour, and their renown went beyond their territory, such as al-Mu'tasim's gardens at Samarra, Iraq;[1358] the great royal parks of the Aghlabid emirs of Tunisia, near Al-Qayrawan, the famous garden of the Hafsid rulers, also in Tunisia;[1359] and the gardens surrounding the

---

[1350] F.R. Cowell: *The Garden as a Fine Art* (Weidenfeld and Nicolson; London; 1978), p. 75.
[1351] R. Ettinghausen: Introduction, op cit, at p. 6.
[1352] A.M. Watson: *Agricultural;* op cit; p. 117.
[1353] R. Ettinghausen: Introduction; op cit; p. 7.
[1354] J. Lehrman: Gardens; Islam; op cit; p. 278.
[1355] A.Schimmel: The Celestial, op cit; p. 15.
[1356] S.M. Imamuddin: *Muslim Spain;* op cit; p. 85.
[1357] Ibid.
[1358] H. Viollet: Description du Palais de al-Mutassim a Samarra; in *Memoires de l'Academie des Inscriptions et des Belles Lettres*; XII; 1913.
[1359] A. Solignac: Recherches sur les installations hydrauliques de kairaouan et des Steppes Tunisiennes du VII au Xiem siecle, in *Annales de l'Institut des Etudes Orientales*, Algiers, X (1952); 5-273. pp 218 ff; G. Marcais: Les Jardins; op cit; p. 237.

royal palaces at Fez and Marrakech.[1360] In Cairo the Mamluk sultan Qalawun (Qala'un) (late 13th century) introduced Syrian plants into his garden in great variety.[1361] In the Yemen, a number of 14th century sultans became so passionately interested in botanical and agricultural research, one of them wrote an agricultural treatise whilst another specialised in adapting exotic trees from distant places.[1362] The Spanish Caliphs, as they did with rare manuscripts, sought plants and seeds of rare species from the furthest places, and with equal determination. Abd Errahman I was so passionately fond of flowers and plants, he sent agents to Syria and other parts of the East to acquire new plants and seeds.[1363] He planted a beautiful garden in imitation of the Rusafah Villa of Damascus.[1364] By the 10th century, the royal gardens at Cordova became botanical gardens, with fields for experimentation with seeds, cuttings and roots brought in from the outermost reaches of the world.[1365] Other royal gardens, in Spain and elsewhere, also became the sites of serious scientific activity as well as places of amusement. A recently discovered manuscript by al-Udhri informs us that al-Mu'tasim, a Taifa king (11th century), brought many rare plants to his garden in Almeria, which even included banana and sugar cane.[1366]

This passion for gardening extended to the population at large, the Muslims using the art of planting to beautify their homes and countryside.[1367] Ettinghausen notes how there were even carefully planned mini gardens with trees, bushes, flowers and central water basins and fountains in the courtyards of countless private homes, owned by men of very limited means.[1368] At Fustat, in old Cairo, multi storey houses were all perfumed with private gardens, and interior courtyards all had their water basins and squares where flowers blossomed.[1369] A visitor to Tunis in 1470 wrote that every citizen had his garden, agreeably pervaded by perfumes from great varieties of flowers, and all sorts of fruit trees; and fountains rising in the middle.[1370] In Spain, Scott writes:

> Love of flowers was a veritable passion among the Spanish Moslems. As they were the greatest botanists in the world, so no other nation approached them in the perfection of their floriculture and the ardour with which they pursued it. The profusion and variety of blossoms of every description were marvellous and enchanting; each had a meaning, by

---

1360 G. Marcais: Les Jardins; op cit; p. 237.

1361 Al-Maqrizi, Ahmad Ibn Ali. *Al-Mawaiz wa'l-itibar fi dhikr al-khitat wa'l-athar*; edited by Ahmed Ali al-Mulaiji. 3 Vols, (Beirut: Dar al Urfan. 1959), II; op cit; p. 119.

1362 M. Meyerhof: Sur un traite d'agriculture compose par un sultan Yemenite du XIV em siecle; *Bulletin de l'Institut d'Egypte*; xxv (1942-3) 54-63; xxvi (1943-4); 51-64; (1942-3) p.58; and (1943-4) pp. 52; 57.

1363 A. Watson: *Agricultural,* op cit, p.118.

1364 S.M. Imamuddin: *Some Aspects of the Socio-Economic and Cultural History of Muslim Spain* (Brill; 1965), p. 82.

1365 Al-Maqqari: *Nafh al-Tib;* ii: 14-5; H. Peres: Le Palmier en Espagne Musulmane; in *Melanges Geodefroy Demombynes* (Cairo; 1935-45), pp. 224-39.

1366 Al-Udhri: *Nusus an al-Andalus*; ed. Abd al-Aziz al-Ahwani (Madrid; 1965), p. 85.

1367 S.M. Imamuddin: *Some Aspects*; op cit; p. 82.

1368 R. Ettinghausen: The Islamic; op cit; p. 5.

1369 G. Marcais: Les Jardins; op cit; p. 236.

1370 Brunschvig, quoted in G. Marcais: Les Jardins; op cit; p. 242.

> which tender sentiments could be conveyed without the instrumentality of speech; they were associated with every public ceremony and with the most prosaic occurrences of domestic life; they dispensed their fragrance from the priceless vase of the palace; they covered the cottage of the labourer; they formed the daily decoration of the luxuriant tresses of the princess and the peasant; their garlands were the common playthings of the infant.[1371]

Amidst greenery there was also cultivated creativity. The Muslims, Gothein says, liked artificial culture, different fruits on one tree; different grapes on one vine, which they thought specially pleasing, and they liked to have flowers of unnatural colours.[1372] In the Tulunid garden (9th century Egypt), they planted saffron and other plants; the gardeners cut plants into various figures, as well as the shapes of letters, and this had to be kept regular, lest a single leaf should stick out.[1373] A tower was made in open work teak to serve as a bird cage, painted in many colours, with paved floors, and little streams purling.[1374] The garden, plants, and animals were all watered with well sweeps, the birds, 'which filled this house with their sweet songs, not only found baths and food there, but also their nests, in pretty coloured pots prepared for them and let into the walls.'[1375] There were also peacocks and fowls, and various wild creatures in great numbers running loose.[1376] At his castle in Baghdad, Caliph al-Qahir had a garden laid out in a court, only a third of an acre in size, but it contained orange trees brought from Basra, Oman and India, and on the regularly planted trees there gleamed yellow and red fruit, bright 'as the stars of heaven' against the dusky foliage.[1377] Around grew all kinds of shrubs, sweet smelling flowers, and plants, and many birds were there: turtle doves, ouzels, and parrots, brought from foreign lands and distant towns.[1378] Fruit trees

> Provided cool shade against the intense heat, flowers supplied fragrance and colour, terraces and canals assisted horticulture and irrigation, while cascades, pools, and fountains cooled and moistened the air, providing gentle sound and visual delight.[1379]

The garden, a symbol of the promised paradise, has, thus, become a little earthly paradise in itself. For the early Muslim, lengthy contemplation of such beauty was enough to replenish life and chase away its sorrows and stresses. An owner would take delight in his garden more by sitting on a rug and cushions in contemplation of

---

[1371] S.P. Scott: *History,* op cit, vol 2; p. 651.
[1372] M.L. Gothein: *A History of Garden Art* (Hacker Art Books; New York; 1979), p. 150.
[1373] Ibid.
[1374] Ibid.
[1375] Ibid.
[1376] Ibid.
[1377] Ibid; p. 151.
[1378] Ibid.
[1379] J. Lehrman: Gardens; Islam; op cit; p. 278.

his pavilion, than by walking through it.[1380] In front of his palace Rumarawayh built a pool of 50x50 cubits filled with mercury on which he floated on an air mattress to cure his insomnia; it was reported to be spectacular by moonlight. And to enjoy his view, Rumarawayh even built a domed kiosk in his palace overlooking the bustan (garden) and the city.[1381] There, inside his artificial Spanish paradise-the site of Soto de Rojas famous poem[1382] could have been chosen by an Arab-'he could enjoy in solitude the voluptuous pleasure produced by different perfumes, colours and shapes in endlessly varied combinations: in sum, it was a place where the refined sensuality of the Muslim sensibility could find full and perfect expression,' says Dickie.[1383]

> It is from this quiet scene of beauty found in the Arabian court garden [Gothein concludes] that their poetry takes its beginning.[1384]

2. The Islamic Garden

Abu Uthman Ibn Luyun al-Tujibi of Almeria (1282-1349) composed in 1348 within the last years of his life a poem in simple verse.[1385] He, thus, designs for us the garden:

> With regard to houses set amidst gardens and elevated site is to be recommended, both for reasons of vigilance and of layout;
> and let them have a southern aspect, with the entrance at one side, and on an upper level the cistern and well,
> or instead of a well have a watercourse where the water runs underneath the shade.
> And if the house has two doors, greater will be the security it enjoys and easier the repose of its occupant.
> Then next to the reservoir plant shrubs whose leaves do not fall and which rejoice the sight;
> And, somewhat further off, arrange flowers of different kinds, and, further off still, evergreen trees,
> And around the perimeter climbing vines, and in the centre of the whole enclosure a sufficiency of vines;
> And under climbing vines let there be paths which surround the garden to serve as margin.

[1380] Ibid.

[1381] Doris Behrens-Abuseif: Gardens in Islamic Egypt: *Der Islam* Vol 69 (1992); pp. 302-312; at p. 304:

[1382] *Parayso cerrado para muchos, jardines abiertos para pocos* 'Paradise closed to many, gardens open to few.'

[1383] J. Dickie: The Islamic Garden; op cit; in *The Islamic Garden* (ed., by E.B. MacDougall and R. Ettinghausen) op cit; pp. 87-106; p. 105.

[1384] M.L. Gothein: *A History of Garden Art*; op cit; p. 151.

[1385] J. Eguaras Ibanes: *Ibn Luyun: Tratado de Agricultura* (Granada; 1975), review in *Garden History*; V; No 2 (1977); pp. 6-8.

And amongst the fruit trees include the grapevine similar to a slim woman, or wood producing trees;
Afterward arrange the virgin soil for planting whatever you wish should prosper.
In the background let there be trees like the fig or any other which does no harm;
And plant any fruit tree which grows big in a confining basin so that its mature growth may serve as a protection against the north wind without preventing the sun from reaching [the plants].
In the centre of the garden let there be a pavilion in which to sit, and with vistas on all sides,
But of such a form that no one approaching could overhear the conversation within and whereupon none could approach undetected.
Clinging to it there be roses and myrtle, likewise all manners of plants with which a garden is adorned.
And this last should be longer than it is wide in order that the beholder's gaze may expand in contemplation.[1386]

The shape of the Islamic garden, Lehrman informs us 'Was nearly always rectangular. It was surrounded by a wall, and an elaborate gateway gave on to a main axis often formed by a water course with one or more subsidiary axes at right angles. Channels and pools were flanked by paths and terraces, often bordered by defined areas of flowers and shrubs with trees for shade; this planting softened the man made geometry. With a pavilion or other form of building in the centre, all vistas were precisely terminated by a further pavilion, gateway, or vaulted recess. Paths were always straight and paved with bricks, stone, pebbles, or mosaic. Although the use of geometry was universal across the Islamic world, there is always a strong sense of place in the garden, with remarkable little uniformity. When sited on a gradient the garden was terraced. In the large royal gardens, especially in India, the public was received only on the lower terrace. The central terrace was private and used for formal audience; the upper terrace was reserved for women. At changes of level, water fell over cascades of carved chutes. On flat sites, channels were given a slight gradient to ensure a flow. Water in pools and channels was always contained in a precise manner.'[1387]
Hyams adds to this overall description, that 'The beds for trees and evergreen or flowering shrubs were sunk below the level of the paths, which were always paved, pebbled or covered with mosaic. Where any flowers at all were grown, they were planted in large earthenware pots or vases. Lawns were unknown; some gardens were paved all over except rectangular beds left uncovered for planting. Walls, balustrades, seats, the sides of fountains and all such vertical surfaces were apt to

[1386] Ibn Luyyun: *Kitab ibda' al-milaha wa-inha al-rijal fi usul sina'at al-Filaha;* in Lerchundi and Simonet; Gestomatia arabigo Espanola (Grenada; 1881); p. 136; in J. Dickie: The Islamic Garden; op cit; p. 94.
[1387] J. Lehrman: Gardens; Islam; op cit; p. 278.

be covered with brightly coloured tiles, a practice which can be best seen today in some old Portuguese gardens such as that of the Pena palace. There were, of course, no statues in Islamic gardens, since the Qur'an forbids the making of graven images.'[1388]

The courtyard and courtyard garden in Islam, and especially the Islamic garden itself, were seen to reflect both human biological and physiological needs as well as the Islamic religious principle of unity and order.[1389] Design reflected 'both the rational and spiritual nature of the human and was expressed in a remarkable unity of concept' that was reflected in gardens from southern Spain to north West India, and common to all was 'the same sense of order, focus on water, and spirit of serenity, yet, each site was unique, and the geometry introduced served only to enhance the genius loci.'[1390]
Within this sense of order, paths of Islamic gardens were never random or winding, but always leading straight to some goal, perhaps a pavilion; sometimes to a view through an ornamental unglazed window in the outer wall; often to a quiet retreat or kiosk made of wood or stone or bricks, brightly tiled, with vines trained over it. The last feature was to become known in later Spanish gardens as 'a glorieta.'[1391] Gloriet comes from glorieta, itself a translation of the Arabic *'aziz*, still surviving at the palace of La Ziza in the royal gardens at Palermo, where an inscription reads:
'Here is the earthly paradise... this is called al-'aziz (the Glorious).'[1392]
This resembles the subsequent greater gardens of medieval France and Britain, the plan with a central pavilion or gloriet, surrounded by flowers, by rows of trees, and by pergola retreats covered with vines on trellis.[1393]

The search for privacy, common to other aspects of Islamic life, was also found in the garden. The garden provided a calm and harmonious retreat from the noisy, turbulent and dusty world outside, and for inner contemplation. The Turkish gardens are rich in kiosks for sitting and reclining in. All foreign travellers remarked on this.[1394] Thévenot noticed it in Syria in the 1660s, where the Turk would sit all day cross-legged on his divan contemplating his garden.[1395] Chardin in Persia a decade later wrote, rather scornfully, that the Persians do not

> Stroll in their gardens as we do, but are satisfied with the sight of what they have, and with breathing the air. They sit down in some spot in the garden when they arrive, and stay there until they leave.[1396]

[1388] E. Hyams: *A History of Gardens and Gardening* (J.M. Dent and Sons LTD; London; 1971), p. 84.
[1389] J. Lehrman: Gardens; Islam; op cit; p. 278.
[1390] Ibid.
[1391] E. Hyams: *A History of Gardens*; op cit; p. 84.
[1392] J. Harvey: *Medieval Gardens;* op cit; p. 44.
[1393] Ibid.
[1394] C. Thacker: *The History of Gardens;* (Croom Helm; London; 1979); p. 34.
[1395] Ibid.
[1396] Ibid.

The Islamic garden was therefore always enclosed, private, and protected.[1397] The differences in psychology between the Muslim and European are accurately reflected in their respective garden traditions, observes Dickie.[1398] Muslims surrounded their gardens with very high walls and then to double the measure of privacy and degree of shade by planting trees-sometimes fruit trees, but chiefly cypresses-inside the walls.[1399] The high walls of the Islamic garden protect its owner from being seen from outside and insulate them against 'the clamour and dirt of the antipathetic life of the streets.'[1400] In this as in so many other matters, Massignon was able to pin-point an essential distinction. The Western garden is landscaped and tends to overcome nature; its long, broad avenues cut through the woodland; its vast meres confine the horizon and its lines of trees 'stand guard over the whole terrain like soldiers.'[1401] The Muslim garden is quite different; its aim is to seclude rather than to open out, to escape attention rather than to draw it.[1402] It has been widened to accommodate 'a fantasy of vegetation,' which is arranged in accordance with Islamic aesthetics and even metaphysics.[1403] In this respect

> It resembles a tapestry, with the greatest possible freedom of frame and line; the lines converge on a central pavilion, where a dreamer sits in melancholy, though not in sadness, and his dream hangs on a thread, almost literally, for it is a thread of water.[1404]

Closely related to this desire for privacy, the facades of Muslim dwellings were bare, betraying nothing of the luxury within.[1405] All were permeated by intimacy and secrecy; access was gained by a twisting passage so that the splendour of the patio should not be seen until after the second turning.[1406] The buildings were simple to the extreme, made of poor quality brick or whitewashed rubblework, but the patios inside, and their secret gardens, undoubtedly contained a profusion of fruit trees and flowers.[1407] This is the origin of the popular song:

> 'Mine is the same condition
> As the house of the Moorish king
> Outside the plaster is rotting
> But treasure lies hidden within.'[1408]

The tall, dense and evergreen enclosure was, as always, on a rectilinear plan, and central to it was at least one canal, probably two or three parallel, and possibly a

---

[1397] J. Lehrman: Gardens; Islam; op cit; p. 278.
[1398] J. Dickie: The Islamic Garden in Spain; op cit; p. 105.
[1399] E. Hyams: *A History of Gardens*; op cit; p. 84.
[1400] J. Dickie: The Islamic Garden in Spain; op cit; p. 105.
[1401] E. Sordo: *Moorish Spain*; (Elek Books; London; 1963); p. 213.
[1402] Ibid.
[1403] Ibid.
[1404] Ibid.
[1405] Marquesa de Casa Valdes: *Spanish Gardens*; tr., E. Tanner (Antique Collectors' Club' Valencia; 1973), p. 27.
[1406] Ibid.
[1407] Ibid.
[1408] Ibid.

whole grid of canals so that water divided the garden in shapes and sizes that enhanced the spirit of harmony, order, peace and stillness.[1409] Jets of water sprang from the canals and fell into them, but there would be other, more elaborate, fountains as well, often in enclosed or cloistered courts.[1410] The most simple place has at least one fine fountain; the paths are very often paved with costly marble and shaded with vines; sometimes the whole court is paved, and in that case the trees are planted in great boxes or in reserve corners where earth has been left.[1411] The beds are bordered with stone, and beside the paths there could be found strong scented plants, or clipped shrubs, salvia, myrtle, and bay hedges, and climbing plants hanging from tree to tree.[1412] Besides the walls there were fountains and there were water cisterns in the middle; through the doors there can be seen the flower garden, where antelopes play about, and in an aviary pigeons fly hither and thither.[1413]

A special feature of the Islamic gardens, little remarked upon and never generally adopted elsewhere, was their sunken flower-beds.[1414] In the medieval Spanish Muslim garden of the Patio de la Aceqia the flower-beds were half a metre (18 inches) below the surrounding paths.[1415] Dickie points out the advantage of such an arrangement.[1416] When the flower blossoms were at feet level, they gave anyone walking on the paths the illusion of treading a floral carpet. At the same time such a design enhanced the geometrical form of the gardens, leaving the architectural features of the adjacent buildings clear and un-obscured by vegetation.[1417] In heavy rain, the soil would not be washed on to the path, as happens with raised flower-beds.[1418] Harvey notes, how, indeed, the Muslim Spanish love of sunk beds beside raised paths, giving the illusion of walking on a carpet formed by the tops of plants-contrasting with northern raised beds, as Gorer suggested, may be due to the climatic need to collect or drain the rainfall.[1419]

The Muslim Spanish garden also shared with the rest of Islamic gardens the same attributes of order, geometry, coolness, privacy, and a focus on water.[1420] There are no large pools, and a local characteristic of large gardens was their division into small enclosures.[1421] Due to hilly terrain, the plans of gardens were slightly irregular, but splendid views were offered. Enclosing walls were of stuccoed

---

[1409] E. Hyams: *A History of Gardens*; op cit; p. 84.
[1410] Ibid.
[1411] M.L. Gothein: *A History of Garden Art*; op cit; p. 151.
[1412] Ibid.
[1413] Ibid.
[1414] F.R. Cowell: *The Garden as a Fine Art;* op cit; p. 75.
[1415] Ibid.
[1416] J. Dickie: The Islamic Garden in Spain; op cit; pp. 98 ff.
[1417] F.R. Cowell: *The Garden as a Fine Art*; op cit; p. 75.
[1418] Ibid.
[1419] J. Harvey: *Medieval Gardens;* op cit; p. 44.
[1420] J. Lehrman: Gardens; Islam; op cit; p. 279.
[1421] Ibid.

masonry, and tiles were used as facing on seats, pools, paths and steps.[1422] There was great use of accessories such as benches and pots, although these might have been a more recent innovation. Ever greens, especially citrus trees, were planted, and flowers were chosen for fragrance, and there was no grass.[1423] The Muslim chronicler, Ibn Said, described the houses and gardens built by sultans and Cordoba's caliphs, and those of rich landowners, as can be found in many extracts of al-Maqqari.[1424] He went on to describe the many palaces and pleasure gardens on the outskirts of Cordova, in particular, especially the one built by Al-Mansur (d.1002), on the banks of the Guadelquevir, then known as *al-Zahira*, with its large lake covered with water lilies.[1425]

The most famous of the earlier Spanish gardens was that of *Madinat az-Zahra*, also near Cordova, built by Caliph Abd Errahman III (r. 912-961).[1426] Ibn Hayyan (d.1076) relates that among the marvels, there were two fountains whose basins were of such gracious form and so priceless for their delicate workmanship that, in his opinion, they constituted the principal ornament of the palace.[1427] Another of the marvels of Madinat al-Zahra was the Hall of the Caliphs, which, in its centre, according to Ibn Backual, had a pond of porphyry filled with mercury. When the rays of the sun reached this apartment the glitter of its walls was dazzling.[1428] One can well imagine the astonishment of the rough northern chieftains Sancho of Leon and Garcia of Navarre when they were made to walk the length of this series of salons.[1429] Miles of clipped box, bay and myrtle hedges divided the garden into many smaller gardens, all rectilinear as was the rule; irrigation canals fed all parts of the garden and worked hundreds of fountains.[1430] On these water works, al-Maqqari comments that after supplying this palace, and irrigating with profusion every corner of its gardens, despite its vast size, the excess water then fell into the Guadelquevir. Every author al Maqqari consulted agrees in saying that this aqueduct, with the reservoir, and the figure pouring the water into it, must be considered 'as one of the most amazing structure ever raised by man;' for by its length, its unfavourable nature on the ground through which it was conducted, the magnitude and solidity of the construction, the height of the piers over which the water was made to flow, sometimes ascending, sometimes descending, 'we shall scarcely find among the works of ancient kings which have reached us anything to be compared to it.'[1431]

[1422] Ibid.
[1423] Ibid.
[1424] Al-Maqqari: *Nafh Al-Tib*; see also Marquesa de Casa Valdes: *Spanish Gardens*; p. 30.
[1425] In Al-Maqqari: *Nafh Al-Tib*, op cit; vol 1; p. 243.
[1426] E. Hyams: *A History of Gardens*; op cit; p. 82.
[1427] In Al-Maqqari: *Nafh Al-Tib*; op cit; vol i; Book iii; chapter iii; p. 236.
[1428] Marquesa de Casa Valdes: *Spanish Gardens*; op cit; p. 30.
[1429] Ibid.
[1430] E. Hyams: *A History of Gardens*; op cit; p. 82.
[1431] Al-Maqqari: *Nafh Al-Tib*; in A. Thomson and M. Rahim: *Islam in Andalus* (Taha; London; 1996), p. 63.

Grenada, wrested last from the Muslims in 1492, has preserved most of the Islamic Spanish garden legacy as is succinctly described by Hyams here.[1432]
'Most famed of its Islamic heritage is the Alhambra, started in the 11th century but the finer parts of which were built from 1248 by Al-Ahmar. Of the numerous original patios or courts only four remain, but from them we can get some idea of what the whole garden was like in say, 1400, and until the re-conquest (1492). First, the Court of the Myrtle consists chiefly of a long, broad pool enclosed by galleries and a colonnade on the north and south sides and by clipped myrtle, which, despite the clipping, flowers deliciously. The much more famous Court of Lions into which it opens through a decorated doorway dates from about 1350, and is surrounded by a peristyle of alabaster columns supporting 'Moorish' arches, with a pavilion at each end of the long axis. The Lion Fountain from which the name derives is central and feeds four small channels, in the manner of the channels of the Villa Adriana, which divide the area into parts now gravelled but originally occupied by shaped citrus trees and possibly by some flowers. The third court, the Court Doraxas, originally for the use of the harem occupants, is contained by walls lined with fine old cypresses and orange trees. Originally they must have been planted regularly, but time has given them a pleasingly scattered or random look. The fountain at the centre looks as if it had been restored in the Renaissance manner and can hardly be called 'Moorish.'[1433]
The beauty of the "garden that has no equal", as Ibn Ammar calls it in his verses-the Generalife, which according to Hernando de Baeza means "the noblest and highest garden of all"-was a byword from the moment of its construction. Al-Khatib praised its leanness, which kept out the sun; Ibn Zamrak called it "Granada's throne"; and Alonso de Herrera in his *Book of Agriculture,* published in Alcala de Henares in 1539, alludes to the curious shapes into which myrtles can be trained "if they are planted as those in the Generalife in Granada."[1434]
The making of the Generalife began later than the Alhambra, but it must have been before 1319, when the Sultan Abu'l-Walid had several repairs carried out in it and filled its walls with inscriptions.[1435] It is on seven levels, the site being a hillside. The highest terrace is the Court of the Canal, which is enclosed on three sides by buildings and on the fourth by an arcade, its name being derived from the narrow canal down the centre of the long axis. Other features of this court are a small mosque, a fountain, and clipped box parterres.[1436] At a lower level on one side is a square walled garden, the walls dotted with decorated windows commanding fine views. On the other side is the Harem court with a horse shaped canal, ancient cypresses, and oleanders, leading to the next terrace through an arched gateway by way of steps and landings ornamented with pebble mosaics.[1437] A belvedere

1432 E. Hyams: *A History of Gardens*; op cit; p. 85.
1433 Ibid.
1434 E. Sordo: *Moorish Spain*; op cit; p. 212.
1435 Ibid; p. 213.
1436 E. Hyams: *A History of Gardens*; op cit; p. 85.
1437 Ibid.

reached by more decorated steps is above this terrace, and from it there is a novel water staircase, the water being carried down the hollow tiled balustrade. Stairs lead to the Mirador from where can be seen the Alhambra, with the sierra in the distance.[1438] It was not the traditional Muslim urge for seclusion alone that caused it to be hidden and enclosed; its situation at a distance from other habitations ensured its safety from prying eyes.[1439]
'Words,' Sordo says, 'are not enough to express the sensation produced by the Generalife: it can only be experienced amid its patios and gardens, its gurgling waters and its whispering glades.'[1440]

3. The Place of Water

Water played the most significant role in Islamic gardens just as it did in every aspect of early Islamic society. Such was the crucial place of water during that period (7th-13th centuries), Muslims developed a whole legal system around water, even water tribunals.[1441] This particular matter will be considered in the chapter on agriculture in the following part. The importance of water is further highlighted by the fact that all Muslim treatises on agriculture, whether Maghribi, Andalusian, Egyptian, Iraqi, Persian or Yemenite, Bolens points out, insist meticulously on the deployment of equipment and on the control of water.[1442] Ibn Luyun (1282-1349), for instance, possibly the last agronomist to live and work in Al-Andalus, in Almeria, wrote his *Kitab Ibda' al-malaha wa-inha' al-rajaha fi usul sina'at al-filaha* (Book on the principles of beauty and the purpose of learning which treats the fundamentals of the art and agriculture) in 1348.[1443] Regarding levelling the earth, Ibn Luyun notes that the soil in a garden bed *(hawd)* should be sloped in such a way that water will distribute itself evenly.[1444] He describes a device for doing this that consists of a cord stretched between two stakes placed fifteen units apart, with a weighted plumb-line *(mizan)* measuring one unit in length dropped from the farthest end of the cord.[1445] He writes that bedding plants should be organised in rows with lengths of string to mark each one, and that the beds should be rectangular following a 1:3 ratio, reaching no more than twelve cubits in length and less if water is scarce.[1446]

[1438] Ibid.
[1439] E. Sordo: *Moorish Spain*; op cit; p. 212.
[1440] Ibid; p. 213.
[1441] S.P. Scott: *History*; op cit; vol 3; pp. 602-3.
[1442] L. Bolens: L'Eau et l'Irrigation d'apres les traites d'agronomie Andalus au Moyen Age (XI-XIIem siecles), *Options Mediterraneenes*, 16 (Dec, 1972), p. 451.
[1443] Ibn Luyun, *Tratado de agricultura.* Ibn Luyun's biography is given in Ibn al-Qadi, *Al-Hijal,* ed. I.S. Allouche (Rabat, 1939).
[1444] D. Fairchild Ruggles: *Gardens, Landscape, and Vision in the Palaces of Islamic Spain;* (The Pennsylvania State University Press; 2000); p. 25.
[1445] Ibid.
[1446] Ibn Luyun, *Tratado,* (Arabic) 61.

The subject of water was at the centre of many sciences and scientific treatises. The mechanical engineers, whether the Banu Musa (fl.early 9th century), or al-Jazari (fl.1206) built machines and mechanisms all related to water; Al-Zarqali built his complex Toledo Clock also around water; Qaysar, the Syrian, built huge water wheels on the Orontes; whilst throughout the Muslim world water power drove mills and industries.[1447] Civil engineers, for their part, excelled at dam construction, excellence proved by the fact that some dams in parts of Spain still working to this day, nearly twelve centuries after they were completed.[1448] In Tunisia, one of the most enduring accomplishments is the Basin of the Aghlabids, an ensemble of reservoirs near Al-Qayrawan dating from the 9th century.[1449] Muslim geographers and travellers focused their minds on water and anything that was related to it. So did the historians, and of course poets, and story tellers.[1450] Mathematicians, too, gave great interest to the subject of water, their geometry, for instance, easing operations of storage, flow, and efficient use of the resource. The Moroccan Ibn al Banna's (b.1256) *Tanbih al-albab*, for instance, studies the calculation of drop irrigation canals.[1451]

The place of water in gardens and gardening was, understandably, central. 'Without water the fruit gardens, which in the Arab consciousness are the gardens of paradise, could not survive,' says Lapidus.[1452] 'Water, principally, we cannot imagine a beautiful Islamic garden doing without,' also says Marcais.[1453] In gardens, just as in courtyards of buildings of a religious nature, water was regarded as a symbol of purity, and since paradise overflowed with water, tanks in mosques and theological colleges were filled to the brim.[1454]

> The Arab knows that only the river that flows through Eden never runs low. He therefore searches constantly for water and when he is successful, he cherishes it, channelling it gently between myrtled banks and spraying it playfully upwards from basins adorned with inscribed verses. Has it not been said that the Arabs caress water as the misers in Flemish paintings let streams of gold coins trickle through their fingers? They handle it greedily and fearfully, knowing that the slightest oversight or disturbance may shatter their dream.[1455]

[1447] For all these points, see, for instance: D.R. Hill: *Islamic Science and Engineering* (Edinburgh University Press, 1993).

[1448] See for instance: N. Smith: *A History of Dams* (The Chaucer Press, London, 1971). A. Pacey: *Technology in World Civilization, a Thousand Year History* (The MIT Press, Cambridge, 1990).

[1449] A. Solignac: Recherches sur les installations hydrauliques de kairaouan et des Steppes Tunisiennes du VII au Xiem siecle, in *Annales de l'Institut des Etudes Orientales*, Algiers, X (1952); 5-273.

[1450] Al-Muqaddasi: *Ahsan at-taqasim;* op cit. Ibn Battuta: *Voyages d'Ibn Battuta*, Arabic text accompanied by French translation by C. Defremery and B.R. Sanguinetti, preface and notes by Vincent Monteil, I-IV (Paris, 1968, reprint of the 1854 ed).

[1451] A. Djebbar: Mathematics in medieval Maghreb; *AMUCHMA-Newsletter* 15; Universidade Pedagógica (UP), (Maputo Mozambique, 15.9.1995).

[1452] I. Lapidus: *Muslim Cities*; op cit; p. 70.

[1453] G. Marcais: Les Jardins; op cit; p. 234.

[1454] J. Lehrman: *Gardens*; op cit; p. 278.

[1455] E. Sordo: *Moorish Spain*; op cit; p. 216.

And the faith, once more, was the greatest of all inspirations. Qura'nic descriptions of Paradise put great stress on the presence of moisture and water, 'equally as or even more important than the soil,' Dickie reminds.[1456] The Qur'an says of the believers:

> 'Theirs shall be gardens of Eden, underneath which rivers flow.' (18: 30.)
>
> 'And for those who believe and do righteous works, We will cause them to enter gardens underneath which rivers flow, to dwell therein eternally: they shall have purified companions, and We will cause them to enter abundant shade.' (4: 57).

Indeed, one can understand neither the Islamic garden nor the attitude of the Muslim toward his garden until one realises that the terrestrial garden is considered a reflection or rather an anticipation of Paradise.[1457] It is a state of blessedness that is promised in the Qur'an as reward to the faithful; reference is made to 'spreading shade;' 'fruits and fountains, and pomegranates;' 'fountains of running water;' and 'cool pavilions'. For believers who perform righteous acts, the Qur'an promises that the 'Gardens of paradise shall be their hospitality, therein to dwell forever, desiring no removal from them.'[1458]

When gardens were made into a paradise on earth, they became a foretaste of the paradise to come after death.[1459]

> 'May rain clouds water his grave and revive it and may the moist garden carry to him its fresh perfume.'

This is, Dickie notes, an Arab funerary inscription. It perpetuates the sensate outlook of the Arabs who, already in the 11th century, sought in their gardens a voluptuous gratification of the senses from their shade, water and scents.[1460]

The gentle trickle of water, in the hot summers of the Islamic land, most particularly, invites contemplation without and within. At the Lion Court in the Alhambra (Grenada), nearly all the main rooms of the palace had water running through them in a marble groove in the floor, and the garden of the Generalife, the summer palace, is typical of the love of gardens with walks and fountains, all arranged in close relation to the living quarters.[1461]

> With the constantly renewed trees and flowers and the flowing and bubbling of its water, the Generalife evokes, even more than the Alhambra, the private life of the Nasrid princes. And the architects of Grenada have never surpassed this perfect alliance of gardens, water, landscape, and architecture, which was their supreme aim, and sets the seal upon their art [says Terrasse].[1462]

[1456] J. Dickie: Rauda, in *Dictionary of the Middle Ages*; vol 10; pp. 261-2.
[1457] J. Dickie: The Islamic Garden in Spain; op cit; p. 90.
[1458] J. Lehrman: Gardens; Islam; op cit; p. 277.
[1459] F.R. Cowell: *The Garden as a Fine Art*; op cit; p. 75.
[1460] Ibid.
[1461] F.B. Artz: *The Mind*; op cit; p. 173.
[1462] H. Terrasse: Gharnata; in *Encyclopaedia of Islam*; op cit; vol 2; p. 1019.

In Cordova, some of the gardens had tempting names, which seem to invite one to rest, escape, and even slumber by the side of the trickling waters, while the sweet scents of the flowers and fruit nearby, together with the trickle, and the faint sight of all, cajole the senses.[1463] Surely at times when the breeze gently blows, when the day is mostly gone, and when the sun is no longer high, whomsoever happens to be around, in the shade of such a setting, idle and silent, alone and still, could only but succumb to all bodily senses at once. The 'Garden of the Water Wheel' gives one a sense of lazy enjoyment, listening to the monotonous creaking of the wheel that pumped up the water to the level of the garden beds; and the 'Meadow of Murmuring Waters' must have been an entrancing spot for the people of Cordova in the hot weather, notes Lane Poole.[1464] In Toledo, King al-Ma'mun (r. 1043-1073) was known as 'the great garden lover.'[1465] One of his estates had a hall called the *Majlis al-Na'ura* (The Seat by the Noria). The *Majlis* had a pool with lion fountains spewing water, and to supply this and irrigate the gardens, water from the river was raised by a wheel, or noria *(na'ura*-hence the name of the *majlis),* which creaked and "groaned like a she-camel after giving birth."[1466] In the chronicle of al-Maqqari, Ibn Badrun also relates that:

> King al-Mamun of Toledo ordered the construction of a lake, in whose centre stood a crystal pavilion; water was lifted to its roof, and from there it ran down to all sides, like artificial rain, into the water below. The pavilion was thus enclosed in a mantle of limpid water which, being constantly renewed, was also fresh, and Al-Mamun could sit inside without being touched by the water.[1467]

On hot summer nights, Al-Ma'mun was also able to sit in the cool place with water all around him by lamplight.[1468]

Water's gentle flow in the garden took an artistic function, and stimulated the talents and creativity of garden designers. Fountains, cascades, channels and pools provided a great variety of sights and sounds, and water could be made 'deep, dark, and tranquil, or swiftly flowing and scintillating.'[1469] Edges of fountains and pools were often carved in stone or marble, whilst at night, candles were set on tiny rafts to reflect in the still water of pools, or glowing lamps were placed behind glistening cascades in carved niches, which during the day contained flower vases.[1470] The Tulunid Sultan Rhumarawaih, in his garden, had many dwarf palms, whose fruit, could be reached and picked by anyone standing up, or even sitting.[1471] Their

---

[1463] S. Lane-Poole: *The Moors in Spain* (Fisher Unwin; London; 1888), pp. 132-3.
[1464] Ibid.
[1465] G.S. Colin: Filaha; *Encyclopaedia of Islam*: New edition (Leiden; 1986), vol 2, p. 901.
[1466] Al-Maqqari: *Analectes sur l'histoire et la literature des Arabes d'Espagne (Nafh al-Tib),* ed., R. Dozy et al; 2 vols in 3; Leiden 1855-1861; London; 1967; i: 426; in D. Fairchild Ruggles: *Gardens, Landscape*; op cit; p. 148.
[1467] In Al-Maqqari: *Nafh Al-Tib*, op cit; vol 2; Book vii; chapter v; p. 263.
[1468] M.L. Gothein: *A History of Garden Art*; op cit; p. 153.
[1469] J. Lehrman: Gardens; Islam; op cit; p. 278.
[1470] Ibid.
[1471] M.L. Gothein: *A History of Garden Art*; op cit; pp. 149-50.

trunks were covered with gilded copper finely wrought, between the copper and the trunk leaden pipes were introduced from which water spurted upward.[1472] The concealed water appeared to come straight out of the palm branches, whence it was collected in a fine basin and was then conducted by canals all through the garden, which, Gothein notes, may perhaps be the original model for artificial fountain trees.[1473]

Turkish gardens are firmly enclosed, and have the same veneration for flowing water in symmetrical basins, for small fountains, for the cypress and the chenar, and for the beauty of individual flowers.[1474] Kiosks in the water garden at Saadabad, in Kagithane, at the end of the Golden Horn, mostly dated from the reign of Ahmet II (1703-30), are beautifully sited over water, either placid or flowing.[1475] A section of river was diverted to form a sequence of three marble-edged pools connected by two shallow ornamental weirs.[1476] The upper and lower weirs have these sequences in different order; the upper has cascades followed by channels, so that the central mirror pool is not disturbed by tumbling water, while the lower weir begins with the channels, followed by the splashing cascade. The kiosks enjoy the various levels and appearances of the water- one perched over the water of the central pool seems to float on its surface.[1477] For coolness, fountains were quite often built inside the kiosks:

> What pleases me best [wrote Lady Montagu (wife of the English ambassador at Istanbul between 1716-1718)] is the fashion of having marble fountains in the lower part of the room, which throw up several spouts of water, giving at the same time an agreeable coolness, and a pleasant dashing sound, falling from one basin to another. In a room in one palace there were falls of water from the very roof, from shell to shell, of white marble, to the lower end of the room, where it falls into a large basin, surrounded with pipes, that throw up the water as high as the room. The walls were in the nature of lattices, and outside vines and woodbines were planted to form a sort of green tapestry, and give an agreeable obscurity to those delightful chambers.[1478]

In Muslim India, the Mughal garden of Shah Jahan's Shalamar in Lahore exhibited:

> Sheets of cool, quiet water contrasted with shawls of fast running white water thrown over chadars; deep throated marble chutes sometimes inlaid with coloured marble. The play of water in countless fountains caused the light to sparkle and covered the surface with ripples. And at night, tiny oil lamps set in marble niches sparkled from behind cascades, while flickering lights were reflected from tiny boats floating across the dark water.[1479]

[1472] Ibid.
[1473] Ibid.
[1474] C. Thacker: *The History of Gardens*; op cit; p. 34.
[1475] Ibid; p. 35.
[1476] Ibid.
[1477] Ibid.
[1478] Ibid.
[1479] The Mughal Garden accessed in 2005 at www.unesco.org/whc/whreview/article1.html

In a 17th century garden in Tunis, there was an immense four cornered basin into which water poured down 'steep as a wall.' There was at either end a grand standing on pillars of marble and mosaic. Other basins, kiosks and tall, shady trees made this place the favourite haunt of the sultan.[1480]

The artistic thrived by the side of the boldness and confidence that marked early Islamic civilisation. At Samarra, impressive architecture was greened by a multitude of gardens, and water occupied the central place, and on a vast scale, erupting out of the barrenness of the desert. The city's founder, Caliph Mu'tasim's (r. 836-876) first concern was to conduct water from the Tigris by canals.[1481] He had trees imported from other parts, and as there was so much water at hand, everything flourished. The geographer al-Ya'qubi in the year 889 remarked how in every garden there had to be a villa, and therewith halls, ponds, and playgrounds for riding and the game of ball.[1482] Mu'tasim's son, al-Mutawakkil, built a palace, entered by wide courts, paved and ornamented with flowering plants in pots. The main palace faced the river and had a large garden in front. One of the palaces had a garden on the river side and was enclosed by a wall, with pillars that ended at the bank with finely decorated pavilions, and at every extremity there was a harbour for boats.[1483] The caliph's palace and its courts stood above the high river bank as on a prominent platform, which might have been a garden, and further inland, one passed through an immense door into a great ornamental garden court, watered by a long canal drawing water from a basin in the centre. At the end there was a sort of grotto, with a basin in front of it, behind and crosswise to the main line was yet another enclosure. By the side of the garden was a large round, deep, space, possibly an arena, maybe a large tank.[1484]

There are two garden kiosks in the grounds of the Topkapi palace, in Turkey, both built in the 1570s.[1485] One, the kiosk of Murad III, retains a broad canal, facing the kiosk, which itself stands over a small extension of the canal, and the other, the kiosk of Siyavush Pasha, is raised up 'like a square island in a square lake, the lake penetrating within the kiosk itself.'[1486] Also in the Topkapi palace, there is the 'Marble Terrace' and its tank and fountains, with a small pavilion built out over the water. This is where the Sultan found solace. This desire to locate the viewing place of the garden be it balcony or pavilion-above water is a major feature of older Turkish gardens.[1487] It developed in a special way, surely inspired

---

1480 M.L. Gothein: *A History of Garden Art*; op cit; p. 150.
1481 Ibid; pp. 146-8.
1482 Ibid.
1483 Ibid.
1484 Ibid.
1485 C. Thacker: *The History of Gardens;* op cit; p. 34.
1486 Ibid.
1487 Ibid.

and also helped by the proximity of the sea along the shores of the Bosphorus, and by the steeply rising terrain at the back of the Sites.[1488]
A spectacular combination of the functional and decorative uses of water is found in the Mughal gardens, where, water, more than soil and vegetation, is the most important element.[1489] Here, as in the terraced garden of Amber resting in its artificial lake, the whole decorative repertoire of Islamic art is found harmoniously combined, although the palace was built for a ruler who in fact was not a Muslim.[1490] The beds are patterned in a geometric combination of stars and polygons that was widely common elsewhere throughout the centuries, in endless permutations, for tile revetments, on metal and earthenware, and on costumes.[1491] The pavilions have patterned screens with similar or contrasting designs. The whole complex is mirrored and framed by the sheet of water that surrounds it. The garden itself is but a part of the great palace, which towers above it, and within the palace itself, there was a sequence of pavilions, courtyards, fountains and pools and channels of water decorated with variations of the same designs.[1492]

Bold designs in water supply always demand a good degree of engineering skills whether in channelling, raising or storing water. In gardens and courtyards water was often lifted to a high storage tank to provide a head for the fountains; from thence it was led to flower beds, kitchen gardens, or fields.[1493] Water was often led from its source along a canal, aqueduct, or pipe to a tank, cistern, or public fountain.[1494] The walled Agdal gardens of Marrakech (under Almohad rule) stretched for two miles south of the Casbah, and were irrigated by water brought from far in the mountain.[1495] The garden is said to have contained huge reservoirs.[1496] In general, in both Muslim North Africa and Spain, gardens in urban areas were irrigated by means of canals led off the watercourses, or, when there were only wells, by means of simple channels leading from basins filled with water by means of norias or simpler water raising devices.[1497] These devices were quite sizeable in places. In the Palace of Galiana situated in the valley of Toledo on the banks of the Tagus, there could be found remnants of the device used by the Muslims to draw the water from the river.[1498] Andrea Navagero, the ambassador sent from Venice in 1526, makes these descriptions of the Palace of Galiana:

> The Tagus rises in Aragon, not far from Calatayud, where it is said Bilbilis, the birthplace of Martial, once stood. Before it reaches Toledo, the river flows

[1488] Ibid.
[1489] D. Jones: The Elements of Decoration: Surface, Pattern, and Light; in G. Michell ed., *Architecture*; pp. 161-75; at p. 174.
[1490] Ibid.
[1491] Ibid.
[1492] Ibid.
[1493] J. Lehrman: Gardens; Islam; op cit; p. 278.
[1494] Ibid.
[1495] M. Brett: Marrakech in *Dictionary of the Middle Ages*; op cit; vol 8; pp. 150-1.
[1496] R. Landau: *Morocco* (Elek Books Ltd, London 1967), p. 81.
[1497] Editor: Irrigation in North Africa and Muslim Spain; *Encyclopaedia of Islam;* under Ma'a; vol 5; p. 877.
[1498] Marquesa de Casa Valdes: *Spanish Gardens*; op cit; p. 25.

> through a plain called Huerta del Rey (King's Orchard) which is watered by norias, wheels invented by the Arabs to draw water from the river. Because of this, the plain is covered by trees and bears much fruit, and the whole of it is cultivated and divided into orchards. They supply the town with vegetables, especially cardoons, carrots and egg-plant, which are much in demand here. In this plain there is an old ruined palace called Galiana. Galiana was the daughter of a Moorish king... The ruins show the palace to have been very fair and its site most peaceful.[1499]

Al-Idrisi, too, tells us in his Description of Spain that the gardens surrounding Toledo are irrigated by canals over which large water wheels have been erected to carry water to the vegetable gardens. These produce remarkable quantities of unusually beautiful and delicious fruit, and on all sides lovely estates and castles can also be admired.[1500]

Muslims made fanciful additions to the flow of water. In the garden of the Alcazar of Cordova, according to al-Maqqari, there was a water jet of surprising strength, reaching a height 'never before seen in East or West.'[1501] The Muslims, as De Casa Valdes reminds us, were the first to construct such vertical water spouts.[1502] At Madinat az-Zahra, the water was so balanced in the complex of lead pipes that the play of every jet was dependent on the play of every other jet, and manipulation of a single valve could alter the water patterns of the whole system.[1503] The fountains of al-Zahira, in the vicinity of Cordoba, were particularly spectacular. Abu Marwan al-Yaziri described one of them:

> 'In the centre of the Hall is a large basin of green water in which the tortoises continually make sounds.
>
> The water pours from the jaws of a lion whose mouth would seem to say something terrible, would it speak.
>
> It is of black amber and around its neck one sees a handsome necklace of pearls.'[1504]

4. Garden Literature

The literature on Islamic farming and botany will be vastly explored in the following part under the chapter on agriculture. The literature here will be therefore kept to a

[1499] Navagero: *Viaje por Espana; in Viajes de Extranjos por Espana*; op cit; p. vol 1; p. 845.
[1500] Al-Idrisi: *Viajes de Extranjeros Por Espana y Portugal*, compiled by J. Garcia Mercada; ed. Aguilar (Madrid; 1952), vol 1; p. 192.
[1501] Al-Maqqari: *Nafh Al-Tib;* op cit; vol 1; p. 208.
[1502] Marquesa de Casa Valdes: *Spanish Gardens*; p. 30.
[1503] E. Hyams: *A History of Gardens and Gardening*; op cit; p. 82.
[1504] J.M. Continente: Abu Marwan al-Yaziri, poeta amiri; *Al-Andalus* 34 (1969); p. 131.

minimum, just enough to illustrate the Muslim use of scientific writing on gardens and gardening.

In 1031 the western caliphate broke up into independent principalities, under the so-called Taifa Kings, the most important centred on Toledo and Seville, and at both were notable palace gardens of the sultans, maintained as scientific botanical gardens.[1505] The two successive superintendents of the princely garden at Toledo, Ibn Wafid (997-1074)[1506] and Ibn Bassal (fl. 11th century),[1507] were amongst the most significant figures in the history of gardening. Their garden was very large, being outside the city on the opposite bank of the Tagus near the modern railways station, and is still known as the Huerta del Rey, the King's Garden.[1508] The sultan whom they served, Al-Ma'mun, made use of the best hydraulic science to provide the garden with water, with a pavilion cooled by streams poured down upon it on each side.[1509] Both Ibn Wafid and Ibn Bassal wrote treatises that have survived.[1510] Ibn Wafid's biographer commented that "he had complete mastery in agriculture and was knowledgeable in its procedures."[1511] His *Collection (Majmu'a)* is divided into eighty-seven chapters followed by an agricultural calendar.[1512] The chapters deal amongst others with soil types; water and how to detect it in the soil; fertilizers; seed selection; how to select sites for vineyards; choosing vine shoots to plant and how to plant them.[1513]

Ibn Wafid was succeeded at Toledo by Ibn Bassal who was both a botanist and also a horticulturist of distinction.[1514] Following the Christian conquest of the city in 1085, Ibn Bassal fled to the court of al-Mu'tamid, the taifa ruler of Seville.[1515] There, in his later career, he experimented in the cultivation of imported seeds.[1516] He travelled widely and collected plants in Sicily, Egypt, Makkah, Khorasan, as well as in various parts of Spain.[1517] Ibn Bassal was also the teacher of an anonymous botanist (who may have been Ibn 'Abdun the *hisba* writer) who later wrote a

---

[1505] J. Harvey: Medieval gardens; p. 40.

[1506] E. H. F. Meyer: *Geschichte der Botanik;* I-IV, Konigsberg (1854-7); vol. 3, pp. 205-8; E. Calvo: Ibn Wafid: in the *Encyclopaedia of the History of Science, Technology, and Medicine in Non Western Cultures*; H. Selin Editor (Kluwer Academic Publishers; Dordrecht/Boston/London, 1997), p. 438.

[1507] Ibn Bassal: *Libro de agricultura*, Jose M.Millas Vallicrosa and Mohammed Azinan ed. (Tetuan: Instituto Muley al-Hasan, 1953).

[1508] J. Harvey: *Medieval Gardens;* op cit; p. 40.

[1509] Ibid.

[1510] Millas Vallicrosa discovered the Arabic manuscript that matched the Spanish-Castilian translation by "Abel Mutariph, Abel nufit" (Ms. 10106, Bibl. Nac. Madrid, originally found in the library of the Toledo Cathedral, Ms. 96-40). "Un manuscrito arabe de la obra de Agricultura de Ibn Wafid," *Tamuda 2* (1954), 87-96; and "Nuevos textos manuscritos de las obras geoponicas de Ibn Wafid e Ibn Bassal," *Tamuda 2* (1954), 339-44. Regarding the attribution of the Castilian version of "Abel nufit," see Dubler, "Fuentes arabes," *Al-Andalus* 6 (1941), 145 ff.

[1511] Ibn al-'Abbar, *Kitab al-takmila li-Kitab al-sila,* n: 551, biographical notice 1557.

[1512] Millas Vallicrosa, "La traduccion castellana del *Tratado de Agricultura* de Ibn Wafid," *Al-Andalus* 8 (1943), 281-332; reprinted as "*El Libro de Agricultura* de Ibn Wafid y su influencia en la agricultura del Renacimiento," in *Estudios sobre la historia de la ciencia espanola,* 2 vols. (Madrid, 1987).

[1513] D. Fairchild Ruggles: *Gardens, Landscape*; op cit; p. 22.

[1514] J. Harvey: *Medieval Gardens;* op cit; p. 40.

[1515] D. Fairchild Ruggles: *Gardens*; op cit; p. 23.

[1516] J. Harvey: *Medieval Gardens;* op cit; p. 41.

[1517] Ibid.

pharmacological treatise for physicians *('Umdat al-tabib fi marifat al-nabat li-kull labib)* (after 542/1147). Ibn Bassal wrote the *Diwan al-filaha* and an abridged version of the same called *al-Qasd wa-l-Bayan* (Concision and Clarity,) the contents of which survive in part because of Ibn al-Awwam's summarisation of them.[1518] Ibn Bassal's work is original, based on his own practical experience.[1519] His manual catalogues with great attention to detail and variety all the known ways of cultivating and controlling soil, water, and growing conditions in order to produce the best plants.[1520] From his list, as well as his reference to the blue lily and various sorts of jasmine he studied on his travels, it becomes obvious that the purely ornamental garden was already highly developed.[1521] This list of flowers and plants combined with the size of garden beds and plant spacing should be informative enough to reconstruct a typical Andalusian garden of the 11th century although it does not tell how they should be arranged.[1522] Most of the plants listed also had commercial value as dye, perfume, and spice, and their cultivation for the market would have been quite different from their arrangement in a formal garden.[1523]

Ibn al-Awwam (fl. End of 12th century), wrote *Kitab al-filaha* (Book of Agriculture*),*[1524] which is the most important Muslim work as well as the most important mediaeval one on the subject.[1525] In this work, which relies on his personal and practical experience, he explains what Muslim gardeners regarded as correct rules for planting, and some of the garden plants which they preferred.[1526] The treatise covers 585 plants, and explains the cultivation of more than fifty different fruit trees, besides containing very interesting observations on the different kinds of soil and manure and their respective properties, on various methods of grafting, on sympathies and antipathies between plants, and many other matters of interest for the gardener.[1527] Ibn al-Awwam, besides dealing with a much larger number of species, breaks new grounds by suggesting, here and there, principles of design.[1528] Thus, cypresses, for instance, might be used to mark corners of beds and in rows alongside main walks, and other trees suitable for planting in rows were cedars and pines, with citrus fruits and sweet bay, while jasmines were presumably intended to be trained on trellis or pergolas.[1529] Ibn al-Awwam insists that all garden doorways should be framed by clipped evergreens, that cypresses should be used to line paths and grouped to mark the junctions of

---

1518 Ibn Bassal: *Kitab al-Filaha. Libro de de Agricultura;* ed., and Spanish tr. J.M. Millas Vallicrosa and M. Aziman; Tetuan; 1955.
1519 J. Harvey: *Medieval Gardens*; op cit; p. 41.
1520 D. Fairchild Ruggles: *Gardens, Landscape*; op cit; p. 23.
1521 J. Harvey: *Medieval Gardens;* op cit; p. 41.
1522 D. Fairchild Ruggles: *Gardens, Landscape,* op cit; p. 24.
1523 Ibid.
1524 Spanish version by Joseph A. Banqueri; 2 vols, folio (Madrid 1802); French version: *Le Livre de l'agriculture*, by Clement-Mullet; 2 tomes in 3 vols (Paris 1864-1867).
1525 G. Sarton: *Introduction*; op cit; vol 2; pp. 424-5.
1526 E. Hyams: *A History of Gardens and Gardening*; op cit; p. 84.
1527 G. Sarton: *Introduction*, op cit, p. 425.
1528 J. Harvey: *Medieval Gardens;* op cit; p. 41.
1529 Ibid.

paths, and he objects to the mixing of evergreen with deciduous trees.[1530] He liked to see canals and pools shaded by trees or bowers, to prevent excessive loss of water by evaporation.[1531] The tree varieties he suggests for that purpose are pomegranate, the elm, poplar and willow.[1532] Amongst the plants he names in his text are lemon and orange trees, pines and most of the common deciduous trees, cypresses, oleander, myrtle and rose as the only flowering shrubs; violets, lavender, balm, mint, thyme, marjoram, iris, mallow, box and bay laurel.[1533] He lays much stress on aromatics, as, indeed, did all the Islamic gardeners.[1534] For hedges, box and laurel could be used, as well as climbing plants such as ivy, jasmine, and the grapevine was considered as an ornament.[1535]

Muslims were extremely fond of flowers, and from early Islamic manuscripts, Dickie compiled a list of the fifty two common flowers mentioned by Muslims up to the 11th century.[1536] Ibn Bassal's most interesting chapter deals with flowers such as the rose, the wallflower and stock, violet, lily, narcissus, basil, marjoram, balm, rue, and camomile.[1537] Between Ibn Bassal and Ibn al-Awwam (roughly 1080-1180) many exotic plants were introduced into Spain, as well as the bringing into cultivation of wild native, expressly advocated by Ibn al-Awwam in connection with ivy and with a great binkweed known as poor man's rope, bearing beautiful bell shaped flowers: these, he suggests, could be trained on a trellis for display.[1538] Violets should be sown in shady and sheltered beds, and also in new perforated flower pots, in either case, laying a bed of crumbled brick and builder's rubbish mixed with an equal quantity of pigeon's dung. The author had himself seen them grown in this way at Seville and Cordova.[1539] Pleasurable scents as well as colours were sought, with jasmine, narcissus, violet, mauve stock, yellow wallflower, red rose, white lily, blue iris, water lily, almond blossom, marguerite, camomile, trumpet narcissus, poppy, pomegranate blossom; myrtle, basil, lavender, carnation, orange blossom, marjoram, oleander, thyme, mint, saffron, lupin, as well as other flowering trees and shrubs: laurel, pear, and plum.[1540] Poetry from the period confirms that the same plants and flowers appeared in pleasure gardens and that they had symbolic meanings.[1541]

One last and important feature to be noted in the Andalusi treatises is their experimental character. Ibn Bassal's personal experiments were remarked upon by

---

[1530] E. Hyams: *A History of Gardens and Gardening*; op cit; p. 84.
[1531] Ibid.
[1532] J. Harvey: *Medieval Gardens;* op cit; p. 41.
[1533] E. Hyams: *A History of Gardens and Gardening*; op cit; p. 84.
[1534] Ibid.
[1535] J. Harvey: *Medieval Gardens;* op cit; p. 41.
[1536] In F.R. Cowell: *The Garden as a Fine Art;* op cit; p. 76.
[1537] J. Harvey: *Medieval Gardens;* op cit; p. 41.
[1538] Ibid; pp. 41-2.
[1539] Ibid.
[1540] F.R. Cowell: *The Garden as a Fine Art;* op cit; p. 76.
[1541] D. Fairchild Ruggles: *Gardens, Landscape,* op cit; p. 24.

his contemporaries, notably al-Tignari of Albolote near Grenada.[1542] From al-Tignari and from other sources we get scraps of information on Ibn Bassal's experimental writing:

> The eminent master Ibn Bassal was learned both in theoretical and experimental agriculture, an expert cultivator who has mastered the subject. He told me that he had seen the Blue lily (?) Iris germanica) in Sicily and in Alexandria; 'I saw this species of garden asparagus sown by Ibn Basal in the sultan's garden: 'all these sorts of jasmine are found in the neighbourhoods of Valencia, Sicily, Alexandria and Khorasan, as I have been told by Ibn Bassal among others.[1543]

Al-Tignari gives details of Ibn Bassal's method of dealing with a disease that infected the orange trees, cutting down and burning those infected, and later making choices among the new shoots from the root. He also carried out experiments in planting the pomegranate, and discovered that the fig and the vine could be planted in any season.[1544]

Ibn Bassal's spirit of experimentation was shared by other Muslim writers, especially Ibn al-Awwam. [1545] Garcia Sanchez remarks that it is their "experimental" character, which has most attracted the attention of later Christian authors such as Gabriel Alonso de Herrera, and which contained the germ of the modern experimental spirit.

> It was this real and direct knowledge of the land [Garcia Sanchez adds] which underlay all the steps taken for the purpose of obtaining good crops; and from it sprang all the technologies based on their knowledge of previous traditions of agriculture, which they received, always, in a critical spirit, and applied to the earth of al-Andalus on which they stood.[1546]

5. Impact on the West and the Impact of History

The Islamic garden impacted considerably on the subsequent Western garden, and was itself to be impacted upon, but in a manner that was much less constructive.

On the pioneering Muslim role, Harvey says:

> In retrospect, we can see that the Muslim Middle East, from India to the Balkans, preceded Western Europe in the development of highly sophisticated gardening. A keen interest in landscape, in Autumn colour, in

[1542] J. Harvey: *Medieval Gardens*; op cit; p. 40.
[1543] Ibid.
[1544] Ibid; p. 41.
[1545] E. Hyams: *A History of Gardens and Gardening*; op cit; p. 84.
[1546] Expiracion Garcia Sanchez: Agriculture in Muslim Spain; in M.G. Morony ed. *Production and the Exploitation of Resources*; (Ashgate; 2002); pp. 204-17; at p. 215.

> the grouping of plants, was being displayed by Turkish princes and their gardeners long before such ideas formed any part of our horticultural currency.[1547]

In the 12th century, Gothein observes, the art of gardening took a most important step forward, for:

> The whole spiritual life of the West was astonishingly uplifted. We are now at the time of the crusades: the Christian soldiery beheld, in the East, gardens of a splendour beyond their wildest dreams. The poets listened to their tales, and from now onward they sang of the East, which was the darling theatre for the adventurous knight errant. Gladly, do we try to depict these distant scenes, and the tale of Herzog Ernst is pleasant enough:
> Near they came to a valley in a garden hall; it was very roomy, and therein stood many cedar trees rich in leafy bowers; they found two rivulets also that rose there and flowed through the grounds, winding as they pleased, and as the master had planned who made all by his skill. They found a bath, too, bright and clean, wrought of green marble, well walled in and overhung with fifty high branches; the streams were brought herein by silver channels. Much water ran out in a silver course from the thicket, and flowed around the castle, in straight or curving lines around the whole castle. All the paths were of white marble, all bridges made where men would walk.[1548]

The influence of the Islamic garden is very obvious in Sicily. There, the 'baptised sultans,' as they were called, of the Norman Hauteville family captured Sicily from the Muslims and took over their gardens; gardens, which resembled those found in other parts of the Muslim world.[1549] The suburbs of Palermo, like the Zisa, whose name derives from the Arabic al-Aziz, "the Splendid",[1550] highlight the Muslim influence, which continued even under William I (The Bad) (r.1154-1166), the heir to Roger II.[1551] He built a number of retreats in the outskirts of Palermo, of which none were more splendid than the "Zisa," the geometric structuring of the design suggesting a relation to woven textile patterns, a frequent means of transmission of ornamental motifs during the middle ages.[1552] The palaces of Emperor Frederick II (1194-1250) showed a marked preference for Muslim customs and architecture, outworks of vast extent protected their approaches, and in all of them were courts and gardens fragrant with the blossoms of jasmine and orange and surrounded by secluded apartments designed for the occupants of the imperial seraglio.[1553] Attached to some of these delightful retreats were

---

[1547] J.H. Harvey; Turkey as a Source of Garden Plants; in *Garden History*; vol 4 (1976); pp. 21-42; at p. 26.
[1548] M.L. Gothein: *A History of Garden Art*; op cit; p. 190.
[1549] E. Hyams: *A History of Gardens and Gardening*; op cit; pp. 91-2.
[1550] J. D. Breckenridge: The Two Sicilies; in *Islam and the Medieval West*; S. Ferber Editor (State University of New York; 1975), pp. 39-59; at p. 55.
[1551] Ibid.
[1552] Ibid.
[1553] S.P. Scott: *History;* op cit; vol 3; p. 51.

extensive menageries, aviaries, and miniature lakes filled with gold and silver fish.[1554]

> There was no appliance of Oriental luxury, no means which could contribute to the gratification of the senses, that was not to be found in the Sicilian palaces of Frederick II [Scott insists.][1555]

Contacts through the Normans settled in Sicily and by way of Spain transmitted the rudiments of walled garden, pool and pavilion to France, England and the Low Countries.[1556] Thus the garden idea, Harvey points out, had preceded most of the cultivated flora by several hundred years.[1557]

Muslims, as noted already, pioneered in the erection of botanical gardens to acclimatise plants and diffuse them. The one at Toledo was founded by Ibn Wafid (999-1075), and his colleague and successor Ibn Bassal continued working there until the Christian conquest of 1085 forced him to flee further south to Seville, where he improved the royal gardens for sultan al Mu'atamid (r. 1061-1091).[1558] This garden, like others, served as a major centre for adapting and then diffusing exotic plants from even far off places. The chapter on agriculture in part II will give many instances of such plants that were received by Spain and then spread in the West, before the Spaniards, centuries later, took them to their colonies in the Americas. The most famous of the botanical gardens was set up a century later at Guadix by Mohammed Ibn Ali Ibn Farah for the Almohad sultan An-Nasir (r. 1199-1214).[1559] Only many centuries later did Europe possess similar botanical gardens which acted as the same kind of medium for plant diffusion that the Muslim world had experienced in the middle ages.[1560] Montpellier was the northern outpost of Muslim-Spanish science, for it belonged to the crown of Aragon from 1202 to 1349. Its university, greatly famed for its medical learning, formed a main international link, and appropriately owned one of the oldest botanical gardens in France, opened by Henry IV in 1593.[1561] Those gardens set up in Pisa (1543) and Padua (1545), Parma and Florence in 1545, Bologna in 1568, Leyden in 1577, Leipzig in 1580, Konigsberg in 1581, Paris (Le Jardin Royal du Louvre) in 1590, Oxford in 1621, and others,[1562] are regarded as the earliest in the world, which forgets the far older gardens of Muslim botanists under the patronage of Muslim rulers (seen above).[1563] The comparative study of plants and the systematic

---

[1554] Ibid.
[1555] Ibid.
[1556] J. Harvey: Turkey as a Source; op cit; p. 21.
[1557] See J. Harvey, The Mediaeval Architect (1972), 59-67; and Early Nurserymen (1975), 15-16, 33-4.
[1558] A. Watson: *Agricultural;* op cit; chap 22.
[1559] J. Harvey: *Medieval Gardens;* op cit; p. 40.
[1560] A. Watson: *Agricultural*, op cit, chap 22.
[1561] J. Harvey: Medieval Gardens; op cit; p. 40.
[1562] See: A. Chiarugi: Le date di fondazione dei primi orti botanici del mondo,' *Nuovo giornale botanico italiano* new ser. LX (1953) 785-839; A.W. Hill: The History and function of botanical gardens; *Annals of the Missouri Botanical Garden;* II (1915); pp. 185-240; 195 fwd; F. Philippi: *Los jardines botanicos* (Santiago de Chile; 1878), etc.
[1563] J. Harvey: *Medieval Gardens;* op cit; p. 40.

introduction of exotic species with experiments in their cultivation derive from the Muslim gardens on European soil.[1564]

Just as it took the idea of botanical gardens from the Muslims, the West filled its gardens with plants and flowers of every variety imported from the Muslim world, Turkey most of all. As Harvey notes, the age of deliberate botanical exploration began, as Miss Alice Coats tells us,[1565] with the travels of Pierre Belon in the Levant in 1546-8.[1566] Belon did not collect seeds or living specimens, as his successors would do, but his observations in the Ottoman Empire opened the way for the first major wave of exotic plants to the West.[1567] The most notable and true pioneer was the imperial ambassador Ogier Ghiselin de Busbecq, who was in Turkey from 1554 to 1562.[1568] Busbecq relates that when he was travelling from Adrianople to Istanbul in the midwinter of 1554, he was presented by peasants 'with large nosegays of bulbous plants,' the narcissus, the hyacinth, and the *tulipan.*[1569] On his return to his native Flanders he carried some tulip bulbs with him, a plant which was almost unknown in Central or Western Europe at this date; and he continued after his return to receive packages of tulips and other rare plants from Istanbul.[1570] In 1562, an Amsterdam merchant imported the first "cargo" of tulip bulbs from Constantinople. The European name of the flower is said to be a derivative from Turkish.[1571] Busbecq, members of his suite, and merchants encouraged by the success of his mission, were responsible for the sudden flood of species, which reached Vienna, Antwerp, Paris and London.[1572] Tulips were not the only import, though. By a process of deduction, based on the species known to have been introduced, we can be sure, Harvey says, that before 1600 the West had derived from or through Turkey the great bulbs: Crown Imperial, Hyacinth, Lilium candidum var. cernuum, L. chalcedonicum, Muscari moschatum, various Narcissi and Tulip; the brilliant Anemones, Carnation, Iris pallida and I. susiana, Love-in-a-Mist, Ranunculus asiaticus and the shrubs Cherry Laurel, Lilac and Syringa (Philadelphus coronarius), and the Oleaster (Elaeagnus angustifolia).[1573] At earlier but unknown dates the West had received the Oriental Plane tree, the Black Mulberry and, indirectly, the Walnut; Hollyhock, White Jasmine, Scarlet Lychnis, 'Female' Peony and Opium Poppy.[1574] More plants were imported into the West in the subsequent decades and centuries, which were to add to the stock inherited from Muslim Spain and Sicily.

[1564] Ibid.
[1565] A.M. Coats: *The Quest for Plants* (1969), 11-3.
[1566] J. Harvey: Turkey as a Source; op cit; p. 21.
[1567] Ibid.
[1568] *The Turkish Letters of Ogier Ghiselin de Busbecq*, tr. E.S. Forster (Oxford 1927/1968).
[1569] B. Miller: *Beyond the Sublime Porte*, AMS Press, New York, 1931, p. 124.
[1570] Ibid.
[1571] H.G. Dwight: *Constantinople, Old and New*, New York, 1915, p. 257.
[1572] J. Harvey: Turkey as a Source; op cit; p. 21.
[1573] Ibid.
[1574] Ibid.

The great value of Islamic botanical treatises was recognised in Christian Spain, where translations of some of them into Castilian were made as part of the great programme of scientific works initiated by Alfonso X (r. 1252-1284). Of these, a substantial part of the versions of the works of Ibn Wafid and Ibn Bassal has come down to our times.[1575] The *Majmu fi'l Filaha* (Compendium of Farming), attributed to Ibn Wafid (Abenguefith), was translated into two romance languages, Catalan[1576] and Castilian.[1577] This work had great influence on the 'Renaissance' work of agronomy, the *Agricultura General* of Gabriel Alonso Herrera (d. c. 1539).[1578] The 11th century farming treatise by Ibn Bassal, which in its abridged form was published at Tetuan in 1955, was translated into Castilian in the Middle Ages.[1579] The significance of these translations, and of the original scientific works produced under Alfonso the Learned, resides largely in the fact that they were in vernacular languages not in Latin.[1580] It is very possible that the users of these works were mainly laymen with a direct interest in craft skills, and for such readers, the guidelines of a practical gardener like Ibn Bassal, writing from his own experience, would be of real importance.[1581] At a later date, there could be found similar attempts to put practical advice into English, along the translations such as those made by John Trevisa, Henry Daniel and others at the end of the 14th century.[1582]

Muslim gardens, as this chapter has shown in great abundance, were grandiose, but, once more, Western literature in general, has endeavoured to phase them out of history, helped in this by the vandalism perpetrated by authorities of diverse ranks. On the first point, briefly, Marquesa de Casa Valdes makes an important remark that:

> Muslim chroniclers have left numerous descriptions of the gardens and fountains that once existed in the palace and town of Medinat al-Zahra. Recent excavations have confirmed these accounts, which had earlier seemed fanciful.[1583]

The Marquesa here insists on how Western writers on Muslim history and civilisation demean its impact, and always refer to scholars' glorification of Muslim civilisation as exaggerated, or mere creations of fertile imaginations.[1584]

[1575] J. Harvey: *Medieval Gardens;* op cit; pp. 43-4.

[1576] The medieval Catalan version can be found in the Bibliotheque Nationale of Paris; Number 93 by A. Morel Fatio, *Catalogue des manuscrits espagnols et des manuscrits Portugais* (Paris, 1982), pp. 332-3.

[1577] Text in Castilian edited by J.M. Millas Vallicrosa: La traduccion castellana del Tratado de Agricultura' de Ibn Wafid; *Al-Andalus;* 8 (1943), pp. 281-332.

[1578] Millas Vallicrosa, "La traduccion castellana; reprinted as "*El Libro de Agricultura* de Ibn Wafid y su influencia en la agricultura del Renacimiento," in *Estudios sobre la historia de la ciencia espanola,* 2 vols. (Madrid, 1987).

[1579] R. B. Serjeant: Agriculture and Horticulture: Some cultural interchanges of the medieval Arabs and Europe; in *Convegno Internationale: Oriente e Occidente Nel Medioevo Filosofia e Scienze;* Aprile 1969 (Academia Nationale Dei Lincei; Roma; 1971), pp. 535-41; at p. 540.

[1580] J. Harvey: *Medieval Gardens;* op cit; pp. 43-4.

[1581] Ibid.

[1582] Ibid.

[1583] Marquesa de Casa Valdes: *Spanish Gardens*; op cit; p. 28.

[1584] Ibid.

More grave is the second form of onslaught on the Muslim legacy that is the physical vandalism:

> Casual visitors to Spain find it difficult to believe that the magnificent villas and gardens of Muslim Spain ever existed or that they were not taken over and enjoyed by some at least of the Christians who came to occupy and rule the land [observes, Cowell.][1585] Such notions [Cowell pursues] are misplaced because they rest upon the tacit assumption that it would have been natural for Christian victors in the holy war against the followers of Islam to have enjoyed gardens as much as the Muslims did or as most people do today. Spanish Christians were sternly forbidden some of the garden joys of the Muslims. To be able to show that anyone had washed in a pool near a mosque, as Muslims ritual required the faithful to do, might set inquisitors to work. Such was the danger that the very name of the Court of the Pool at Grenada had to be changed to the Court of the Myrtle Hedges. Railings and barriers were erected to shut away the charm of such Moorish garden pools that were allowed to remain, while the rigidly orthodox displayed an aversion to water that remained for too long among their less pleasant characteristics.[1586]

Hyams is even harsher, holding, that:

> Just as they were to destroy the great civilisations of Central and South America, the Spaniards destroyed the Muslim civilisation of Andalusia.[1587]

This destruction is underlined by Scott in a lengthy tirade, here abridged for the sake of convenience; he says:

> In the land illuminated by his genius and enriched by his industry, the Spanish Muslim is forgotten or absolutely unknown to the majority of the people The effects and the influence of his civilization are disputed or depreciated; his sites mutilated or entirely destroyed; his palaces transformed into the squalid haunts of mendacity and vice, while the leather-clad shepherd watches his flock on the once famous site of gardens adorned with magnificent villas and beautiful with all the luxuriant and fanciful horticulture of the East. Barbaric violence has annihilated the palaces, which lined the Guadalquevir, and whose richness and beauty were the admiration of the world.[1588]

The same happened in Sicily, where, as Scott continues:

> The unrelenting hostility of the See of Rome to everything connected with Islam may account for the total disappearance of the superb architectural monuments which history informs us abounded during Muslim rule. The sumptuous edifices which abounded in every city have disappeared or have been mutilated almost beyond recognition. Ignorance and prejudice of

---

[1585] F.R. Cowell: *The Garden as a Fine Art*; op cit; p. 76.

[1586] Ibid.

[1587] E. Hyams: *A History of Gardens and Gardening*; op cit; p. 84.

[1588] S.P. Scott: *History;* op cit*;* Vol II; pp. 537; 553; 557-8.

> successive generations, in addition to the above named destructive agencies, contributing their share, and no unimportant one, to the obliteration of these memorials of Muslim taste and ingenuity.[1589]

In Spain, few of the Muslim gardens still remain.

> The gardens of delight with their bright tiles, their fountains and their deep calm pools that had brought a breath of the far distant Orient to the western limits of Europe faded away.[1590] In their place [Cowell asserts] came the glum austerity of monasticism, progressively degenerating by spiritual inbreeding and ritualistic monotony. Its nadir is to be seen in the funeral gloom of the Escorial, while in Cordoba the great Mosque with the remnants of courtyards and patios still contrive under the southern sun, amid the scented glory of orange blossoms and golden fruits, to recall some of the pleasant features of Islamic paradises and to stir thoughts of distant lands and ways of long ago, of muezzins and camel bells, when the caliph's word was law from the Indian to the Atlantic Ocean.[1591]

The three principal survivors of Spanish Muslim gardens are the Alhambra and the Generalife in Granada, the Alcazar in Seville; the surviving and smaller patio de los Naranjos at Cordova mosque is older than any of these.[1592] Hardly anything of Muslim origin remains of the others. Neglect of irrigation systems had a worse effect than the breakdown of ornamental waterworks: as the irrigation system failed the gardens died, and as the gardens died, the villas decayed.[1593]

The fate of the patio of Orange trees (de Los Naranjos) in the Mosque of Cordova is a very good example of such decay. This is perhaps the most ancient walled garden in the world. It was begun by Abd Errahman II about the year 776, then, Al-Mansur enlarged the mosque in 987-990 adding eight naves to its eastern side, so that the pond was no longer at its centre. The Mosque's floor plan shows the Patio of Orange Trees was designed and planted in conjunction with this final addition.[1594] According to Mrs Villiers Stuart, each row of orange trees was aligned with the pillars inside the mosque and with the nineteen arches that once opened onto the garden in the Arab fashion. One can imagine, she says, moments of prayer in the mosque; the light filtering through the rows of orange trees must have formed an impressive image of seclusion and poetry.[1595] An anonymous author, M, on a journey to Spain around the year 1700, described the Patio of Orange Trees as

> A square garden of nearly three acres, planted with very fine large orange trees forming beautiful avenues, just as our elms do in France. This was the

---

[1589] Ibid.
[1590] F.R. Cowell: *The Garden as a Fine Art*; op cit; pp. 76-7.
[1591] Ibid.
[1592] E. Hyams: *A History of Gardens and Gardening*; op cit; p. 85.
[1593] Ibid; p. 84.
[1594] Marquesa de Casa Valdes: *Spanish Gardens*; op cit; p. 27.
[1595] Ibid; p. 28.

work of the Moors, and that country is still richly endowed with their legacy.[1596]

At the beginning of the 19th century, Count Alexander Laborde wrote his *Picturesque and Historical Journey Through Spain*, an account, which, without any doubt, is the most detailed of its kind ever published. About the garden of Cordova, he says:

> It is a sort of raised garden over a vast cistern: the four or five feet of earth that cover its vaults suffice to support and feed these lovely trees, among which there are orange trees thirty five or forty feet high and palm trees about sixty feet high. In the centre of this vegetation above the front of the building which forms the fourth façade of the enclosure, rises a square windowed tower crowned with a rotunda that serves as a belfry.[1597]

The patio has since fallen into neglect. The arches have since been filled in order to construct chapels.[1598] The cistern has apparently been used as an ossuary and access to it is difficult, the hundred year old orange trees described by Laborde at the beginning of the 19th century can no longer be seen, and those that remain lack symmetry, and are no longer aligned with the pillars inside the mosque.[1599]

The same can be said of the 13th century garden discovered in the Patio de la Cequia in the Generalife in 1959.[1600] Although the primary aim was to repair damage caused by the fire of 1958, the archaeologist Jesus Bermudes not only found the pavement of the Muslim paths, revealing thereby the primitive cruciform design of the garden, but, underneath the accumulated debris of almost five centuries, located the primitive level of the parterres (50 cm. below that of the paths) and even, pierced in the flanking paths of the watercourse, the outlet holes which made possible the watering of the flower beds.[1601]

> Now, for some obscure reason [Dickie remarks] other authorities have disfigured once more the Patio de la Acequia, sealing the outlet holes, burying the Muslim level under half a metre of earth and debris as before and planting once more upon this false surface the no less false plants unknown to the Muslims.[1602]

In Sicily, nearly everything Islamic is gone today, and late medieval travellers in the 14th century, such as Alberti and Fazello, could find only poor remains, which were strung round the city of Palermo, like a 'necklace of a fair lady's neck.'[1603] Alberti does describe the Villa la Ziza, which is still standing, but so completely rebuilt that one can barely find the court with the fountain that he admired so much.[1604] The whole of the house floor is crossed by a stream, with a fine

---

[1596] Anonymous M: *Viajes;* Ed Aguilar (Madrid; 1952), vol iii; p. 97.
[1597] A. Laborde: Voyage en Espagne; *Revue Hispanique*; ed. Fouche Delbose; (Paris; 1925); p. 491.
[1598] Marquesa de Casa Valdes: *Spanish Gardens*; op cit; p. 28.
[1599] Ibid.
[1600] J. Dickie: The Islamic Garden; op cit; p. 98.
[1601] El-Generalife depues del incendio de 1958,' *Cuadernos de la Alhambra;* I (1965); pp. 9-39.
[1602] J. Dickie: The Islamic Garden; op cit; p. 98.
[1603] M.L. Gothein: *A History of Garden Art*; op cit; p. 159.
[1604] Ibid.

decorated hall above it two storeys and a vaulted roof. In front of the hall, Alberti saw a wonderful fishpond, into which streamed the fountain water, and the middle of it was a kiosk, attached by a bridge to the land.[1605]

Another Muslim villa, which lay between Palermo and Montreale, is mentioned by Bocaccio in the sixth tale of the fifth day, calling it Cuba, from Arabic Kubba or domed pavilion.[1606] Traces of an important orchard, about two thousand feet long, have been preserved:

> There was a splendid garden [says the 14th century Italian traveller, Fazello, following older accounts] with all possible combinations of trees, ever flowing waters, and bushes of laurel and myrtle. From entrance to exit there ran a long colonnade with many vaulted pavilions for the king to take his pleasure in. One of these is still to be seen. In the middle of the garden is a large fish pond, built of freestone, and beside it the lofty castle of the king.[1607]

Hardly anything resembling such late medieval descriptions can be seen today.

Final Words on the Islamic Garden

Islamic gardens are nearly all gone today, and not just in former Muslim lands of the Christian West, but also in the Muslim world of today. From the eastern realm of Islam to its western end, time, invasions, vandalism, neglect, crassness, vulgarity and coarseness, have erased nearly all such gardens from existence. In a land where the green, the natural, the truly beautiful have no place, even the concept that a garden is a beautiful thing is lost. To our great fortune, there remains today the memories, accounts from contemporaries and from modern day passionate Western lovers of Muslim gardens, and also beautiful lines such as these by Armesto on which to end this chapter:

> The strict unity, which characterised Islam was shattered in the 10th century by political schism, the proclamation in both Spain and Egypt of rival caliphates... and other difficulties which made the caliph's rule only nominal. Yet, a sense of comity survived, and travellers could feel at home throughout Dar al-Islam, or to use the language of the poets-in a garden of Islam, cultivated, walled against the world, yielding for its privileged occupants, shades and tastes of paradise.[1608]

[1605] Ibid; pp. 159-60.

[1606] Ibid; p. 160.

[1607] Ibid.

[1608] F. Fernandez Armesto: *Millennium;* op cit; p. 35.

Four

LEARNING AND SCHOLARSHIP

When the Muslims were about to begin their conquest of Sicily, describing a scene of beating drums, neighing horses and waving banners with huge crowds of citizens in attendance, the historian al-Maliki reported a short speech by Asad Ibn al-Furat, supreme commander of the expeditionary forces,[1609] delivered on that Spring day in 827 at the end of which he quoted the Qur'anic injunction:

> Exert your minds and bodies in the search and pursuit of knowledge; increase it and be patient with its intensity, for with it you will gain this world and the next.[1610]

Part two of this work will be solely devoted to Islamic sciences, and will be critical of the way mainstream history has dealt with such sciences. Thus in this chapter, focus is on Islamic learning as a whole, and its general aspects only. This is still a vast subject which, in its own right, requires a whole book, but just as with other matters mentioned above, only a superficial summary can be made.[1611] The main points looked at here are the dominant aspects of Islamic learning; the place of faith and faiths in this experience; the accomplishments of scholars and scholarship, a brief view of the Islamic impact on the Christian West, and books and libraries in early Islamic civilisation.

1. Dominant Aspects of Islamic Learning

In the lines of Mutahhr b. Tahir al-Maqdisi (fl 966):

> Learning only unveils herself to him who wholeheartedly gives himself up to her; who approaches her with unclouded mind and clear insight; who seeks God's help and focuses an undivided attention upon her; who girds up his robe and who, albeit weary, out of sheer ardour, passes sleepless nights in pursuit of his goal rising, by steady ascent, to its topmost height.[1612]

[1609] S and N. Ronart: *Concise encyclopaedia of Arabic civilization; The Arab West;* Djambatan; Amsterdam; 1966; p. 38.

[1610] Al-Maliki: *Riyad al-Nufus*; Cairo; Maktabat al-Nahdah al-Misriya; 1951; pp. 187-8; W. Granara: Islamic Education and the transmission of knowledge in Muslim Sicily; in J.E. Lowry et al: *Law and Education in Medieval Islam*; (E.J. W. Gibb Memorial Trust; 2004); pp. 150-73; at p. 154.

[1611] For more see works such as: J. Ribera: *Dissertaciones y opusculos;* 2 vols (Madrid, 1928). George Makdisi: *The Rise of Colleges* (Edinburgh University Press, 1981). George Makdisi: *The Rise of Humanism in Classical Islam and the Christian West* (Edinburgh University Press, 1990). J. Pedersen: *The Arabic Book*; tr., by G. French (Princeton University; 1984).

[1612] Mutahhr b. Tahir al-Maqdisi (fl 966) *Livre de la Creation et de l'Histoire*, ed., and tr. C. Huart (Paris, 1899-1910) I, 4-5.

The 10th century belletrist Ibn Abd Rabbihi of Cordova (860-940) devoted a whole book to knowledge and education: *Al-Iqd al-farid* (The Unique Necklace).[1613] In this work, he reiterates an already established tradition, stressing the importance of knowledge, its usefulness and virtue, exhorting people to pursue it.[1614] He refers to the leading scholars, their qualities and prominent positions, and he defines knowledge and education as:

> The pillars upon which rests the axis of religion and the world. They distinguish man from the beast, and the rational from the irrational being. They are the substance of the intellect, the lantern of the body, the light of the heart, and the pole of the soul... The proof is that the intellect grasps the sciences in the same manner sight receives colours, and hearing receives sound. Indeed, the intelligent person who is not taught anything is like one who has no intellect at all. And if a child were not educated and taught to read and write he would be the most stupid of animals and the most wandering beast.[1615]

Knowledge is one of those concepts that have dominated Islam and given Muslim civilisation its distinctive shape and complexion, insists Rosenthal.[1616] In fact, there is no other concept that has determined early Muslim civilisation in all its aspects to the same extent as knowledge.[1617]

Learning, by which is meant the whole world of the intellect, Pedersen also notes, engaged the interest of Muslims more than anything else during the golden age of Islam and for a good while thereafter.[1618]

> The life that evolved in the mosques [Pedersen says] spread outward to put its mark upon influential circles everywhere. Princes and rich men gathered people of learning and letters around them, and it was quite common for a prince, one or more times a week, to hold a concourse (majlis), at which representatives of the intellectual life would assemble and, with their princely host participating, discuss those topics that concerned them, just as they were accustomed to do when meeting in their own milieu.[1619]

In the search for knowledge, I.R and L.L Al Faruqi explain, 'everybody felt himself to be a conscript.'[1620]

> Never before and never since [admits Briffault] on such a scale has the spectacle been witnessed of the ruling classes throughout the length and breadth of a vast empire given over entirely to a frenzied passion for the acquisition of knowledge. Learning seemed to have become for them the

---

1613 Edition A. Amin (Cairo 1948-53).

1614 A. Chejne: *Muslim Spain, Its History and Culture* (The University of Minnesota Press; Minneapolis; 1974), pp. 166-7.

1615 Ibn Abd Rabihi: *Al-Iqd al-Farid;* vol 2; p. 206.

1616 F. Rosenthal: *Knowledge Triumphant: The Concept of Knowledge in Medieval Islam* (Leiden; E.J. Brill, 1970), p. 2.

1617 Ibid.

1618 J. Pedersen: *The Arabic*; op cit; p. 37.

1619 Ibid.

1620 I.R. & L.L. Al Faruqi, *The Cultural Atlas;* op cit; at p. 320

> chief business of life. Caliphs and emirs hurried from their Diwans to closet themselves in their libraries and observatories. They neglected the affairs of the state to attend lectures and converse on mathematical problems with men of science.[1621]

And where and when the ruler was absent, it was the closest in family ties on to whom this duty fell. In Muslim Spain, for instance, Al-Mondhir, a brother of Caliph Al-Hakem (r. 961-972), who, in the absence of the sovereign, presided over the contests of the famous literary institute in which the talents and the learning of the aspiring scholars of the land were exhibited.[1622]

Early in the 9th century, under the sponsorship of enlightened rulers, such as al-Ma'mun, al-Mutawakkil, Abd Errahman II, and the Aghlabid rulers of al-Qayrawan, there were established centres for advanced learning in the Muslim world. By the end of the 11th century 'university-type institutions' were established in most of the chief cities.[1623] Earliest among such institutions was *Bayt al-Hikmah*, or House of Wisdom, which was established in Baghdad in the 9th century. It had a library, scientific equipment, a translation bureau, and an observatory. Instruction was given in diverse subjects.[1624] At the end of the 9th century, under Aghlabid rule, a *Bayt al-Hikmah* (House of Wisdom) was established in Al-Qayrawan, Tunisia, rivalling its counterpart in Baghdad in the study of medicine, astronomy, engineering and translation.[1625] There, intellectual debate raged, around a number of subjects.[1626] Two centuries later, in 1065, Artz notes, a great university (The Nizamiya) (not in the sense we know universities today) was founded in Baghdad by the Seljuk minister, Nizam al-Mulk, and then, in 1234, a second, even more advanced, was set up. This one, he adds, had magnificent buildings, including quarters for four law faculties. The institution also included dormitories, a hospital, and a library, where it was easy to consult the books, and where pens, paper and lamps were supplied free to the students. The students were maintained thanks to endowments.[1627] Similar institutions had also been established at Fes, Al-Azhar in Cairo, at Cordova, and even as far east as in Ghazna, where Sultan Mahmud (r. 997-1030) made the city one of the cultural centres of the Orient, amongst other things with a scientific organisation comparable to an early university.[1628] The leading institution at the time, the Qarawiyyin of Fes, was first built in 859, for some time one of the three or four schools of the city, before it became the principal centre of higher learning in

---

[1621] R. Briffault: *The Making of Humanity* (London: George Allen and Unwin Ltd, 1928), p. 188.
[1622] S.P. Scott: *History*; op cit; vol 3; p. 465.
[1623] W.M. Watt: *The Influence of Islam*; op cit; p. 12.
[1624] F.B. Artz: *The Mind*; op cit; p. 151.
[1625] M al-Rammah: The Ancient Library of Kairaouan and its methods of conservation, in *The Conservation and Preservation of Islamic Manuscripts*, Proceedings of the Third Conference of Al-Furqan Islamic Heritage Foundation (1995), pp. 29-47; p. 29.
[1626] H. Djait et al: *Histoire de la Tunisie* (le Moyen Age) (Societe Tunisienne de Difusion, Tunis).
[1627] F.B. Artz: *The Mind;* op cit; pp.151-2.
[1628] A. Mieli: *La Science Arabe et son role dans l'evolution scientifique mondiale* (Leiden: E.J. Brill. 1938), p. 99.

Morocco.[1629] It pioneered in providing an advanced curriculum and in its organisation.[1630] Endowed principally by royal families, it received students from near and far, from the Maghrib, the Sahara and also Europe. These students lived in residential quadrangles, which contained two and three storey buildings, accommodating 60-150 students, who all received assistance with food and accommodation.[1631] This Moroccan institution was impressive within and also without. Its dazzling beauty, in terms of architecture and design, is perfectly caught by Burckhardt's work on the city.[1632]

A predominating trademark of Islamic learning was its universality. Learning, for the first time in human history, crossed boundaries of class, territory, and social function. In scarcely any other culture, Pedersen holds, has the literary life played such a role as in Islam.[1633] Science, once secluded amongst the few, became 'hobby of the masses, paupers and kings competing to obtain knowledge.' Islam's religious encouragement of science broke the monopolies of the hermits, of churches and temples, say I.R and L. Al-Faruqi.[1634] In Muslim Spain, Scott notes, there was not a village where 'the blessings of education' could not be enjoyed by the children of the poorest peasant, and in Cordova there were eight hundred public schools (surely an exaggerated figure) frequented alike by Muslims, Christians, and Jews, and where instruction was by means of lectures.[1635] The Spanish Muslim was taught at the same time and under the same conditions as the literary pilgrims from Asia Minor and Egypt, from Germany, France, and Britain.[1636] And in the great Muslim 'university' of Cordova, both Jews and Christians attained to acknowledged distinction as professors.[1637]

> During the most splendid period of Islamic Spain [Scott adds] ignorance was regarded so disgraceful that those without education concealed the fact as far as possible, just as they would have hidden the commission of a crime.[1638]

Women, alongside men sought such knowledge, such as at Al-Qayrawan, for instance.[1639] Scott contrasts the situation between Western Christendom and the land of Islam. 'The degradation of women belonging to the remaining orders of society can scarcely be conceived, nor were these conditions materially improved for centuries,' he notes.[1640] Even so late as 1750, the laws of England made it possible to treat women with a severity almost barbarous. During the reign of Charles II, illiteracy was almost universal; learning amongst women was decried

---

[1629] B. Dodge: *Muslim Education in Medieval Times* (The Middle East Institute, Washington D.C, 1962), p. 27.
[1630] Ibid.
[1631] Ibid.
[1632] T. Burckhardt: *Fez City of Islam* (The Islamic Text Society; Cambridge; 1992).
[1633] J. Pedersen: *The Arabic Book*; op cit; p. 37.
[1634] I.R. and L.L. Al Faruqi: *The Cultural*; op cit; p. 232.
[1635] S.P. Scott: *History;* op cit*;* Vol 3, at pp. 467-8.
[1636] Ibid.
[1637] Ibid.
[1638] Ibid; p. 424.
[1639] M.M. Sibai; *Mosque Libraries: An Historical Study* (Mansell Publishing Limited: London and New York: 1987), p. 58.
[1640] S.P. Scott: *Moorish Empire;* op cit; Vol 3; p. 656.

as pedantry or worse; it was rarely that a housewife could write her name; and even the princesses of the royal blood were unable to speak or spell grammatically.[1641] Eight hundred years before, women of Cordova had established an enviable reputation for their proficiency in all the arts, which contribute to the rich culture of nation:

> For the skill which they exhibited in every department of scientific research; for their profound acquaintance with the models of classic antiquity; for their originality in poetical composition; for the signal success they achieved in the literary congresses, wherein they were forced to compete with the assembled genius and learning of the empire. They were treated with the dignified respect and courtesy which were due to high mental attainments, as well as dictated by the regulations of chivalry which governed the conduct of every Moorish cavalier.[1642]

Tuition in colleges was free, and in some cases government or philanthropy paid both the salaries of the professors and the expenses of the students.[1643] Caliphs such as Al-Mutawakil (r.847-61) favoured the sciences and extended protection to men of science, many of whom were Christians.[1644] Early Arab authors also give lists of teachers, some of whom taught without remuneration.[1645] However, the thousands of Muslim educational institutions set up between the 7th and 13th century, and even later, were maintained by endowments (waqf), income generating sources of one form or another.[1646] In Aleppo, for instance, it is known that a share of the profits from lands and orchards, mills and shops, and baths was devoted to the financing of madrasas (and also mosques and hospitals.)[1647] In Fustat, old Cairo, investments from a number of persons, and also revenues from caravanserais were devoted as waqfs for the up-keep of madrasas.[1648]

At the peak of Muslim civilisation, Pedersen notes, the search for knowledge drove intellectuals to travel widely to hear eminent personages discussing their works.[1649] The teacher counted for more than the text, except in the case of the Qur'an: boys studied men rather than books and students would travel immense distances 'to engage the mind of a famous teacher.'[1650] Every scholar who sought a high standing at home had to hear the master scholars of Makkah, Baghdad, Damascus, and Cairo.[1651] The many books written about learned men left a strong

---

[1641] Ibid.
[1642] Ibid; pp. 656-7.
[1643] Mac Donald: Aspects of Islam; 289; 301 in W. Durant: *The Age of Faith*; op cit; p. 236.
[1644] T. Thomson: *The History of Chemistry*; (H Colburn and R. Bentley Publishers London; 1830), p. 113.
[1645] G. Wiet et al: *History;* op cit; p. 450.
[1646] Such as: B. Dodge: *Muslim Education in Medieval Times* (The Middle East Institute, Washington D.C, 1962). K. A Totah: *The Contribution of the Arabs to Education* (New York: Columbia University Press, 1926). J. Pedersen: *The Arabic Book*; op cit;
[1647] S. Denoix: Bilans: in *Grandes Villes Mediterraneenes;* op cit*;* p. 294.
[1648] D. Behrens Abouseif; S. Denoix, J.C. Garcin: Cairo: in *Grandes Villes;* op cit; p. 188.
[1649] J. Pedersen: *The Arabic Book*; op cit; p. 21.
[1650] W. Durant: *The Age of Faith*; op cit; p. 236.
[1651] Ibid.

impression of this intense life of study, which led young and old from one end of the far flung world of Islam to the other.[1652] One person claimed hundreds of teachers, both men and women, and another sold all that he had inherited from his merchant family and spent the money, instead, in search of learning; so that he had to travel on foot to Isfahan and Baghdad, carrying his books on his back. [1653] Travel in search of knowledge was key modality of scientific communication, Glick remarks.[1654] Merchants and scholars when they returned to their homelands disseminated both books and ideas among their more sedentary colleagues.[1655]

The community of a world already tightly linked by commercial networks explains the rapidity by which certain ideas and techniques spread.[1656] This, however, was not the only factor. Just as with commerce, the frontierless nature of the Islamic state played a major part and so did the absence of boundaries between ethnic groups and races. There was, Arnold notes, a period during which the traveller could pass from the confines of China to the Pillars of Hercules, from the banks of the Indus to the Cilician Gates, from the Oxus to the shores of the Atlantic, without stepping outside the boundaries of the territory ruled over by the Caliph in Damascus or Baghdad.[1657] Even after this vast empire broke up into separate principalities, the journey of the Muslim traveller was facilitated by

> That brotherhood of Islam which gives to the Muslim world its cosmopolitan character, and enables a community of faith to wipe out all differences of race and origin.[1658]

The great age of Muslim civilisation achieved 'a truly lofty ideal of the savant,' says Von Grunebaum.[1659] However many hundreds of miles the Muslim might journey from his native town, he could confidently hope to find a welcome and generous hospitality at the hands of his co-religionists, especially if he had any reputation for piety or religious knowledge, and he might even come across a fellow townsman, even though his wanderings had carried him into 'the land of the infidels,' far beyond the boundaries of the Muslim land.[1660] In many cases the wandering scholar received not only free instruction at the madrasa (college), but, for a time, also free lodging and food.[1661] As a result of this, from the Atlantic to the Himalayas the fraternity of scholars thrived.[1662] One can only ponder about

---

[1652] J. Pedersen: *The Arabic Book*; op cit; p. 21.
[1653] A.S. Tritton: Muslim Education in the Middle Ages; *The Muslim World*; vol 43; pp. 82-94, at p. 92.
[1654] T. Glick: Communication; T. Glick, S.J. Livesey, F. Wallis Editors: *Medieval Science, Technology and Medicine; An Encyclopaedia*; (Routledge; London; 2005); pp. 135-8; at p. 138.
[1655] Ibid.
[1656] T. Glick: Communication; op cit; p. 138.
[1657] T.W. Arnold: Arab Travellers and Merchants; AD 1000-1500; in A.P. Newton: *Travel and Travellers of the Middle Ages*; (Kegan Paul; London; 1926); pp. 88-103; at p. 89.
[1658] Ibid.
[1659] G.E. Von Grunebaum: *Medieval Islam* (The University of Chicago Press, 1954), p. 243.
[1660] T.W. Arnold: Arab Travellers; op cit; p. 89.
[1661] S.K. Bukhsh: Studies; 195 in W. Durant: *The Age of Faith*; op cit; p. 236.
[1662] J. Pedersen: *The Arabic Book;* p. 20.

the exchanges between this remarkable community, meeting anywhere in the vast land of Islam. In this respect, the experience lived by the Moroccan traveller/scholar Ibn Battuta is quite edifying.[1663] Ibn Battuta (b. Tangier 1304; d. 1368-9) tells us how on his arrival in a town in China, which he calls Kanjanfu, the Muslim merchants there came out to receive him with flags and a band of musicians with trumpets, drums and horns, bringing horses for him and his party, so that they rode into the city in a triumphal procession. During his stay there he heard of the arrival of a highly respected doctor of the law among the Muslims of that part. His friends asked his permission to introduce this person to him, and he was named as Mawlan Qiwam al-Din of Ceuta. As Ceuta was near his own birthplace, Tangier, Ibn Battuta was naturally struck by the name and gazed at him eagerly. After they had been talking a while, the visitor said, "You seem to be looking at me as though you knew me." "From what country do you come?" asked Ibn Battutta. "From Ceuta." "And I am from Tangier," replied the traveller, and they wept together at the thought of this strange meeting at the other end of the world, so far from their distant home in the west. After some further conversation Ibn Battuta realised that they had met before in India, in the capital, Delhi, which Qiwam al-Din had visited as a young man with his uncle, a Spanish Muslim. The Sultan of Delhi had tried to lure the young man to settle in India, but he refused as he had set his heart on visiting China; and there he soon acquired a high position and considerable wealth. Some years later, after his return home, Ibn Battuta started off to explore Central Africa and met a brother of this same man in a town in the Western Sudan.[1664] Ibn Battuta comments on the considerable distance that separated these two brothers from one another. This incident, Arnold points out, is characteristic of Muslim society during the Middle Ages; it reveals the enterprise that merchants and travellers showed in journeying such enormous distances, and the facilities, which their co-religionists provided for those who braved the perils of such arduous journeys.[1665]

Muslim civilisation imposed the highest scholarly standards, and it also rewarded them.

> Whether judge or theologian of Islam [Artz insists] they were required to be experts in Islamic tradition, canon law, and scholastic theology; and the state administrator, the civil servant, and the educated noble or merchant were supposed to be thoroughly trained in grammar, rhetoric, and history.[1666]

Among all these professions, proficiency and excellence in written expression, mastery of etiquette, and a fine command of handwriting were considered great

---

[1663] Ibn Battuta: *Voyages d'Ibn Battuta*, Arabic text accompanied by French translation by C. Defremery and B.R. Sanguinetti, preface and notes by Vincent Monteil, I-IV, (Paris, 1968, reprint of the 1854 ed; Paris; 1858); IV; pp. 281-2.
[1664] Ibid.
[1665] T.W. Arnold: Arab Travellers; op cit; at p. 90.
[1666] F.B. Artz: *The Mind*; op cit; pp. 151-2.

accomplishments.[1667] The highest echelon of social respect was owed to the scholar; a respect that is a frequent topic of Muslim tradition, as Tritton notes:

> All creatures lament the death of a scholar, the birds in the air and the fish in the sea, because they profited by his exposition of the law concerning them and his knowledge saved them from ill-treatment. The scholar should not be satisfied in his acts and thoughts with what the law allows: he should aim at the highest. An ignorant teacher is a mockery of religion and to say: 'I do not know' is half of knowledge. To cease learning is to be ignorant.[1668]

2. Faith, Faiths and Learning

The Prophet is quoted as saying:

> 'Acquire knowledge because he who acquires it in the way of the Lord performs an act of piety; who speaks of it praises the Lord; who seeks it, adores God; who dispenses instruction in it, bestow alms; and who imparts it to its fitting objects, performs an act of devotion to God. Knowledge enables its possessor to distinguish what is forbidden from what is not; it lights the way to heaven; it is our friend in the desert, our society in solitude, our companion when bereft of friends; it guides us to happiness, it sustains us in misery; it is our ornament in the company of friends; it serves as an armour against the enemies. With knowledge, the servant of God rises to the heights of goodness and to a noble position, associates with sovereigns in this world, and attains to the perfection of happiness in the next.'[1669]

The Prophet reiterates this message in countless circumstances:

> 'There is nothing greater in the eyes of God than a man who has learned a science and who has taught it to people.'
>
> 'The bearers of knowledge are the successors to the prophets in this world and the martyrs in the Hereafter.'
>
> 'Scholars and teachers are partners in reward, and there are no better people than they.'
>
> 'The knowledge that is not used is like a treasure from which nothing is spent. Its possessor laboured in collecting it, but never benefited from it.'
>
> 'And if God directs you to one single man [who is learned], it is better for you than the whole world and all in it.'[1670]

[1667] Ibid.

[1668] A.S. Tritton: Muslim Education in the Middle Ages; op cit; p. 82.

[1669] Qoted by Syed Ameer Ali: *The Spirit of Islam;* rev. ed.; (London, 1922) pp. 360-361.

[1670] Ibn Khayr: *Fahrasah;* ed., F. Codera and J. Ribera (Saragossa; 1893; Baghdad; 1963), in A. Chejne: *Muslim Spain;* op cit; p. 175.

The acquisition of knowledge, thus, Kramers notes, was in the first place a compliance with a religious command, but at the same time it had to serve the transmission of knowledge to others, and the complete fulfilment of the divine command of 'exhorting to good and admonishing against evil.'[1671] So the scholar was at the same time a teacher, a 'doctor', and his school was that original centre of political and religious life in Islam: the mosque.[1672] There is no branch of Muslim intellectual, religious, political, or the daily life of the average Muslim that remained untouched by the all pervasive attitude towards 'knowledge' as something of supreme value for the Muslim.[1673]

'Ilm (science/learning/knowledge),' says Rosenthal, 'is Islam.'[1674]

Religion dominated learning in the Christian world, too: all aspects of society were permeated by religion, the emphasis clearly seen in the intellectual and cultural life of the period.[1675] But there were fundamental differences with Islam.

Firstly, Western education was almost the exclusive province of the clergy. Devons outlines how (the Bishop of Lincoln) Grosseteste's disciple, Roger Bacon was the Franciscan 'Dr Mirabilis' of Oxford and Paris; the renowned Albertus Magnus 'Dr Universalis' of Cologne, Provincial of the German Dominican Order and Bishop of Ratisbon. Albertus' disciple, Witelo, was a Silesian Dominican at the Papal court at Viterbo; John of Peckham was Archbishop of Canterbury; Theodoric of Freiberg a Dominican leader of German preachers, and so on.[1676] In Islam, in contrast, it was not just that other faiths and groups were part of the intellectual upsurge, but also, and most importantly, the scholars, with rare exceptions, had no official links with the faith (e.g as Imams, or religious scholars.)[1677]

Secondly, in the Christian West, medieval education, music, art, and architecture were motivated by, permeated with, or channelled into religious goals, and the most highly regarded branch of learning 'the Queen of the Sciences,' as it was called-was theology, the study of doctrines concerning God.[1678] Painting and sculpture dealt mainly with religious subjects; the most magnificent, most costly buildings were churches and cathedrals, and for the medieval period, then, the Latin phrase *ad maiorem Dei gloriam* (to the greater glory of God) was meaningful and relevant for all activities, notes Geanakoplos.[1679] The opposite was the case of Islam. Although God's guidance was always sought, and each and every work opened with the customary 'In the name of God the gracious and merciful,' matters addressed were

[1671] J.H. Kramers: Sciences in Islamic Civilisation. *Analecta Orientalia: Posthumous Writings and Selected Minor Works of J.H. Kramers*; vol 2 (Leiden; Brill; 1956), p.86.

[1672] Ibid.

[1673] F. Rosenthal: *Knowledge Triumphant;* op cit; p. 2.

[1674] Ibid.

[1675] D. J. Geanakoplos: *Medieval Western Civilisation, and the Byzantine and Islamic Worlds* (D.C. Heath and Company, Toronto, 1979), p. 307

[1676] S. Devons: Optics through the eyes of the medieval Churchmen; in *Science and Technology in Medieval Society*: Edition Pamela O Long: *Annals of the New York Academy of Sciences*, vol 441 (New York, 1985), pp. 205-24; at p. 206.

[1677] See entries on Muslim scholars in *Dictionary of Scientific Biography;* op cit.

[1678] D. J. Geanakoplos: *Medieval Western Civilisation,* op cit; p. 307.

[1679] Ibid.

remarkably endless in scope and diversity. They included all the sciences, as will be extensively shown in the next part, and more importantly, they applied to very practical, earthly matters. Muslims wrote about stars, water, markets, animals, taxation, diseases, mysterious lands, climate, arrows and weapons, the good and the bad ruler, ethics, and all that attracted their interest and fancy. Moreover, although faith driven, Islamic learning was not restricted by the faith. It provided absolute freedom to study, a boon which was enjoyed only by those who lived under the shadow of 'the Arab empire.'[1680] Nothing was neglected, and everyone said pretty much what they liked without fearing the heavy hand of the mosque weighing on him, or feeling the threat of the stake. Even the Greeks did not grant such freedom as did the Muslims. 'Did not the Greeks condemn Socrates to drain a lethal draught on the grounds that he was corrupting youth by training them to think?' asks Farukh.[1681]

Muslim civilisation was profoundly marked by its multi ethnic and multi faith character.

> Of all world religions, Islam has been most successful in overriding barriers of colour and nationality. No line is drawn except between believers and unbelievers [says Artz.][1682]

Islamic thinking made for a greater mingling of races; there was in it no conception of nationhood as distinct from the religious community.[1683]

> For the first time in history [says Sabra] science became international on a really wide scale and one language, Arabic, became its vehicle. A large number of scholars belonging to different nations and professing different beliefs collaborated in the process of moulding into this one language materials which had previously existed in Greek, Syriac, Persian or Sanskrit. It is this enduring character of the scientific enterprise in medieval Islam which is being emphasised when the phrase 'Arabic science' is used.[1684]

Arabic science is a misnomer. Indeed, its scholars were mostly non Arabs: Turks, Berbers, Iranians, Spanish Muslims and non Muslims, white and black, and Chinese, too. Even the 'great masters' of the Arabic language were not of Arab ancestry.[1685] Thus, 'Arabic civilisation becomes Muslim civilisation.'[1686]

Most particularly, Muslim civilisation, in its glory centuries, brought together Muslims, Christians and Jews,[1687] all under the mantle of Islam. The Great virtue of

---

[1680] O.A. Farukh: *The Arab Genius in Science and Philosophy* (American Council of Learned Societies, Washington, D.C, 1954), p. 10.

[1681] Ibid.

[1682] F.B. Artz: *The Mind*; op cit; p. 140.

[1683] G. Wiet et al: *History*; op cit; p. 545.

[1684] A.I. Sabra: The Scientific Enterprise; in *Islam and the Arab World*; ed., by B. Lewis (London; 1976), pp. 181-92, at pp. 182-3.

[1685] G.E. Von Grunebaum: *Medieval Islam*, op cit; p. 201.

[1686] Ibid.

[1687] S. Pines: *Studies in Arabic Versions of Greek Texts and in Mediaeval Science* (The Magnes Press, Brill, Leiden, 1986), p. 354

the Arabs, Hyams points out, was that they gave the diverse people under their aegis a chance to do their best.[1688] Sarton's prolific *Introduction to the History of Science* is an excellent window on this amalgam of ethnic groups, but most of all on all faiths that met on the Muslim scientific ground.[1689] Commenting on this, he observes:

> The great racial and cultural complexity of Islam, even in those early days, is a very curious spectacle. How strong must the religious bond have been to keep together such disparate elements! to begin with, the Abbasid court was entirely permeated with foreign influences-Persian, Jewish, and Nestorians.[1690]

Again, this tradition of opening up to other faiths went back to the early example set by the Prophet, and in Islam, Sunni Islam above all, the Qur'an, and the example set by the Prophet are the two guiding principles. Hence, the first Muslim physician we have any record of is Harith Ibn Kalada al-Thakeshi, born near Makkah, who, after practicing medicine for many years in Persia, returned to his native Arabia, and became the friend and physician of the Prophet.[1691] Harith, although the physician of the Prophet, never embraced Islam, and may have been a Christian. This act of the Prophet, Major points out, in selecting a non-Muslim as his physician, was doubtless a powerful example to his followers. Indeed. Islam earliest and most prominent scientists at the Abbasid court, Ishaq Ibn Hunayn and Hunayn Ibn Ishaq were Nestorian Christians. Thabit Ibn Qurrah, the astronomer, was a Sabean. The Bakhishtu family who held most prominent positions in the court in the 9th century were Christians, too, and so was the historian-physicist Abu'l Faraj. So were others of the same profession: Ali Ibn Ridwan, Ibn Djazla of Baghdad, and Isa Ibn Ali. Yaqut al-Hamawi, one of Islam's greatest geographer-historians, was of Greek antecedents, and so was Al-Khazini (the author of the *Balance of Wisdom*). The Jews, as obvious in Sarton's introduction,[1692] in their tens, and possibly in their hundreds, experienced the most glorious pages of their civilisation under Islam, too. From Maimonides to Hasdai Ibn Shaprut, to Petrus Alfonsi, to the Ben-Tibbons, all reached fame and prominence under Islam. Draper observes that in Cordova, Granada and other large cities, the universities were frequently under the superintendence of Jews because, for the Muslims, the maxim was that:

> The real learning of a man is of more public importance than any particular religious opinion he may entertain.

A liberality, which Draper notes, was in striking contrast with intolerant Europe.[1693] Even enlightened Byzantium, though artistic and learned, Atroshenko and Collins note, was cruel and intolerant in a way which the world came to

[1688] E. Hyams: *A History of Gardens and Gardening*; op cit; p. 82.
[1689] G. Sarton: *Introduction*; op cit.
[1690] Ibid; vol I, at p. 524.
[1691] R.H. Major: *A History of Medicine*; 2 vols (Blackwell; Oxford), vol 1; p. 229.
[1692] G. Sarton: *Introduction;* op cit.
[1693] J.W. Draper: *A History of the Intellectual Development*, op cit; vol 2; p. 36.

associate with the spread of Christian dogma.[1694] Condemned heretics and expelled philosophers found refuge in the tolerant Muslim world, where the Arabs themselves were, as such, a tiny minority, and Jewish, Zoroastrian and Christian minorities flourished.[1695]

There seems to be a major deficiency in the multi-ethnic character of Muslim civilisation, though, as Sarton points out:

> Although the Persians had introduced into the Caliphate a greater love of beauty, urbanity, intellectual curiosity, and much fondness for discussion, all favourable to the progress of science, free thought was often followed by libertinage and immorality. No wonder that the genuine Arabs looked down upon the Persian intruders even as the old Romans looked down upon the Greeks. The fact is that every civilisation acts as a poison upon those who have not been properly inoculated; it would act that way even were it perfectly pure and did not contain (as it always does) evil elements. The Arabic strength and virtue were gradually undermined by Persian urbanity.'[1696]

Sarton's point, that the Persians undermined Arabic strength, somehow runs against the opinions of those who grant the Persians all good part in Muslim civilisation. In response to Sarton's point, the undermining of Arabic strength lies only partly in this Persian intrusion, and surely not in the so called Turkish intrusion, nor in the Berber intrusion (whose impact will be examined in the final part of this work). All these ethnic groups, Persians, Turks, Berbers and others, had their points of strengths and weaknesses. True the Turks and Berbers, just like the Arabs and Kurds, fought and died for the spread and defence of the faith whilst the Persians never did. All ethnic groups, however, gave Muslim civilisation a huge amount, but not everything. The Muslims became corrupt in urbanity, their harems and the like, not just where the Persians had an influence, but all over the Muslim world, even in Muslim Spain, which had little Persian influence in its midst. As for the maligned Berbers and Turks, especially the Ottomans, it was they who fought the most decisive battles that saved the Muslim world from the successive invaders and threats. The real, the true, intrusion that truly destroyed Islamic civilisation was the 13th century Crusade-Mongol concerted push, one coming from the east and the other from the west.[1697] This assault did not just cause destruction, slaughter and mayhem; it led above all the Muslim realm to alter its priorities: fighting for survival, instead of scholarly creativity. This matter will be returned to in great detail in the final part of this work.

[1694] V.I. Atroshenko and J. Collins: *The Origins of the Romanesque*; (Lund Humphries; London; 1985); p. 34.
[1695] Ibid.
[1696] G. Sarton: *Introduction*; op cit; p. 524.
[1697] See, for instance, Baron G. D'Ohsson: *Histoire des Mongols;* op cit. J.J. Saunders: *Aspects of the Crusades* (University of Canterbury Publishing; Canterbury; 1962). P. Pelliot: *Mongols and Popes; 13th and 14th Centuries* (Paris; 1922).

3. The Place of Arabic

> Islam, and also the Arabic language [Jurji insists,] are the two ostensible factors in the creation of that gigantic melting pot in the centre of whose orbit rose the scientific leaders of the Arabic speaking world.[1698]

This international community of letters was made possible, indeed, by the fact that throughout the Islamic world-whatever its diversity of peoples-the language of learning and literature was Arabic.[1699] Arabic, the language of Revelation, of diplomacy and polite intercourse, thus becoming that of science.[1700] From the end of the 8th century to the end of the 11th the intellectual leaders had been mostly Muslims, according to Sarton, and the most progressive works had been written in Arabic: during these three centuries the Arabic language was the main vehicle of culture.[1701] As Von Ranke observes, leaving Latin aside, Arabic is the most important of all the languages of the world for universal history.[1702] The language that ranks so high 'for purposes of eloquence and poetic flight' lent itself to the demands of exact and positive expression.[1703] Sapir, in his *Language*, lists it as the third among those which have had an overwhelming significance as carriers of culture. English and French are conspicuous by their absence from this list. Montgomery, in the *Haverford Symposium*, also asserts that Arabic has had the most unique development and spread of all the tongues of the earth and that only within the last two centuries has English come to rival it.[1704] Archer,[1705] goes further, asserting that Arabic is a richer and more flexible tongue than Latin or Greek, no Western tongue equalling it in the variety of its forms and verbal nouns.[1706] The impact of Arabic on other languages, and not just Spanish (for obvious reasons,) such as French is particularly strong.[1707]

The development of Arabic into a language of religion, state and culture constitutes the most fascinating chapter of Muslim history.[1708] During the rise of Islam in the 7th century, Arabic was basically a tribal language lacking a written grammar, lexicon and the terms of the sciences as they were known in the great urban centres of the Near East.[1709] However, soon after the expansion of Islam over a wide territory, including the area from the Indus River to the Atlantic

---

[1698] E.J. Jurji: The Course of Arabic Scientific Thought: in *The Arab Heritage;* Edition: N.A. Faris (Princeton University Press, 1944), pp. 221-50; at p. 221.
[1699] W. Durant: *The Age of Faith*; op cit; p. 236.
[1700] E.J. Jurji: The Course; op cit; p. 224.
[1701] G. Sarton: *Introduction*; op cit; Vol II, p. 109.
[1702] In P.K. Hitti: America and the Arab heritage; op cit; p. 5.
[1703] E J. Jurji: The Course; p. 222.
[1704] P.K. Hitti: America; op cit; p. 5.
[1705] J.C. Archer: Our debt to the Moslem World, *The Moslem World*, XXXIX (1939), p. 259.
[1706] P.K. Hitti: America; op cit; p. 5.
[1707] Salah Guemriche: *Dictionnaire des mots français d'origine arabe et turque et persane : accompagné d'une anthologie littéraire: 400 extraits d'auteurs français, de Rabelais à Houellebecq*, Seuil, 2007, réédition poche Points 2012 et 2015.
-Salah Guemriche: *Dictionnaire Des Mots Francais D'origine Arabe*, Mass Market Paperback – 20 Jan 2015.
[1708] For the rise and role of Arabic, see A. Chejne: *The Arabic Language: Its role in History* (Minneapolis; 1969).
[1709] A. Chejne: *Muslim Spain;* op cit; pp. 182-3.

Ocean, special care was taken to study the language in which the Qur'an was revealed and to preserve its purity in conformity with the Holy Book, pre-Islamic poetry and Bedouin speech as it was known in and around the city of Makkah.[1710] This interest in the language eventually led to intensive linguistic studies, which included not only grammar and lexicography but also every aspect of the language.[1711]
A great number of Muslim scholars contributed to the emergence of Arabic as a powerful tool of communication. Ibn Sidah was one of the prominent philologists of the 11th century, and he had a great influence on Arabic lexicography.[1712] He was born blind in Murcia, and received his early education from his father. He developed an extraordinary memory, which made it possible for him to compile voluminous lexicons.[1713] His lexicon, *al-Muhkam,*[1714] was arranged alphabetically, each letter constituting a section divided into chapters, each entry explained, giving, for instance, the verb, its imperfect, verbal nouns, and derivatives.[1715] *Al-Muhkam* was followed by a larger work, *al-Mukhassas.*[1716] In this, Ibn Sidah provided a long discussion of various aspects of the language, mainly the excellence and the origin of language.[1717] He took a middle position between those who advocated divine origin of language and those who held that language resulted from human convention. He maintained that he had pondered this question for a long time and found that each of the opposing views had some convincing arguments, but he concluded that 'Arabic is so noble, perfect, and elegant that God must have helped to make it so through His teaching and inspiration.'[1718]

There were positive factors which helped to give impetus to Arabisation as outlined by Chejne.[1719] Although the newcomers (the Arabs) were the minority, their numbers increased through marriage, principally, and their offspring became Muslims and learned the languages of both father and mother. As the numbers of converts to Islam increased, the Arabic language came to have a wider significance and served as the medium of unity among Muslims, first, and among these and non-Muslims afterwards. The Umayyads, who were proud of their Arab ancestry, and who came to rule the land of Islam after the first four caliphs (from 661 to 750), also made Arabic the official language. Their rule over

---

[1710] Ibid.
[1711] For general works on Arabic philology, see: Ibn Faris: *Al-Sahih fi fiqh al-lughah* (Cairo; 1910); Al-Suyuti: *Al-Muzhir* (Cairo; 1958); A Gonzales Palencia: *Historia de la Literatura Arabigo-Espanole* (Barcelona; 1928); J. Haywood: *Arabic Lexicography* (Leiden; 1960).
[1712] On Ibn Sidah, See Ibn Bashkuwal: *Al-Silah*; ed., by Fr Codera (Madrid; 1882-3); ed. Izzat al-Itar al-Hussayni; 2 vols (Cairo; 1955), vol 2; pp. 396 ff; See also J. Haywood: Arabic Lexicography; op cit; pp. 66 ff.
[1713] A. Chejne: *Muslim Spain*; op cit; p. 191.
[1714] Ibn Sidah: *Al-Muhkam wa'l muhit al-a'zam* (Cairo; 1958).
[1715] A. Chejne: *Muslim Spain*; op cit; p. 191.
[1716] *Al-Mukhasas;* 17 pts; Edition Bullaq (1316-1321 (H).
[1717] A. Chejne: *Muslim Spain*; op cit; p. 191.
[1718] Ibn Sidah: *Al-Mukhassas;* op cit; pp. 3-6.
[1719] A. Chejne: *Muslim Spain*; op cit; pp. 184-5.

Muslim Spain from roughly the 750s to 976 also played a part in spreading the language there. From the 9th century onward, Arabic increasingly became the language of daily communication and the instrument of literary expression for Muslims and non-Muslims.[1720]

From the 8th to the 12th centuries, Arabic was the intellectual and scientific language of the entire scholastic world. The men of letters and science in both the eastern and western lands had to know Arabic if they wanted to produce works of arts or sciences.[1721] During these centuries, Andalusia by itself produced more works in Arabic than were produced in all the languages of Europe.[1722] The libraries in Muslim Spain, some containing over half a million manuscripts, had no match in all the other countries of Europe.[1723] It is then not strange, Salloum and Peters note, that the Arabic molded in those 500 years has survived and flourished until our time.[1724] How Arabic rose to a prominent role so as to become the vehicle of science and culture is elaborated upon by Sarton:

> The vehicle of the new Muslim civilisation was a language that had never been used for any scientific purpose. Almost every bit of knowledge had to be translated either from Greek or from Sanskrit, or from Pahlawi before it could be assimilated. And not only that, but these interpretations necessitated the creation of a philosophic and scientific terminology, which did not exist. When one takes all this into consideration, instead of being surprised at the relative smallness of the first harvest, one cannot help admiring the immensity of the effort. This effort was of such a nature that no people could have endured it for a long time, but only during a period of exaltation and youthful optimism.[1725]

Hence a double accomplishment, not just in turning a non scientific language into one upon which modern science was built but also in acting as the crucial unifying element of so many disparate nations and groups. Without such a language, uniform through a vast land, little progress in science would have taken place, except in insignificant pockets. This was also the first instance of universality of the language of science, and it was possible thanks to the Arabic language itself.

The primary role of Arabic is its semantics, its flexibility enabling the scholar to coin exact scientific and technological vocabularies 'capable of expressing the most complicated scientific and technical ideas.'[1726] Arabic is also exceedingly rich, and it can be increased almost indefinitely, because a very complex and elegant morphology makes it easy to create new derivatives.[1727] From its own inner

[1720] Ibid.

[1721] H. Salloum and J. Peters: *Arabic Contributions to the English Vocabulary*; (Librairie du Liban; 1996); p. x.

[1722] Ibid.

[1723] Ibid.

[1724] Ibid.

[1725] G. Sarton: *Introduction* vol I, at p. 523.

[1726] A. Y. Al-Hasan; D.R. Hill: *Islamic Technology* (Cambridge University Press, 1986, p. 10.

[1727] G. Sarton: *The Incubation of Western Culture in the Middle East*, A George C. Keiser Foundation Lecture, March 29, 1950 (Washington; DC 1951), p. 19.

resources, Arnold and Guillaume point out, it could evolve by autogenous processes the *mot juste* (the perfect word) which new arts and new sciences demanded for their intellectual expression.[1728]

The place of Arabic in the scientific-cultural medieval outburst was such that not just the translators of sciences (Gerard of Cremona, Robert of Chester, John of Seville...), but nearly every man of learning of Western Christendom had to be knowledgeable in it, or be able to access it (through intermediaries). Arnold of Villanova (d.1311), for instance, mastered Arabic, and in his enthusiasm for Muslim medicine translated a series of its important works into Latin.[1729] Roger Bacon (1220-1294) asserted that all thought and science in his day could base themselves only upon familiarity with the Arabian authors.[1730]

Western poetry and literature were particularly impacted on by the Arabic language. The whole of Dante's work illustrates this.[1731] In respect to all his major works, whether *Vita Nuova,* or *Convivio,* or the *Divine Comedy*, Dante's indebtedness to Muslim authors, al-Farghani in particular, was decisive.[1732] In Spain, the Poema de Yussuf, entirely Arabic in inspiration, is the work of an Aragonese poet who used Arabic characters when he wrote in his native language.[1733] Al-Maqqari reproduced a copy of these poems which Christian poets had composed in Arabic.[1734] Arabic poetry, itself, impacted on the poetry of the French southern region of Provence, which itself impacted on the literature of the rest of the Christian West. This latter impact is looked at under the following heading.

Arabic for many centuries at the time of Muslim apogee symbolised all that was sophisticated, and superior.

> Material wealth and comfort for Western Europeans, must have at times appeared to go hand in hand with the ability to read Arabic [Menocal points out.][1735]

Thus, with great bitterness, Alvarus (9th century), subsequently a Christian martyr, conceded:

> Who is there among the faithful laity sufficiently learned to understand the Holy Scriptures, or what our doctors have written in Latin? Who is there fired with love of the Gospels, the Prophets, the Apostles? All our young Christians... are learned in infidel erudition and perfected in Arabic eloquence. They assiduously study, intently read and ardently discuss

[1728] Preface in A. Guillaume, T. Arnold: *The Legacy of Islam*; first Edition; (Oxford; 1931;) p. vi.

[1729] R. I. Burns: Muslims in the Thirteenth Century Realms of Aragon: Interaction and Reaction, in *Muslims under Latin Rule, 1100-1300;* J.M. Powell: editor (Princeton University Press, 1990), pp. 57-102; at pp. 90-1.

[1730] R. Bacon: *Opus Majus*, ed. S. Jebb; London; 1735; p. 44.

[1731] R.S. Briffault: *The Troubadours*; tr. from French by author; edited by L.F. Koons; (The Indiana University Press; Bloomington; 1965); p. 161.

[1732] P. Toynbee, *Dante Studies and Research* (London, Methuen, 1902), pp. 56-77.

[1733] J. FitzmauriceKelly, in *Encyclopaedia Britannica*, 14th ed., 1938, Vol. XXI, p. 155.

[1734] Al-Maqqari: Nafh al-Tib; in R.S. Briffault: *The Troubadours*; tr.; Note 22; p. 19.

[1735] M R Menocal: *The Arabic Role in Medieval Literary History* (University of Pennsylvania Press, Philadelphia, 1987), p. 63.

> Arabic books.... The Christians are ignorant of their own tongue; the Latin race does not understand its own language. Not one in a thousand of the Christian communion can write an intelligent letter to a brother. On the other hand there are great numbers of them who expound the Arabic splendour of language, and metrically adorn, by mono-rhyme, the final clauses of songs, better more sublimely than other peoples.[1736]

Even Church and secular authorities expressed their assiduity for the language. A manuscript of ecclesiastical decrees at Madrid contains a dedication in Arabic verse by a priest named Vincent.[1737] King Alphonso, the Wise, who had one of the better appreciated Arab fantasies diffused throughout European literature, the tale of the statue and the ring; his brother, Fadriquez, who was the author of the *Libro de los engaños et los asaiamentos de las mujeres*; Duns Scotus, who was a poet as well as a theologian, were all familiar with Arabic poetry.[1738] Juan Ruiz, Archpriest of Hita, the most illustrious of the medieval Spanish poets, knew Arabic poetry well and imitated it.[1739]

Although Spain was the principal point of impact, Muslim influence also spread to Europe from Sicily after its conquest.[1740] In addition, the Crusaders returning from Syria and Palestine brought back to Dark Ages Europe many new products and ideas.[1741] After the crusaders' returned, English and the other European languages were enriched with numerous words in the fields of architecture, agriculture, food, manufacturing, the sciences and trade.[1742] It was only natural that the borrowing of words would travel from east to west, for in those times, Salloum and Peters note, the Muslim lands were the most advanced in the world. In the same fashion today, English being the language of industry and science, its words creep into foreign tongues, so it was with Arabic in the era of the Crusades.[1743]

The impact of Arabic on Western science and culture remained strong down to the late 17th century. The skeptical attitude to Latin translations from Arabic of Muslim works made in the 12th century, Russell notes, provided the grounds for an examination of Arabic sources.[1744] In the ensuing textual criticism, Ibn Sina's *Canon,* 'the bible of the academic medical profession,' took center stage as a key text.[1745] In the second Giunta edition of the *Canon* (Venice, 1595), its 12th century

---

[1736] Alvari Cordubensis Indiculus Luminosus in Migne, *Patrologia Latina* (Paris; 1857-1912); 121, cols. 555-6. Quotation in English from R. Dozy: *Spanish Islam: a History of the Muslims in Spain;* tr. F.G. Stokes (London; 1913), p. 268.

[1737] A. Gonzalez Palencia: *Historia de la literatura arabigo-espanola*, (Barcelona-Buenos Aires; 1928); p. 272 f.

[1738] R.S. Briffault: *The Troubadours*; Note 22; p. 19.

[1739] Menéndez y Pelayo: *Estudios de critica literaria*, 2 da Serie, p. 390; J. FitzmauriceKelly, in *Encyclopaedia Britannica*, 14th ed., (1938), Vol. XXI, p. 155.

[1740] H. Salloum and J. Peters: *Arabic Contributions*; p. xi.

[1741] Ibid.

[1742] Ibid.

[1743] Ibid; pp. xi-xii.

[1744] G.A. Russell: Introduction: The Seventeenth Century: The Age of Arabick; in G.A. Russell Ed: *The Arabick Interest of the Natural Philosophers in Seventeenth Century England;* (E.J. Brill; Leiden; 1994); at p. 6.

[1745] Ibid.

Latin version by Gerard of Cremona was corrected against the more recent retranslation of Andrea Alpago.[1746] To consult the Arabic sources, however, scholars needed, in addition to linguistic skills, access to the actual texts, and preferably in print since the manuscripts were difficult to read. Ibn Sina's *Qanun* became available as one of the first texts to be printed (1593), using Arabic font, by the newly set up Medici Press in Rome.[1747] Jewish scholars, largely from the Iberian Peninsula in the aftermath of the Inquisition and of forced conversions to Christianity, provided the crucial need for expertise in Arabic.[1748] Amatus Lusitanus (1511-68), a 'Marrano' physician, for instance, gained refuge in the Ottoman city of Salonica.[1749] Amatus illustrated the deficiencies of the Latin translation of Ibn Sina's *Canon* with actual examples of mis-readings in Arabic and the disastrous consequences of such mistranslations for medical practice.[1750] By demonstrating the importance of reading medical and scientific texts in the original for textual accuracy, such analyses underlined the essential relevance of Arabic to scholarship, and the need for Arabic glossaries and dictionaries.[1751] As a result, Arabic interest emerged for the first time specifically for philological purposes. By the 17th century, the case for Arabic, made by Biblical scholars as well as physicians, formed the basis of apologies in lectures and orations for the purpose of establishing its study in universities.[1752] In England, Hebraic scholars, who fled war-torn Central Europe in the wake of the Catholic-Protestant wars (1618-1648), further promoted the study of Arabic.[1753] Already by the 1620s, there was interest large enough not only at Cambridge, where the ground was laid by Bedwell, but also at Oxford where Matthias Pasor, professor of mathematics and theology from Heidelberg, found a highly favourable environment to his proposal of introducing Arabic lectures.[1754] Those who gave support were not only theologians and physicians, but also mathematicians (such as Henry Briggs and John Bainbridge) because of their interest in reading Arabic mathematical texts.[1755]

Reflecting the dominance Arabic once had in the scientific field, are the numerous words of Arabic origin in the modern scientific sphere. In astronomy, for instance,

---

[1746] The first 'Giunta' edition of 1564 was published in Venice by the editors G.P. Mongius and J. Costaeus, both of whom were medical men. The second edition was greatly enlarged by corrections of Cremona's version against Alpago's with a detailed commentary which summarised previous discussions of the text. It marks a high point of Renaissance scholarship. See the Wellcome Institute *Exhibition List,* p. 10.

[1747] G.A. Russell: Introduction; op cit; p. 6.

[1748] Ibid.

[1749] G.A. Russell: 'Physicians at the Ottoman Court,' *Medical History,* 34 (1990), p. 258.

[1750] G.A. Russell: Introduction: op cit; p. 6.

[1751] See H. Friedenwald, 'Amatus Lusitanus,' *Bulletin of the Institute for the history Medicine,* 5 (1937), pp. 603-53. In the seventeenth century, these textual criticisms, in fact, stimulated physicians to learn Arabic. For example, Peter Kirsten (1575-1640) printed a part of the *Canon* in Arabic with an accompanying glossary to facilitate the study of the text. See, Hamilton, *Bedwell,* ch.iv, pp. 72-3 and 146.

[1752] G.A. Russell: Introduction; op cit; at p. 7.

[1753] Ibid.

[1754] Ibid.

[1755] For a description and bibliography of Arabic studies at Oxford, see M. Feingold, 'The Oxford Oriental School' in *The History of the University of Oxford.*

as Erbstosser notes, and as Kunitzsch has abundantly shown, almost all the names of constellations and the basic terms of astronomy come from Arabic.[1756] Much the same is the case for other sciences, as the next part highlights. The Arabic words in architecture, agriculture, art, commerce, geography, industry (including armaments, fabrics, glass making, leather work, paper making, and silk making) literature, mathematics, mechanics, medicine, music and physics, clearly outline the impact of Arabic.[1757]

Beyond this, it was the beauty of Arabic, which has caught the imagination of linguists, readers, and the lettered throughout the centuries. Joel Carmichael in his book *The Shaping of the Arabs* writes:

> As the defenders of Arabic uniqueness would point out, where Greek often has only one word for several objects, Arabic has many words for one object. The stunning phonetic beauty of the language is matched, they say, by its staggering wealth of synonyms. The possibilities in Arabic for the use of figurative language are endless; its allusiveness, tropes, and figures of speech place it beyond the reach of any other language. Arabic has numerous stylistic and grammatical peculiarities that are quite unique; hence nothing can be translated from Arabic satisfactorily. The Arabic version of something foreign is always shorter than the original. Arabic loses on translation but all other languages being translated into Arabic gain; thus it is quite understandable, says a well known writer, that upon being expelled from paradise Adam was naturally forbidden to speak Arabic and had to talk Syriac instead, and when he repented God let him go back to Arabic.[1758]
>
> We can only express our wonder and 'say mashallah' (God willed it) [comments Sarton.] How it so happened (and this the Prophet could not foresee unless he had some divine insight) that the only language he knew was one of the most beautiful languages in existence.[1759]

4. The Scope and Accomplishments of Muslim Scholarship

The success of the Muslim renaissance, Sarton holds, was:

> Essentially due to the wave of enthusiasm and energy which lifted these people up for a time almost above themselves.[1760]

[1756] M. Erbstosser: *The Crusades;* op cit; p. 185; P. Kunitzsch: *The Arabs and the Stars: texts and traditions on the fixed stars, and their influence in medieval Europe*; (Variorum; Aldershot; 1989).
[1757] H. Salloum and J. Peters: *Arabic Contributions*; op cit; p. xii.
[1758] J. Carmichael: *The Shaping of the Arabs*; New York; 1967; in H. Salloum and J. Peters: *Arabic Contributions*; op cit; p. x.
[1759] G. Sarton: The Incubation; op cit; p. 19.
[1760] G. Sarton: *Introduction*, vol I, at p. 549.

The life and works of the poet Abu'l Ala al-Ma'ari, briefly summarised by Durant,[1761] are quite impressive:

'Abu'l Ala al-Ma'ari (10th-11th centuries) was born at al-Ma'arat, near Aleppo. Smallpox left him blind at the age of four; nevertheless he took up the career of a student, learned by heart the manuscripts that he liked in the libraries, travelled widely to hear famous masters, and returned to his village. During the next fifteen years his annual income was thirty dinars (some twelve dollars a month), which he shared with servant and guide; his poems won him fame, but as he refused to write encomiums, he nearly starved. In 1008 he visited Baghdad, was honoured by poets and scholars before returning two years later to Ma'arat, became rich, but lived to the end with the simplicity of a sage. He was a vegetarian a l'outrance, avoiding not only flesh and fowl, but milk, eggs, and honey as well; to take any of these from an animal world, he thought, was rank robbery. On the same principle he rejected the use of animal skins, blamed ladies for wearing furs, and recommended wooden shoes.[1762] He died at eighty four; and a pious pupil relates that 180 poets followed his funeral, and eighty four savants recited eulogies at his grave.'[1763]

A similar picture, but at the level of royalty, is illustrated by the life of Abd Errahman III of Spain (r. 912-961).[1764] As a ruler, he fought and quashed the threats to the kingdom, both from within and from without. Under his rule, commerce thrived and so did agriculture, horticulture and industrial production. His contribution to arts, learning, and civilisation was enormous and he was also known for his building of the famed al-Zahra (the Bright One) at Cordova. The city's mosques, schools, baths, gardens, and scholarly circles of his time were only rivalled by those of Baghdad.[1765] Then, Abd Errahman virtually abandoned the administration of the empire to his heir, Al-Hakem II. He renounced the frivolities of the court and attached himself to the ascetic Abu Ayub, in whose company he passed much of his time in fasting, prayer, and the distribution of alms. He focused his mind on learning and reading, drawn to intellectual matters of various sorts. After the king's death, in a journal which recorded his most secret thoughts, were found his reflections on 'the disappointments of life and the delusive attractions of human greatness and imperial ambition':

> I have reigned fifty years in peace and in glory, beloved by my people, feared by my enemies, respected by my allies. My friendship has been sought by the great kings of the earth. I have wanted nothing that the heart of man could desire, neither renown, nor power, nor pleasure. During this long life, I have counted the days when I have enjoyed complete happiness

---

[1761] W. Durant: *The Age of Faith*, op cit; p. 265:

[1762] Nicholson: Islamic poetry; 133-7 in W. Durant: *The Age of Faith*, op cit, p. 265.

[1763] A.F. Rihani: The Quatrains of Abu'l Ala (Al-Maari); vii; in W. Durant, op cit, p. 265.

[1764] Extracts from: E.L. Provencal: *Histoire;* op cit. S.P. Scott: *History*; op cit. S and N. Ronart: *Concise Encyclopaedia of Arabic civilization; The Arab West;* (Djambatan; Amsterdam; 1966).

[1765] S and N. Ronart: *Concise; op cit;* p. 15.

> and they amount to only fourteen! Praise be to Him who alone possesses eternal glory and omnipotence, there is no other God than He![1766]

Abd Errahman's predilections for a sedentary life, and his intimate relations with the learned, Scott points out:

> Were viewed with contempt by the barbarous Christians, who considered war as the peculiar calling of a man of spirit, and the acquisition of knowledge as only fit for monks, an order whose pacific occupations did not, nevertheless, exclude even its members from the profession of arms.[1767]

Two figures from the scholarly world reinforce this picture of passion for learning and accomplishments in the world of the intellect that marked the Muslim world in its phase of glory. Abbas Ibn Firnas (d.887) of Cordova, first, had such a boundless imagination and inventive faculty, he could decipher even the most incomprehensible hieroglyphics.[1768] On one occasion, as Levi Provencal narrates, when a merchant returned to Spain with Khalil's treatise on the Arab metrical system, nobody could make anything of these rules of prosody and scansion. Ibn Firnas had the manuscript brought to him, and, retiring to a corner of the palace, he examined it and, quickly, after grasping its meaning, proceeded to explain it to a dumbfounded audience.[1769] Ibn Firnas was also a poet under three successive rulers, a mathematician, an astronomer, and a pioneer in many fields.[1770] He might have imported the numeral system after a trip to Iraq.[1771] Ibn Firnas also invented spectacles, complex chronometers, and a rudimentary flying machine.[1772] He was accustomed with the scientific properties of glass, and contributed to early experiments with lenses and the idea of using them to magnify script.[1773] He also lent his skills to the glass making furnaces of Cordova, and made a representation of the sky in glass, which he was able at will to make clear or cloudy, with lightning and the noise of thunder at the press of a finger.[1774] He also made some of the earliest attempts at flying by building artificial wings.[1775]

Al-Biruni (973-1050) is possibly one of the greatest minds that ever lived. Other than his contributions to geography, medicine and physics, which will be amply looked at in the following part, he dealt with many astronomical issues, and provided solutions and explanations to many phenomena. An important astronomical problem tackled by him was the calculation of the acceleration of the rotation of the earth.[1776] The data that he obtained in the investigation has

---

1766 S.P. Scott: *History*; op cit; vol 1; pp. 632-3.
1767 Ibid; vol 1; p. 638.
1768 L. Provencal in G. Wiet et al: *History;* op cit; p. 455.
1769 Ibid.
1770 S. N. Ronart: A *Concise*; op cit; p. 142.
1771 Ibid.
1772 W. Durant: *The Age of Faith*; op cit; pp. 298.
1773 A. Djebbar: *Une Histoire;* op cit; 272-4.
1774 Levi Provencal, in G. Wiet et al: *History*; op cit; at p. 336.
1775 A. Djebbar: *Une Histoire;* op cit; p. 274; S and N. Ronart ed., *A Concise*; op cit; at p. 142.
1776 S. Pines la Theorie de la Rotation de la Terre a l'Epoque d'Al-Biruni; *Journal Asiatique*; 244; 1956; pp. 301-5; Paris.

been used by a modern scientist writing on this problem.[1777] An issue of ancient astronomy on which al-Biruni wrote to great effect was the computation of the length of daylight.[1778] He also wrote a study of transits, now available in English translation.[1779] Further he analysed the light of the moon during an eclipse, as well as the appearance of fire during a solar eclipse.[1780] Al-Biruni's trigonometrical teaching is developed in the third book of *al-Qanun al-Masu'di.*[1781] It has been suggested that he was the first writer to approach trigonometry as an independent subject,[1782] although the credit for this has generally been, wrongly, given to Nasr al-Din a-Tusi.[1783] It should be noted that al-Biruni developed conical and cylindrical projections in cartography some 550 years before Mercator.[1784] Further he wrote a geometrical treatise, *Kitab istikhraj al-autar fi al-da'irah* (translated into German by Suter (1910)),[1785] which deals with theorems concerning the chords in circles.[1786] Al-Shahrazuri, one of his earliest biographers, wrote about him:

> He (Al-Biruni) never had a pen out of his hand, nor his eyes ever off a book, and his thoughts were always directed to his studies, with the exception of two days in the year, when he was occupied in procuring the necessaries of life on such a moderate scale as to afford him bare sustenance and clothing.[1787]

Early scholars of Islam distinguished themselves by their monumental written output. It was not just the better known figures of Ibn Sina or Al-Razi, whose works *The Qanun* and *The Continens* were so voluminous they could scarcely be edited whole, or kept in one location, but many others. Thus, Ibn Hayyan of Cordova (b.987-88 d. 1076), not to be confused with the earlier chemist, Jabir Ibn Hayyan, was the author of an immense history of Spain in 60 volumes (*Kitab al-matin, Liber solidus*) and of a shorter work, in 10 volumes, dealing with the biographies of Hispano-Muslim scholars (*Kitab al-Muqtabis fi Tarikh al-*

[1777] R.R. Newton: The Earth's acceleration as deduced from al-Biruni's solar data; *Memoirs of the Royal Astronomical Society*; 76 (1972); pp. 99-128; Oxford.

[1778] M. Lesley: Biruni on Rising times and daylights lengths; *Centaurus* 5 (1937); 121-41; Copenhagen.

[1779] *Al-Biruni on Transits*; (American University of Beirut. Beirut; 1969).

[1780] T. Jarzebowski: Astronomical Works of al-Biruni; *Afghanistan* 26 (1973); pp. 6-14. G.R: Aziz: Al-Biruni and his academic conquests; in H.M. Said ed. *Al-Biruni's Commemorative Volume;* (Karachi; Hamdard Academy; 1979); pp. 158-9.

[1781] K. Schoy: *Die Bestimmung...al-Biruni;* (Berlin; 1925).

[1782] M.A. Kazim: Al-Biruni and Trigonometry; (Iran society; 1951); pp. 161-70. O. Qudsi: Al-Biruni's Methodology and its sources; in H.M. Said Ed; *Al-Biruni's Commemorative Volume;* pp. 594-604.

[1783] For more technical discussions of al-Biruni's trigonometrical work see A.D. Bradley: Al-Biruni's table of Cords; *The Mathematics Teacher*; 63 (1970); pp. 615-6. A.S. Saidan: the Trigonometry of al-Biruni; in H.M. Said Ed; *Al-Biruni's Commemorative Volume;* pp. 681-90. It might be mentioned here that J.H. Kramers: Al-Biruni's determination of Geographical Longitudes by measuring the Distances; *Iran Society*; 1951; pp. 177-93. retranslates the second chapter of the sixth book (on calculating longitude by measuring distances).

[1784] M. Fiorini: Le projezioni cartographiche di Alberuni; *Bolletino della Societa Geografica Italiana*; 39 (Roma; 1891); pp. 287-94. Syed Hasan Barani; Al-Biruni's Scientific Achievements; *Indo-Iranica* 5; (1952); 37-48; Calcutta; p. 43. M. Anas: Al-Beruni's mathematics and Astronomy; *Afghanistan*; 26; 76-85; at p. 83.

[1785] H. Suter: Das Buch...al-Biruni; *Bibliotheca Mathematica* 3rd series; (Leipzig; 1910); 11; pp. 11-78.

[1786] M. Saud: A Part of al-Biruni's Istikhraj al-Autar fi al-dairah; in H.M. Said ed; *Al-Biruni's Commemorative Volume*; op cit; pp. 691-105.

[1787] J.S. Mishra: New Light on Al-Biruni's Stay in India; *Central Asian Journal;* 15; 1972; 302-12; p. 305.

Andalus).[1788] Ibn al-Khatib of Cordoba, who died in the 10th century, is credited with nearly 110 works on metaphysics, history and medicine, whilst Ibn Hassan composed 450 works on philosophy and jurisprudence.[1789] Ibn Hazm (994-1064) lived for a considerable length in Xatiba, near Valencia, and in the Algarve, and died there; his writing include around 400 volumes, nearly 80,000 pages.[1790] Al-Tabari, born in 839, in Amul, in the province of Tabaristan, which gave him his surname, began his studies in Amul, he then left for many cities: Ravy, Baghdad, Basra, Kufa, different Syrian centres of learning, then Fustat in Egypt, then back to Baghdad.[1791] Al-Tabari, according to Yaqut (d. 1229), had planned a commentary on the Qur'an ten times more voluminous than the one he completed that is 30,000 pages rather than 3,000. It was only the anxious protests of his pupils that led him to cut the size to the latter number.[1792] Al-Tabari is also said to have projected the precise number of pages for his universal history, 30,000 only to reduce that to the same 3000, because of the same protests.[1793] Yaqut al-Hamawi himself managed altogether 33,180 pages on the poets and men of literature,[1794] whilst Al-Marzubani, who died shortly before the year 1000, wrote over 37,580 pages, according to Ibn al-Nadim's *Fihrist.*[1795] According to the catalogue established by Al-Biruni, the writings by al-Razi (854-934-5) can be classified as follows: 56 medical works; 33 works on natural sciences; 8 on logic; 10 on mathematics; 17 on philosophy; 6 on metaphysics; 14 on theology; 23 on chemistry; 10 on varied subjects; and 7 on explanations or summaries of other philosophical or medical works.[1796] Ibn al-Jawzi, an encyclopaedist (b. ca. 1115-d. 1201), was one of the most learned men of his time, and his immense literary activity was equalled in Islam only by al-Suyuti's (second half of the 15th century.)[1797] His almost innumerable writings cover history, philology, biography, Hadith, Fiqh, the Qur'an, ethics, medicine, geography, and other subjects. His most important work seems to be a history of the world from the creation to 1180, entitled *Kitab al-muntazam wa multaqat al-multazam.* He prepared a critical edition of al-Ghazzali's *Ihya.* He wrote a treatise on medical generalities called *Luqat al-manafi fi'l-tibb*, and another on spiritual medicine, *Kitab al-Tibb al-Ruhani.* Also a sort of autobiography in the form of a letter to his son, *Liftat al-Kabid*, followed by a list of his writings, he compiled two other lists of these.[1798] Ibn al-Banna, also known as Abu'l-Abbas Ahmad ibn Muhammad ibn

---

1788 G. Sarton: *Introduction,* vol I, op cit; p. 734.
1789 S.P Scott: *History;* op cit; vol 3 p. 425.
1790 A. Mieli: *La Science Arabe;* op cit; p. 183.
1791 J. Dahmus: *Seven Medieval Historians* (Nelson-Hall, Chicago, 1982), p. 83.
1792 Ibid; p. 85.
1793 Ibid.
1794 Yaqut al-Hamawi: *Irshad al-arib ila marifat al-adib*, also referred to as *Mu'ujam al-udaba*, edited by D. S. Margoliouth (London, 1907-1926) V, 110. Yaqut is also the author of a geographical encyclopaedia: *Mu'jam al-Buldan* (Dictionary of countries).
1795 Ibn al-Nadim: *Al-Fihrist;* pp. 132-4 in J. Pedersen: *The Arabic Book*, op cit, p. 37.
1796 A. Mieli: *La Science Arabe;* op cit; p. 91.
1797 G. Sarton: *Introduction*; vol II, p. 362.
1798 Criticism: Ibn Khalikan: Biographical Dictionary; tr. MacGukin de Slane; 6 vols (Paris-London; 1843); vol 2, 96-98, L. Leclerc: *Medecine Arabe;* vol 2, 36, (1876). F. Wustenfeld: *Geschchtschreiber der Araber*, 102-104 (1881). All in G Sarton: *Introduction*; Vol II, p. 362.

Uthman al-Azdi, was born in 1256 in the city of Marrakech, or the region of Marrakech.[1799] Ibn al-Banna wrote a large number of works, in fact 82 are listed by Renaud.[1800] Based on the inventory that was made at the time by Ibn Hayder, Ibn al-Banna seems to be in fact the author of more than 100 titles, of which 32 deal with Mathematics and Astronomy, the others being dedicated to Linguistics, Rhetoric, Astrology, Grammatics and Logic.[1801] Al-Nuwayri (1279-1332), a close associate to the Mamluk Sultan, al-Nasir, was deeply interested in the art of writing, with an output of eighty pages a day, completing an encyclopaedia entitled *Nihayat al-arab fi funun al-adab*, which aimed at encompassing all sociological sciences needed for the prominent secretaries.[1802] Pursuing the tradition, Ibn Khaldun's (1332-1406) *Muqqadimmah* was not just immense in size, but also dealt with many subjects, ranging from history, to political administration, economic and social institutions.[1803]
And, of course, the sheer number of scholars themselves is quite impressive, Hammer Purgastall counted 5,218 Muslim authors who lived and wrote prior to the end of the 11th century.[1804] In his *Geschichtschreiber der Araber*, written in 1882, Wustenfeld counted no less than 590 historians who flourished in the first thousand years of Islam.[1805]

Muslim biographical dictionaries, as Young observes, combine and also anticipate the features of both Who's Who and works such as the *Dictionary of National Biography*.[1806] Biography, Young explains, seeks to understand individuals and those features of character that make them unique, the space devoted to each being proportional to their accomplishments and status. The entries cover principally the subjects' date of death, their lineage, education and travels; appointments, their intellectual and moral qualities and interesting anecdotes related to them. Also included are philological notes on the form of the subjects' name, a brief description of their physical appearance and, in the case of authors, a list of their works.[1807] The earliest biographical dictionary was the *Kitab tabaqat al-muhaddithin* of al-Mawsali, who died in 800, but of which no copy is thought to have survived. Many more followed, and included not just the names of men but also of women; encompassing all classes of important people, as in such works as *Kitab Wulat Misr wa Qudatiha* (Book of the Governors and Judges

[1799] J J O'Connor and E F Robertson: *Arabic Mathematics, a Forgotten Brilliance* at: http://www-history.mcs.st-andrews.ac.uk/history/index.html
[1800] Ibid.
[1801] Al-Balagh and Djebbar, 1995 b, in A. Djebbar: Mathematics in Medieval Maghreb; *AMUCHMA-Newsletter* 15; Universidade Pedagógica (UP), (Maputo Mozambique, 15.9.1995).
[1802] I.J. Krckovskij: *Izbrannye Socinenja* (chosen works); Vol 4 (Moscow, 1957), pp. 439-42.
[1803] Ibn Khaldun: *The Muqqaddimah*, tr. F. Rosenthal; 3 vols (New York, 1958).
[1804] S.K. Bukhsh: 'The Islamic Libraries.' *The Nineteenth Century and After*' (July 1902) 125-39; at p. 127 (there is unfortunately no figure for the period after that date, especially in the 12th –13th centuries.)
[1805] P.K. Hitti: America and the Arab heritage: in *The Arab Heritage*, op cit; pp. 1-24; p. 5.
[1806] M.J. L Young: Arabic Biographical Writing, in *Religion, Learning and Science in the Abbasid Period,* Ed M.J. L. Young, J.D. Latham and R.B. Serjeant (Cambridge University Press, 1990), pp. 168-187; p. 173.
[1807] Ibid.

of Egypt) by Muhammad b. Yusuf al-Kindi (d 961) and *Qudat Qurtuba* (The Judges of Cordova) by al-Khushani (981).[1808] The *Fihrist,* completed by the Baghdad bookseller, Ibn al-Nadim, in 987,[1809] gives the most detailed account of all works by Muslim scholars up to the last decade of the 10th century.[1810] It is divided into ten 'discourses,' the first, for instance, describing the language of both Arabs and non Arabs, the varieties of their scripts and related matters. The second mainly deals with grammar; the third with *Belles Lettres*, biography, genealogies; other chapters deal with various other subjects. From *al-Fihrist* the scale of loss of Muslim works becomes obvious, for the majority of works it cites are no longer extant.[1811] Ibn al-Asqalani in his *al-Durar al-kaminah* has over 5000 entries, while Ibn al-Athir in his *Asd al-ghabah fi maarifat al-sahabah* has over 7000.[1812] The most used Muslim Biographical sources are those of Ibn-al-Qifti (d.1248), who wrote *The History of the Philosophers* on the lives of 414 philosophers and scientists; Ibn-Abi-Usaybi'ah, who wrote the *Tabaqat al-Atibba (*The Classes of the Physicians) (in 1242), and the bibliographer Hajji Khalifa (d.1658) whose work contains 18,500 indications of Oriental works, with the names of the authors and a bibliography of each of them.[1813] Ibn Khallikan (1211-1282) in his *Wafayat al-'Ayan* (Obituaries of Men of Note) wrote brief anecdotal lives of over 850 distinguished Muslims.[1814] Regarding the latter, whilst Durant finds the work remarkably accurate, Ibn Khallikan nevertheless apologised for its imperfections: 'God has allowed no book to be faultless except the Qur'an.'[1815]

It would require a vast amount of space to study the role Muslim scholarship had in shaping many of our modern ideas. Al-Farabi, Al-Ghazali, Ibn Khaldun, and many of he great scholars of Islam are, indeed, behind many of our supposedly Western concepts. Here, we examine briefly the contribution of one of Islam's great scholars: Al-Razi, better known for his medical and chemical works. Al-Razi, Myers observes, is noted for his *The Spiritual Physic,* which shows him a thoughtful psychologist and outstanding physician.[1816] Some of his ideas have a strikingly modern ring:

> Mutual helpfulness is closely related to division of labour. Each man must eat, be clothed, have shelter and security, though he may contribute directly to only one of these activities. The good life is thus attained by division of labour and mutual helpfulness. Each labours at a single task and is simultaneously servant and served, works for others and has others

[1808] Ibid.
[1809] R.P. Multhauf: *The Origins of Chemistry;* op cit; p. 124.
[1810] B. Dodge: *The Fihrist of al-Nadim.* A Tenth Century Survey of Muslim Culture, Columbia Records of Civilisation: Sources and Studies, No LXXXIII, 2 vols (New York and London; 1970). See also M. Nakosteen: *History,* op cit, for extracts from *al-Fihrist*, pp. 29-33.
[1811] B. Dodge: *The Fihrist;* op cit.
[1812] M.J. L Young: Arabic Biographical Writing; op cit; at p. 169.
[1813] G Le Bon: *La Civilisation;* op cit. p. 358.
[1814] W. Durant: *The Age of Faith*; op cit. p. 319.
[1815] Ibid.
[1816] E.A. Myers: *Arabic Thought and the Western World;* (Frederick Ungar Publishing Co; New York; 1964); p. 13.

> work for him. As a healthy and effective social organization is possible only on the basis of cooperation and mutual help, it is every man's duty to give assistance to his fellow man in one way or another and to work to the best of his abilities to that end, avoiding at the same time the two extremes of excess and deficiency.
>
> If he toils all his life to earn more than he requires or needs for his old age without disposing of his earnings in such ways as will yield him comfort, he is really the loser and has enslaved himself; for he will have given away his own energy without obtaining in return a proper compensation. Such a man has not bartered toil against toil and service against service; his toil will have yielded profit only to his fellows, while their toil on his behalf will have passed him by.
>
> The man who follows this rule in earning his living will have received in exchange toil for toil and service for service.[1817]

Al Razi's expressions "cooperation," "mutual help," "mutual assistance", Myers points out, have had a revival in Pëtr Kropotkin's *Mutual Aid,* published in 1902 as refutation to Darwin's theory of the survival of the fittest.[1818] While the Darwinists declared competition and struggle for existence to be the governing law of nature, Kropotkin, like al Razi, emphasided the principle of mutual aid in which 'he no less saw a fundamental law of nature.[1819]

It is crucial to raise, with King (David), what is possibly the most important point in respect to the scope of Islamic scholarship, its great loss, and the present failure to bring to light what has survived. From the 9th to the 15th century, King says, Muslim scholars excelled in every branch of scientific knowledge: their contributions in astronomy and mathematics are particularly impressive.[1820] Any brief survey of the categories of Islamic astronomical literature, for instance, will not do justice to the scope of a corpus of literature compiled over a thousand year period, in a society, which gave great consideration to the subject. Anyone who reads through the pages of Fuat Sezgin's volume 6 of his *Geschichte des arabischen Schrifttums* dealing with astronomy will see the amount of scientific material available from the first four centuries of Islam.[1821] The amount of material available from later centuries is even much greater. Even though there are an estimated 10,000 Islamic astronomical manuscripts and close to 1000 Islamic astronomical instruments preserved in libraries and museums, and even if all of them were properly catalogued and indexed, the picture that we could reconstruct of Islamic astronomy, especially for the 8th, 9th and 10th centuries,

---

[1817] A. J. Arberry, *The Spiritual Physick of Rhazes* (London, John Murray, 1950), pp. 89-90.
[1818] E.A. Myers: *Arabic Thought and the Western World;* op cit; p. 13.
[1819] Ibid.
[1820] D.A. King: Astronomy in the Islamic World; in H. Selin ed: *Encyclopaedia of the History of Science, Technology, and Medicine in Non Western Cultures*, (Kluwer Academic Publishers. Boston/London, 1997); pp. 125-33; at p. 125.
D.A. King: Astronomy; in M.J.L. Young et al ed. *Religion, Learning and Science in the Abbasid Period;* (Cambridge University Press; 1990); pp. 274-89; at p. 288.
[1821] F. Sezgin: *Geschichte des Arabischen Schrifttums* (vol vi for astronomy); (Frankfurt; 1978).

would be quite deficient.[1822] Most of the available manuscripts and instruments date from the later period of Islamic astronomy, that is, from the 15th to the 19th century, and although some of these are based or modelled on earlier works, many of the early works are extant in unique copies and others have been lost almost without trace, and are only known through their titles.[1823] The 13th century Syrian scientific biographer Ibn al-Qifti relates that the eleventh-century Egyptian astronomer Ibn al-Sanbadi heard that the manuscripts in the library in Cairo were being catalogued and so he went to have a look at the works relating to his field. He found 6500 manuscripts relating to astronomy, mathematics, and philosophy; not one of these survives amongst the 2500 scientific manuscripts preserved in Cairo today.[1824] The surviving manuscripts thus constitute but a small fraction of those that were actually copied: nevertheless they preserve a substantial part of the Islamic scientific heritage, certainly enough of it for us to judge its level of sophistication.[1825] And yet, even this small fraction is hardly being studied, in fact it remains untouched. Very few Islamic astronomical works have been published or have received the attention they deserve. Three out of close to 200 Islamic Zijs (astronomical tables) have been published in the optimum way (text, translation, and commentary). Many of the published Arabic scientific texts were printed in Hyderabad, most with no critical apparatus.[1826] There is a great need for reproducing in printed form of manuscripts of particular importance, since the historian of Islamic astronomy has to rely mainly on microfilms of manuscripts, which some libraries are unable or unwilling to supply.[1827] With respect to Islamic observational instruments, although most are lost and known to us only through texts, the state of documentation of the other, smaller Islamic astronomical instruments that do survive leaves much to be desired.[1828] Many of the most important writings on instruments are still unpublished, and much that has been written on instruments is on a very amateur level.[1829] In 1845, L.A. Sédillot (who wrote the best work on Muslim astronomical instruments to date), whose privilege it was to have access to the rich collection of Arabic and Persian scientific manuscripts in the Bibliothéque Nationale in Paris, noted how 'Each day brings some new discovery and illustrates the extreme importance of a thorough study of the manuscripts of the East.'[1830] Sédillot also realised the importance of Islamic astronomical instruments. Given the vast number of manuscripts and instruments now available in libraries and museums elsewhere in Europe, the United States, and

[1822] D.A. King: Astronomy in the Islamic World; (H. Selin); op cit; at p. 125.
[1823] Ibid.
[1824] Ibid.
[1825] Ibid.
[1826] Ibid; p. 133.
[1827] D.A. King: Astronomy (Young); op cit; p. 288.
[1828] D.A. King: Astronomical Instruments in the Islamic World; in *Encyclopaedia* (H. Selin ed); op cit; pp. 86-8; at p. 86.
[1829] Ibid.
[1830] L.A. Sedillot: Memoire sur les instruments astronomique des Arabes, *Memoires de l'Academie Royale des Inscriptions et Belles Lettres de l'Institut de France* 1: 1-229; (Reprinted Frankfurt, 1985).

the Near East, and the rather small number of people currently working in this field, King concludes, 'Sedillot's statement is no less true today than it was a century and a half ago.'[1831]

5. Order, Accuracy and the Need for Evidence as Foundations of Islamic Learning

> Out of their different circumstances of life [Jurji observes] the wielders of the new scientific style travelled their numerous pathways till they met together at a single crossroad. Common to most of them was the unwearied attempt to simplify and to make lucid. Herein resided their own unchallengeable genius. They could, despite certain persistent opinions to the contrary, make generalizations and propound a subtle synthesis. They had a solid mastery over their materials, necessary in creative work. They could classify and enumerate, above all, they possessed untarnished the simple gift of orderliness.[1832]

Organising, systematising, and classifying sciences were indeed shared preoccupations of Muslim scholars, from Al-Farabi to Al-Ghazali, to Ibn Sina, Ibn Hazm, and many more. Al-Farabi's *Ihsa al-Ulum* (Catalogue of the Sciences, ca 900) was widely used by Muslim authors as an introduction to philosophical study, and was twice translated into Hebrew, and into Latin in the 12th century.[1833] The preface offers a classification of all the recognised sciences, or branches of learning, their parts, and their contents.[1834] Al-Farabi identifies five major sciences: grammar, logic, mathematics, the science of physics and metaphysics, and political science, which includes the Islamic religious disciplines of jurisprudence (*fiqh)* and dialectical theology (*kalam*).[1835] The preface concludes with some remarks on the purpose and utility of such an enumeration:

> It will indicate the proper beginning and order of the study of the sciences and will orient the student to the study he is about to undertake; it will show him the relative value of various disciplines; and it will alert him to those who profess expertise in some or all of the sciences but who are in fact charlatans.[1836]

Prior to the classifications made by Muslim scholars, science was a bulk of knowledge, where the scientific mingled with the folkloric, which was very obvious with both Greek and early Muslim learning. It was thus very common to

[1831] D.A. King: Astronomy in the Islamic World in *Encyclopaedia* (H. Selin ed); op cit; p. 133.
[1832] E. J. Jurji: The Course; op cit; pp. 222-3.
[1833] D.L. Black: Al-Farabi in Medieval Philosophers; *Dictionary of Literary Biography;* vol 115; edited by J. Hackett; A Bruccoli Clark Layman Book; Detroit; pp. 184-95, at p. 189.
[1834] Ibid.
[1835] Ibid.
[1836] Ibid.

find the chemist dabbling with the magician, and it was extremely hard to delimit the boundaries, or prevent the non scientific taking over the scientific. Science also had no distinct parameters within which it could be addressed. The Muslim classification of sciences, thus, somehow refined the whole matter, contributing to the emergence of what was centuries later to be our modern learning system in departments, faculties, and courses. And then, within the sciences, further subdivisions were made. Al-Razi and Jabir Ibn Hayyan (722-815) performed this to perfection in chemistry. In his work *Secret of Secrets*,[1837] Al-Razi, for instance, divided natural substances into earthly, vegetable and animal substances, to which he also added a number artificially obtained such as lead oxide, caustic soda, and various alloys. Al-Razi again, in his medical treatises gathered all knowledge, formerly disorganised, into a perfect synthesis, thus providing his users with a framework for learning, understanding, and developing medical subjects.[1838]

A significant example of botanical work in Muslim Spain during the 10th and 11th centuries is the great book entitled "The physician's support for the knowledge of plants", by an anonymous author.[1839] A study of this book was published by the Spanish Arabist Asin Palacios, who pointed out its considerable importance to the history of science and to that of the early Spanish writers in the Iberian Peninsula.[1840] The following description of the work by Millas Vallicrosa gives us an idea on its meticulousness and precision, besides the care for detail that defined an early Muslim scientist's works.[1841] The author of this manuscript was a botanist and agronomist as well as a doctor and chemist; and his dictionary, whose chapters follow the order of the Arabic letters in the Western alphabet, lists the names of all plants, whether medicinal or not, giving a separate entry to each under the name by which it was most usually known in classical Arabic, and providing cross-references under its other names. The main entries, so large that in some instances they take up several pages, are classified as follows: botanical genus to which the plant belongs, and its different species and varieties; morphological description of each of these, with an analysis of its component parts (root, stem or trunk, branches, leaves, flower, fruit, sap, gum or resin), mentioning the consistency, structure, colour, aspect and other physical characteristics (size, hardness, taste, smell, stickiness, and the like) that distinguish them, defining these by means of comparison with other and more familiar plants and conveying size by the simplest means such as the length or thickness of a finger, the height of a man, the length of the arm, and so on. The author refrains from asserting dogmatically the genus, species and variety of the

---

1837 Translated into Latin by Gerard of Cremona in the 12th century; see chapter on sciences, and chemistry section.

1838 See chapter on sciences and section on medical sciences.

1839 J. M. Millas Vallicrosa: Arab and Hebrew Contributions to Spanish Culture; in *Cahier d'Histoire Mondiale;* 6; (1960); pp. 732-51; p. 746.

1840 *Glosaria de voces romanas registradas por un botanico anonimo hispano-musulman (siglos XI-XII),* (Madrid-Granada, 1943).

1841 J. M. Millas Vallicrosa: Arab and Hebrew Contributions; op cit; pp. 746-7.

different plants according to his own opinion; but rather he first sets forth the views found in earlier treatises, or in those of his contemporaries, and then discusses these with scientific impartiality before rejecting or accepting them as the case may be. He gives the names of each plant in different languages, and sometimes he even differentiates between the various local forms of Spanish-al-Andalus (that of Muslim Spain), Galician, the speech of the Upper Marches (corresponding to the North-East of the peninsula)-and *afranj,* or French, and so on. The description of the plant nearly always includes its geographical location, with particulars of the nature of the soil in which it grows wild or is cultivated (dry, damp, marshy or fluvial, mountain, valley, steppe, ravine, or other settings) and the regions where the author has seen it or gathered it or ascertained that it is to be found; all this being described in such minute detail as to guide other herbalists who might want to locate the plant at the exact spot, without hesitation or risk of going astray. The author concludes by describing the pharmaceutical, industrial and domestic purposes to which the plant can be applied, mentioning whether it is edible, suitable as a condiment, combustible, cosmetic, whether it can be used in tanning, or for timber, for fodder, for the extraction of resin, or for textile purposes. If it is medicinal he explains which ailment it should be used for, how it should be administered to produce the best results, in what circumstances it is harmful instead of curative, and so on.[1842] Moreover, Millas Vallicrosa points out, the work of this 11th century Muslim Andalusian botanist, who was closely associated with other botanists, such as Ibn Bassal and Ibn Luyyun-both of Toledo-makes him an obvious forerunner of the modern system of classification of flora invented by Cuvier, for which the only precedents hitherto encountered-and those very imprecise-had been those in the work of the 16th century Italian botanists, Cesalpino and Matthioli.[1843]

The search for maximum accuracy remained a constant concern in the endeavours of Muslim scholarship. So keen were biographers, for instance, to achieve accuracy that persons bearing the same name had whole books devoted to them, one such book being The *Kitab al-Mushtabih fi Asmaa al-Rijal* (Book of Names of Authorities Resembling Each Other) by Al-Dhahabi (d.1348). Biographers also went to great lengths to differentiate between degrees of certainty, near certainty and doubt. Abd al-Ghani Hasan, hence, mentions the method of Yaqut in his *Irshad al-Arib,* whereby 'he does not state something positively when he is not certain; only using 'I think,' 'I reckon,' and similar expressions indicative of mere supposition. On the other hand, when confident about the matter, he says: 'that which I know is,' 'that with which I am acquainted is' and similar phrases indicative of certainty.[1844]

[1842] Ibid.
[1843] Ibid; p. 747.
[1844] *Al-Tarajim wa'l siyar*, 84, in M.J.L. Young: Arabic; op cit, p. 178.

This keen search for accuracy that identified early Muslim scholarship followed on the legacy of Imam al-Bukhari. Al-Bukhari (b. 810) travelled the length of the land of Islam, and for years, in search of accurate texts of tradition, selecting the 7,275 most trusted Prophet's sayings out of an initial total of 300,000 of a more doubtful or spurious character.[1845] He and his fellow Hadith collectors made certain to the maximum of the reliability and accuracy of such hadiths. In this respect they classified the hadith into four main categories: *Sahih* or authentic; *Hasan* or good, likely to be authentic; *Daif*: weak, or likely to be unauthentic; and *Mawdu'* or forged, and hence not a hadith.[1846] One of the criterion for a hadith to be qualified as *Sahih* was that it should be universally related by at least four or sometimes as many as 310 different reporters in exactly the same form of meaning without contradiction by any.[1847] All *sahih* hadiths were classified according to the chapters of common law, and helped form a complete system of concrete jurisprudence. This approach was the earliest example of such critical activity in the world, with remarkably high standards of accuracy.[1848] Such accuracy relied on an earlier oral tradition: recitation. Recitation alone gave the certainty of avoiding confusion, and in the words of Shwab, for whom oral transmission was the method of high fidelity as compared with 'the professional blunderings of never ending copyists,' the more so in view of the 'heights of perfection long ago attained in memorizing techniques.'[1849]

Every author, or every person involved in scholarship, whether as producers of scholarly text, or its readers, perfectly realises the importance of accurate referencing to what they claim. Any academic work without notes/sources, at least to this author, is worth absolutely nothing. In giving the sources of their claims/facts, often to beyond the dreary, again, medieval Muslim scholars pioneered in this practice. And again, this goes back to the times of the Prophet, or soon after. This is remarkably explained by Sezgin as follows:

> The quest of recording in writing the Prophet's biography and his conquering expeditions as well as the biographies of his successors paved the way to the development of a variegated historiography of enormous proportions, including the separate treatment of the history of science that emerged quite early on as well.
>
> To my knowledge the issue of the significance of this historiography, which arose in a purely Islamic intellectual milieu, and of the methodology developed within it has not at all or at least not adequately been treated as yet in the context of the universal history of the subject. Even Arabists underestimate the historical content of the majority of the historical writings that arose primarily in the first three centuries of Islam (7th-9th

---

[1845] E. Gibbon: *The Decline;* op cit; chap L; part iv.
[1846] Al-Faruqi: *The Cultural Atlas;* op cit; p. 261.
[1847] Ibid.
[1848] Ignaz Goldziher: *Progress of Islamic Science*; St Louis Congress of Arts and Sciences, vol 2, 1906, pp. 497 sq., 502.
[1849] In G. Wiet et al: *History*; op cit; p. 446.

> centuries) because of the peculiar method of quoting their sources. The individual historical reports in those works which are, in most cases, preceded by a chain of transmitters as evidence of their authenticity, and which can, in some cases, be accompanied by the respective authors' own remarks or comments, are unfortunately considered, either as reports that were handed down orally for centuries, or as personal views of a particular transmitter written down according to certain tendencies one or two generations before the book in question was composed. Without going into further details in this introduction, it may be stated that those chains of transmitters contain the names of the authors of written sources as well as their transmitters, who were authorised, according to strict rules, to hand down certain named sources. In modern terms, the chains of transmitters appearing in Arabic works on history can be considered as references to the sources, somewhat like those given in the footnotes of our books.'[1850]

Muslim learning also distinguished itself in striking the perfect balance between authority and experiment. Ibn Hazm comments on reliance upon authority:

> We know with certainty that never could man have acquired the sciences and arts by himself guided only by his natural abilities and without the benefit of instruction (this applies, for instance,) to medicine, the knowledge of the physiological temperaments, the diseases and their causes, in all their numerous varieties, and the invention of adequate treatment and cure of each of them by drugs or preparations, which could never have been actually tried out. For how could anyone test every prescription on every disease since this would take thousands of years and necessitate the examination of every sick person in the world? And what goes for medicine goes for other sciences.[1851]

The trust in authority, however, is balanced against the need for proof and experiment. For a long time, Jurji notes, interpretation was the Muslim's legitimate monopoly. 'Soaring high above the mean levels of confusion' they did not seem satisfied till full proof and concrete evidence had been meticulously offered in their writings.[1852] Thus, for al-Maqdisi:

> He (the scholar) should not yield to bad habits or permit himself to be led astray by vicious tendencies. Nor must he turn his eyes from truth's depth. He should discriminate between the doubtful and the certain, between genuine and spurious, and should always stand firm by the clear light of reason.[1853]

[1850] Fuat Sezgin: *Science and Technology in Islam;* 5 vols; tr., into English by R. and S.R. Sarma; Institut für Geschichte der Arabisch–Islamischen Wissenschaften an der Johann Wolfgang Goethe-Universitat Frankfurt am Main, 2010, vol 1; p. 6.

[1851] *Kitab al-fisal fi'l-milal*, I, 72. In G. Le Bon: *La Civilisation;* p. 329.

[1852] E. J. Jurji: The Course; op cit; p. 223.

[1853] Mutahhr b. Tahir al-Maqdisi (fl 966) *Livre de la creation* op cit; I: pp. 5-6.

Checking, measuring, and experimenting in order to determine truth were thus central to Islamic learning, and affected all branches of sciences. Following the examples set before him by Al-Kindi (801-873) and Ibn Sahl (fl. 985), Ibn al-Haytham (965-1039), for instance, was able to determine optical rules through experimentation rather than the speculative exercise current with the Greeks.[1854] Muslim astronomers devised astronomical tables through observations and calculations, and used for the first time sophisticated apparatus for such operations.[1855] In chemistry, the pioneering role in this went to Jabir:

> The first essential in chemistry is that you should perform practical work and conduct experiments, for he who performs not practical work nor makes experiments will never attain to the least degree of mastery. But you, O my son, do your experiment so that you may acquire knowledge.
>
> Scientists delight not in abundance of material; they rejoice only in the excellence of their experimental methods.[1856]

And beautiful lines from al-Zamashhari:

> Knowledge is for the practitioner what the string is for the builder.
> And practice for the learned what the cord is for him who hauls water.
> Without string building will not be exact.
> Without cord the thirst will not be slaked.
> Who aspires to perfection.
> Let him both be learned and practise.[1857]

An account by an early Muslim astronomer, Habash al-Hasib (9th century), whose *Kitab al-ajsam wa'l-ab'ad* (Book of Bodies and Distances) is extant,[1858] outlines this spirit of Islamic learning. The passage is as follows:

> The commander of the faithful Al-Mamun desired to know the size of the earth. He inquired into this and found that Ptolemy mentioned in one of his books that the circumference of the earth is so and so many thousands of stades. He asked the commentators about the meaning of stade, and they differed about the meaning of this. Since he was not told what he wanted, he directed Al-Marwarrudhi, Isa al-Astrulabi, and al-Dhari with a group of surveyors and some of the skilled artisans including carpenters and brass-makers, in order to maintain the instruments which they needed. He transported them to a place which he chose in the desert of Sinjar. Al-Marwarrudhi and his party headed for the north pole of *Banat Na'sh* (Ursa

---

[1854] D.C. Lindberg: *Studies in the History of Medieval Optics* (London, Variorum; 1983).
G.A. Russell: Emergence of Physiological optics, in *Encyclopaedia of the History of Arabic Science* 3 vols; ed R. Rashed (Routledge, London, New York: 1996), pp. 672-715.

[1855] See for instance: L. Sedillot: Memoire sur les instruments astronomique des Arabes, *Memoires de l'Academie Royale des Inscriptions et Belles Lettres de l'Institut de France* 1: 1-229 (Reprinted Frankfurt, 1985).B. Hetherington: *A Chronicle of Pre-Telescopic Astronomy* (John Wiley and Sons; Chichester; 1996). R.P. Lorch: The Astronomical Instruments of Jabir Ibn Aflah and the Torquetom; *Centaurus* (1976) vol 20; pp. 11-34.

[1856] E.J. Holmyard: *Makers of Chemistry* (Oxford at the Clarendon Press, 1931), p. 60.

[1857] Az-Zamashhari: *Atwaq ad-dahab*, ed. tr. Barbier de Meynard (Paris, 1876), maqal 77, p. 172.

[1858] Y. Tvzi Langermann: The Book of Bodies and Distances of Habash al-Hasib; *Centaurus*; 28; (1985); pp. 108-28.

> Minor), and Isa and al-Dhari and their party headed to the south pole. They proceeded until they found that the maximum altitude of the sun at noon had increased, and differed from the noon altitude which they had found at the place from which they had separated, by the amount of one degree, after subtracting from it the sun's declination along the path of the outward journey, and there put arrows. Then they returned to the arrows, testing the measurement a second time, and so found that one degree of the earth was 56 miles, of which one mile is 4,000 black cubits. This is the cubit adopted by al-Mamun for the measurement of cloths, surveying of fields, and the distribution of way stations.[1859]

The dominant elements of Muslim science are, thus, obvious from this passage just cited. On top of the role of the rulers in the scientific drive, we note the involvement of teams of scholars in specific scientific tasks; the need to check and clarify extant knowledge; experiment, and, obviously, the importance of knowledge derived from such endeavours.

6. A Word on the Islamic Impact on Modern Culture

The impact of Muslim sciences and civilisation on the West has been vastly explored by this author in another work,[1860] and will be touched upon intermittently in the following part. It is, thus, unnecessary to dwell on this matter here. All that is necessary here is, first, to take note of the reverence held for Muslim scholarship and science in the medieval period, despite the hostility to the Islamic faith. The first English scientist, Adelard of Bath (fl. early 12th) referred to Muslims only as his masters, and travelled for many years so as 'To investigate the learning of the Arabs as best as he could.'[1861] For the Muslim educated Jewish scholar, Petrus Alphonsi (b.1062 or 1063), who converted to Christianity, and was one of King Henry's physicians in England from 1112 to 1120:[1862]

> The ignorant had to be educated in Islamic science, and he (Petrus) has laboured hard-'*magno labore.... et summo studio*' to translate Islamic works for the benefit of the Latin.[1863]

[1859] In R. Mercier: Geodesy; in *History of Cartography in Prehistoric, Ancient and Medieval Europe, and the Mediterranean;* J.B. Harley and D. Woodward ed (Chicago; 1987), volume 2; Book 1; Cartography in the Traditional Islamic and South Asian Societies; pp. 175-88; at pp.178-9.

[1860] S.E. Al-Djazairi: *The Hidden Debt to Islamic Civilisation*; 2 vols; MSBN Books 2015; available on Amazon Kindle Books.

[1861] Adelard of Bath: *Die Questiones Naturales des Alardus von Bath*; ed. M. Mueller; p. 4 in D. Metlitzki: *The Matter of Araby*; op cit; p. 13.

[1862] See J.H.L. Reuter: Petrus Alfonsi: an examination of his works; their scientific content, and their background.' Unpublished Ph.d thesis; (Oxford; 1975); p. iii.

[1863] D. Metlitzki: *The Matter*; pp. 24-5.

The Tunisian, known as Constantine the African (d.1087), who brought Muslim medical science from the great seat of learning of al-Qayrawan to Salerno (south of Rome,) from whence it spread to the rest of Western Christendom,[1864] was called the "Miracle man from the Orient."[1865] More instances could be given to highlight the awe in front of which Western Christendom stood; in fact not just Islamic learning, but all aspects of Muslim culture and civilisation.

The borrowing was not, as it is represented today in modern scholarship, scant, or highly selective, or limited to translations of sciences from Arabic, it was, in fact, a wholly encompassing exercise, which, if investigated thoroughly (as has not been the case yet) would reveal the Islamic foundations of the whole of modern science, civilisation and culture. This is not the place to go into this issue. All that is appropriate here is to show (however succinctly) how powerful and encompassing, and even crucial, was the Islamic influence. Three particular matters are identified here, relating to the knowledge of our planet; the reconciliation of faith and science, and thirdly the appreciation by the creative mind and soul of the literary form.

With regard to the knowledge of our planet, and without going into all the detail of the issue of the great discoveries of the Americas, which will be addressed under the chapter on Geography in part two, it is well accepted that the first explorers, responsible for the great discoveries were the Iberian people. The reasons for their success are obvious. It was amongst them that Muslim knowledge was most prevalent (for both countries (Spain and Portugal) were under Islamic rule for centuries (early 8th till mid late 13th centuries (with the exception of Grenada remaining Muslim until 1492). It was known amongst the Iberians that the earth was a sphere, and the theory had long been put forward that it was possible to reach the East by sailing west.[1866] It was Muslim scholarship, which was first to make the claims as found in *Hudud al-Alam,* written in 982, where the author, in his *Discourse on the Disposition of the Earth with Regard to its Cultivation or Lack of Cultivation*, says:

> '1. The Earth is round as a sphere and the firmament enfolds it turning on two poles, of which the one is the North Pole and the other the South Pole.
>
> 2. If on any sphere you trace two large circles *(dayira)* intersecting one another at right angles, those two circles will cut that sphere into four parts. The Earth is likewise divided into four parts by two circles, of which the one is called horizon *(da'irat al-afaq* and the other Equator *(khatt alistiwã).* As regards the Horizon, it starts from the eastern parts, passes by the limit of the inhabited lands of the Earth, which (is) at the South Pole; then it passes by the western parts until it reaches again the East. And this

---

[1864] K. Sudhoff: *Essays in the History of Medicine;* (New York; 1926). M. Mc Vaugh, `Constantine the African,' *Dictionary of Scientific Biography*, 3: pp. 393-5.

[1865] L.M. Sa'adi: Reflection of Arabian Medicine at Salerno and Montpellier; in *Annals of Medical History*; vol V; pp. 215-25; at p. 218.

[1866] A. Villiers: *Monsoon Seas*; (Mc Graw Hill Book Company, New York; 1952); p. 124.

circle is the one which separates this visible inhabited half of the Earth from the other hidden half which is beneath us. The Equator is a circle which starts from the eastern limit and follows the middle of the Earth by the line farthest distant [equidistant] from both poles until it reaches the West, and it goes on in the same way until it comes back to the East.
3. Within the northern quarter, the inhabited lands lie in that half (of it) which adjoins the Equator. And there are also some inhabited lands in the southern quarter, in the half (of it) adjoining the Equator. The amount of the inhabited lands of the North is: 63 degrees of breadth by 180 degrees of length, because the largest circle traceable round the Earth is of 360 degrees. The measure of the inhabited lands lying in the southern parts is somewhat over 17 degrees by 180 degrees. The measure of the area *(masaha)* of these two forms one-ninth of the whole of the Earth. All the cities of the world, the different kingdoms, the seas, the mountains, and the rivers and (in general) all the places possessing animals and fishes are within this ninth part of the Earth which we have mentioned.'[1867]

These ideas anticipated similar ones in the West by centuries. They were not alone, of course, in helping the great discoveries, and many technical breakthroughs were necessary. As Villiers points out, the ships were useless if no one understood the science of conducting them safely from place to place.[1868] Stars and familiar landmarks were all very well for short passages, to which men were accustomed. But 'to blaze out into the unknown and, finding what was there hidden, bring back account and directions of it good enough for men to follow-these were different skills.' To navigate successfully required instruments, skill in using them, nautical tables showing the movements of the heavenly bodies, and accurate charts. There were already then early navigators with skills in astronomy who, having measured the angle of the sun at its midday height, knew how to compute from that the distance of the ship, measured in degrees from the place where the sun was overhead. But for such methods to work, the navigator in his ship must have tables showing where the sun was overhead, at all times of the year, for the sun was in constant move. There was nothing easy about these problems, and they had to be overcome, insists Villiers.[1869] And so they were. Answers to these questions, the necessary instruments, such as the astrolabe and the compass, charts, the lateen sails, and many other pre-requisites, were all supplied by Muslims, both scholars and mariners between the 9th and 13th centuries, for the Muslims, already, had centuries of experience of ocean sailing and shipping between Arabia and China, and were going through their scientific,

---

[1867] *Hudud Al-Alam* (982) tr., and explained by V. Minorsky; Luzac and Co; (London; 1937); p. 50.
[1868] A. Villiers: *Monsoon Seas*; op cit; p. 121.
[1869] Ibid.

primarily, mathematical, astronomical and geographical, renaissance.[1870] The following part will dwell on these issues at great length.

With regard to philosophical thought, and most principally the idea of reconciling faith with science, the Muslim impact through al-Ghazali, Ibn Rushd, Ibn Sina, Ibn Baja, and Al-Farabi, most particularly, was immense.[1871] Here, it is looked briefly at the impact of Al-Farabi on Christian thought, on Albertus Magnus, first, then, most particularly on the father of modern Christian thought: Thomas Aquinas.[1872] This impact has been well summed up by Myers, from whose work much of the following is derived.[1873] In his writing, Albertus Magnus (1206-1280), theologian, philosopher, and teacher quoted quite freely from al Farabi, particularly on matters dealing with metaphysics.[1874] Albertus Magnus and St. Thomas Aquinas, his pupil, made it the goal of their lives to reconcile Muslim philosophy with Christian theology. They discarded those of Al-Farabi's theories that conflicted with Christian teaching and adopted those that appeared to them reconcilable with Christianity.[1875] The impact by Al-Farabi on Thomas Aquinas (c.1225-1274) is particularly obvious as in these extracts. On the *Theory of Knowledge,* Al-Farabi says:

> Every idea comes from sense- experience according to the adage "There is nothing in the intellect that has not first been in the senses." The mind is like a smooth tablet on which nothing is written.
> It is the senses that do all the writing on it. The senses are five:
> sight, hearing, smell, taste, and touch. Each of these has a proper sensible thing for its object. In every sensation the sense receives the form or species of sensible things without the matter, just as wax receives the form of a seal without any of the matter of it.[1876]

T. Aquinas says:

> Now, sense is a passive power, and is naturally changed by the exterior sensible. Wherefore the exterior cause of such change is what is directly perceived by the sense, and according to the diversity of that exterior cause are the sensitive powers diversified.

[1870] G. Ferrand: *Relations de Voyages et textes geographiques Arabes, Persans and Turks relatifs a l'Extreme orient du VIIIem au XVIIIem Siecles* (Ernest Leroux, Paris, 1913-4.) For Muslim scientific renaissance and its impact, the best work remains G. Sarton: *Introduction to the History of Science*, in 3 vols; Carnegie, Washington, 1927ff.

[1871] T. Arnold -A. Guillaume ed. *The Legacy of Islam*; (Oxford; 1931).

[1872] R. Hammond, *The Philosophy of al Farabi and Its Influence on Medieval Thought* (New York, Hobson Press, 1947).

[1873] E.A. Myers: Arabic Thought; op cit; pp. 15-30; Myers notes that extensive use has been made of this scholarly work in conjunction with al Farabi, *The Jami (Collections)* which include *The Gems of Wisdom; The Sources of Questions; A Letter in Reply to Questions; The Intellectual and the Intelligibles* (Cairo, Egypt, Saadeh Press, 1907); al Farabi, *Political Regime* (Cairo, Nile Press, 1927); and al Farabi, *Fusul al Madina,* ed. with English translation by D.M. Dunlop (New York, Cambridge University Press, 1961).

[1874] E.A. Myers: *Arabic Thought*; op cit; p. 16.

[1875] Ibid; Thomas Aquinas, *Summa Theologica,* translated by Fathers of the English Dominican Province, 2nd and rev. ed. (London, Burns, Oates and Washbourne, 1911), and in Thomas Aquinas, *Summa Contra Gentiles,* translated by the English Dominican Fathers from the latest Leonine edition (London, Burns, Oates and Washboume, 1924).

[1876] *The Jami,* op cit, p. 149.

> Now, change is of two kinds, one natural and the other spiritual. Natural change takes place by the form of the changer being received, according to its natural existence, into the thing changed, as heat is received into the thing heated. Whereas spiritual change takes place by the form of the changer being received, according to a spiritual mode of existence, into the thing changed, as the form of colour is received into the pupil which does not thereby become coloured. Now, for the operation of the senses, a spiritual change is required, whereby an intention of the sensible form is effected in the sensible organ.[1877]

More importantly, as noted above, it was al-Farabi's *Ihsa al-Ulum* (Catalogue of the Sciences, ca 900) which first organised scientific knowledge.[1878] Through its translation into Latin this work had a decisive impact on the Christian West. Two Latin translations are in fact known: one was by Gerard of Cremona, and the other, much more importantly, was by the much influential: Domingo Gundisalvo.[1879] Domingo Gundisalvo (c. 1120-1180) was a prolific translator and also author of works based on Ibn Sina and Al-Farabi, most particularly. Gundisalvo's work *On the Divisions of Philosophy* was widely distributed in the Christian West, and on Al-Farabi's methodology was built subsequent classification of sciences.[1880] Alexander Nequam expected students to be reading the newly translated texts in the divisions as Gundisalvo had passed them on.[1881] Robert Kilwardby wrote a text called "On the Rise of the Sciences," which was directly dependent on Gundisalvo's *Divisions*.[1882] Nearly contemporary with him, Vincent of Beauvais copied almost all of "On the Sciences" into his *Speculum doctrinale,* which was one of the most widely read books of the Middle Ages.[1883] Significant disputes arose in the new University of Paris about the way the sciences should be organised, learned, and taught, but the fact was that a new way organising knowledge for teaching and learning had spread in Europe, and despite its detractors, Weber insists, it was never to be stopped.[1884]

With regard to literature, Arabic poetry stood at the source of medieval poetry and subsequent literature of the Christian West.[1885] One particular region that was most influenced by Muslim poetry was the French southern region of Provence. This impact took place in the 12th century, and the principal source of influence was Muslim Spain. Giammaria Barbieri (1519-75) was the first scholar

---

[1877] *Summa Theologica* Part 1, Third Number [Questions LXXV-CXIX] and Question LXXVIII, Article 3, p. 80.

[1878] D.L. Black: Al-Farabi in Medieval Philosophers; *Dictionary of Literary Biography;* Vol 115; edited by J. Hackett; A Bruccoli Clark Layman Book; Detroit; pp. 184-95; at p. 189.

[1879] Alonso: Traducciones del Arc. Gundislavo; pp. 298-308; in J. Puig: Arabic Philosophy; op cit; p. 16.

[1880] M. C. Weber: Gundisalvo Domingo; in T. Glick, S.J. Livesey, F. Wallis Editors: *Medieval Science, Technology and Medicine; An Encyclopaedia*; (Routledge; London; 2005); pp. 208-10; p. 210.

[1881] M. C. Weber: Gundisalvo Domingo; p. 210.

[1882] Ibid.

[1883] Ibid.

[1884] Ibid.

[1885] See, most particularly: H.A.R. Gibb: Literature; in *The Legacy of Islam*; (Arnold-Guillaume ed); pp. 180-209; see also part three of this author's *Hidden Debt*, under appropriate headings.

to advocate the theory that contact with Muslim Spain contributed to the rise of the troubadour lyric in the 12th century.[1886] Barbieri explained that the Arabs in the 6th or 7th century invented rhymed verse, took it to Spain with them (following their arrival and conquest of the country: 711 onwards), and Provence learnt the art from Spain.[1887] Rymer (1641-1713) in his *Short History of Tragedy* insisted that modern poetry originated in Provence and that Provencal was the first of the modern languages.[1888] Warton's *On the Origin of Romantic Fiction in Europe* stated that poets of Provence have laid the foundations for modern polite literature.[1889] Warton declared that prose romances reached Europe from Muslim Spain through wars and commercial intercourse.[1890] As regards the poetical art of the troubadours, he also sided with the Hispano-Arabic thesis, which, with the decline of Neoclassicism and the rise of literary historiography, was in the ascendant.[1891] Xavier Lampillas (1731-1810) insisted that Spain should be accorded 'the honour and distinction of having contributed to the development of both the modern Italian language and its poetry, through Provencal.'[1892] The Jesuit, Juan Andres, discussed the scientific and literary achievements of Hispano-Arabic culture, and reached the same conclusion regarding the origin of Provencal poetry.[1893] Andres argued that Provencal genres corresponded to those in use amongst the Arabs, and that poetic academies in Italy, France and Spain were modelled on similar Arabic institutions.[1894]

It was this Provence poetry that was at the foundation of all forms of Western literary expressions. The troubadours were proclaimed the initiators of 'Modern taste' and the harbingers of Romanticism.[1895] The 'courtesy' of 12th century Provence reappears in 17th and 18th century 'gallantry'; it comes up again in the novel of the 19th century.[1896] The vital debt of Italian poetry to the Provençal was freely owned from the first.

> It is universally recognized and is beyond doubt [wrote Cardinal Bembo] that the Tuscan language is mainly indebted for its poetry to the poets of Provence, who are our masters.... Our tongue itself, which was still uncouth and poor in resources at the time, was refined and enriched by what it borrowed from that foreign store.[1897]

Italian poets of the 13th century composed exclusively in Provencal. Rambertino Buvalelli, of Bologna, who was Podesta of Milan in 1208, and of Genoa in 1220,

---

[1886] G. Barbieri: *Dell'origine della poesia rimata*; ed., Girolamo Tiraboschi, (Modena, 1790); (written c. 1570).

[1887] Ibid.

[1888] T. Rymer: *A Short History of Tragedy;* (London; Richard Baldwin; 1693).

[1889] T. Warton: *On the Origin of Romantic Fiction in Europe*; 3 vols; (London; 1775-81).

[1890] Ibid, I, pp. 2-3.

[1891] In R. Boase: *The Origins and Meaning of Courtly Love;* (Manchester University Press; 1977); p. 16.

[1892] Xavier Lampillas: *Saggio storico-apologetico della letteratura spagnola* (1778-81).

[1893] J. Andres: *Dell'origine, progressi e stato attuale d'ogni letteratura*; 8 vols; (Parma; 1782-1822); II, p. 48.

[1894] I, p. 25-4.

[1895] R. Boase: *The Origins and Meaning*; op cit; p. 2.

[1896] R.S. Briffault: *The Troubadours*; op cit; p. 200.

[1897] P. Bembo: *Della Volgare Lingua*; ed., Sonzogno; (Milan 1880); pp. 151 ff.

distinguished himself for his Provencal verse.[1898] The Romance speech of Italy, north of the Apennines, differed but slightly from the language of the troubadours, and was much closer to it than to Tuscan Italian. To this day, Briffault points out, a Milanese is able to converse quite intelligibly with an inhabitant of Marseilles, each using his own idiom.[1899] A great number of Provencal troubadours made long stays in Northern Italy. The court of Count Alberto Malaspina, in Lunigiana, was a noted meeting-place of the Provencal poets. Rambaud de Vaqueiras appears to have spent the greater part of his life in Italy; Peire Vidal, Gauceim Faidit, Uc de Saint Cyr, Peire Ramon, Aimeric de Perguilhan were frequent visitors to that country.[1900] On the other hand, almost all the Italian troubadours, Lanfranc Cigala, Nicoletto, Ferrari, Ugo di Grimaldo, and the most famous and influential among them, Sordello of Mantua, spent a great deal of time in Provence, and like the Provencal poets, visited the courts of Spain.[1901]

Another route of influence on the literature of the Christian West was the most Islamised of all courts, the Court of Frederick II of Sicily (1194-1250). It was under his rule, Briffault explains, that Muslim culture on the island reached its peak and had a far reaching civilising influence over 'Barbaric Europe.'[1902] In his preference to be surrounded by Muslim rather than Christian influence, he was 'half Muslim in his own ways,' according to Sarton.[1903] The role of Sicily in the awakening of Europe, and its imprint on modern civilisation have been well studied by the best source, unequalled to this day, Michele Amari's *Storia dei Musulmani di Sicilia*, Amari who said:

> Sicily owes its civilisation to the Arabs, and the whole of Italy owes to Sicily its initiation to the masterpieces of Arabic civilisation.[1904]

The new Italian vernacular poetry was known as "Sicilian," although it was composed in the purest Tuscan, whose quality was acknowledged long before Dante, owing to its closer approach to literary Latinity.[1905] Nor was the "Sicilian" manner by any means confined to the court of Palermo. It soon spread to every part of the peninsula, and the term became applied to all Italians who composed verses in the Provencal style.[1906] Among these were the Sienese poet Folcachieri, Urbicciani of Lucca, the Florentine Dante da Majano, and Chiaro Davanzati.[1907] To the youthful Dante Alighieri, no other Italian poetry was known but the "Sicilian." The first verses we have of him are a series of five sonnets in a *tenson*, or

[1898] R.S. Briffault: *The Troubadours*; op cit; pp.161-2.
[1899] Ibid; p. 162.
[1900] Ibid.
[1901] Ibid.
[1902] Ibid, p. 212.
[1903] G. Sarton: *Introduction,* op cit, vol 2; p. 575.
[1904] Michele Amari: *Storia dei Musulmani di Sicilia;* 3 vols in 4. Lvi + 2086 pp.; (Ristampa dell'edizione di Firenze, 1854; 1858; 1868; 1872; Catania; F. Guaitolini); in M. Souissi: La Presence Arabo-Islamique dans la culture Sicilienne; in *Cahiers de Tunisie*; Vol 29: (1981); pp. 211-19; p. 211.
[1905] R.S. Briffault: *The Troubadours*; op cit; p. 164.
[1906] Ibid.
[1907] Ibid.

exchange of verses.[1908] Italian did not at first wholly displace Provencal. Many who dabbled in the Sicilian poetry continued at the same time to compose in Provencal. Dante da Majano wrote in both languages.[1909] Guittone d'Arezzo says of one of his friends that his Provencal poems are better than those he composed in Italian.[1910]

Italy, in turn, impacted on other countries such as England. 'The manner, style, metrical models, and the very themes and conceits of the troubadour tradition, which had moulded Italian lyrical poetry,' Briffault remarks, 'became transported bodily into England.'[1911] The English poets, Raleigh, Spenser, Sidney, Marlowe, Shakespeare, while probably unaware of those Provencal origins, were fully conscious of their Italian connections and of that migration.[1912] Foremost in bringing about the latter was a poet whom Sir Arthur Quiller-Couch regards as "one of the glories" of English poetry and "one of the heroes of our literature," Sir Thomas Wyat.[1913] He had spent some time in Italy, and it was he, chiefly, who brought 'the flame of lyrical poetry to England, the flame of the Petrarchists, caught from the Troubadours.'[1914] It is of interest to note that Wyat, who led English poets to Italy and introduced the sonnet and much else that became characteristic of a new phase of English poetry, Briffault points out, showed a particular liking for an archaic stanzaic form, which was no longer fashionable among the Italian poets themselves. That form is no other than the Hispano-Mauresque *murabaa,* 'the technological seed of the whole lyrical evolution.'[1915]

The abundant importation of novels, fables, narratives, and other sorts of literary expressions from the Islamic world to the West is generally recognised. Gibb, in particular, made an excellent study of this in the first edition of *The Legacy of Islam*.[1916] Gaston Paris, for his part, writes:

> Whence came these tales which were so widely spread throughout Europe, many of which are popular even today? Most of them have their origin in the East... The Arabic importations took place through two very different locations: Syria and Spain... In the East, the crusaders, who lived very intimately with the Moslem population, received many of these tales by word of mouth.[1917]

The extent of this light type of literature is so great that Paris devoted a whole volume to its study.[1918] The *Disciplina Clericalis* was translated into French, German, Italian, English, Catalan, the language of Bearn and Icelandic; it gave rise

[1908] Ibid.
[1909] A. Gaspary: *Die Sicilianische Dichtershule*; (Berlin; Leipzig; 1878); pp. 17; 25; 30 ff.
[1910] Guittone d'Arezzo: *Rime,* 2 vols; (Florence; 1828); xxii.
[1911] R.S. Briffault: *The Troubadours*; op cit; p. 194.
[1912] Ibid.
[1913] Arthur Quiller Couch: *The Art of Writing*; (Cambridge; 1916); Lecture; IX;
[1914] Ibid.
[1915] R.S. Briffault: *The Troubadours*; op cit; p. 194.
[1916] H.A.R. Gibb: Literature; in *The Legacy of Islam*; op cit; pp. 180-209.
[1917] Gaston Paris: *Melanges de Littérature française au moyen age,* (Paris; 1912); p. ix f.
[1918] *Les Contes orientaux dans la literature francaise du moyen age.*

to a whole line of tales.[1919] A vast literature of *fableaux* and *fablieux* extended through the time of Boccaccio and the Italian story-tellers, up through the 16th and 17th centuries.[1920] In France, *Floire et Blanche Fleur, Aucassin et Nicoleite,* the *Estormi* of Huoun Peucele, Rutebeuf's *Testament de l'ane,* the *Longue nuit,* the *Vilain mire,* from which Moliere took the theme of his (Le Medecin Malgre Lui) "The Doctor Despite Himself," are derived directly from the repertories of the Arab and Hispano-'Moorish' story-tellers.[1921] The very novels of chivalry are adorned in oriental garb and sometimes, as for example in the case of *Enfance Vivien,* are actually Arabic stories. Even hagiology and the lives of the saints are derived from the same source, as for example, *Barlaam et Josaphat.*[1922]

*****

It is, maybe, best to end this section with these extracts for the meaning they carry. First are lines about the poet Saadi, narrated by Durant. Saadi knew every hardship, and all degrees of poverty; he complained that he had no shoes, until he met a man without feet, 'whereupon I thanked Providence for its bounty to myself.'[1923] In India he exposed the mechanism of a miracle-working idol, and killed the hidden Brahmin who was the god of the machine. He recommended the same summary procedure with all quacks:

> 'You too, should you chance to discover such a trick,
> Make away with the trickster; don't spare him; be quick!
> For if you should suffer the scoundrel to live,
> Be sure that to you he no quarter will give.
> So I finished the rogue, notwithstanding his wails
> With stones, for dead men, as you know, tell no tales.'[1924]

Then, these wonderful lines on early Muslim wisdom, brought to our knowledge by Graham:

Men Are Four

He who knows not, and
Knows not he knows not—
He is a fool—shun him.

He who knows not, and
Knows he knows not—
He is a child—trust him.

He who knows, and

[1919] R.S. Briffault: *The Troubadours*; op cit; p. 78; note 149.
[1920] Ibid.
[1921] Ibid.
[1922] G. Paris, op. cit., pp. 233 ff.
[1923] Saadi: Gullistan, ii; 30 in W. Durant: *The Age of Faith*, op cit, at p. 326.
[1924] E.G. Browne: *History of Persia*; II; p. 530, in W. Durant: *The Age of Faith,* op cit, at p. 326.

Knows not he knows—
He is asleep—wake him.

He who knows, and
Knows he knows—
He is wise—follow him.[1925]

7. Muslim Libraries

The passion for books in early Islam is well expressed by the words of al-Jahiz (776-868):

> The book is the companion with whom you do not get bored; it is the friend who does not tire you; it is the colleague who does not deprive you of what you possess through his flattery... If you study the book, it will increase your store of knowledge, sharpen your wit, add to your power of speech, increase your vocabulary, broaden your mind, accord you the respect of people and confidence of kings. Moreover you can learn from books in only a month's time what you cannot learn from people's mouths in ages.... As long as you associate yourself with them (books), you do not need anybody else and you are not forced to prefer loneliness over bad companionship; it relieves you of your worries regarding scarcity of wealth and material prosperity and absence of joy and merriment in your life. In fact, the one who keeps company with books has been bestowed with great privilege and highest favour.[1926]

According to Yaqut, when Nuh Ben Mansur offered a governorship to al-Sahib b. Abbad (938-995), the latter declined it. He justified his decision on the ground that it would be difficult to carry his books, estimated at 400 camel-loads. Obviously, he much preferred the company of his books to the appointment.[1927] For Al-Hakam II (r. 961-976) of Spain, books were 'a more consuming passion than his throne.'[1928] In the 10th century we hear of autograph hunters, and book collectors who paid great sums for rare manuscripts.[1929] The book loving mentality of early Islam is noted by Erbstosser through an episode in which a Muslim figure, whose ship had been wrecked and plundered on the coast of the crusader states, complained that:

[1925] T.F. Graham: *Medieval Minds*; *Mental Health in the Middle Ages*; (London; Allen and Unwin; 1967); p. 38.
[1926] Al-Jahiz: *Kitab al-Hayawan (the Book of Animals)* ed. F. Atawi; vol1; pp. 33-5, in A.L.A. Ibn Dohaish: Growth and Development of Islamic Libraries; in *Der Islam*, vol 66; pp.289-302, at p. 299.
[1927] Yaqut, ibn-' Abd Allah al-Hamawi, *Irshad al-Arib ila Ma'rifat al-Adib*, also referred to as *Mu'jam al-Udaba*, (Dictionary of Learned Men,) ed., D.S. Margoliouth (Luzac, 1907 ff); vol II, p. 315.
[1928] R. Mackensen: Moslem Libraries and Sectarian propaganda, in *The American Journal of Semitic Languages* (1934-5), pp 83-113; at p. 108.
[1929] S.K. Bukhsh: Studies; 49-50; in W. Durant: *The Age;* op cit; p. 236.

> The well being of my children, the children of my brother and of our wives allowed me to accept the loss of my wealth with ease. What distressed me was the loss of my books. These were four thousand volumes, all precious works. Their loss was the cause of life long sorrow for me.[1930]

A Muslim scholar, of the 8th century, Al-Zuhri, had a huge collection of books, to which he devoted himself, and so much so, his wife lamented, 'I would prefer three rival co-wives to his love for books.'[1931]

From these extracts, it becomes obvious that, just as it had a passion for gardens, early Islamic society had a passion for books, which contrasts sharply with the generalised contempt for reading amongst Muslims today (with ever fewer exceptions), a passion for books in early Islamic society that attracted the interest of many historians of Islam such as Quatremere and Hammer Purgastall.[1932] This passion, whose basic inspiration was the faith, led to two revolutionary changes: the emergence of the public library, and the production of books on a vast scale.

a. The Islamic Library: Foundation, Rise and Scope

Islam the faith was, once more, central to the demand for books. Reichmann notes how God created the pen as His great gift to humanity, and all past and future actions of humans are noted in the heavenly books, (as evidenced by the term *maktub,* (it is written).[1933]

There are many quotations from the Qur'an in praise of writing, for instance, 'writing is the tongue of the hand.' The word Qur'an stems from *qara'a*: to read, or Qur'an 'recitation'.[1934] The writing of Islamic books was a religious commitment, the reading of the Qur'an was and still is a sacred duty demanded from every believer, and to know the entire Qur'an by heart was and still is meritorious and highly rewarded.[1935] In fact, as Ettinghausen notes, next to the mosque the most sacred institution in Islam was Arabic writing. Writing was the vehicle of the Qur'an, the basis of the whole religion and civilisation.[1936] This accounts for Islamic civilisation becoming a book culture.[1937] A culture of the book could only result in the institutionalisation of book collection and distribution, hence, the library.

[1930] M. Erbstosser: *The Crusades;* op cit; p. 136.

[1931] Ibn Khallikan: *Wafayat al-Ayan;* vol iii; p. 317, in A.L.A. Ibn Dohaish: Growth and Development; p. 292.

[1932] M. Quatremere: Memoires sur le gout des livres chez les Orientaux; in *Journal Asiatique*; VI; (1830); pp. 35-78.

-H. Purgastall: Additions au memoire de M. Quatremere sur le gout des livres chez les Orientaux; *Journal Asiatique*; XI (1848), pp. 178-98.

[1933] F. Reichmann: *The Sources of Western Literacy* (Greenwood Press; London; 1980), p. 205.

[1934] Ibid.

[1935] Ibid.

[1936] R. Ettinghausen: Interaction and Integration in Islamic Art; in *Unity and Variety in Muslim Civilisation*; ed. by G.E. von Grunebaum; (The University of Chicago Press; 1955); pp. 107-31; at p. 122.

[1937] A. Grohmann: Arabische Palaeographie; Vienna; Osterreichische Akademie der Wissenschafte; *Denkschriften* 94 (1967-1971) in F. Reichmann: *The Sources of Western Literacy*; op cit; p. 205.

The origin of the Muslim library went as far back as to the early Umayyad rule (661-750), when Caliph Mu'awiya (661-80) established at Damascus in the early period of his reign a library called *Bayt al-Hikma* (House of Wisdom), housed in a large building, and containing a large collection of books.[1938] Khalid Ibn Yazid followed suit, and also established a special library that accumulated a large number of books, including his favourite subject, chemistry.[1939] Successive caliphs, whether east or west, did the same at different times in the history of early Islam. Abu Ya'qub, the Almohad ruler of Morocco and Muslim Spain (r. 1163-1184), Deverdun says, 'had a great soul and love for collecting books.'[1940] He founded a great library, which was eventually carried to the Casbah, and turned into a public library, under the management of erudite Moroccan scholars. Their service, says Ibn Farhun, was one of the privileged state positions, for which only the best scholars were selected.[1941] Some books in the library even constituted part of the Almohad treasury, and were as prized as precious metals.[1942]

Libraries were densely spread throughout medieval Muslim society, from one end of the realm to the other.[1943] Baghdad, for instance, prior to the Mongols, had 36 public libraries[1944] and over a hundred book-dealers, some of whom were also publishers employing a corps of copyists.[1945] The last such libraries in the city was that of the vizier Ibn al-Alkami (who connived with the Mongols, in fact, and was eventually killed by them).[1946] He owned 10,000 books, placed in a library in Baghdad, which was destroyed by the Mongols in 1258 alongside the others.[1947] In Marrakech, the Kutubiya Mosque was so named because around 200 Kutubiya or book sellers had assembled their booths around that Mosque erected by the Almohad ruler Abd al-Mumin.[1948] In the 10th century, Fes, one of the chief seats of Islamic learning, had a library of 300,000 volumes.[1949] Muslim Spain alone had seventy public libraries.[1950] The Cordoban people of the caliphate had a great love for books. In the western suburb of the city alone about 170 women earned their living by copying manuscripts.[1951] Every year 60,000 books were produced in Cordoba (perhaps a figure that should be cut ten times, a total of 6,000 being more realistic).[1952] The Caliph, it is held, built up a library of 400,000 volumes

---

[1938] Y. Eche: *Les Bibliotheques Arabes;* Institut Francais de Damas (Damascus; 1967), p. 11.
[1939] A.L.A. Ibn Dohaish: Growth and Development; op cit; p. 295.
[1940] G. Deverdun: *Marrakech*; Editions Techniques Nord Africaines (Rabat; 1959), p. 265.
[1941] Ibid.
[1942] Ibid.
[1943] O. Pinto: 'The Libraries of the Arabs during the time of the Abbasids,' in *Islamic Culture* 3 (1929), pp. 211-43.
[1944] S.K. Padover: Muslim Libraries; in *The Medieval Library*; edited by J.W. Thompson (Hafner Publishing Company; New York; 1957 ed.), pp. 347-68; at p. 352.
[1945] A. Von Kremer: *Culturgeschichte des Orients under den Chalifen* (Vienna; 1877), II; p. 483.
[1946] See G. D'Ohsson: *Histoire des Mongols*; op cit; vol 3.
[1947] S.K. Padover: Muslim Libraries; op cit; pp. 351-2.
[1948] R. Landau: *Morocco;* op cit; p. 80.
[1949] F. Reichmann: *The Sources of Western Literacy;* op cit; p. 208.
[1950] G. Le Bon: *La Civilisation*; op cit; p. 343.
[1951] E. Sordo: *Moorish Spain*; (Elek Books; London; 1963); p. 55.
[1952] Ibid.

(again an exaggerated figure,) and the nobles followed his example. There was a flourishing book market where rare or 'de luxe books' were auctioned.[1953] In Merw, around 1216-1218, there were 10 libraries, two in the main mosque and the remainder in the madrasas,[1954] which were also to perish following the first Mongol invasion of 1219-1221.[1955] The geographer Yaqut (d.1229), who lived through the episode, in fact narrowly escaped the Mongol advance, and fled, clutching his manuscripts, across Persia to Mosul.[1956] He tells us:

> I remained there (in Merw) three years... Were it not for what happened after the coming of the Tartars to that land and its devastation... I surely would not have left it till death because of the people's generosity, kindness, and sociability, and the multitude of sound fundamental books there. For when I left it there were in it ten endowed libraries, the like of which, in numbers of books, I had never seen. Among them were two libraries in the mosque, one of them with 12,000 volumes... and there is the library of Sharaf al-Mulk, the accountant; and the library of Nizam al-Mulk in his mosque; and two libraries (belonging to the Samani faculty), and another library in the Amiduia College. And a library belonging to Majd al-Mulk, one of the later viziers there; and the Khatuniya (princess) libraries in the mosque-college; and the Damiruja.[1957]

So widespread were public book collections that it was impossible to find a mosque or a learning institution of any sort without a collection of books placed at the disposal of students or readers.[1958] The medieval Islamic public library, Eche states, 'did not just serve the parent institution in the accomplishment of its scientific purpose, which it reflected scrupulously, as a place for permanent storage; it perpetuated the best scientific works, kept the most precious documents, and even scientific instruments.'[1959]

One of the most famed libraries of Islam was that of Tripoli (northern Lebanon, today).[1960] Tripoli was a natural port in what was then Syria, and was very prosperous thanks to its farm products and its manufacture. When the crusaders sacked it in 1109, it possessed a splendid mosque, rich bazaars, and houses from four to six storeys high, and had a population of 20,000 chiefly engaged in the making of glass and paper.[1961] According to Michaud, four thousand workmen were involved in textile manufacturing,[1962] whilst the large paper workshop

---

[1953] Ibid.
[1954] Yaqut: Mu'jam in J. Pedersen: *The Arabic Book*, op cit; p. 128.
[1955] See final part under appropriate heading for the fate of Muslim libraries.
[1956] W. Durant: *The Age of Faith*; op cit; p. 329.
[1957] Yaqut, Ibn Abd Allah al-Hamawi: *Jacut's Geographisches Worterbuch*, ed. F. Wustenfeld. 6 vols (Leipzig, 1866-70), vol iv; p. 509; I. 9, in S.K. Padover: Muslim Libraries; op cit; p. 355.
[1958] A. Shalaby: *History of Muslim Education* (Dar Al Kashaf; Beirut; 1954), p. 95.
[1959] Y. Eche: Les Bibliotheques; op cit; p. 299.
[1960] M. Quatremere: Memoires sur le gout des livres chez les Orientaux; op cit.
[1961] R. Rohricht: *Geschichte des konigreichs Jerusalem* (Innsbruck; 1898), p. 78.
[1962] M. Michaud: *Histoire des Croisades* (Paris; 1825), II; p. 54.

helped spread the making of books.[1963] Already, at the time of Al-Ma'ari, cited above, the city had many public libraries organised under waqf endowments.[1964] The largest of these was founded some time in the 11th century.[1965] It was one of the richest and best endowed in the Muslim world, and according to Ibn Abi Tay, it included 3 million works (which is much higher and much exaggerated than the figure given by Al-Nuwayri) and it employed 180 copyists, who were remunerated for day and night work.[1966] The city's ruling dynasty, the Banu Ammar gave their care and support to this library, and they sent their agents to all places to acquire works to put in their library.[1967] Under their rule, Tripoli became the centre of attraction for scholars, who worked in their service.[1968] The library sheltered an active scholarly life involving students and scholars, but this life was cut short following the crusades.[1969] In 1109, the crusaders besieged the city, eventually forcing it to surrender to them. The outcome here as elsewhere was looting and devastation on a vast scale, and the thorough destruction of the great library by flames, and the great loss of many and irreplaceable scientific works.[1970]

Rulers and leading figures played a crucial part in the rise and the life of the libraries. The Al-Mustansiriya of Baghdad had a rich library composed largely of books transferred from the very private library of the Caliph.[1971] In Damascus, Nur Eddin Zangi gave large collections of books to the many libraries of the city,[1972] whilst in Cairo, al Qadi al-Fadil presented his schools with thousands of volumes on various subjects for the use of students.[1973] In Spain, Al-Hakam II's collection was estimated at tens of thousands of books.[1974] The list of catalogues recording only the names of the authors and the titles of the books consisted of 44 volumes.[1975] He engaged copyists and bookbinders, and had agents sent to every province to obtain books for him by purchase and by transcription.[1976] The Reyes of Tayfas, princes who succeeded the Umayyads in Spain (early 11th century), also became celebrated for their libraries at Saragossa, Granada, Toledo, and elsewhere.[1977] Back in the East, Adud al-Daula (d.983), founded a library in Shiraz, which, in the words of al-Muqaddasi was:

[1963] Kurd Ali: *Khitat al-Sham;* Damascus; 6 vols (Al-Matbaa al Haditha, 1925-8), VI; p. 191.
[1964] Al-Dahabi: *Tarikh al-Islam*; Aya Sofya; 4009; vol XI; year 499 H.
[1965] Y. Eche: *Les Bibliotheques Arabes;* op cit; p. 118.
[1966] Al-Nuwayri BN, ar. 1578; 116 r. in Y. Eche: *Les Bibliotheques Arabes;* op cit; p. 118.
[1967] Y. Eche: *Les Bibliotheques Arabes;* op cit; p. 118.
[1968] Ibn Al-Furat: *Tarikh al-Duwal wa'l Muluk*; Ms National Library of Vienna; A.F. 117; I; p. 38.
[1969] Y. Eche: *Les Bibliotheques Arabes;* op cit; p. 119.
[1970] Sibt al-Jawzi in *Recueil des Historiens Orientaux des Croisades* (Paris; 1884), III; 536.
[1971] Ibid; p. 102.
[1972] Ibid.
[1973] Al-Makrizi: *al-Khitat*, op cit, II, p. 366.
[1974] J. Pedersen: *The Arabic Book,* op cit, p. 120.
[1975] Al-Maqqari: *Nafh al-Tib*, op cit II, p. 180.
[1976] J. Pedersen: *The Arabic Book*; op cit; p.120:
[1977] Ibid; p. 121.

> A complex of buildings surrounded by gardens with lakes and waterways. The buildings were topped with domes, and comprised an upper and a lower storey with a total, according to the chief official, of 360 rooms.... The library, which contained much scientific literature was in the charge of a director, a librarian and a superintendent. The books were stored in a long arched hall, with stack rooms on all sides. Against the walls stood book-presses, six feet high and three yards wide, made of carved wood, with doors which closed from the top down, each branch of knowledge having separate book cases and catalogues. In each department, catalogues were placed on a shelf... the rooms were furnished with carpets...[1978]

These thriving book collections are remarkable when considering the technological limits of the time, and also when considering that in comparison, in the 14th century, King Charles the Wise could gather in his royal library of France nine hundred volumes, of which only a third were not dealing with theology.[1979]

A considerable number of private libraries thrived, too, amongst the scholars in particular. There was none of them who could be found without a collection of books, Shalaby, thus, concluding, that the number of these libraries equalled the number of learned people.[1980] Book collection was an indispensable tool for the scholar, and it included, in general, all the works that his never interrupted studies allowed him to buy or copy.[1981] There are countless instances of such libraries. Al-Waqidi, at his death, in the year 823, left 600 boxes of books, each so heavy that two men were needed to carry it.[1982] Al-Baiqani (1033) had so many books that it required sixty three hampers and two trunks to transport them, whilst a 10th century scholar, Mohammed ben al-Husain of Haditha, had a collection of rare manuscripts that was so precious that it was kept under lock and key.[1983] The library of the physician Ibn al-Mutran had, according to Ibn Abi Usaybi'a, more than 3000 volumes; and three copyists worked constantly in his service.[1984] And we hear of a private library in Baghdad, in the 9th century, which required 120 camels to move it from one place to another.[1985] Under Almohad rule, in Morocco, there was the famed 13th century Maktaba (Library) of Ibn Tarawa, who was a great lover of chroniclers, besides being a manuscript writer.[1986] Also famed were the Maktaba of al-Qaysi and the Maqtaba of Ibn as-Suqr, the main librarian of the imperial library, his collection requiring five full camel loads to be carried.[1987] Eche notes how the

---

[1978] Al-Muqaddasi: *Ahsan al-Taqasim;* edited by de Goeje, op cit; p. 449; Von Kremer: *Culturgeschichte des Orients under den Chalifen*; op cit; II; pp. 483-4.

[1979] G Le Bon: *La Civilisation;* op cit; p. 343.

[1980] A. Shalaby: *History,* op cit, p. 107.

[1981] Y. Eche: *Les Bibliotheques;* op cit; p. 282.

[1982] E.G. Browne: *Literary History of Persia* (1908), I; p. 275.

[1983] S.K. Padover: Muslim Libraries; op cit; pp. 351-2.

[1984] In F. Micheau: The Scientific Institutions in the Medieval Near East, in *The Encyclopaedia* (Rashed ed.), pp. 985-1007, at p. 988:

[1985] F.B. Artz: *The Mind*; op cit; p. 153.

[1986] G. Deverdun: *Marrakech*; op cit; p. 265.

[1987] Ibid.

richness of any scholar's library was valued according to its scientific content, a collection, which nearly always ended in public libraries, thus enriching them considerably.[1988]

Private libraries were numberless amongst other groups, for it was a fashion among the rich to have an ample collection of books.[1989] The library of Abu al-Mutrif (d. 1001), a Cordovan judge, was sold at auction in the mosque for a whole year, bringing in 40,000 dinars.[1990] Al-Maqqari quotes this passage from Ibn Said who held:

> To such an extent did this rage for collection increase that a man in power or holding a situation in the government considered himself obliged to have a library of his own and would spare no trouble or expense in collecting books merely in order that people might say 'such a one has a very fine library.'[1991]

Muslim scholars' bequests of books, and the establishment of waqfs for the purpose, considerably enriched public libraries. Al-Khatib al-Baghdadi (d. 1070) constituted into a waqf all his works and writings for the benefit of Muslims.[1992] The Faqih al-Humaydi (d. 1095), also known as man of letters, loved books so much that he worked at night copying them. He also constituted his collection into a waqf for the benefit of those engaged in scientific work.[1993] This must have been a rich collection, for he copied much and gathered plenty of notes. Al-Mustazhari (d. 1115), a very pious and generous figure, also constituted as a waqf for the learners of Tradition, a good number of books, which included the *masnad* of Ibn Hanbal.[1994] Al-Katib (d. 1218), the last representative of the family of writers of Banu Hamdan, constituted as a waqf for the benefit of students a good part of his collection, made up of many original works.[1995] Ibn Harit (d. 1322), a Faqih, a reader and lexicographer constituted his book collection as well as his properties into a waqf.[1996] The chief of physicians, Al-Muhaddab Ibn Ali al-Dawhar (d. 1230) made of his house south of the Umayyad Mosque in Damascus a madrasa devoted to medicine. He had himself copied a large number of works in his meticulous hand-writing, and these books, estimated at over a hundred volumes on medicine and other sciences, were constituted into a waqf for the madrasa for the use of Physicians.[1997]

[1988] Y. Eche: *Les Bibliotheques*; op cit; p. 282.
[1989] W. Durant: *The Age of Faith*; op cit; p. 236.
[1990] W. Gottschalk: Die Bibliotheken der Araber im Zeitalter der Abassiden; *Zentralblatt fur Bibliothekswesen*; XLVII (1930); pp. 1-6.
[1991] P. De Gayangos: *The History of the Mohammedan Dynasties in Spain* (extracted from *Nifh Al-Tib* by al-Maqqari); 2 vols (The Oriental Translation Fund; London, 1840-3), Vol 1; pp. 139-40.
[1992] Y. Eche: *Al-Habib al-Baghdadi* (Damascus; 1364), pp. 92-137.
[1993] Al-Dahabi: *Tadkirat al-Hufaz*; Hydarabad; ND; IV; p. 20; Al-Maqqari: *Nafh al-Tibb*; I; p. 382.
[1994] Muntazam; ed. Haydarabad; IX; p. 183; in Y. Eche: *Les Bibliotheques*; op cit; p. 196.
[1995] Al-Dubayti: *Dayl Tarikh al-Salam;* Mss at the Bibliotheque Nationale (Paris); ar. 2133; 173 v.
[1996] Al-Safadi: *Al-Wafi bi'l wafayat;* Ms of Ahmad III; Istanbul; No 2920; ed. Ritter; I; p. 232.
[1997] Sibt al-Jawzi: *Mir'at al-Zaman;* Ms of Bibliothque Nationale; ar. 1505; 1506; 5866; ed by J. Richard (Chicago; 1907) and Ms Fayd Allah 1524; IX; 88 v.; in Y. Eche: *Les Bibliotheques*; op cit; p. 236.

One of the most notable traditions long held by the Muslims was to bequeath their manuscripts and book collections, sometimes thousands of volumes, to mosques.[1998] As Pedersen notes, because mosques were not just devoted to worship, but were also seats of learning, it was normal that people should give their libraries to mosques, and an entire book collection might be transferred to a mosque as a self contained library or *dar al-kutub*.[1999] Al-Jaburi reported that Naila Khatun, a wealthy widow of Turkish origin, founded a mosque in memory of her deceased husband, Murad Afandi. She attached to the mosque a madrasa and a library for which she reportedly bought many valuable books and manuscripts.[2000] In Iraq, the Abu Hanifa mosque had an impressive library, which benefited from the gifts of private collections, amongst which was one by the physician, Ibn Jazla (d 493H/1099) and the writer historian al-Zamakhshari (d 538H/1143).[2001] In Aleppo, the largest and probably the oldest mosque library, the Sufiya, located at the city's Grand Umayyad Mosque, contained a large book collection of which 10 000 volumes were reportedly bequeathed by the city's most famous ruler, Prince Sayf al-Dawla.[2002] The famed historian, Abu'l Fida, built in the city of Hama a beautiful mosque and constituted into a waqf a collection of books, numbering seven thousand volumes of all sorts of sciences, a collection, which it was said, was without equal.[2003] It included works he had collected with considerable effort from various parts of the east and the west.[2004] Yaqut, the famed geographer, also left his collection as waqf to the Zaidi mosque library.[2005] In Al-Qayrawan, the manuscripts were endowed to students by those 'who sought Allah's favour and pleasure,' as was recorded on many such manuscripts.[2006] In the year 1548, the Qarawiyyin teacher, Abu Abd Allah Muhammad al-Ajmawi, bequeathed his large work, *al-Qawl al-Mutabar* to the students of the mosque,[2007] which came after Ibn Khaldun had bequeathed to the same Mosque library his *Kitab al-'Ibar*, to be lent 'only to trustworthy men for the period of two months.'[2008] Most often, this gesture was a mark of gratitude by the scholar towards the mosques for their upkeep and support.[2009]

[1998] R. Mackensen: Background of the History of Muslim libraries; in *The American Journal of Semitic Languages and Literatures,* vol 51; Four Great Libraries....', op cit.

[1999] J. Pedersen: *The Arabic Book*, op cit, p. 126.

[2000] Al-Jaburi, Maktabat al-Awqaf... op cit, p. 89, in M. Sibai: *Mosque Libraries*, op cit, p. 92.

[2001] M. Sibai: *Mosque Libraries*, op cit, p. 81.

[2002] Ibid; p. 71.

[2003] M. Kurd Ali: *Khitat al-Sham*; 6 vols, (Damascus: Al-Matbaa al Haditha, 1925-8), IV; p. 193. Y. Eche: *Les Bibliotheques*; op cit; p. 248.

[2004] Ibn Higga: *Tamarat al-awraq* (Cairo; 1339), I; p. 75.

[2005] Ibn al-Imad: *Shaderat al-dahab*, v: 122, in A. Shalaby: *History*, op cit, p. 101.

[2006] M. al-Rammah: The Ancient Library of Kairaouan and its methods of conservation, in *The Conservation and preservation of Islamic manuscripts*, Proceedings of the Third Conference of Al-Furqan Islamic Heritage Foundation (1995), pp. 29-47, p. 32.

[2007] A. al-Fasi: *'Khizanat al Qarawiyyin wa nawadiruha,'* Majallat Mahad al-Makhtutat al-Arabiya 5 (May 1959): 3-16. p. 9.

[2008] W. Heffening: Maktaba; in *Encyclopaedia of Islam*, op cit; vol VI, p. 199.

[2009] M. Sibai: *Mosque Libraries*, op cit, p. 90.

b. Muslim Libraries: Their Public Role and their Management

Mackensen notes that the contrast between the Christian West and medieval Islam was not just in terms of size of book collections, but also extended to the fact that whilst Western Christendom restricted access to books, Islam encouraged it.[2010] The Muslim attitude, again, derives from the Prophet's summons:

> 'The first blessing that accrues to a person occupied with the transmission of traditions consists of the fact that he has the opportunity to lend books to others.'[2011]

This summons permeated all echelons of Muslim scholarship and society; the scholar abided by it, and elaborated on it. Ibn Jammah advised his students in his *Books as the Tools of the Scholars*, written in 1273:

> Books are needed in all useful scholarly pursuits. A student, therefore, must in every possible manner try to get hold of them. He must try to buy, or hire, or borrow them, since these are the ways to get hold of them. However, the acquisition, collection, and possession of books in great numbers should not become the student's only claim to scholarship.... Do not bother with copying books that you can buy. It is more important to spend your time studying books than copying them. And do not be content with borrowing books that you can buy or hire.... The lending of books to others is commendable, if no harm to either borrower or lender is involved. Some people disapprove of borrowing books, but the other attitude is the more correct and preferable one, since lending something to someone else is in itself a meritorious action and, in the case of books, in addition serves to promote knowledge.[2012]

Many libraries were founded for the sole purpose of lending books.[2013] We even find in the waqf stipulations the basic rule for book lending. Thus, in *luga* 42 of the Zahiriya Library, the following rule stipulated by the waqf said:

> Gifted for the profit of all Muslims and deposited at the madrasa al-Jawziyya of Damascus. Those who require such works can use them and then after use must return them back to the madrasa.[2014]

In Islam, in fact, caliphs, viziers, and scholars, were extremely generous in supporting access to, and use of libraries, including their own. In the Grand Palace of Ali b. Yahya al-Munajjim (897) in Iraq, there was a great library with the name *Khizanat al-Hikmah* visited by people who travelled from different places to study.

[2010] R. Mackensen: Moslem Libraries; op cit; p. 109.
[2011] In M. Sibai: *Mosque Libraries,* op cit; p. 105.
[2012] In F. Rosenthal: *Technique and Approach of Muslim Scholarship;* (Rome; Pontificum Institutum Biblicum; 1947), pp. 8-9.
[2013] Y. Eche: *Les Bibliotheques Arabes;* op cit; p. 384.
[2014] Ibid.

Accommodation was available for those amongst them who sought to live in the library wing, and food too was made available.[2015] In the 900s, a *Dar al-Ilm* (House of Learning) was established in Mosul, northern Iraq, by Mohammed Ibn Hamdan al-Mawsili (854-934).[2016] It included books in all sorts of sciences, especially philosophy and astronomy.[2017] The library was open to all seekers of knowledge who were supplied with paper as well as books.[2018] Ibn Hamdan was in the habit of visiting this library every day.[2019] The geographer Yaqut al-Hamawi (d. 1229) adds that the library was bequeathed in favour of all seekers of knowledge, and no one was denied access to it: even if a stranger wished to enter it he was allowed to do so.[2020] Admission was not just granted to everyone, but poor students could be financially supported, too.[2021] The scholar Ibn Abbad (938-995) had a library, whose book list filled ten catalogues.[2022] He was interested in philosophy, science and techniques, and was very generous with scholars; he gave each, it was said from 100 to 500 dirhems and a garment.[2023] At Basrah (Basra), Abu 'Ali b. Sawwar, a learned man and a patron of learning, founded two libraries, where students could read and copy books, and could also be fed.[2024] Ibn Hibban (d. 965), the qadi (judge) of Nishapur, bequeathed to the city a house with a library and quarters for foreign students and provided stipends for their maintenance.[2025] In Ispahan, a rich landowner established a library in 855, and is said to have spent 300,000 dirhems on books.[2026] In Morocco, the Merinid sultan Abu Inan, an avid reader and book collector, founded at the Qarawiyyin of Fes the Abu Inan Library, in which he deposited books on various subjects for the readers, who found not only room for consultation of such books but also items such as paper, pens, and other materials.[2027]

The organisation and management of Muslim libraries was quite remarkable, and descriptions of both public and private libraries speak of the classification of books and their arrangement in separate cases or even in separate rooms in the Baghdad libraries.[2028] Great care, says Olga Pinto, was taken concerning the buildings which were to serve as public libraries. Some of them, like those of Shiraz, Cordova and Cairo, were placed in separate structures, with many rooms for different uses: galleries with shelves in which the books were kept, rooms where the visitors could read and study, rooms set apart for those in charge of making

---

[2015] Yaqut: *Muujam al-Udaba*, op cit; V, p. 467.
[2016] O. Pinto: Le Biblioteche degli Arabi nell eta degli Abbasidi; in *Bibliofilia di L. Olschki;* vol XXX; p.151.
[2017] R.S. Mackensen: Background; op cit.
[2018] W. Durant: *The Age of Faith*; op cit; p. 237.
[2019] Y. Eche: *Les Bibliotheques Arabes;* op cit; p. 99.
[2020] Yaqut al-Hamawi quoted in A.L.A. Ibn Dohaish: Growth and Development; op cit; p. 297.
[2021] Yaqut: *Mu'jam*; op cit; II, p. 420.
[2022] S.K. Padover: Muslim Libraries; op cit; p. 353.
[2023] A. Mez: *Die Renaissance des Islams* (Heidelberg; 1922), p. 95.
[2024] A Shalaby: *History;* op cit; p. 98.
[2025] S. Khuda Bukhsh: The Renaissance of Islam; *Islamic Culture*; IV (1930), p. 297.
[2026] Ibid; p. 295.
[2027] M. Sibai: *Mosque Libraries,* op cit; p 55.
[2028] F.B. Artz: *The Mind*; op cit; pp.152-3.

copies of manuscripts, rooms which served for literary assemblies, and rooms for other literary activities.[2029]
There was accurate cataloguing of all contents to help readers, whether the library was private or public. One single private collection required 10 volumes,[2030] whilst in Spain, the catalogue for the works in Al Hakam's library is alleged to have consisted of 44 volumes.[2031] The contents of each section of a bookshelf were also registered on a strip of paper attached to the shelf outside; which bore indications of works which were incomplete or lacking in some part.[2032] Book lending, too, followed strict regulations, such as that readers were urged to take great care of borrowed books, not to write comments or correct any mistakes found in the book, but instead to report them to the librarian; and return the borrowed items by a given date.[2033]

It was the practice to appoint a librarian to take charge of the affairs of the library,[2034] but such duty was only granted to the most learned amongst Muslims; only men 'of unusual attainment' were allowed the privilege to be custodians of the libraries.[2035] The Sufiya of the Grand Mosque of Aleppo library, for instance, had in charge of it Muhammad al-Qasarani, an accomplished poet and a man well versed in literature, geometry, arithmetic and astronomy.[2036] The Nizamiya library of Baghdad had as one of its earlier custodians Abu Yusuf Ibn Dawud, who was a faqih, a methodologist, a man of letters, calligrapher and poet.[2037] Another of its custodians was Abu Zakaria al-Tabrizi, a man of letters, author of many masterpieces, who was also appointed as teacher of literature and philosophy in the Nizamiya madrasa itself.[2038] In Spain, in the provinces, the custody of the assembled manuscripts was entrusted to a noble of distinction; but at the capital the charge of the magnificent library of Al-Hakem was considered an employment worthy of royalty itself, and was committed to Abd-al-Aziz, a brother of the caliph.[2039] Such men, Mackensen notes, were themselves pleased to act as librarians.

> It speaks highly for the generosity of the patrons as well as for the really important work carried out in these libraries that men of marked ability in various fields felt it worth their while to undertake the duties of custodian.[2040]

[2029] O. Pinto: The Libraries; op cit; p. 227.
[2030] F.B. Artz: *The Mind;* op cit; p.153.
[2031] Al Maqqari: *Nafh al-Tib*, op cit; I, p. 186.
[2032] O. Pinto: The Libraries; op cit; p. 229.
[2033] A. Shalaby: History; op cit, pp. 82-3.
[2034] E.L. Provencal: *Nukhab Tarikhiya Jamia li Akhbar al-Maghrib al-Aqsa* (Paris: La Rose, 1948), pp. 67-8.
[2035] R.S. Mackensen: Background, op cit; p. 24.
[2036] Y. Eche: *Les Bibliotheques Arabes,* op cit; p. 134.
[2037] Asnawi: *Tabakat al-Safi'ya;* ms of the Zahiriya; Tarikh; 56; 18 v. and 19 r.; Al-Subki: *Tabaqat al-Safi'ya* (Cairo; 1323), IV; p. 29.
[2038] Yaqut: *Irsad al-Arib*; ed. Margoliouth; vol vii; p. 286.
[2039] S.P. Scott: *History;* op cit; vol 3; p. 465.
[2040] R.S. Mackensen: Background; op cit; p. 24.

Equally intensely sought after were copyists and it was the generalised rule in Muslim libraries to employ many of them together with calligraphists, and to employ the most illustrious of them.[2041] Caliph al-Hakam II of Spain gathered around him men with great skills in the art of copying,[2042] including the famed Zifr al-Baghdadi, whom he had brought specially from Baghdad.[2043] The Abbasid Caliph Al-Musta'sim did the same in the search of copyists for his library at the Mustansiriya.[2044] Abu al-Mutrif (d.1001), a Cordovan judge, possessed a magnificent library, consisting largely of rare books and masterpieces of calligraphy.[2045] He employed six copyists, who were constantly at work, and bought books in large quantities.[2046] The judge never lent a manuscript, but had copies made as gifts.[2047] Regarding the craft of copying, generally, as Watts explains, a master would slowly read out a scholarly work and scribes would copy down what he said.[2048] Depending on how many scribes he employed, ten or fifteen or more copies of a 300 page book could be produced in a few weeks.[2049] It was in this way that the great Library in Muslim Cordoba built up its large collection before it was burnt in 1236 when the Christians captured the city.[2050] To conform to the original, the work of the copyist, however meticulous he was, necessitated not just skills in writing, but also exactitude, and once the text was copied, other scholars checked it.[2051] Often, a famed scholar took on this task, and corrected copies; al-Farisi (d. 983), for instance, was employed two days a week in the correction of the *Tadhkira of Sahih* of Ibn Abbad, which was copied for the library of *Kafi al-Kifaya.*[2052] The search for exactitude also prompted the search for the copyist who knew best the work to be copied, or the person owning the best of the manuscripts.[2053]

From the point of view of their role in Muslim society and their place in human civilisation, their organisation and functions, their size and impact, and their innovative character, Islamic public libraries, Eche concludes, did not just surpass by far any similar institution that might have existed elsewhere, but they were only surpassed by modern libraries by around the 17th century after mass printing made possible the production of books on a grand scale.[2054]

[2041] Y. Eche: *Les Bibliotheques;* op cit; p. 273.
[2042] Ibn Khaldun: *Al-Ibar wa diwan al-mubtada wa 'l-habar*; ed Bullaq (1284 (H); IV; p. 146.
[2043] Ibn al-Abbar: *Kitab al-Takmila* (Madrid; 1886), vol I; p. 86.
[2044] Al-Safadi: *Al-Wafi bi'l wafayat;* Ms of Ahmad III; Istanbul; No 2920; XIX; p. 118 v.
[2045] S.K. Padover: Muslim libraries; op cit; p. 362.
[2046] Ibid.
[2047] Ibid.
[2048] S. Watts: *Disease and Medicine in World History* (Routledge; 2003), p. 40.
[2049] Ibid.
[2050] Ibid.
[2051] Y. Eche: *Les Bibliotheques;* op cit; p. 274.
[2052] Ibid; p. 275.
[2053] Ibid.
[2054] Ibid; pp. 396-7.

c. The Rise of the Book Industry

The early Muslim passion for books did not just lead to the rise of one of the greatest institutions of human civilisation, it also led to the advent and advancement of some essential functions, crafts and trades, which had dramatic effects on the worlds of intellect and industry.

First and foremost, as noted above, Muslims were great book collectors, and this stimulated a flourishing book trade.[2055] At its foundation was the *Warraq* profession (waraq being the Arabic word for paper), which developed considerably.[2056] The *Warraqeen* (plural of Warraq) traded mostly in paper, but also copied rare manuscripts they managed to obtain from often distant places, and made them available to the public at reasonable prices.[2057] The manuscripts that the warraqs transcribed during public dictations had little value unless they carried the *ijaza* (licence), that they were copies authorised by their authors.[2058] The function of getting the *ijaza* and distributing the approved manuscripts was performed by the warraqs, a process, which was long and complicated, but which ensured that the rights of the author were preserved and plagiarism was avoided.[2059] Once the warraq made a copy of the author's work, it was read back to him three or more times in public; each time, the author making amendments or additions which required further readings.[2060] Only when the author was finally satisfied, did he place the *ijaza* on the copies that he approved; the *ijaza* signifying that he granted permission 'to transmit the work from him' in the form as approved. If the author of a particular work was dead, then the copy was read out by a distinguished scholar for a fee, and he gave his *ijaza* to the manuscript if satisfied with the work.[2061] The *ijaza* did not give the warraq copyright over the work; it was simply an assurance that he passed the book in the form determined by the author and was empowered to transmit the book in the same form to others.[2062]

Baghdad, most probably, was the first place where the Warraqeen bookshops appeared.[2063] Ya'qubi (d. 897) says that in his time Baghdad had over a hundred booksellers.[2064] The bookshops were often situated around the city's central mosque; scholars and men of letters used them as places where they could gather.[2065] It was in these shops that al-Jahiz would pay for the privilege of being

---

[2055] F.B. Artz: *The Mind;* op cit; p. 152.
[2056] M. Sibai: *Mosque Libraries*, op cit, p. 41.
[2057] Ibid.
[2058] Z. Sardar-M.W. Davies: *Distorted Imagination*; op cit; p. 99.
[2059] Ibid.
[2060] Ibid.
[2061] Ibid.
[2062] Ibid.
[2063] W. Durant: *The Age of Faith*; op cit; p. 319.
[2064] Ibid; p. 236.
[2065] G. Wiet et al: *History*; op cit; p. 448.

locked in all night in order to read a copy that he wanted.[2066] From Iraq, bookshops spread westward. In Cairo, according to Ibn Zulaq, under Tulunid and Ikhlisid rule (9th– early 10th century), there was a special bazaar for the *Warraqeen* where books were sold and debate took place.[2067] The intellectual role of such places in Egyptian life was subsequently studied by al-Makrizi (d.1442).[2068] In the bazaars of Cordova, which possessed the largest book market in Spain, manuscripts were bought and sold like any other commodity.[2069] Such an intellectual flourish was not strange to Muslim Spain, where Zainab and Hamda, the daughters of Zaid, the bookseller who lived at Wadi al-Hima in the neighbourhood of Grenada, were 'excellent poetesses, thoroughly versed in all branches of learning and science.'[2070]

The profession of warraq also stimulated a diversity of trades, here well outlined by Durant. The Warraqs, he said:

> Made ever lovelier Kurans for Seljuk, Ayyubid, or Mamluk mosques, monasteries, dignitaries, and schools, and engraved upon the leather or lacquer bindings designs as delicate as a spider's web. Rich men spent small fortunes in engaging artists to make the most beautiful books ever known. A corps of papermakers, calligraphers, painters, and bookbinders in some cases worked for seventeen years on one volume. Paper had to be of the best; brushes were put together, we are told, from the white neck hair of kittens not more than two years old; blue ink was sometimes made from powdered lapis lazuli, and could be worth its weight in gold; and liquid gold was not thought too precious for some lines or letters of design or text.[2071]

Paper, a Chinese invention, was turned by the Muslims into an industry that led to the massive production of books. The literary necessities of a highly educated population, the multiplication of manuscripts, the requirements of innumerable institutions of learning, and the need to stack the shelves of libraries, in turn stimulated the industry.[2072] The use of paper rather than papyrus or parchment, in turn, made books relatively cheap.[2073] Thus, whilst elsewhere books were 'published' only through the tedious labour of copyists, in the Muslim world hundreds, even thousands of copies of reference materials were made available to those wishing to learn.[2074]

All this had decisive impacts subsequently when transmitted to the West. The Europeans of the Middle Ages wrote only on parchment but its high price was a

---

[2066] Yaqut: *Mu'jam al-Udaba*; op cit; Vol VI, p. 56.
[2067] Ibn Zulaq, *Akhbar Sibawiy al-Misri*, pp. 33, 44 MS 1461; Tarikh Taimur, Egypt; in A. Shalaby: *History,* op cit, p. 27.
[2068] Al-Makrizi: *al-Khitat*, vol I, p. 361, Vol II p. 96.
[2069] S.K. Padover: Muslim Libraries; op cit; p. 361.
[2070] Sayid Amir 'Ali, in A. Shalaby: *History,* op cit, p. 28.
[2071] W. Durant: *The Age of Faith;* op cit; p. 319:
[2072] S.P. Scott: *History;* op cit; vol 2; p. 387. J. Pedersen: *The Arabic Book*; op cit; pp. 50 sq.
[2073] F.B. Artz: *The Mind;* op cit; p. 152.
[2074] M. Nakosteen: *History*, op cit, p. 37.

serious obstacle to the multiplication of written works.[2075] The shift in production from Islam to Western Christendom took place in the 13th century when Valencia was captured from the Muslims (in 1238.)[2076] The Valencian exports doubtless originated in Xativa, where the Muslim community received royal support for the continued production of paper; and virtual monopoly in the kingdom of Valencia.[2077] The gathering of rags for the paper industry was a profession in itself.[2078] Other than Spain, the other route for the introduction of paper into Christian Europe was Italy. This owes once more to the impact of the crusades. When the mastery of the sea fell to the Italian republics, which had given first assistance to the crusades, Western tradesmen purchased from the Levant paper called *charta damascena* for which rags of linen were used as a raw material.[2079] This Italian-Eastern connection is found in the name for paper *carta cuttonea*, derived from the Arabic for linen, *kattan.*[2080] Paper sold in the south of Europe was taken north to cities and fairs, and soon the Italians started producing paper themselves. In 1250 a centre to supply Europe with paper was set up near Ancona.[2081] One of the first paper mills was set up in Bologna in 1293.[2082] Germany followed suite in the late stages of the 14th.[2083] The impact of such transfers is well known: a revolution in learning, a decisive step in laying the foundations of our modern civilisation. It is thus quite fitting to conclude with Pedersen, who remarks that:

> By making use of this new material, paper, and manufacturing it on a large scale, the Muslims accomplished a feat of crucial significance not only to the history of the Islamic book but also to the whole world of books[2084]

[2075] G Le Bon: *La Civilisation*; op cit; p. 391.
[2076] T. Glick: *Islamic and Christian Spain*; op cit; p. 242.
[2077] M. Lombard: *L'Islam*, p. 191; Madurell, Paper a terres catalanes, ii: 963-8; Valls i Subira, `Caracteristiques del paper,' pp. 319-21; in T. Glick: *Islamic and Christian Spain*; p. 242.
[2078] M. Levey: *Medieval Arabic Book Making and its Relation to Early Chemistry and Pharmacology*; (Philadelphia: American Philosophical Society, 1962), p. 10.
[2079] N. Elisseeff: Les Echanges; op cit; p. 46.
[2080] F. Reichmann: *The Sources of Western Literacy;* op cit; p. 205.
[2081] N. Elisseeff: Les Echanges; op cit, p. 46.
[2082] D. Hunter: *Papermaking*; op cit; p. 474.
[2083] R. Garaudy: *Comment l'Homme devint Humain,* (Editions J.A, 1978); p. 207.
[2084] J. Pedersen: *The Arabic Book*, op cit, p. 59.

And thus is the Reason; and Why decline of Muslim Society Will Persist Until...

When we reach this point and ponder about the accomplishments of medieval Muslim society, we can only lament the state of Muslim society today. How come Muslims of over a thousand years ago could accomplish more than those of today? We might venture the following thoughts:

-Muslim 'Scholars' of today (a few exceptions aside) have titles and cvs the length of a large essay and demeanours of medieval popes, but they glean and complete their academic papers out of the first entries found on the internet.

-As this author repeatedly sat at the university library entrance with one or two other witnesses, he always said: 'see how many Muslims would enter the library, and see how many non-Muslims would.' The witnesses were always astounded by the virtually Muslim free library floors.

-This author was emailed countless times by angered/despondent/offended Muslims who referred to how non Muslim observers cited facts reflecting lack of Muslim contributions to the human intellectual output, today's output by all Muslims together (in terms of inventions, publishing, print, or any form of intellectual output) being much lower than Spain's (that is unfortunately modern 2016 Spain, not medieval Spain). Muslim anger was not with the fact but was at being reminded how intellectually impotent they have become.

-Indeed, it is delusion which is the enemy, it is Muslims' belief in their present 'greatness' whilst they are swamped by the mediocre which is their greatest enemy, and until the day they seek out, and only, the excellent/the best/the superior, then mediocrity, at best, is their fate.

Concluding Words to Volume One

This volume has outlined how Islamic civilisation affected most aspects of learning and culture, on a much wider scale than any other civilisation had done. Only Islamic civilisation has had a lasting impact on trade, industry, architecture and design, water supply and gardening, universal learning and book manufacturing, as well as the sciences. No other civilisation had brought as many diverse sections of the community, as well as other communities, into shared effort. This first volume has also shown that Islamic civilisation, in all its fundamental manifestations, whether with regard to trade, banking, scholarship, garden design, or the universality of learning, and other aspects, was fundamentally inspired by the faith, Islam. This part has also raised the matter of distortions that have plagued our understanding of Muslim civilisation and its role in human civilisation. The following parts will lend greater focus to this latter issue. Whilst this first volume has dealt with generalities, the following two will address every matter in greater detail.

BIBLIOGRAPHY

-Ibn al-Abbar: *Kitab al-Takmila*; Madrid; 1886.
-D. Abulafia: *Commerce and Conquest in the Mediterranean, 1100-1500*, Variorum, 1993.
-J L. Abu-Lughod: *Before European Hegemony,* Oxford University Press, 1989.
-C.R. Ageron: *Modern Algeria*, tr., by M. Brett, Hurst and Company, London, 9th ed., 1990.
-S.M. Ahmad: *Muslim Contribution to Geography;* Lahore: M. Ashraf, 1947.
-S.M.Z Alavi: *Arab Geography in the Ninth and Tenth Centuries*, Department of Geography, Aligrah Muslim University, Aligrah, 1965.
-H Alleg; J. de Bonis, H.J. Douzon, J. Freire, P. Haudiquet: *La Guerre d'Algerie*: three volumes, Temps Actuels, Paris, 1981.
-N. AlSayyad: *Cities and Caliphs*; Greenwood Press; London; 1991.
-M. Amari: *La Storia dei Musulmani di Sicilia*; 3 vols in 4. Lvi + 2086 p; Ristampa Dell'edizione di Firenze, 1854; 1858; 1868; 1872; Catania; F. Guaitolini.
-G. Anawati: Science, in *The Cambridge History of Islam*, vol 2, ed., P.M. Holt, A.K.S. Lambton, and B. Lewis, Cambridge University Press, 1970, pp. 741-79.
-K.R. Andrews: Sir Robert Cecil and Mediterranean Plunder; in *The English Historical Review*; Vol 87 (1972); pp. 513-32.
-F.F. Armesto: *Millennium*; A Touchstone Book; New York; 1995.
-F F Armesto: *Before Columbus*: MaCMillan Education; London, 1987.
-F.F. Armesto ed., *The Global Opportunity*; Variorum; Ashgate Publishing; London; 1995.
-T. Arnold and A Guillaume ed., *The Legacy of Islam;* 1st edition Oxford; 1931.
-F.B. Artz: *The Mind of the Middle Ages*; third edition revised; The University of Chicago Press, 1980.
-O. Aslanapa: *Turkish Art and Architecture;* 1971.
-E. Atil, ed., *Turkish Art;* 1980.
-A.S. Atiya: *Crusade, Commerce and Culture*; Oxford University Press; London; 1962.
-S. Athar ed.; *Islamic Perspectives in Medicine*; American Trust Publications, Indianapolis, 1993.
-Ibn al-Athir: *Al-Kamil fi'l Tarikh;* 12 Vols; ed., C.J. Tornberg; Leiden and Uppsala; 1851-76.
-Ibn Al-Awwam: *Le Livre de l'Agriculture* d'Ibn al-Awwam, tr., from Arabic by J.J. Clement-Mullet, Vol I, Paris, 1864.
-Al-Bakri: Descriptions de l'Afrique Septentrionale; in *Journal Asiatique*; 5th series; XII.
-Al-Baladhuri: *Futuh al-Buldhan*; Leyden; Brill; 1866.

-Banu Musa: *The Book of Ingenious Devices*, tr., and annoted by D. R. Hill, Dordrecht: Reidel, 1979; Arabic text, ed. A.Y. al-Hassan; Aleppo: Institute for the History of Arabic Science, 1981.
-Ibn Bassal: *Libro de Agricultura*, Jose M. Millas Vallicrosa and Mohammed Azinan ed., Tetuan: Instituto Muley al-Hasan, 1953.
-Ibn Battuta: *Travels in Asia and Africa;* translated and selected by H.A.R. Gibb; George Routledge and Sons Ltd; London, 1929.
-Ibn Battuta: *Voyages d'Ibn Battuta*, Arabic text accompanied by French translation by C. Defremery and B.R. Sanguinetti, preface and notes by Vincent Monteil, I-IV, Paris, 1968, reprint of the 1854 ed.
-Ibn al-Baytar (1874) *Kitab-ul-Jami fil Adwiyah al-Mufradah*, Cairo, 1291, French translation by Lucien Leclerc, I-III, Paris, new ed. 1977-83.
-D Behrens-Abuseif: Gardens in Islamic Egypt: *Der Islam,* Vol 69 (1992); pp. 302-12.
-Issa Bey: *Histoire des Hopitaux en Islam*; Beirut; Dar ar ra'id al'arabi; 1981.
-A. Bir: *The Kitab al-Hiyal of Banu Musa Bin Shakir*; IRCICA, Istanbul; 1990.
-Al-Biruni: *Chronology of Ancient Nations*, tr. E. Sachau (London, 1879).
-D.R. Blanks, and M. Frassetto ed., *Western Views of Islam in Medieval and Early Modern Europe;* St. Martin's Press; New York; 1999.
-S. Blair and J. Bloom: *God is Beautiful and Loves Beauty, the Object in Islamic Art and Culture.* Connecticut: Yale University Press, 2011.
-S. Blair and J. Bloom: *Rivers of Paradise: Water in Islamic Art and Culture.* Connecticut: Yale University Press, 2009.
-S. Blair and J. Bloom: *The Grove Encyclopedia of Islamic Art and Architecture.* Oxford: Oxford University Press, 2009.
-S. Blair and J. Bloom: *The Art and Architecture of Islam 1250-1800.* Connecticut: The Pelican History of Art: Yale University Press, 1994.
-S. Blair, J. Bloom: *Images of Paradise in Islamic Art.* Hanover, NH, 1991.
-J. Bloom: *Paper Before Print: The History of Paper Making in the Islamic World.* Connecticut: Yale University Press, 2001.
-L. Bolens: L'Eau et l'Irrigation D'apres les Traites D'agronomie Andalus au Moyen Age (XI-XIIem siecles), *Options Mediterraneenes*, 16 (Dec, 1972).
-S. Bono: *I Corsari Barbareschi*; Torino; 1964.
-J. Boswell: The Royal Treasure: *Muslim Communities Under the Crown of Aragon in the Fourteenth Century*, New Haven, 1977.
-C. Bouamrane-L. Gardet: *Panorama de la Pensee Islamique*, Sindbad; Paris, 1984.
-F. Braudel: *Grammaire des Civilisations*; Flammarion, 1987.
-H. Bresc: *Un Monde Mediterraneen: Economies et Societe en Sicile*, 1300-1450: 2 vols, Rome-Palermo, 1986; vol 2.
-H. Bresc: *Politique et Societe en Sicile; XII-XVem Siecle*; Variorum; Aldershot; 1990.
-R. Briffault: *The Making of Humanity*, George Allen and Unwin Ltd, 1928.
-E.G. Browne: *Arabian Medicine*; Cambridge University Press, 1962.

-Maurice Bucaille: *The Bible, The Qur'an and Science,* tr., from French by A.D. Pannell & the author. 7th ed., (revised). Seghers; Paris (1993).
-T. Burckhardt: *Moorish Culture in Spain*, George Allen & Unwin, London; 1972.
-T. Burckhardt: *Fez City of Islam;* The Islamic Text Society; Cambridge; 1992.
-C. Burnett ed., *La Connaissance de l'Islam Dans l'Occident Medieval*; Variorum; 1994.
-C.E. Butterworth and B.A Kessel ed., *The Introduction of Arabic Philosophy Into Europe*; Brill; Leiden; 1994.
-C. Cahen, 'Le Service de L'irrigation en Iraq au Debut du XIem Siecle,' *Bulletin d'Etudes Orientales*, Vol 13, 1949-51, pp. 117-43.
-C. Cahen: *Orient et Occident au Temps des Croisades*, Aubier Montaigne, 1983.
-A. Caiger-Smith: *Tin Glazed Pottery*; Faber and Faber; London; 1973.
-A.F. Calvert: *Moorish Remains in Spain*; John Lane; London; 1906.
-*The Cambridge Medieval History*, vol IV; edited by J. R. Tanner, C. W. Previte; Z.N. Brooke, 1923.
-*The Cambridge History of Islam*, vol 2, ed., P.M. Holt, A.K.S. Lambton, and B. Lewis, Cambridge University Press, 1970.
-D. Campbell: *Arabian Medicine and its Influence on the Middle Ages*; Philo Press; Amsterdam; 1926.
-M. Canard: Les Relations de voyage d'Ibn Fadlan chez les Bulgares de la Volga; In *Annales de l'Institut d'Etudes Orientales*; Vol 16; 1958; pp. 41-146.
-S. Carboni: *Glass from Islamic Lands.* London: Thames and Hudson, 2001.
-G. Casale: *The Ottoman Age of Exploration;* Oxford University Press; 2010.
-A. Castro: *The Structure of Spanish History*, English tr., with revisions and modifications by E A. King, Princeton University Press, 1954.
-A. Castro: *The Spaniards. An Introduction to Their History;* tr. W.F. King and S L. Margaretten. Berkeley, The University of California Press, 1971.
-A K Chehade: *Ibn an-Nafis*, Institut Francais, Damas, 1955.
-A. Chejne: *Muslim Spain, Its History And Culture*; The University of Minnesota Press; Minneapolis; 1974.
-A. Cherbonneau: *Kitab al-Filaha* of Abu Khayr al-Ichbili, in *Bulletin d'Etudes Arabes*, vol 6 (1946); pp. 130-144.
-S. Chew: *The Crescent and the Rose;* New York; 1974.
-C.R. Conder: *The Latin Kingdom of Jerusalem;* The Committee of the Palestine Exploration Fund; London; 1897.
-O.R. Constable: *Trade and Traders in Muslim Spain*; Cambridge University Press; 1994.
-M.A. Cook ed., *Studies in the Economic History of the Middle East*; Oxford University Press; London; 1970.
-Y. Courbage; P. Fargues: *Chretiens et Juifs dans l'Islam Arabe et Turc*, Payot, Paris, 1997.
-F.R. Cowell: *The Garden as a Fine Art*; Weidenfeld and Nicolson; London; 1978.
-G.W. Cox: *The Crusades*; Longmans; London; 1874.

-K.A.C. Creswell: *Early Muslim Architecture*, 2 vols, 1932-40.
-M. Danby: *Moorish Style*; Phaidon Press; London; 1995.
-N. Daniel: *The Cultural Barrier*, Edinburgh University Press, 1975.
-N. Daniel: *The Arabs and Medieval Europe*; Longman Librairie du Liban; 1975.
-N. Daniel: *Islam, Europe and Empire*, Edinburgh University Press, 1966.
-N. Daniel: *Islam and the West*; Oneworld; Oxford; 1993.
-M.L. De Mas Latrie: *Traites de Paix et de Commerce, et Documents Divers, Concernant les Relations des Chretiens avec les Arabes de l'Afrique Septentrionale au Moyen Age*, Burt Franklin, New York, originally Published in Paris, 1866.
-T.K Derry and T.I Williams: *A Short History of Technology*; Oxford Clarendon Press, 1960.
-G. Deverdun: *Marrakech*; Editions Techniques Nord Africaines; Rabat; 1959.
-*Dictionary of the Middle Ages*; J.R. Strayer Editor in Chief; Charles Scribner's Sons; New York; 1982 ff.
-*Dictionary of Scientific Biography;* Editor Charles C. Gillispie; Charles Scribner's Sons, New York, 1970 fwd.
-Al-Dimashqi (al-Dimashki): *Kitab nukhbat al-dahr fi ajaib al-barr wal bahr* (Selection of the Age on the Wonders of the Land and the Sea) edited by A.F. Mehren; quarto, 375 pp. St Petersburg; 1866.
-Al-Dimashqi: *Mahasin al-Tijara*; tr. H. Ritter, Ein arabisches handbuch der handelswissenschaft; in *Der Islam*; vol VII; 1917; pp. 1-91.
-A.N. Diyab: Al-Ghazali: in *Religion, Learning and Science in the Abbasid Period;* ed., by M.J.L. Young; J.D. Latham; and R.B. Serjeant; Cambridge University Press; 1990; pp. 424-44.
-H. Djait et al: *Histoire de la Tunisie* (le Moyen Age); Societe Tunisienne de Difusion, Tunis.
-A. Djebbar: *Une Histoire de la Science Arabe*; Le Seuil; Paris; 2001.
-B. Dodge: *Muslim Education in Medieval Times*; The Middle East Institute, Washington, D.C. 1962.
-R. Dozy: *Spanish Islam: a History of the Muslims in Spain*; tr. F.G. Stokes; London; 1913.
-J.W. Draper: *A History of the Intellectual Development of Europe*; Revised edition; George Bell and Sons, London, 1875.
-J.W. Draper: *History of the Conflict Between Religion and Sciences;* Henry S. King and Co; London; 1875.
-J.L.E. Dreyer: *A History of Astronomy from Thales to Kepler*; Dover Publications Inc, New York, 1953.
-D.M. Dunlop: *Arab Civilisation 800-1500 A.D*, Longman Group Ltd, 1971.
-W. Durant: *The Age of Faith*, Simon and Shuster, New York; 6th printing; 1950.
-Al-Duri: *Tarikh al-Iraq*; Baghdad; 1948.
-P. Earle: *Corsairs of Malta and Barbary*; London; 1970.
-Y. Eche: *Les Bibliotheques Arabes, Publiques et Semi Publiques en Mesopotamie, en Syrie et en Egypte au Moyen Age*. Damascus: Institut Francais. 1967.

-*Encyclopaedia of Islam*, Leyden; Brill.

-A.M. Fahmy: *Muslim Naval Organization*; Second edition; Cairo; 1966.

-D. Fairchild Ruggles: *Gardens, Landscape, and Vision in the Palaces of Islamic Spain;* The Pennsylvania State University Press; 2000.

-N.A. Faris editor: *The Arab Heritage*; Princeton University Press; New Jersey; 1944.

-O.A. Farukh: *The Arab Genius in Science and Philosophy*; American Council of Learned Societies, Washington, D.C, 1954.

-I.R. al-Faruqi and L.L al-Faruqi: *The Cultural Atlas of Islam;* Mc Millan Publishing Company New York, 1986.

-G. Ferrand: *Instructions Nautiques et Routiers Arabes et Portugais des XV et XVI Siecles*, 3 Vols, Paris, 1921-8.

-G. Ferrand: *Relations de Voyages et Textes Geographiques Arabes, Persans et Turks Relatifs a l'Extreme Orient du VIIIem au XVIIIem Siecles*; E. Leroux, Paris, 1913-4; re-edition by F. Sezgin, Frankfurt, 1986.

-S. Ferber ed., *Islam and the Medieval West*; State University of New York at Binghamton; 1975.

-Abu al-Fida: *Geographie d'Aboulfeda*, ed. and tr. M. Reinaud. 3 vols. Paris, 1840-83.

-W. Fischel: The Origins of Banking in Medieval Islam: *JRAS;* 1933; pp. 339-52.

-G. Fisher: *The Barbary Legend*; Oxford; 1957.

-R.J. Forbes: *Studies in Ancient Technology*; vol II, second revised ed., Leiden, Brill, 1965.

-A. Frothingham: *Lustre Ware of Spain*; Hispanic Society of America; New York; 1951.

-R. Garaudy: *Comment l'Homme Devint Humain,* Editions J.A, 1978.

-R. Garaudy: *Appel aux Vivants*, Le Seuil, Paris, 1979.

-M. Garcia-Arenal: Historiens de l'Espagne, Historiens du Maghreb au 19em siecle. Comparaison des Stereotypes *ANNALES: Economies, Societes, Civilisations*: vol 54 (1999); pp. 687-703.

-J.C. Garcin et al: *Etats, Societes et Cultures du Monde Musulman Medieval*; vol 2; Presses Universitaires de France; Paris; 2000.

-P.De Gayangos: *The History of the Mohammedan Dynasties in Spain* (extracted from *Nifh Al-Tib* by al-Maqqari); 2 vols; The Oriental Translation Fund; London, 1840-3.

-D.J. Geanakoplos: *Medieval Western Civilisation, and the Byzantine and Islamic Worlds,* D.C. Heath and Company, Toronto, 1979.

-Al-Ghazali: *Fatihat al-Ulum;* Cairo 1904.

-Al-Ghazali*: Ayyuha l'Walad*: UNESCO, Beirut 1951 (Arabic text, Fr tr).

-E. Gibbon: *The Decline and Fall of the Roman Empire*; vol 5; ed. W. Smith; London, 1858.

-T. Glick: *Islamic and Christian Spain in the Early Middle Ages,* Princeton University Press, New Jersey, 1979.

-T. Glick, S.J. Livesey, F. Wallis Editors: *Medieval Science, Technology and Medicine; An Encyclopaedia*; Routledge; London; 2005.

-S.D. Goitein: *A Mediterranean Society*, 5 Vols, Berkeley, 1967-90.

-V.P. Goss ed., *The Meeting of Two Worlds*; Medieval Institute Publications, Michigan, 1986.

-M.L. Gothein: *A History of Garden Art*; Hacker Art Books; New York; 1979.

-T.F. Graham: *Medieval Minds; Mental Health in the Middle Ages*; London; Allen and Unwin; 1967.

-Salah Guemriche: *Dictionnaire des mots français d'origine arabe et turque et persane : accompagné d'une anthologie littéraire: 400 extraits d'auteurs français, de Rabelais à Houellebecq*, Seuil, 2007, réédition poche Points 2012 et 2015.

-Salah Guemriche: *Dictionnaire Des Mots Francais D'origine Arabe*, Mass Market Paperback – 20 Jan 2015.

-S.K. Hamarneh: *Health Sciences in Early Islam*, 2 vols, edited by M.A. Anees, vol I, Noor Health Foundation and Zahra Publications, 1983.

-A. Hamdani: Columbus and the Recovery of Jerusalem; in *Journal of the American Oriental Society*; 99; 1979; pp. 39-47.

-A. Hamdani: Ottoman Response to the Discovery of America and the New Route to India; in *Journal of the American Oriental Society*; Vol 101; 1981; pp. 323-30.

-J.B. Harley and D. Woodward ed: *The History of Cartography*; Volume 2; Book 1; Cartography in the Traditional Islamic and South Asian Societies; The University of Chicago Press; Chicago and London; 1992.

-J. Harvey: *The Master Builders: Architecture in the Middle Ages*: Thames and Hudson, London, 1971.

-J. Harvey: Turkey as a source of garden plants, *Garden History*; vol 4; 1976.

-J. Harvey: *Medieval Gardens;* B.T. Batsford Ltd; London; 1981.

-J. Harvey: The Development of Architecture, in *The Flowering of the Middle Ages*; ed., J. Evans; Thames and Hudson; 1985; pp. 85-105.

-C.H. Haskins: *Studies in the History of Mediaeval Science.* Frederick Ungar Publishing Co. New York; 1967.

-C.H. Haskins: *The Renaissance of the Twelfth Century*, Harvard University Press, 1927.

-A.Y. Al-Hassan; D.R. Hill: *Islamic Technology*: Cambridge University Press, 1986.

-J.R. Hayes ed., *The Genius of Arab Civilisation*, Source of Renaissance, Phaidon, Oxford; 1976.

-Gene. W. Heck: *Charlemagne, Muhammad, and the Arab Roots of Capitalism;* Walter de Gruyter; Berlin; New York; 2006.

-C. Hess Editor: *The Arts of Fire, Islamic Influence on Glass and Ceramics of the Italian Renaissance*, The J. Paul Getty Museum, Los Angeles, 2004.

-B. Hetherington: *A Chronicle of Pre-Telescopic Astronomy*; John Wiley and Sons; Chichester; 1996.

-W. Heyd: *Histoire du Commerce du Levant au Moyen Age*; Leipzig; 1885-6; reedit; Amsterdam 1967.

-D.R. Hill: *Islamic Science and Engineering*, Edinburgh University Press, 1993.
-D.R. Hill: *A History of Engineering in Classical and Medieval Times;* Croom Helm; 1984.
-J.M. Hobson: *The Eastern Origins of Western Civilisation*, Cambridge University Press; 2004.
-J.M. Hobson: *The Role of the Arab Islamic World in the Rise of the West;* edited by Al Rodhan R.F*;* New York: Macmillan, 2012; pp. 84-115.
-E.J. Holmyard: *Makers of Chemistry*; Oxford at the Clarendon Press, 1931.
-E.J. Holmyard: A Critical examination of Berthelot's work upon Arabic chemistry. *ISIS,* vol 6; pp. 479-99; reprinted from *Chemistry and Industry Review*, Published by the Society of Chemical Industry; vol 42. 958-63; 976-80; London; 1923.
-E.J. Holmyard: Jabir Ibn Hayyan; in *Proceedings of the Royal Society of Medicine*; vol 16; 1923; pp. 46-57.
-G.F. Hourani: *Arab Seafaring in the Indian Ocean in Ancient and Early Medieval Times*; Princeton University Press; 1971.
-W. Howitt: *Colonisation and Christianity*: Longman; London; 1838.
-Paul Egon Hubinger: *Bedeutung Und Rolle des Islam Beim Ubergang Vom Altertum Zum Mittelalter*, Darmstadt, 1968.
-S.F.D. Hughes: Scandinavia in Arabic Sources; *Dictionary of the Middle Ages*; Vol 10, pp. 706-8.
-E. Hyams: *A History of Gardens and Gardening*; J.M. Dent and Sons Ltd; London; 1971.
-Al-Idrisi: *Opus Geographicum;* v; Naples-Rome; 1975.
-Al-Idrisi: *Description de l'Afrique et de l'Espagne;* ed and Fr tr., by R. Dozy and M.J. de Goeje; Leiden; 1866.
-S.M. Imamuddin: *Muslim Spain;* Leiden; Brill; 1981.
-S.M. Imamuddin: Maritime Trade under the Mamluks of Egypt (1250-1517); *Hamdard Islamicus*; vol 3; no 4; 1980.
-C. Imber: *The Islamic Legal Tradition*; Edinburgh; 1997.
-T.B. Irving: Dates, Names and Places: The End of Islamic Spain; in *Revue d'Histoire Maghrebine;* No 61-62; 1991; pp. 77-93.
-Al-Istakhri: *Kitab Masalik wal-Mamlik*; ed. De Goeje; Leyden; 1927.
-Al-Istakhri: *Das Buch der Lander*, tr. A.D. Mordtmann. Hamburg, 1845.
-Al-Jabarti: *Al-Jabarti's Chronicle of the First Seven Months of the French Occupation of Egypt*; ed and tr by S. Moreh; Leiden, 1975.
-Al-Jahiz: *Tria Opuscula*, ed. G. van Vloten; Leiden, 1903.
-Al-Jahiz: *Al-Tabasseur bi'l Tijara;* edited by H. Abd al-Wahab; *Revue de l'Academie Arabe de Damas;* XII; 1932.
-Al-Jazari: *The Book of Knowledge of Ingenious Mechanical Devices*, tr. D.R. Hill; Dordrecht, Boston, 1974.
-G.G. Joseph: *The Crest of the Peacock*; Penguin Books; 1991.
-Ibn Jubayr: *The Travels of Ibn Jubayr*; tr. R.J.C. Broadhurst; London; 1952.
-R. Kabbani: *Europe's Myths of the Orient*; Mc Millan; 1986.

-E.S. Kennedy: *Astronomy and Astrology in the Medieval Islamic World*; Aldershot; Variorum; 1988.
-Ibn Khaldun: *Kitab al-Ibar*; ed. Bulaq; 1847; Beirut: 1956.
-Ibn Khaldun: *The Muqaddimah*, tr. F. Rosenthal, Bollingen series, XLIII; New York, Princeton University Press, 1958.
-Ibn Khalikan: *Wafayat al-Iyan* (Biographical Dictionary,) tr., M. De Slane Duprat, Paris and Allen & Co., London, 1843.
-H. Khalileh: *Islamic Maritime Law*; Leyden; 1998.
-Al-Khazini: *Kitab Mizan al-Hikma*, Hyderabad; partial English translation by N. Khanikoff (1859); 'Analysis and extracts of *Kitab Mizan al-Hikma* (Book of Balance of Wisdom), *Journal of the American Oriental Society*, vol, 6: pp. 1-128.
-D.A. King: *World Maps for Finding the Direction and Distance to Mecca*; Al-Furqan Islamic Heritage and Brill; Leiden; 1999.
-D.A. King: The Astronomy of the Mamluks; *ISIS* vol 74; 1983; pp. 531-55.
-P. Kraus: *Jabir Ibn Hayyan*. Textes choisis, Paris, Cairo, 1935.
-I.J. Krckovskij: *Izbrannye Socinenja*; Moscow, 1957.
-P. Kunitzsch: *The Arabs and the Stars: Texts and Traditions on the Fixed Stars, and Their Influence in Medieval Europe*; Variorum; Aldershot; 1989.
-Al-Khwarizmi: *Surat al-Ard*, ed., Hans v. Mzik, Leipzig, 1926.
-M. Kurd Ali: *Khitat al-Sham*. 6 Vols. Damascus: Al-Matbaa al Haditha, 1925-8.
-A. Lane: *Early Islamic Pottery*; Faber and Faber; London; 1947.
-R. Landau: *Morocco*: Elek Books Ltd, London 1967.
-S. Lane-Poole: *The Moors in Spain;* Fisher Unwin; London; 1888.
-I.M. Lapidus: *Muslim Cities in the Later Middle Ages*: Harvard University Press; Cambridge Mass; 1967.
-H.C. Lea: *A History of the Inquisition in Spain;* 4 vols; The Mac Millan Company, New York, 1907.
-H.C. Lea: *The Moriscos of Spain;* Burt Franklin; New York; 1968 reprint.
-G. Le Bon: *La Civilisation des Arabes*; IMAG; Syracuse; Italy; 1884.
-N.L. Leclerc: *Histoire de la Medecine Arabe*; 2 vols; Paris; 1876.
-G. Le Strange: *The Lands of the Eastern Caliphate*, London, 1905.
-R. Letourneau: *Fes avant le Protectorat*; Paris; 1949.
-M. Levey: *Early Arabic Pharmacology*; E. J. Brill; Leiden, 1973.
-M. Levey: Medical Ethics of Medieval Islam with special reference to Rahawi's 'Practical Ethics of the physician. *The American Philosophical Society*, vol 57, 1967; part 3, pp. 1-99.
-E. Levi Provencal: *Histoire de l'Espagne Musulmane*; Paris, Maisonneuve, 1953.
-R. Lewcock: Architects, Craftsmen and Builders: Materials and Techniques; in G. Michell Ed: *Architecture of the Islamic World*; Thames and Hudson; London; 1978; pp. 129-43.
-A.R. Lewis: *Naval Power and Trade in the Mediterranean, 500-1100*; Princeton University Press; 1951.

-A.R. Lewis ed.: *The Islamic World and the West*; John Wiley and Sons; London; 1970.

-D.C. Lindberg: *Studies in the History of Medieval Optics*; London, Variorum; 1983.

-D.C. Lindberg ed., *Science in the Middle Ages*. The University of Chicago Press. Chicago and London. 1978.

-M. Lombard: *The Golden Age of Islam*; tr. J. Spencer; North Holland Publishers; 1975.

-M. Lombard: *Les Textiles Dans le Monde Musulman du VII au XIIem Siecle*; Mouton Editeur; Paris; 1978.

-M. Lombard: Arsenaux et Bois de Marine dans la Mediterranee Musulmane; in *Le Navire et l'Economie Maritime du Moyen Age au 18em Siecle*; Deuxieme Colloque International d'Histoire Maritime; Paris; 1958; pp. 53-106.

-E. Lourie: Anatomy of Ambivalence; Muslims under the crown of Aragon in the late thirteenth century; in E. Lourie: *Crusade and Colonisation; Muslims, Christians and Jews in Medieval Aragon*; Variorum; Aldershot; 1990, pp. 1-75.

-C.G. Ludlow and A.S. Bahrani: Mechanical engineering during the early Islamic period; in *Chartered Mechanical Engineering*; Nov 1978; pp. 79-83.

-Ibn Luyyun: *Kitab ibda' al-malaha wa-inha al-rajal fi usul sina'at al-filaha;* in Lerchundi and Simonet; Gestomatia Arabigo Espanola; Grenada; 1881.

-S.C. Mc Cluskey: *Astronomies and Cultures in Early Medieval Europe*; Cambridge University Press; 1998.

-E.B. Macdougall and R. Ettinghausen ed., *The Islamic Garden*, Dumbarton Oaks; Washington; 1976.

-R.S. Mackensen: Background of the History of Muslim libraries. *The American Journal of Semitic Languages and Literatures* 51 (January 1935) 114-125, 52 (October 1935) 22-33, and 52 (January 1936), pp. 104-10.

-G. Makdisi: *The Rise of Colleges*, Edinburgh University Press; 1981.

-G. Makdisi: *The Rise of Humanism in Classical Islam and the Christian West*; Edinburgh University Press, 1990.

-Al-Maqqari: *Analectes sur l'histoire et la literature des Arabes d'Espagne (Nafh al-Tib),* ed. R. Dozy et al; 2 vols in 3; Leiden; 1855-61; London; 1967.

-Al Maqrizi: *Histoire des Sultans Mamlouks de l'Egypte*, Etienne M. Quatremere, tr. 2 vols; (1837-1845).

-Al Maqrizi: *Kitab Al-Mawaiz wa'l Itibar fi Dhikr al-Khitat wa'l-Athar*, Bulaq 1863, vol. II.

-Al Maqrizi: *Kitab al-Suluk,* ed. M.M. Ziada; 2 vols; Cairo; 1936-58; vol ii; pp. 726-87; tr. G. Wiet: La Grande Peste Noire en Syrie et en Egypte; in *Etudes d'Orientalisme Dedies a la Memoire de Levi Provencal;* 2 vols; Paris; 1962; vol I; pp. 368-80.

-G. Marcais: *Melanges d'Histoire et d'Archeologie de l'Occident Musulman*; 2 vols; Gouvernement General de l'Algerie; Alger; 1957.

-D. Matthew: *The Norman Kingdom of Sicily*: Cambridge University Press; 1992.

-J. Mathiex: Trafic et Prix de l'Homme en Mediterranee au 17 et 18 Siecles; *ANNALES: Economies, Societes, Civilisations*: Vol 9: pp. 157-64.
-L.A. Mayer: *Islamic Astrolabists and Their Works;* Albert Kundig; Geneva; 1956.
-M.R. Menocal: *The Arabic Role in Medieval Literary History,* University of Pennsylvania Press, Philadelphia, 1987.
-D. Metlitzki: *The Matter of Araby in Medieval England*, Yale University Press, 1977.
-M. Meyerhof: 'Esquisse d'histoire de la pharmacologie et de la botanique chez les Musulmans d'Espagne,' *Al-Andalus* 3, 1935, pp. 1-41.
-G. Michell ed., *Architecture of the Islamic World*; Thames and Hudson; London; 1978.
-A. Mieli: *La Science Arabe et Son Role Dans L'Evolution Scientifique Mondiale.* Leiden: E.J. Brill; 1938.
-J.M. Millas Vallicrosa: Arab and Hebrew Contributions to Spanish Culture; in *Cahier d'Histoire Mondiale;* 6; 1960; pp. 732-51.
-J.M. Millas Vallicrosa: *Estudios sobre historia de la ciencia espanola*, Barcelona, 1949.
-A. Miquel: *La Geographie Humaine du Monde Musulman*, vol 4, Ecole des Hautes Etudes en Sciences Sociales, Paris, 1988.
-M. Morsy: *North Africa 1800-1900*; Longman; London; 1984.
-D.C. Munro: The Western attitude toward Islam during the period of the Crusades; *Speculum;* vol 6 No 4, pp. 329-43.
-J.H. Munro: Technology Treatises in *Dictionary of the Middle Ages*; vol 11; New York; pp. 641-2.
-Al-Muqaddasi: *Ahsan al-Taqassim li-Ma'arifat al-Amaqin;* (The Best Divisions for Knowledge of the Regions,) tr. B.A. Collins, Centre for Muslim Contribution to Civilization, Garnet Publishing, Reading, 1994.
-A.S.S. Nadvi: *Arab Navigation*; S. M. Ashraf Publishers; Lahore; 1966.
-M. Nakosteen: *History of Islamic Origins of Western Education: 800-1350*; University of Colorado Press; Boulder; Colorado; 1964.
-C.A. Nallino: *Raccolta di Scritti Editi e Inediti*, Roma, 1944.
-A. Nallino: *Albateni Opus Astronomicum* (Arabic text with Latin translation), 3 vols, Milan 1899-1907 reprinted Frankfurt 1969.
-G.G. Neill Wright: *The Writing of Arabic Numerals*; University of London Press; London; 1952.
-Al-Nuwayri: *Nihayat al-Arab;* Cairo, 1923.
-*Occident et Orient au Xe Siecle: Actes du IXe Congres de la Societe des Historiens Medievistes de l'Enseignement Superieur Public* (Dijon, 2-4 Juin, 1978); Societe des Belles Lettres, Paris, 1979.
-J J O'Connor and E F Robertson: Arabic Mathematics: a Forgotten Brilliance, at: http://www-history.mcs.st-andrews.ac.uk/history/index.html
-Baron G. D'Ohsson: *Histoire des Mongols,* in four volumes; Les Freres Van Cleef; la Haye and Amsterdam; 1834.

-Z. Oldenbourg: *The Crusades*; tr., from the French by A. Carter; Weinfeld and Nicolson; London; 1965.
-A. Pacey: *Technology in World Civilization, a Thousand Year History*, The MIT Press, Cambridge, 1990.
-S.K. Padover: Muslim Libraries; in *The Medieval Library*; edited by J.W. Thompson; Hafner Publishing Company; New York; 1957; pp. 347-68.
-R. Palter ed., *Toward Modern Science*; The Noonday Press; New York; 1961.
-K.M. Panikkar: *Asia and Western Domination*; George Allen and Unwin Ltd; London; 1953.
-J. Pedersen: *The Arabic Book,* (1928) tr., by G French; Princeton University Press; 1984.
-P. Pelliot: *Mongols and Popes; 13th and 14th Centuries;* Paris; 1922.
-O. Pinto: 'The Libraries of the Arabs during the time of the Abbasids,' in *Islamic Culture* 3 (1929), pp. 211-43.
-H. Pirenne: *Mohammed and Charlemagne*; F. Alcan; Paris-Bruxelles; 7th edition; 1937.
-H. Prutz: *Kulturgeschichte der Kreuzzuge*; Berlin, 1883.
-T. Pushmann: *History of Medical Education*; tr., and ed., E. Hare; London; 1891.
-Al-Qazwini, *Works* edit. Wustenfeld, Cottingen, 1849, vol II.
-*The Meaning of the Glorious Qur'an*; an explanatory translation by M.M. Pickthall; Taha Publishers; ltd; London; first printed 1930.
-R. Rashed (with collaboration of R. Morelon): *Encyclopaedia of the History of Arabic Science*, 3 vols, Routledge, London, 1996.
-J. Ribera: *Disertaciones Y Opusculos,* 2 vols. Madrid 1928.
-D.S. Richards ed., *Islam and the Trade of Asia*; Oxford; 1970.
-M. Rodinson: *Europe and the Mystique of Islam*; tr. R. Veinus; I.B. Tauris and Co Ltd; London; 1988.
-M. Rodinson; *Islam and Capitalism;* tr., by R. Pearce; Allen Lane; London; 1974.
-F. Rosen ed.: *The Algebra of Mohammed ben Musa (al-Khwarizmi)*. London: Oriental Translation Fund, 1831, Reprint: Hildesheim, Olms, 1986.
-B. Rosenfeld and E. Ihsanoglu: *Mathematicians, Astronomers and Other Scholars of Islamic Civilisation*; Research Centre for Islamic History, art and Culture; Istanbul; 2003.
-F. Rosenthal: *Knowledge Triumphant: The Concept of Knowledge in Medieval Islam*, Leiden; E.J. Brill, 1970.
-S. Runciman: *A History of the Crusades*, Cambridge University Press, 1962.
-J. Ruska: *Das Buch der Alaune and Salze*, Berlin, 1935.
-G.A. Russell Ed: *The Arabick Interest of the Natural Philosophers in Seventeenth Century England;* E.J. Brill; Leiden; 1994.
-Ibn Rustah: *Al-A'alaq-un-Nafisa*; Leyden; 1891.
-H.M. Said; A. Z. Khan: *Al-Biruni: His Times, Life and Works*; Hamdard Foundation, Pakistan, 1981.
-Z. Sardar; M.W. Davies: *Distorted Imagination*; Grey Seal Books; London, 1990.

-Z. Sardar ed., *The Touch of Midas; Science, Values and Environment in Islam and the West*, Manchester University Press, 1984.
-G. Sarton: *Introduction to the History of Science*; 3 vols; The Carnegie Institute of Washington; 1927-48.
-J.J. Saunders ed., *The Muslim World on the Eve of Europe's Expansion*; Prentice Hall Inc; New Jersey; 1966.
-A. Sayili: *The Observatory in Islam;* Publications of the Turkish Historical Society, Series VII, No 38, Ankara, 1960.
-R. Schwoebel: *The Shadow of the Crescent: The Renaissance Image of the Turk*; Nieuwkoop; 1967.
-L.A. Sedillot: *Histoire Generale des Arabes*, 2 Vols, Paris 1877.
-H. Selin Ed: *Encyclopaedia of the History of Science, Technology, and Medicine in Non Western Cultures*, Kluwer Academic Publishers. Boston/London, 1997.
-K. I. Semaan ed: *Islam and the Medieval West*. State University of New York Press/Albany; 1980.
-M. Serres: *A History of Scientific Thought;* Blackwell, 1995.
-F. Sezgin: *Geschichte des Arabischen Schrifttums*; 13 vols; Frankfurt; 1978.
-Fuat Sezgin: *Science and Technology in Islam;* 5 vols; tr., into English by R. and S.R. Sarma; Institut für Geschichte der Arabisch–Islamischen Wissenschaften an der Johann Wolfgang Goethe-Universitat Frankfurt am Main, 2010, vol 1.
-A. Shalaby: *History of Muslim Education*: Dar Al Kashaf; Beirut; 1954.
-M. Sibai: *Mosque Libraries: An Historical Study*: Mansell Publishing Limited: London and New York: 1987.
-Sibt al-Jawzi: *Al-Muntazam fi tarikh al-muluk wa'l umam*; X; Hyderabad; 1940.
-C.J. Singer et al: *History of Technology*; 5 vols; Oxford at The Clarendon; vol 2 (1956).
-D.E. Smith: *History of Mathematics*; Dover Publications; New York; 1958.
-N. Smith: *A History of Dams,* The Chaucer Press; London; 1971.
-N. Smith: *Man and Water; A History of Hydro Technology*; Peter Davies; London; 1975.
-A. Solignac: Recherches sur les Installations Hydrauliques de Kairaouan et des Steppes Tunisiennes du VII au XIem siecle, in *Annales de l'Institut des Etudes Orientales*, Algiers, X (1952); pp. 5-273.
-E. Sordo: *Moorish Spain*; Elek Books; London; 1963.
-R.W. Southern: *Western Views of Islam in the Middle Ages*, Harvard University Press, 1978.
-M.S. Spink and G.L. Lewis: *Abulcasis on Surgery and Instruments*; The Wellcome Institute, London, 1973.
-B. Spuler: *History of the Mongols*; London, Routledge& Kegan Paul, 1972.
-L. Suryadinata: *Admiral Zheng He and South East Asia*. Singapore: Institute of South-East Studies (ISEAS)/International Zheng He Society, 2005.
-H. Suter: *Die Mathematiker und Astronomen der Araber und ihre Werke (1900)*; APA, Oriental Press, Amsterdam, reedit; 1982.

-Al-Suyuti: *Tarikh al-Khulafa*; Cairo 1350 (H).
-Al-Suyuti: *Lub al-Lubab*; Leiden; 1840.
-Al-Suyuti: *Al-Muzhir*; Cairo; 1958.
-J.W. Sweetman: *Islam and Christian Theology*; Lutterworth Press; London; 1955; Vol I; Part II.
-J. Sweetman: *The Oriental Obsession*: Cambridge University Press, 1987.
-N. Swerdlow and O. Neugebauer, Mathematical Astronomy in Copernicus's *De Revolutionibus*, New York: Springer Verlag, 1984.
-D. Talbot Rice: *Islamic Art;* Thames and Hudson; London; 1979.
-R. Taton ed., *Ancient and Medieval Science*; Thames and Hudson; London; English tr. 1963.
-J. Taylor: *Muslims in Medieval Italy*; Lexington Books; New York; Oxford; 2003.
-H. Terrasse: *L'Art Hispano Mauresque des Origins au 13em Siecle;* Paris; 1933.
-A. Thomson: *Barbary and Enlightenment:* Brill; Leiden; 1987.
-A. Tibawi: *Islamic Education*, Luzac and Company Ltd, London, 1972.
-A. Tibawi: English Speaking Orientalists; in *Islamic Quarterly*; vol 8; pp. 25-45.
-J.V. Tolan ed., *Medieval Christian Perceptions of Islam*; Routledge; London; 1996.
-K.A Totah: *The Contribution of the Arabs to Education;* New York: Columbia University Press, 1926.
-D.M. Traboulay: *Columbus and Las Casas*; University Press of America, New York, London, 1994.
-H.R. Turner: *Science in Medieval Islam*, Austin Texas, 1997.
-A.L. Udovitch: Trade, in the *Dictionary of the Middle Ages*; vol 12; Charles Scribner's Sons; New York; 1980-; pp. 105-8.
-A.L. Udovitch: *Bankers Without Banks; The Dawn of Modern Banking*; N. Haven; Yale University Press; 1979.
-A.L. Udovitch: Urbanism; in *The Dictionary of the Middle Ages*; vol 12; pp. 306-10.
-Al-Udhri: *Nusus an al-Andalus*; ed., Abd al-Aziz al-Ahwani; Madrid; 1965.
-Ibn Al-Ukhuwwa: *Ma'alim al-Qurba fi Ahkam al-Hisba*; ed., R. Levy; Arabic text with abridged English translation (Gibb Memorial Series); London; New Series; 1938.
-Ibn Abi Ussaybia: *Uyun al-anba fi tabaqat al-attiba'*, edited by A. Mueller, Cairo/Konigsberg; 1884, reprint, 1965.
-L. Valensi: *Le Maghreb Avant la Prise d'Alger;* Paris; 1969.
-L. Valensi: *North Africa Before the French Conquest; 1790-1830*; tr. by K.J. Perkins; Africana Publishing Company; London; 1977.
-Carra de Vaux: *Les Penseurs de l'Islam*, Paris, Librairie Paul Geuthner, 1921, vol 2.
-J. Vernet: *Ce que la Culture doit aux Arabes d'Espagne*, translation by Gabriel Martinez Gros, Paris, 1985.
-A. Villiers: *Monsoon Seas*; Mc Graw Hill Book Company, Inc; New York; 1952
-J. Waardenburg: Some institutional aspects of Muslim higher learning, *NVMEN*, 12, pp. 96-138.
-C. Waern: *Medieval Sicily*; Duckworth and Co; London; 1910.

-Wan Mohd Nor Wan Daud: *The Concept of Knowledge in Islam*; Mansell: London and New York; 1989.
-A.M. Watson: *Agricultural Innovation in the Early Islamic World*; Cambridge University Press; 1983.
-A.M Watson: A Medieval Green Revolution: New Crops and Farming Techniques in The Early Islamic World, in *The Islamic Middle East 700-1900;* edited by A. Udovitch; Princeton; 1981; pp. 29-58.
-J.B. West: *Essays on the History of Respiratory Physiology*. Washington, D.C.: American Physiological Society/Springer, 2015.
-D. Whitehouse: Glass in *Dictionary of the Middle Ages*; vol 5; pp. 545-8.
-G.M. Wickens: 'What the West borrowed from the Middle East,' in *Introduction to Islamic Civilisation*, edited by R.M. Savory, Cambridge University Press, Cambridge, 1976, pp. 120-5.
-G. Wiet; V. Elisseeff; P. Wolff; and J. Naudu: *History of Mankind;* vol 3: The Great Medieval Civilisations; tr., from French; G Allen &Unwin Ltd; UNESCO; 1975.
-E.R. Wolf: *Europe and the People Without History*; University of California Press; Berkeley; 1982.
-J.K. Wright: *The Geographical Lore of the Time of the Crusades*; Dover Publications; New York; 1925.
-F. Wustenfeld: *Geschichte der Arabichen Aertze und Naturforscher*; Gottingen; 1840.
-Yaqut Ibn-'Abd Allah al-Hamawi: *Irshad al-Arib ila Ma'rifat al-Adib*, also referred to as *Mu'jam al-Udaba*, (Dictionary of Learned Men,) ed., D.S. Margoliouth; Luzac, 1907 ff.
-Yaqut al-Hamawi: *Mu'Ajam al-Buldan*; Wustenfeld Edition; in six volumes; Leipzig; 1866.
-M.J.L. Young, J.D. Latham and R.B. Serjeant ed., *Religion, Learning and Science in the Abbasid Period*; Cambridge University Press, 1990.

Printed in Great Britain
by Amazon